JORDAN SINCE 1989

JORDAN SINCE 1989
A Study in
Political Economy

Warwick Knowles

I.B. TAURIS

LONDON · NEW YORK

Published in 2005 by I.B. Tauris & Co Ltd
6 Salem Road, London W2 4BU
175 Fifth Avenue, New York NY10010
www.ibtauris.com

In the United States of America and in Canada distributed by Palgrave Macmillan, a division of St Martins Press, 175 Fifth Avenue, New York NY 10010

International Library of Modern Middle East Studies 47

ISBN   1 85043 633 9
EAN   978 1 85043 633 1

A full CIP record for this book is available from the British Library
A full CIP record for this book is available from the Library of Congress

Library of Congress catalog card: available

Printed and bound in Great Britain by TJ International Ltd, Padstow, Cornwall
Camera-ready copy edited and supplied by the author

Contents

List of Tables

List of Figures

CHAPTER FIVE
The Changing Face of Rentierism: 1989-2002

CHAPTER SIX
Donor Community Involvement: 1989-2002

CHAPTER EIGHT
The State-Market Interface: Which Political Economy?

CHAPTER Nine
Concluding Comments

Abbreviations

ACC:	Amman Chamber of Commerce.
ACI:	Amman Chamber of Industry.
AMIR:	Access to Microfinance and Improved Implementation of Policy Reform Program.
APC:	Arab Potash Company.
ASE:	Amman Stock Exchange.
BWI:	Bretton Woods Institution.
CBJ:	Central Bank of Jordan.
CCFF:	Compensatory and Contingency Financing Facility.
DM:	Deutsche Mark.
ECC:	Economic Consultative Council.
EFF:	Extended Fund Facility.
EIB:	European Investment Bank.
ERDL:	Economic and Reform Development Loan.
FDI:	Foreign Direct Investment.
FJCC:	Federation of Chambers of Commerce.
FTA:	Free Trade Agreement.
GFCF:	Gross Fixed Capital Formation.
GST:	General Sales Tax.
GTZ:	Deutsche Gesellschaft für Techische Zusammenarbeit.
IDB:	Industrial Development Bank.
JBA:	Jordanian Businessmen Association.
JCFC:	Jordan Cement Factory Company.
JD:	Jordanian Dinar
JEA:	Jordan Electricity Company
JIC:	Jordan Investment Corporation.
JICA:	Japan International Cooperation Agency.
JPMC:	Jordan Phosphate Mines Company.
JPRC:	Jordan Petroleum Refinery Company.
JTC:	Jordan Telecommunications Company.
JUSBP:	Jordan-United States Business Partnership.
JV2020:	Jordan Vision 2020.
KfW:	Kreditanstalt für Wiederaufbau.
OECD:	Organization for Economic Cooperation and Development.
OPEC:	Organisation of Petroleum Exporting Countries.

£E:	Egyptian Pounds.
£P:	Palestinian Pounds.
PTC:	Public Transport Corporation.
QIZ:	Qualifying Industrial Zone.
RJ:	Royal Jordanian.
SAL:	Structural Adjustment Loan.
SAP:	Structural Adjustment Programme.
SDR:	Special Drawing Right.
SEZ:	Special Economic Zone.
SME:	Small- and Medium-Sized Enterprise.
SO:	Strategic Objective.
SOE:	State Owned Enterprise.
SSC:	Social Security Corporation.
TCC:	Telecommunications Corporation.
UNDP:	United Nations Development Programme.
USAID:	US Agency for International Development.

Acknowledgements

This book is drawn heavily from my PhD and as such I would like to retain the same set of acknowledgements. However, a couple of additions need to added: to Maryam Nemazee, thanks for belatedly introducing me to the concept of the semi-colon! to Chris Temple for final editing help and especially to Anna Stead for riding to my rescue on a white charger.

Many people warned me that undertaking a PhD was a very solitary undertaking. However, I found the opposite; a PhD, although written by one person, is very much a team effort. Now those of you who know me will recognise the direction this acknowledgment is going in—football. The first person to whom I must give thanks is the coach and manager Dr. Emma Murphy—the Sir Alec Ferguson, Sir Matt Busby, Jock Stein and Bill Shankly all rolled into one (what more can I say). The goalkeepers are my parents who have saved me on many occasions prior to and during the PhD. My defence, the people that tried to reduce my many mistakes (especially where commas are concerned!) are the editorial team (any remaining mistakes are solely mine): Nick Keegan, Louise Haysey, Anna Stead and Declan O'Sullivan. The creative midfielders have added the artistic touches to the thesis: Anna Stead (the figures). The ball-winning midfielders, those players that do the hard work (in this case all foreign language sources), are my translators: Hassan Barari, Ahmed Al-Rajhi, Omar Laghrouche and Michaela Prokop. The goal scorers, those that gave substance to my thesis are the interviewees and people of Jordan, who provided considerable assistance during my spell in their country. And speaking of substance, the caterers, Chang Cheng Liu (food) and Lesley-Anne Robson (drink), have kept my stomach full and head sore! The team chauffeurs have been Ibrahim Serafi and Omar Laghrouche. The Centre for Strategic Studies at the University of Jordan, Amman supplied me with a pitch to play on in Jordan— the facilities in which to study and stay. As any football player will tell you without the backing of the crowd no team can be successful. In this case the crowd (some of whom are also the players) are all my friends and family (too numerous to mention individually) who like all football supporters have continually given their amazing support, even in the dark times. In these days of big money transfers, the moneymen are vital: I was lucky enough to receive a three-year scholarship from the University of Durham. The championship winning University Library F.C. has helped me to relax and win trophies (even at my age). Finally, but most importantly, without the support of Moira this thesis would not have been possible.

YOU ARE THE CHAMPIONS. A MASSIVE THANKS TO YOU ALL.

1

Introduction

The Hashemite Kingdom of Jordan has proved to be one of the world's most vulnerable countries to external political, economic and security events. The country has been rocked by the effects of apparent inherent regional instability, including: the ongoing conflict in Israel/Palestine, which can be traced back to before the creation of Transjordan in 1921; the wave of radical revolutions that swept through the Arab world in the 1950s and 1960s; and the various Gulf Wars (Iran-Iraq in the 1980s, the invasion of Kuwait in 1990 by Iraq and the subsequent freeing of Kuwait by the US-led coalitions, and the invasions of Afghanistan and Iraq following the declaration of the war-on-terrorism by President George W. Bush in September 2001). The country also found itself caught up in the repercussions of the Second World War and the subsequent Cold War. Despite the lack of an indigenous hydrocarbon industry, the economy has also subjected to the vagaries of the international oil market as oil prices rocketed in the 1970s from US$2.60 per barrel to over $40 per barrel before collapsing in the 1980s. Nevertheless, despite these threats the Hashemite regime has managed to preserve (and even enhance its position) in the political economy of Jordan.

In part the Hashemite regime has been able to maintain its position because of the flows of international economic assistance, which have been an enduring feature of the political economy since the establishment of Transjordan. The sources of these flows of aid have varied depending on the changing international, regional and domestic environment. Importantly, as one source of aid has evaporated the ruling elite has ensured that other sources have been available. This aid dependency has resulted in a number of writers using rentier theory to discuss the political and economic developments in Jordan, on the basis that economic assistance is a form of rent. Since the start of the 1970s a further flow of rent that of remittances, has entered the economy further influencing the political economy of the Kingdom.

Since the late 1980s two significant changes have occurred which have the potential to alter the nature of the political economy. These changes are: the transformation from an economy primarily based on official economic assistance (aid) (which tends to be distributed by the state) to one primarily based on remittance income (which tends to be distributed through the private sector); and the increased depth of involvement of the donor community, led by the International Monetary Fund (IMF) and the World Bank, which has as its stated aim the desire to increase the involvement of the private sector in the economy at the expense of the state. In relation to these changes the book sets out to answer two important questions. Firstly, what does rentier theory tell us about the effects of these changes on the nature of the state and the private sector and the relationship between the two in Jordan? In order to set the context for the first question, a second question is also addressed, namely: how has the nature of the relationship between the donor community and the state altered since the start of the active IMF involvement in 1989?

OUTLINE

The second chapter introduces rentier theory, clarifying the somewhat ambiguous uses of the various concepts associated with the theory, including rent and the three types of rentier economy. The models that are used to measure the degrees of rent and the characteristics associated with the differing rentier economies are also introduced. These characteristics are used in later chapters to assess to what degree rentier aspects are exhibited at various stages of the economic development of the Kingdom. The second part of the chapter defines and then discusses how the main concepts the state, the private sector, the regime, and the rentier élite, are used throughout the thesis.

The third chapter turns away from the theoretical and conceptual discussion to assess the changing nature of rent in the Jordanian economy between 1921 and 1989. The study acknowledges the effects of the changes in the global, regional and domestic ideological, political and economic environments on the levels of rent entering the economy. These levels of rent are then measured using the models discussed in the second chapter. The third chapter concludes that the high point for the induced rentier-state economy was the late 1970s, since when aid has become progressively less important. In contrast, the levels of the private sector rentier economy have grown from virtually zero in 1970 to high-level by the end of the decade, at which level it has remained.

The foundations laid in chapter three are built on in the fourth chapter, which evaluates the changing levels of state involvement in the economy as measured by the five-continua state-market model. Thereafter, the chapter assesses which characteristics of rentierism are present. The premise is that the presence of these characteristics would affect how the various actors (the state, the rentier élite and the private sector) will react to the conditions imposed by or negotiated with the IMF. The conclusion reached is that by 1989, although the economy was becoming more dependent on remittances, the political economy maintained the prime characteristics of induced state rentierism. By 1989, the rentier élite, which dominated the economic and political decision-making processes, was beginning to display signs of internal divisions. However, the division between the private and public sectors remained extremely blurred and was manifested in four areas: state involvement in productive companies; state intercession in the market; the use of access to the economy by the state for political purposes; and the institutional structure of the private sector being tied to state purposes.

The main analysis of the thesis follows in the next four chapters. In chapter five, the collapse of the economy, which resulted in the introduction of the first of four (to date) structural adjustment programmes (SAPs), is discussed. Thereafter the changing patterns of rent throughout the 1990s are assessed using the measures of induced rentier state economy and private sector rentier economy. The chapter concludes that by the turn of the century the induced rentier state economy was in decline, while private sector rentier economy remained strong.

The involvement of the donor community from 1989 is analysed in chapter six. The analysis bears in mind the changing patterns of rent, the changing international, regional and domestic environments and the new-found ability of the donor community to insist on economic conditions being attached to new aid. The chapter identifies the main members of the donor community, both in terms of volume of assistance and influence within the community. Each of the main donors (multilateral and bilateral) is then studied to assess its individual impact. The analysis highlights that the differing interests within the donor community have allowed the state as an institution to maintain a rentier mentality. However, by the end of the period, the reduced volumes of aid available have helped to close the door to a considerable extent on the state's ability to continue to attract aid.

The analysis in chapter seven switches to an assessment of the ability of the state as an institution to resist/accept the conditions sought by the donor community. In addition, the reactions of the rentier élite to the threats and opportunities posed by the proposed change of economic direction are discussed, as are possibility of splits within the rentier élite. Three case studies (privatisation, sales tax and subsidies) are explored to assess the objectives of the chapter. The conclusion is that the state has become more willing to implement economic liberalisation, particularly since 1998. This change seems to have coincided with increasing differences within the rentier élite and a greater acceptance of the need to introduce economic change.

In the penultimate chapter the five-continua state-market model is re-introduced to assess the changes in the state-private sector relationship since 1989. The analysis concludes that the evidence points to a move towards the market end of the continuum. However, the state has been able to maintain a role (albeit different) by reducing direct intervention but increasing indirect intervention, via policies such as regulation. In the second part of the chapter the changes in the rentier aspects of the political economy (the economy, the nature of the state and the private sector, and the relationship between the two) are assessed. Although the policies of the donor community have been aimed at reducing the characteristics of induced state rentierism, these aspects have only weakened, not disappeared. In addition, because of the importance of remittances in the economy the move has not been completely in the direction of a market-based economy but has been subverted to include increased features associated with private sector rentierism.

In the final chapter the first section gives a brief review of the preceding chapters. The second part recommends a number of areas for future research. The third section assesses the impact of the study on the debate on rentierism in the Middle East and North African context, while the final section turns from the theoretical implications to the implications for the actors involved. An important recommendation is that the IMF and World Bank packages must take into account the political economy of rentierism if the aim of the policies is to establish an economy based on the market rather than the extraction and allocation of rent.

2

Theoretical Considerations

INTRODUCTION

The chapter introduces the lens through which the study is viewed: rentier theory and concludes by clarifying how the concepts of the state, the regime, the rentier élite, and the private sector are used. The discussion on rentier theory starts by introducing the concept of rent, before extending the debate to describing a rentier economy. Three sub-sets of a rentier economy are then presented (figure 2.1): The pure rentier state economy, primarily based on oil rent; the induced rentier state economy, primarily based on aid; and the private sector rentier economy, primarily based on remittances.

The resulting differences in the nature of both the state and the private sector, and the relationship between the two are then developed using a model derived from those occurring in a 'normal' market economy. The emphasis is on induced state rentierism and private sector rentierism, as both are directly relevant to the case study of Jordan. The other main concepts of the thesis, state, regime, rentier élite and private sector, are discussed in the following section.

RENTIER THEORY

THE CONCEPTS OF RENTIERISM

The huge flows of wealth created by the oil price rises in the early 1970s re-awakened discussion concerning the idea of rent at the national level.[1] In particular the question was raised as to how the accumulation of rent affected the nature and role of the state in its relationship with society. As Beblawi correctly argues, the impact of oil income on "the role of the state and on economic behaviour in general has been so profound in the Arab world during the seventies as to justify special treatment."[2] Mahdavy, in 1970, first used the concept of rentierism in the context of the Middle East in his analysis of economic development in Iran, since when the usage has evolved through the writings of Beblawi and Luciani, among others. However, the theoretical discussion has become distorted by different terms being used for similar concepts.[3] For example, Beblawi defines a rentier economy as "an economy substantially supported by expenditure from the state whilst the state itself is supported by rent accruing from abroad,"[4] a definition, which as will become apparent, ought to be applied to a rentier state. The following analysis clarifies the theoretical debate in order to establish the effects of rent on the primary aspect of the book, the relationship between the state and the private sector but also on the relationship between the state and the donor community.

Before discussing the concepts of a rentier economy, a rentier state economy, a pure rentier state economy, an induced rentier state economy and a private sector rentier economy, the term 'rent' requires explanation. Adam Smith was the first to draw a distinction between rent as a reward for the ownership of natural resources, including land and minerals, from other income (wages and profit).[5] Rent, therefore, differed from normal income because it did not link work/risk with reward. Marshall, in 1920, gave a similar definition arguing that rent was "the income derived from the gift of nature."[6] However, the concept of rent has been extended from income accruing from natural resources to include "the amount earned that is above the cost of production of the resource/service."[7] In short, rent is that anathema of both liberal and radical economics: unearned or undeserved income. Five different types of rent can be distinguished at the national level:[8] portfolio, external capital, quasi-rents, natural resources and locational rent (table 2.1).

Table 2.1   **Typologies of Rent**

Type of Rent	Example	Accrues to State/ Private Sector	Importance to Jordan
Portfolio	Dividends, Interest	State or Private Sector	Negligible
External Capital	Aid	State	High
Quasi-Rents	Remittances	Private Sector	High
Natural Resources	Oil, Phosphates	State	Low
Locational	Transit Trade	State	Low

Jordan has accrued rent from each of the five types over the years but the two most consistently important have been external capital (in terms of grants and soft loans (i.e. aid)) and quasi-rents (in the form of remittances). Arguably, significant sums of locational rent, to ensure the stability of the regime, have also been received. However, the support has almost invariably been in the form of aid, and to differentiate between aid as external capital and as locational rent would prove impossible. Rent from phosphates and potash has also accrued to the state but, perhaps, apart from the mid-1970s, this source of rent has been insignificant.[9] Portfolio and other forms of locational rent have been equally insignificant. Therefore, the analysis will focus on aid and remittances.

Before continuing with the theoretical discussion a number of important features of aid and remittances require to be highlighted. As will become obvious throughout the book an important aspect of aid is that the donors' motives are seldom concerned with the economic development of the recipient country but are related to political, economic and security interests of the donor country. Thus aid is delivered for national interests not altruism. However, the relationship between the donor community[10] and recipient countries has evolved through a number of stages since the end of World War II. The most profound of which occurred during the 1980s. The debt crisis among the developing countries,[11] the lack of a coherent southern position on aid,[12] the recession in the West with the consequent ideological change to monetarism and the introduction of SAPs[13] all placed the IMF in pole position to dictate the new aid policy agenda. Other members of the donor community, including the World Bank, the Paris Club and the bilateral donors linked their funding to the recipient's agreement and adherence to the SAPs.

For aid, the result was the overthrow of the hegemony of development economics based on Keynesian theory and the intervening state by the counter-revolution of the new development paradigm "based on markets, competition, and private initiative and enterprise"[14] and a minimalist state. Aid was now provided almost purely in support of the SAPs through Structural Adjustment Loans (SALs), which were granted on the proviso that the countries adhered to strict economic conditions of the SAPs. In order to help achieve compliance the funds were issued in tranches. Thus aid became an instrument to achieve the economic policy desired by the neo-liberal counter-revolution and was used not for the direct relief of poverty (indeed arguably it was now used to create poverty) but for short-term macro-economic relief, with the stated aim of long-term economic growth.

The implementation of economic conditionality or what Stokke terms "first generation conditionality"[15] meant a significant change in the already asymmetrical relationship between the donor and the recipient in favour of the latter. In the previous eras aid usually came with various conditions attached, but these were invariably micro-economic and did not attempt to change the economic policy direction of the state.[16] The ability of the IMF to apply conditions to its lending had been incorporated into its Articles of Agreement as early as 1969,[17] but was not used extensively until the 1980s.[18]

Although exponents of SAPs, such as Krueger,[19] argue that conditionality is a result of policy dialogue between the IMF and the recipient, this position ignores totally the asymmetrical power relationship between the two parties. The key element of conditionality is "the use of pressure, by the donor, in terms of threatening to terminate aid, or actually terminating or reducing it, if conditions are not met by the recipient."[20] Thus the emphasis is on coercion rather than encouragement and is concerned with future rather than past conditions.[21] The increasingly asymmetrical relationship globally between the donor community and the recipients from the 1980s informs the context of the main body of the thesis.

The second important flow of rent to Jordan is remittances, which are considered as the portion of international migrant workers' earnings sent from the country of employment to the country of origin,[22] usually to the immediate family of the expatriate workers. These remittances can be the equivalent of a substantial proportion of the merchandise exports in a number of countries.[23] However, despite an IMF definition of remittances,[24] as with aid, severe problems are associated with the measurement of these flows. Inconsistencies in the interpretation of the reporting result in difficulties of calculating the exact figures. Secondly, not all remittances are in the form of cash: in-kind transfers also occur.[25] Furthermore, the level of remittances is understated as the figures recorded apply only to those remittances received through official channels. However, no reliable estimates are available for the transfers using the unofficial channels, although Abella, writing in 1989, estimates that in countries such as Pakistan, the Philippines, Sudan and Egypt the total could be tripled.[26]

The actual volumes of remittances depend on a number of factors, including the size of the migrant workforce, the level of their earnings and their willingness to remit. The final factor is, in turn, dependent on macro-economic factors, such as the economic conditions in the host country, the differential in interest rates between the two countries, the exchange rate, and incentives offered by the labour-exporting country. In addition, socio-demographic characteristics affect the levels remitted, including the length of time spent abroad (generally, the longer the time abroad the less the value of the remittances).[27]

Although the transfers increase the standard of living of the recipients, not all the macro-economic effects are positive. Remittances may be used by the recipients in a number of ways, such as investing in productive or non-productive assets, consumed through the acquisition of domestically produced goods/services and/or imported goods/services, or saved domestically or abroad. However, as discussed previously, the increase in the standard of living encourages spending on imports, creating difficulties in the balance of trade of the labour-exporting country. Furthermore, countries, such as Jordan, have regularly adopted policies aimed at ensuring high levels of remittances, including maintaining high interest rates and an over-valued currency. However, these policies have a detrimental effect on promoting the supposed prime objective of creating an export-oriented industrial economy.

Remittances have formed an important part of the Jordanian economy since the mid-1970s and in terms of their share of the rent, remittances have become progressively more important. This relative increase forms a core element of the final chapters of the thesis.

Returning to the discussion the focus is turned to what is a rentier economy? Two important elements contribute to the concept. Firstly, as is apparent from the five different types, rent will exist in all national economies. However, in a rentier economy rent is the predominant contributor to the national income. Secondly, as the concept is being defined for the purposes of analysing the relationship between the state and the private sector, the rent in question must be external. A preponderance of internal rent would have no effect on this relationship, merely creating a strong rentier class or group but still requiring the existence of a strong productive sector in order to be maintained.[28] Consequently, a rentier economy is one in which external rent contributes significantly to the national income or, as Mahdavy argues, a "rentier economy is an economy which relies on substantial external rent."[29]

However, this definition is subjective: when does external rent become significant? At this stage the analysis is concerned with producing an economic measure for rent. Once an economy has been proved to contain a degree of rent, the analysis will then assess what the political implications are. Furthermore, establishing a base line figure, above which an economy is deemed to be rentier and below which it is productive, is too cut and dry. Indeed, an economy can switch over time between these categories. Consequently, a preferable method is to analyse the degree of rent from low, through medium to high, based on the model developed later in the chapter. Admittedly, this measure can be open to accusations of vagueness but without a comparative analysis of a number of rentier economies (which is beyond the scope of this study), it is impossible to design a more objective method.

While this measure may not seem contentious, assessing the value of any type of rent is not straightforward as the previous discussion has indicated.[30] Furthermore, different reputable sources, such as the IMF, the World Bank and the Organisation for Economic Cooperation and Development (OECD), can give considerably different figures for what ought to be the same unit/phenomenon. Remittances suffer equal problems of measurement in that they regularly by-pass the official banking system and therefore cannot be calculated accurately. Given the problems facing official economic figures in Jordan until very recently, the difficulties of estimating the levels of remittances by-passing the official system would involve a further research project. In addition, a question arises as to what proportion of the remittance can be classified as rent. Should the full amount repatriated be considered or merely the excess over the amount which could have been earned in the home country? While this discussion is appropriate, the need to delve as deeply is beyond the ambit of this study. Consequently, as the analysis is primarily based on figures over a period of time, the overall imperative is to use one measure (and as far as possible one source) to ensure continuity of comparison.

STATE RENTIERISM VERSUS PRIVATE SECTOR RENTIERISM

So far, the discussion has concentrated on external rent accruing to the national economy. An important distinction is now introduced: to which particular sector, private or public, the rent accrues. This difference creates what this study terms 'state rentierism' and 'private sector rentierism', dependent on the sector to which the rent accrues. A rentier economy can comprise of either, or a combination of both: thus both a rentier state economy and a private sector rentier economy can be considered a sub-set of a rentier economy (figure 2.1). In the majority of rentier economies in the Middle East, rent accrues predominantly to the state in the form of oil revenues (e.g. Saudi Arabia), portfolio income (Kuwait), locational rent (Suez Canal revenues in Egypt), and/or aid[31] (Jordan until mid-1970s). However, since the 1970s oil boom, large-scale rent in the form of remittances has been channelled into the private sector in a number of labour-exporting countries, such as Egypt, Yemen and Jordan. These funds are not received by the state but by individuals/families, and therefore the state can only access the funds through indirect means, such as taxation or the creation of public sector controlled savings schemes. The funds represent latent capital that may be invested in productive or non-productive assets, consumed through the acquisition of domestically produced goods/services and/or imported goods/services, or saved domestically or abroad. In each case, with the exception of 'saved abroad', the funds tend to benefit the private sector, admittedly to varying degrees but in each case directly, whereas the government can only benefit on a secondary or indirect level. The state has no control over the rent, although it may adopt policies that allow access to the rent circuit.

According to rentier theory, the accrual of rent to the state creates a particular set of relations between the state and society in general, and, consequently, between state and the private sector. In addition, a particular set of relations between the domestic economy and the international economy is formed. This latter relationship impinges directly on how the regime interacts with certain international actors, such as the donor community in the case of aid. The accrual of significant sums of rent to the private sector has the potential to change considerably the relationship between the state and the private sector and, to a lesser degree, the state and the donor community. This aspect of rentierism has suffered from a lack of research,[32] which this study aims to help rectify.

Figure 2.1   **Types of Rentier Economy**

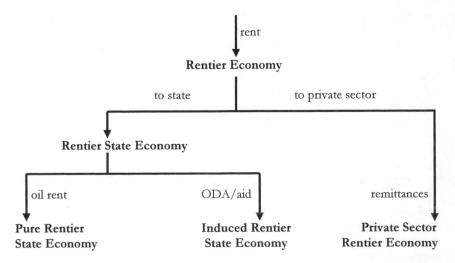

Based on rent accruing to the state or to the private sector, the two poles of a rentier economy that can be envisaged are an unadulterated rentier state economy and an unadulterated private sector rentier economy. As has been highlighted, these polar opposites are only possible in theory; in reality, an economy will contain elements of each, which will vary over time. The study will now clarify the various terms that are used in rentier writings before discussing the effects of rent on the state-private sector and state-donor relationships. The next section discusses the difference between a 'normal' production economy and a rentier economy.

PRODUCTION ECONOMY VERSUS RENTIER ECONOMY

The starting point for the following discussion is that a rentier economy differs in important elements from a production economy. In the production economy the national income is predominantly composed of firstly the productive activities of the citizens through wages, and secondly businesses through profit. The state raises revenue through direct and indirect taxation of these productive activities in order to continue to recreate itself. In the production economy, the production/redistribution/extraction[33] state "has an interest in expanding the income base on which taxes can be levied"[34] to ensure its continued role. As the state is limited in size by the amount of domestic revenue that can be raised, economic policies formulated by the state have the aim of creating economic growth for the economy as a whole in order to sustain the state. A degree of consensus is built round the level of taxation levied: in the words of Vanderwalle an "historic compromise."[35] The private sector, on the other hand, is concerned with profit maximisation, which in production economies is a corollary of economic growth.[36] The relationship between the state and the private sector can be viewed as one in which the private sector expects the state to provide a degree of security and protection, without impinging directly on its activities. The two actors are clearly delineated, but with a degree of interdependence. Importantly, the private sector is not homogenous but is comprised of many different groups, not all necessarily pulling in the same direction. The bureaucracy is built around the extractive capacity of the state, and is seen to act as a mediator between the state and the private sector, through its rules and procedures.   On the external level, the state's economic relations with the international community are formulated on the need to attract investment and to increase exports. Both these measures, if successful, will increase the taxation base and therefore sustain the existence of the state. One final point should be borne in mind: the state can also expand its activities by borrowing domestically and/or internationally. However, the servicing of such debts is merely part of government expenditure and is therefore still constrained by the revenue-raising capacity. Thus in the production economy the state remains reliant on the economic development of the private sector.

By contrast, the rentier economy, which is an economy where the substantial part of its revenue accrues from foreign sources and under the form of rent but "the rent need not accrue directly to state,"[37] produces a different relationship between the state and the private sector, and the state and international community based on a "rentier mentality."[38]   This mentality breaks the conventional work/risk and reward causation found in the production economy, with the result that "[g]etting access to the rent circuit is a greater pre-occupation than reaching productive efficiency."[39] However, the rentier mentality is not only about gaining access to the rent circuit but also it allows those with the available resources to attempt to gain control of the rent.[40] Finally, protecting control and access becomes an integral part of economic strategy. Thus, the bread riots, which have erupted occasionally in the Arab world following the withdrawal or reduction of subsidies, can be seen as expressions of rentier mentality. The importance of gaining and maintaining access or control means "[s]pecial social and economic interests are organised in such a manner as to capture a good slice of ... rent."[41] Government policy takes on a two-dimensional role that involves maintaining control of and access to rent, while pursuing a politically-driven expenditure policy. Thus, the scene is set for a different relationship between the state and the private sector and the state and the donor community in a rentier economy than that which occurs in a production economy.

However, these relationships are further dependent on the type of rent. Two important variables occur between the types of rents: to whom the rent accrues, and whether a third party plays a significant role (table 2.2). Oil rent accrues directly to the state, without the significant intervention of a third actor resulting in pure-state rentierism.[42] Aid also accrues to the state, but is dependent to a major degree on the political interests of the donor, resulting in an induced rentier state economy. This dependence exacerbates the volatile nature of rent, which can result in threats of instability for the incumbent regime.   The pure rentier state economy (oil) and induced rentier state economy (aid) can be considered sub-sets of the rentier state economy (figure 2.1). Remittances accrue to the private sector (i.e. a private sector rentier economy), on the forbearance of a third party: the state in which the expatriates work. The oil revenue slump of the 1980s and the Gulf crisis of 1990 illustrated the vulnerability of Jordanian remittances to external crises.

Table 2.2   **Differences in Types of Rent**

Rent	Accrues To	Third Party	Relevance to Jordan
Oil	State	No	Insignificant
Aid	State	Donor Community	Highly Relevant
Remittances	Private Sector	Labour-Importing State	Highly Relevant

The rentier state is one in which "the *government* is the principal recipient of the external rent in the economy."[43] Alternatively, a number of writers prefer the term allocative or allocation state.[44] Rather than concentrating on the source of revenue the term arises from the main activity of the rentier state, which rather than extracting revenue from the population, allocates the rent to the population. Nevertheless, the two terms can be used interchangeably. Luciani actually sets a precise figure for when a state attains rentier status: "all states whose revenue derives predominantly (more than 40 per cent) from oil or other foreign sources and whose expenditure is a substantial share of GDP."[45] To clarify then two different styles of rentier state economy are found, based on the type of rent accruing to the state: 1) pure rentier state economies, (oil revenue based); and 2) induced rentier state economies (aid).

The following section discusses the first of these and the effects on the nature of the state and the private sector, and the relationship between the two.

PURE RENTIER STATE ECONOMIES: OIL RENT

The pure rentier states form the basis for the following analysis of the political correlates of the rentier state. The initial discussion ignores the influence of the third party, which can be found in aid rent but not in oil rent. Once the basis of the state-private sector relationship has been established in a pure rentier state, the analysis will be extended to account for possible third party intervention, in the form of aid.

In the pure rentier state, the state is the prime economic power. As discussed earlier, the influence of the rentier mentality results in the state adopting a two-dimensional policy-making process: maintaining control of and access to rent and allocating expenditure rather than the raising of domestic revenues (figure 2.2a). The first dimension is focused outwards on the source of the rent. Thus in the case of Saudi Arabia, policy would be aimed around maintaining the price of oil and ensuring a smooth supply to the world market. The second dimension, namely a politically-inspired "expenditure policy",[46] can be seen in a number of outcomes: 1) infrastructure development, which will be led through state-controlled development plans; 2) state-controlled or state-supported enterprises; 3) subsidies both of basic necessities, such as bread, electricity and water, and those aimed at favoured businesses, such as cheap loans and tax breaks; 4) contracts from the state to favoured businesses; 5) 'Royal' favours, such as free land in return for political support; 6) bureaucracy built around allocative, rather than extractive, mechanisms; 7) regulations aimed at preferred businesses, such as partnership agreements in Saudi Arabia, which allow foreigners to establish trades and professions in conjunction with a Saudi national; and 8) the state as a major source of employment. The majority of these features impact significantly on the development of a private sector, which then becomes dependent on the state for its growth.

The outcomes of the expenditure policy help to legitimise the rule of the state without the necessity for democratic institutions. Citizenship becomes a source of economic benefit whether through subsidies or employment, while in return the state expects loyalty without political participation. As Najmabadi claims, the traditional tribal/kinship networks, already in existence prior to the formation of the Middle East rentier state, provide "the new economic and political élite, the backbone of the new state bureaucracies, and to a large extent they also provided a ready-made distribution network for the new wealth."[47] Consequently, pure state rentierism has been able to "reinforce traditional forms of tribal networks, linking business and government through kinship networks, tribal loyalties and business partnerships."[48] The second aspect is that economic policy is used to build and reinforce the state, not only through a sizeable bureaucracy, but also through industrialisation policies. The state moves into the productive sector, either at the expense of, or in co-ordination with, elements of the private sector. Thirdly, the expenditure policy creates a short-termism aimed at increasing rent, not at long-term policies predicated on achieving sustainable economic growth. The failure of the Gulf oil states, in general, to diversify into other sectors to reduce their dependency on oil can be seen as a classic example of this short-termism. Similarly, in the induced rentier state, the periodic 'world' tours of King Hussein pleading for extra aid, rather than actively promoting a restructuring of the domestic economy, were a perfect example of this policy. Indeed, one of King Abdullah's first moves, on acceding to throne, was to embark on a world tour with this aim in mind. However, the outcome was largely unsuccessful, laying the foundations for the new King's acceptance of the need to implement wholesale economic liberalisation.

What, then, are the effects of pure rentier state rentierism on the private sector and on its relationship with the state? Firstly, pure state rentierism creates an imbalance between production and the standard of living. Levels of consumption are greater than could be afforded in an economy that was reliant only on the productive sector. Economically, the high levels of consumption translate into higher than expected levels of imports (although these are more than offset by export revenues from oil—indeed one of the main features of a pure rentier state economy are high balance of trade surpluses), as the higher levels of private consumption are directed towards imports. The imbalance skews the interests of the private sector towards catering for the imports needed to feed the level of consumption. The private sector tends, therefore, to move towards the service sector, failing to form a vibrant industrial sector. Secondly, as with other forms of rentierism the private sector adopts a rentier mentality: rent-seeking rather than profit-seeking becomes the order of the day. The rent seeking is manifested in the formation of businesses designed to access the allocation of rent by the state, such as construction companies, and to access the indirect or second-level rent in the economy, e.g. import companies. As these companies become directly and/or indirectly reliant on the state for survival they build close relations with it. In addition, individual members of the regime are able to establish similar companies to gain access to the rent that they themselves disburse.

The result is state-private sector relations become blurred, as the distinction between public and private interests breaks down, or is not clearly differentiated from the outset. The blurring is manifested in a plethora of ways. Among the examples is the involvement of the state in part-ownership of 'private' companies; "élite circulation"[49] with the appointment of state officials to the boards of private companies and the reverse case with the appointment of élite private sector representatives sitting on the boards of state companies; and the voluntary co-optation of the private business associations, such as Chambers of Commerce and Industry and, in the case of Jordan, the Jordanian Businessmen Association (JBA). In addition, formal relations between the two sectors based on institutions tend to be by-passed and/or fall into disuse, while informal contacts become the order of the day.[50] Although accusations of corruption are regularly heard, little or no action is usually taken to stop the use of public resources to boost private interests. The state acts to provide special favours via legislation, subsidies, 'royal' favours, contracts, etc. Rather than being seen as a competitor to the private sector in, for example, industrialisation, the state becomes a friend to particular private sector interests.

The blurring discussed earlier means that a distinct private sector, as would be found in a production economy, is not evident. The élites of the private sector and the state found in the production economy are subsumed in the pure rentier state into a combined rentier élite. Importantly, this rentier élite is hierarchical, with the main power centre equated with the ruling regime. Thus in Saudi Arabia, the al-Saud family is considered the prime element of the rentier élite, while in Jordan the Hashemites fulfil the same role. However, for analytical purposes three characteristics of a private sector that evolves from this form of rent can be adduced. The first is that the main actors in the private sector are relatively homogenous in their outlook, with the rentier mentality creating a bias towards the service sector. Secondly, the private sector becomes heavily dependent on the state for its profits and its continued survival. Finally, the private sector becomes 'captured' by the state, acting as a tool for the political and economic interests of the élite. Thus an independent private sector fails to emerge, but a relatively homogenous dependent captive private sector evolves. On the other side of the equation, as a consequence of the flows of rent, a different type of state from that of the production state develops. The pure rentier state is able to use the rent to buy political support from various groups in society, including the private sector élite. Indeed due to the resources at its disposal the state can eliminate old classes and create new ones, as occurred with the business élite in Saudi Arabia.[51] In addition, what was a political state élite has now become what can be described as a political state élite with private sector economic interests, as the élite has expanded its activities through direct intervention in the economy, including the ownership of productive assets. The *raison d'être* of the pure rentier state is drawn from the rentier mentality and is concerned with controlling and gaining access to the flows of rent.

Although intuitively this state would seem to be strong and therefore autonomous from society in general and from the private sector in particular, the reverse is actually the case. This apparent paradox occurs because of the rentier élite, which is politically and economically bound to the political and economic structures created by the oil-rent. Thus when levels of rent decline, as happened during the mid-1980s, the apparently strong state is unable to implement the change demanded by the international community to overcome the potential collapse of the economy.[52] The close relationship between the state and private sector based on the new rentier élite acts as a major impediment to the threat of change. The élite, with its short-term rentier mentality, lobbies against changes that they perceive are not to be in their immediate interest. The political and economic interests of the élite have become dependent on the status quo. Rather than becoming autonomous, oil rentierism creates a state whose links with the private sector make wholesale, speedy change almost impossible to implement.

INDUCED RENTIER STATE ECONOMIES: AID RENT

Having discussed pure state rentierism (i.e. no third party involvement) the analysis now assesses the differences between oil rent and aid rent. Firstly, an important difference between these rents is the relative importance of each in the economy. In the pure rentier state, oil rent can account for in excess of 90% of the GNP, whereas in induced rentier states based on aid rent the importance is considerably less, but nevertheless still remains significant. As the level of rent accruing to the state is less, the influence of the state in the economy is also reduced. However, the overall effect will be to dilute, but certainly not negate, the various features of the state-private sector relationship in comparison with a pure rentier state. Thus, as opposed to the pure rentier state, the two sectors will still become blurred but the rentier élite will be less homogenous and less powerful. In addition, the state will less easily be able to create and destroy classes, and the private sector will be captured to a lesser degree. The symbiosis between the two sectors will nonetheless ensure that the adoption of any change of economic direction, which threatens the immediate interests of the élite, will be challenged.

Secondly, aid is dependent on a third party, the donor, whose interests are invariably political, thus resulting in the funds, and, therefore, the state being highly vulnerable to political and economic events outside its control. With oil rent, the state controls the source of the rent (but certainly not all the market conditions), in contrast to aid where the donor controls the flow of rent. In order to continue to access aid the state has to adopt, or be seen to attempt to adopt, policies (whether in the field of security, politics or economics), which meet the criteria of the donor, without affecting the short-term stability of the regime.[53] However, until the end of the 1980s in the bipolar Cold War world the recipient state was often in a position to threaten the donor with a change of allegiance, thus maintaining high levels of aid. The result was that states such as Jordan became hooked on the 'cocaine' of aid, adopting a rentier mentality at the external level of economic decision-making in order to avoid the 'cold turkey' of withdrawal. Since the late 1980s, the move towards the imposition of political and economic conditions by donors on the recipients has reduced the leeway for the rentier state to implement domestic economic, and to a lesser degree political, policies outside the global norm. In addition, the scope for playing one donor off against another has diminished, almost to zero, since the end of the Cold War. These two factors have reduced the autonomy and space for manoeuvre of the rentier state *vis-à-vis* the donor community, providing a rein on the rentier mentality. How the support of the donor community for the enhancement of the private sector's role in the economy changes the relationship between the state and the private sector, given the existence of a relatively homogenous rentier élite, is one of the questions that will be addressed in the following chapters. A further question that will be addressed is: whether the state can prove resilient in the face of donor conditionality due to historical state-private sector relationship?

A further difference from the pure rentier state is that the induced rentier state can afford to run budget deficits (excluding aid). As the deficits are funded by the aid, a higher level of government expenditure is possible paralleling the higher consumption levels of the private sector in the pure rentier state. In times of recession, this feature allows the donor community to be able to apply extra pressure in having the recipient state adapt new economic policies.

To summarise, the characteristics of the induced rentier state economy are: 1) a dependency on aid; 2) a high level of imports, which help to create a chronic balance of trade deficit (in comparison high earnings from oil revenues more than offset high levels of imports in a pure rentier state economy); 3) a high level of state expenditure resulting in continual budget deficits (excluding aid); 4) economic sectoral imbalances in favour of services; and 5) high levels of consumption in comparison to GDP. Meanwhile, the state follows a two-dimensional policy of maintaining control of and access to rent and pursuing a politically motivated expenditure policy (figure 2.2b) and has the ability to create and destroy classes. The private sector is: 1) relatively homogenised in outlook; 2) dependent on the state; and 3) service oriented. The relationship between the private and public sectors is blurred, which results in: 1) the creation of a rentier élite; 2) élite circulation between the two sectors; 2) voluntary co-optation or 'capture' of the private sector by the state; 3) informal rather than formal contacts between the private sector and the state; and 4) endemic corruption.

Regularly, rentier theory analysis uses only the one measure, rent as a percentage of GNP, to assess the degree of rent in the economy. However, this indicator does not reveal the full picture. Therefore this study uses a model based on a combination of six measures to present a more accurate reflection of the situation with regard to the induced rentier state economy. Although calculating aid as a percentage of GNP can assess the importance of aid to the economy, this measure does not necessarily reflect the position fully. The funds must be circulated within the economy, not merely redirected externally for debt repayments or to private banks in Switzerland.[54] If the funds are circulated within the economy the effects can be seen in government expenditure. Thus the higher the percentage of expenditure accounted for by aid, the greater the level of state rentierism, as the aid and oil rent allows the state to contribute a higher share of the GNP than would be the case in a production economy. Thirdly, the government retains the ability to raise revenues domestically, via taxation. The less the government relies on domestic revenue the greater the effects of the induced rentier state economy ought to be. The overall effects on government expenditure and revenue are reflected in the budget deficit, which can be offset by the use of aid. Persistent trade deficits can also be compensated for by regular inflows of aid, sustaining an unbalanced economy. Finally, the volume of aid in relation to the population must also be considered, as relatively bigger populations will dilute the effects of aid. In order to take account of these factors, the thesis will use six measures to assess the degree of the induced rentier state economy: 1) gross aid as a percentage of GNP; 2) gross aid as a percentage of government revenue; 3) gross aid as a percentage of government expenditure; 4) gross aid as a percentage of budget deficit, excluding aid; 5) gross aid as a percentage of trade deficit; and 6) gross aid per capita. In normal circumstance, a high degree of correlation ought to exist between the six measures.

PRIVATE SECTOR RENTIER ECONOMIES: REMITTANCES

The discussion now moves from state rentierism to the opposite end of the rent continuum, private sector rent in the form of remittances. An economy based on remittances displays a number of similarities to state rentierism, but significant differences are also apparent. As with other forms of rent, the predominance of remittances in the economy ensures that a rentier mentality is adopted by both the private and public sectors. This rent-seeking mentality is again manifested in the public sector in a dual policy (figure 2.2c). Firstly, in order for the state to reproduce itself the continuing flow of remittances must be ensured. Policy-making, as far as possible, becomes directed at maintaining relations with the labour-importing countries.[55] Secondly, the state adopts economic policies that attempt to ensure access to the flow of remittances, as the state is unable directly to control or access the flows of rent, as it was able to do under state rentierism. For example, although direct taxation on inward capital transfers is possible, this method either discourages the transfer of remittances or else unofficial channels are used to by-pass the taxation. Therefore, the state's most realistic option for raising domestic revenue on remittance income is via indirect taxation, for example through custom duties on the imports fed by the remittance economy. Thus, although significant trade deficits are experienced, policies will rarely be taken to cut the levels of imports. In addition, businesses with direct access to the flow of rent will be encouraged by the state, via different types of incentives. These businesses can then be subject to taxation, further allowing the state to gain indirect access to the flow of remittances. The state can also access the flow by establishing compulsory or voluntary savings schemes under its control. However, the lack of direct access to the rent flow results in less finance being available to the state, which in turn is less able to move directly into economy but also is unable to provide the level of social services associated with both a production economy (paid for by taxes) and a rentier state economy (paid for by rent).

Although the private sector ought to be able to move into the productive sector three factors combine to produce a private sector that is service-oriented. As in the case of aid, remittances create an imbalance between production and consumption, since higher standards of living than would be expected can be maintained, and again this extra consumption is disproportionally directed towards imports. In addition, the adoption of the rentier mentality ensures the private sector is geared towards providing the services that are needed by the remittance economy, such as banks and the import trade sector. Finally, as discussed above, the policies of the public sector reinforce the bias towards the service sector.

On the other hand, the private sector is able to develop independently of the state. Remittances can guarantee "the financial independence of the private sector."[56] Indeed in Chaudhry's study of the Yemen, the author found that the private sector was able to replace the state in areas of social welfare, such as education and health provision.[57] Although, the economy as a whole develops a bias towards the service sector, the flow of remittances does allow the private sector to form a series of different interest groups, similar to the production economy. Overall, the private sector therefore becomes service-oriented, independent of the state and relatively heterogeneous.

The relationship between the two sectors is therefore based on an apparently weak state and a strong private sector. The result is that the formal lines of communication between the two either atrophy (if they existed originally) or fail to develop as fully as in a production economy. In addition, the independence of the private sector from the state ensures that the informal contacts of the rentier state do not materialise.

Intuitively, the outcome would seem to be a strong and autonomous private sector and a weak state with little control over the private sector. However, in times of the retrenchment of remittances, the independence of the state from the private sector allows the former to adopt a policy of economic change. The reason for this set of affairs is due to the development of separate élites under private sector rentierism. In her study, Chaudhry[58] found that remittances helped to boost the position of the "traditional southern Sunni merchant class,"[59] with the northern tribes continuing to staff the apparatuses of the state such as the bureaucracy and the army.[60] Thus remittances "accentuated the longstanding disequilibria in the social composition of the bureaucracy and army on the one hand and the merchant class on the other."[61] In other words, under private sector rentierism the state and private sector élites are able to develop independently of each other, in contrast to induced state rentierism. The lack of élite rotation, voluntary co-optation of the private business associations and informal contacts between the two sectors allowed the state and private sectors to remain separate entities. Thus when remittances retreated in the mid-1980s the apparently weak state was able to implement policies that were detrimental to powerful private sector interests.

Similarly to the case of the induced rentier state economy a model, on this occasion using four measures, has been developed to assess the degree to which an economy can be termed as a private sector rentier economy. The first measure of the level of the private sector rentier economy is the ratio of remittances to GNP. Again, however, this indicator does not paint the full picture. Firstly, the volume of remittances will be diluted when spread over a larger population. In addition, remittances are often used to fuel levels of imports, producing a trade deficit, which, as with aid, can be sustained by remittances. Finally, the relative importance of remittances to aid needs to be established in order to distinguish which of the two is more likely to have the greater effect on state-donor and state-private sector relations. Consequently, the analysis uses four measures of private-sector rentierism: 1) remittances as a percentage of GNP; 2) remittances per capita; 3) remittances as a percentage of trade deficit; and 4) remittances as a percentage of aid.

INDUCED STATE RENTIERISM AND PRIVATE SECTOR RENTIERISM

This discussion of the different forms of rentierism has allowed the diverse outcomes caused by different types of rent to be drawn out. The first difference highlighted has been the relationship between the type of rent, the state and the private sector (figures 1.2a, 1.2b and 1.2c). In the case of the pure rentier state economy, the state has significant control over the allocation of rent, which itself is relatively more important in the economy than in the case of the induced rentier state economy. In the latter case, the state is also constrained by the influence of the donor community. The state's role is further diluted in the case of the private sector rentier economy, as it cannot control the flow of rent but can only adopt policies that will allow it access to the flow of rent.

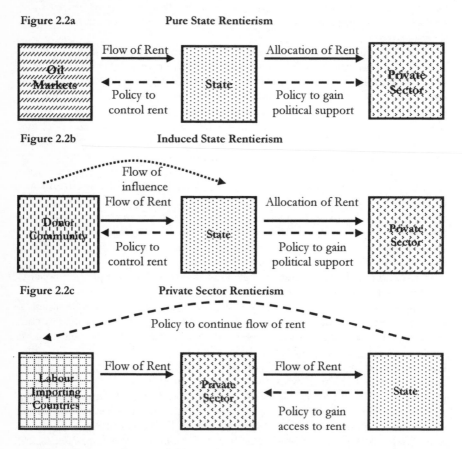

Figure 2.2a   **Pure State Rentierism**

Figure 2.2b   **Induced State Rentierism**

Figure 2.2c   **Private Sector Rentierism**

The primary concerns of this study are the cases of the induced rentier state economy (aid) and private sector rentier economy (remittances). In each case a certain set of characteristics are apparent: in the case of the induced rentier state economy these characteristics have been termed induced state rentierism, and for the private sector rentier economy, they are referred to as private sector rentierism. The theoretical discussion has highlighted that private sector rentierism has similarities to induced state rentierism in that both: 1) are dependent on rent (albeit of different types); 2) suffer from chronic balance of trade deficits due to the high levels of imports; 3) show high levels of consumption in comparison to GDP; and 4) produce economies that tend to be service-oriented. However, vital differences are also in evidence. Under private sector rentierism: 1) the state does not have control over rent but adopts different policies that allow it access to the rent. In addition, the level of expenditure policy is necessarily more restrained due to the restricted level of revenues; 2) the private sector becomes more heterogeneous; 3) the private sector develops independently of the state; 4) the political and economic élites remain separate; and 5) the relationship between the private and public sectors is based on formal but weak institutions.

In the case of Jordan, aid has been an important (if somewhat fluctuating) aspect of the economy from its inception. Only from the early 1970s, however, have remittances become a significant feature on the economic landscape. Chapters three and four investigate what happens to the state-private sector relationship in a case where remittances become an important factor in an economy in which the state and the private sector have already formed a symbiotic relationship, based on induced state rentierism. Theoretically, remittances ought to allow a private sector élite to (re-) emerge, and thus to (re-)gain independence from the state, but the rentier élite may be able to access the flow of remittances due to its close relationship with the private sector, ensuring no change in the balance of power in the economy.

STATE, REGIME, RENTIER ÉLITE AND PRIVATE SECTOR

This section discusses how the final four concepts (the state, the regime, the rentier élite and the private sector) are understood and used in the context of the study. The state and the market (a nebulous concept which can be represented institutionally by the private sector) interact in the modern world to create 'political economy'.[62] Neither the state nor the market exists in pure form, and both have changed with time, along with the balance of power within their interdependent relationship. International political economy analyses how these "two organising principles of social life"[63] interact at the global level: indeed a number of writers view international political economy as a battleground between the two concepts,[64] proscribing prescriptive solutions in favour of either.

THE STATE, THE REGIME AND THE RENTIER ÉLITE

At the beginning of the 21st century one of the major debates in international political economy revolves around whether the state is in retreat or whether it has merely repositioned itself in the face of the changing international climate driven by the end of the Cold War and globalisation. A major flaw in the whole debate is the lack of agreement over the nature of the state. Despite (or perhaps because of) the extensive usage and the longevity (over four centuries)[65] of theoretical debate over the nature of the state, this concept remains "the most opaque term in the whole of political vocabulary."[66] Indeed, Held argues that the term is the most contested in political and social theory.[67]

Among the many uses of the term, three stand out: 1) the state as a sovereign political entity with international recognition, its own boundaries and its national symbols;[68] 2) the state as a single entity, which is able to define a coherent rational approach to decision-making in the national interest; and 3) the state as an arena of contestation, in which economic decision-making is the outcome of interaction between various domestic and international forces.

In rentier theory, the state is used in both the latter two senses. In the single entity sense, the state is an actor that is able not only to destroy and create classes but also to follow a two-dimensional policy of gaining access to rent and expenditure policy in order that it can continue to recreate itself. In the second sense, the state is an arena of contestation, in which the rentier élite uses the apparatus of state, such as the political system, the bureaucracy and the security forces, to maintain its position of dominance.

Throughout the study, the state is used in all three senses discussed earlier. When referring to the state of Jordan, the first sense of a sovereign political entity is used. The state as a single entity forms much of the analysis in defining the degrees of rentierism in the economy, when the state-market continuum is used as a measure (chapters three and five). The state as an arena of contestation can be seen throughout the thesis with the analysis of the rentier élite's attempts to maintain access to the sources of rent, whether aid or remittances. This method of analysis follows the model used by Owen in his recent article.[69]

As with the term state the concept rentier élite is open to debate. For the purposes of this study the rentier élite is broadly defined as an informal group that holds the key positions in the political decision-making set-up (including the top posts in the bureaucracy and the security services), as well as the leading decision-makers and power-brokers in the economic field. In Jordan, membership of the group has traditionally been based around a network of families with close ties to the ruling Hashemite dynasty. Indeed, descendents of Emir Abdullah's original supporters when he first came to Transjordan remain within the rentier élite. However, the composition of the group is dynamic as new members are able to join, while previously important families can be by-passed. An important aspect of the rentier élite has been the degree to which this group have been able to dictate the political and economic agenda of Jordan for their own purposes, within the constraints imposed by the international, regional and domestic environment.

In the rentier state in the Middle East, the principal actors are the state, the regime and the rentier élite. The three are interdependent and overlapping, with the rentier élite forming one part of the state. However, the ability of the rentier élite to gain access to and to control the preponderance of rent in the economy allows it to dominate the decision-making process. The regime is at the apex of the rentier élite: in the case of Jordan this is the Hashemite royal family. Ultimately in this relationship the regime attempts to use the state to maintain its position of dominance but different elements within the state, such as the bureaucracy, are able to subvert (to varying degrees depending on the issue and their access to resources) the policy for their own interests. Indeed the regime's interests may not always equate with those of the wider rentier élite. The tension among these three actors, within the constraints of the structures of the global and domestic political, economic and security structures, provides the context for the analysis of the thesis.

THE PRIVATE SECTOR

The private sector is that "part of an economy in which goods and services are produced and distributed by individuals and organizations that are not part of the government or state bureaucracy."[70] In a market-based economy, the private sector is considered the antithesis of the state. This public/private dichotomy has informed much of the thinking behind the IMF's SAPs, which considers state involvement in the economy divisive but, in contrast, the private sector is considered as the potential engine for economic development. However, as the discussion on rentier theory highlighted, the division between the two is not clearly defined in a rentier state, particularly at the important élite level. The blurring does not mean that an independent private sector is not present, merely that the one that exists is unable to exert any significant influence on the economic and political decision-making process.

Although the thesis tends to use the private sector as a single entity, for example in the measures on the state-market continuum, it cannot always be conceived of as a homogenous actor. Different sectors require or seek different types of interaction with the state at different times. For example, broadly speaking, industrialists may seek protection from imports through the imposition of customs duties and quotas. On the other hand, those involved in the export/import business do not want these barriers to trade. This heterogeneity must be borne in mind throughout the study.

Finally, the perception of the Transjordanian-Palestinian divide in Jordan remains strong with the former being associated with the public sector and perceived as obstructive to the private sector, which is associated with latter. Although a number of recent studies have challenged this dichotomy particularly at the level of the élite, the perception remains powerfully embedded in the minds of many Jordanians and scholars of Jordan. This perception has a powerful influence in disguising the blurred nature of the relationship between the state and the private sector.

SUMMARY

This chapter has established the theoretical and conceptual foundations of the study. The next chapter sets the context for the later analysis by highlighting the historical evolution of the rentierism in the economy of Jordan from its formation as a state under the British mandate in 1921 to the start of the IMF's SAP in 1989.

3

Changing Patterns of
the Rentier Economy

INTRODUCTION

The next two chapters set the context for the analysis of the effects of the involvement of the IMF-led donor community on state-private relations after 1989. The changing rentier elements in the period prior to 1989 helped forge the nature of both the state and the private sector, and a particular set of relations between the two. These historic rentier aspects then inform the reactions of the rentier élite to the IMF's attempts to change the structure of the Jordanian economy. This chapter establishes the changing nature of the rent in the economy from 1921 to 1989, while chapter four highlights the effects of the changes on the nature of the state and the private sector, and on the state-private sector relationship.

Aid and remittances are highly dependent on external conditions and to a lesser degree on internal conditions. Thus the analysis is based on four different but overlapping time-spans, which are differentiated by the changes in the political, economic and security environment. The four eras are: Mandate Transjordan: from the early 1920s to the mid-1940s; state-building in independent Jordan: from the late 1940s to the early 1970s; the 'years of plenty': from the early 1970s to the early 1980s; and the 'years of lean': from the early 1980s to the late 1980s. The last two eras are analysed together because of the difficulty of defining a clean break between the 'plenty' and the 'lean'.

Each era is assessed in a similar pattern. Firstly, the important external and internal political, geo-strategic and ideological factors are discussed. These factors are then related to their effects on the levels of the two major sources of rent in Jordan and their relative importance to the economy. Over the period, aid has fluctuated considerably in terms of amount, the relative level of grants and the sources. These aspects will be briefly discussed before aid is measured against GNP, per capita, government revenues and expenditure, budget deficit and trade deficit, in order to assess the changing degrees of the induced rentier state economy. In addition, remittances are assessed against the balance of trade deficit, GNP, per capita and aid to discover the depth of the private sector rentier economy.

An important consideration concerning the relationship between the defining events and the changes in rent is raised: the state cannot be considered to be merely a blank slate in the equation. For example, with each change in the regional geostrategic relationship, the state was required to reposition itself in relation to the members of the donor community. The two constants in the international relations dynamic of the region from post-World War II until 1989 were the security threats of the Cold War and the threats to regional stability, especially in relation to the Arab-Israeli dispute. The ability of the Hashemite regime to portray itself as a factor for stability in a region of apparently inherent instability enabled Jordan to replace its main sponsor on a number of occasions. Thus Britain was the main donor from the 1920s to 1950. From 1950 to 1956 Britain and the UN were the main donors. Thereafter the USA took over until 1973, while Arab bilateral assistance then dominated the donor community until 1989.

MANDATE TRANSJORDAN: THE EARLY 1920s TO THE MID-1940s

The creation of Transjordan can be seen as the result of a confluence of a number of events and ideas, none of which took into account the long-term economic viability of the country. These political and strategic factors included the need to reward the Hashemites for their assistance during the First World War, the question as to what should be done with the area to the east of the Jordan, the principle of the mandate system, and, perhaps most importantly, the need to satisfy British and French national interests in the region. Britain accepted the installation of Emir Abdullah "because it required no troops and it was tentative enough not to prejudice other, perhaps better, arrangements that might be possible in the future."[71] For his part Abdullah accepted it as a stepping-stone to greater aspirations, such as becoming the ruler in Damascus.[72] This marriage of convenience was to have a profound effect on the future of Jordan. The country itself was a political creation with no sense of national identity. The ruler was an imposed foreigner, and the political élite were in the main foreigners, all of whom were expressing Arab nationalist ambitions rather than narrow Transjordanian national interests.

The League of Nations formally approved the British mandate in July 1922, which was followed by the Anglo-Transjordanian agreement of the 25th March 1923 that provided for an autonomous administration under Abdullah. The formal political system was not established until five years later, following the signing of the 1928 Anglo-Transjordanian Treaty. A number of laws were promulgated, including the Organic Law of 1928 (in effect the constitution), the Electoral Law of 1928,[73] and the 1928 Nationality Law.

By the end of the 1920s, the confluence of events that resulted in the formation of Transjordan had laid the basis for the future development of the country. Domestically, Emir Abdullah was at the apex of power, with few formal constraints on his actions, but as an outsider he found it necessary to purchase his legitimacy, often via financial means.[74] Further constraints on Abdullah were the British control of the financial subsidy (which not only allowed for the patrimonial political system to be sustained but also kept the country afloat), of the security apparatus (not just financially but in terms of leadership) and of foreign policy.

The relationship between Britain and Abdullah has been described correctly as:

a product of marginal utility ... . Marginal utility, however, did not mean equality. Abdullah, for Britain, was only one piece in the interlocking patterns of allies and protégés stretching from Egypt to Iran which maintained Britain's overall position of superiority in the region. Without him the pattern might not be so neat, but Britain would still have been able adequately to protect its interest and its position.[75]

The 1928 treaty, in which "Britain laid down the conditions ... with inequality written into every clause, was the price of his [Abdullah's] position and one that he was willing to pay."[76]

The period of the mandate until the declaration of independence in 1946 saw five major developments:[77] the creation of a state bureaucracy and security apparatus; the building of a limited physical infrastructure; the suppression of internal revolts which initially threatened Hashemite supremacy; the stifling of external aggression, in particular from the nascent state of Ibn Saud in the south; and perhaps most importantly "the detribalisation of the desert which allowed for the integration of the Bedouin into the state."[78] The latter was achieved through the use of land settlement[79] and through employment in the Arab Legion where the Bedouin were inculcated with the ideas of the modern state.[80] Mazur adds a further two developments, the introduction of the tax system and the change of land ownership from *mushaa* to individual.[81] Significantly, development in the Mandate period, although steady, was always "as a junior associate of ambitious Palestine."[82]

THE CREATION OF THE INDUCED RENTIER STATE ECONOMY

The focus now turns to how the internal and external developments in the mandate era affected the levels of aid. From the creation of Transjordan, the country has been reliant on external economic assistance. As previously argued, British involvement in Jordan was motivated by political and geo-strategic concerns rather than by thoughts of economic development. The paucity of development of the local economy, the lack of natural resources and the absence of any centralised state apparatus meant that economic subsidies were necessary from day one. Emir Abdullah was initially granted £5,000 per month, which increased to £100,000 annually by the mid-1920s. By the mid-1940s the sum had reached £2m annually, although by this stage the budget was under the control of the British rather than the Emir[83] (see figure 3.1). The actual subsidy is understated due to a number of accounting procedures, which saw London and the Palestinian budget being used for spending relative to Transjordan.[84] The subsidy was in two forms: budgetary support and establishing and maintaining the Arab Legion. However, budgetary support was limited and primarily concerned with the maintenance of the governmental administration, with only small sums made available for welfare purposes and even less available for development purposes.

What, then, was the importance of the British subsidy in terms of the economy? Unfortunately, neither the national income nor the population figures are available for the period of the Mandate. Furthermore, as government expenditure was linked to the amount of revenue available, no deficits were experienced in this era, thereby negating the value of the measure of aid as a percentage of budget deficit. Thus the three measures of aid against GNP, per capita income and budget deficit cannot be used.

Figure 3.1   **British Subsidy, 1921/22-1943/44**

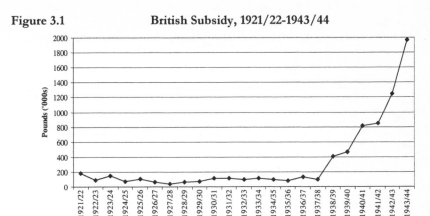

Sources: 1921/22 to 1923/24, Shwardan, B., (1959), *Jordan: A State of Tension*, (New York: Council for Middle Eastern Affairs Press), p. 164; 1924/25 to 1935/36, Naval Intelligence Division, (1943), *Palestine and Transjordan*, (no place of publication, Naval Intelligence Division), p. 500 and 1936/37 to 1943/44, Konikoff, A., (1946), *Transjordan: An Economic Survey*, (Jerusalem: Economic Research Institute of the Jewish Agency for Palestine), p.115.

As can be seen from table 3.1, the average percentage share of the British subsidy was over 50% of revenue over the period 1924/25 to 1943/44. However, the average hides a sharp change in relative and absolute terms from the year 1938/39, before which the subsidy had been running at an average of 26.8% of total revenue, ranging from a high of 38.2% in 1924/25 to a low of 16% in 1927/28. The initial reason for the change was the funding of the Baghdad to Haifa road that followed the route of the Iraqi Petroleum Company pipeline through Transjordan. Grants totalling around £P1m during the period 1938-39 to 1941-42 were received from the UK for that purpose. Thereafter, British war needs resulted in an increase in military expenditure, which in turn saw a jump in the subsidy. Similar results are also experienced in the relationship between the subsidy and government expenditure. Thus on both measures from the financial year (FY) 1938/39 a sharp increase in the degree of the induced rentier state economy is highlighted.

The final measure of the level of induced rentier state economy in the Mandate period is aid as a percentage of trade deficit. Unfortunately, figures for balance of trade (including re-exports) are not available prior to 1937. As is apparent from table 3.2 a significant increase in the induced rentier state economy is experienced, with the percentage of aid against the trade deficit increasing from a low of 15.2% in 1938 to 164.8% by 1944. The trade surplus recorded in 1943 was an abnormality, with the war forcing up the prices of agricultural exports to Palestine. Thus, even with the truncated data available, the evidence supports the other measures of an increasing induced rentier state economy.

The creation of Transjordan for strategic British interests, along with the imposition of a foreign ruling élite, which required the establishment of a degree of political legitimacy, resulted in the establishment of a state based on economic largesse. The lack of development and sources of raw materials compounded the need to rely on external rent. However, not until the late 1930s with the advent of the building of the Iraqi Petroleum Company road, and then the Second World War, could Transjordan have been declared a high-level induced rentier state economy.

Table 3.1: Aid as Percentage of Revenue and Expenditure, 1924/25-1943/44

Fiscal Year	Grants (£P)	Government Revenue (£P)	Grants as % of Revenue	Government Expenditure (£P)	Grants as % of Expenditure
1924/25-1937/38	1,305,330	4,864,236	26.8	4,859,644	26.9
1938/39-1943/44	5,741,090	8,375,516	68.5	8,615,645	66.6
1924/25-1943/44	**7,046,420**	**13,239,752**	**53.2**	**13,475,289**	**52.3**

Sources: Adapted by author. For years 1924/25 to 1933/34 Naval Intelligence Division, (1943), *Palestine and Transjordan*, (no place of publication, Naval Intelligence Division), p. 500. For years 1934/35 to 1943/44, Konikoff, A., (1946), *Transjordan: An Economic Survey*, (Jerusalem: Economic Research Institute of the Jewish Agency for Palestine), p.95.

Table 3.2   Aid as Percentage of Trade Deficit, 1937-1944

Year*	Balance of Trade Deficit** (£P)	Grants (£P)	Aid as % of Balance of Trade
1937	523,928	130,510	24.9
1938	664,003	100,990	15.2
1939	714,870	404,005	56.5
1940	827,037	465,201	56.2
1941	1,423,977	809,214	56.8
1942	1,044,067	850,333	81.4
1943	(46,016)	1,245,013	n.a.
1944	1,194,041	1,967,324	164.8

Source: Konikoff, A., (1946), *Transjordan: An Economic Survey*, (Jerusalem: Economic Research Institute of the Jewish Agency for Palestine), p.63.
* In the case of the balance of trade the figures are for the calendar year, whereas the grants refer to the FY. Thus the figures for 1937 refer to the balance of trade deficit for that year, but the grants are for 1936/37.
** Includes re-exports.

STATE-BUILDING AND POLITICAL INSTABILITY: LATE 1940 TO EARLY 1970

Between 1946 and 1948 a number of events occurred which altered the direct rule of Mandate Transjordan by Britain to the indirect rule of an independent Jordan. In March 1946 a new treaty was signed between Transjordan and the UK, which nominally gave independence to the former. As Dann argues, "the body of the treaty was innocuous, but an annex and an exchange of notes made clear that sovereign Transjordan would remain a military dependency of Britain."[85] As a result, the USA withheld recognition of the independence until the 31st January 1949. The treaty was followed in May 1946 by the adoption of Emir Abdullah as King Abdullah, and in February 1947 a new constitution was published replacing the Organic Law of 1928. In March 1948, a new treaty, which "softened some of the asperities of its predecessor",[86] was signed between Britain and Jordan. However British involvement remained to such an extent that it was able to dictate the speed and direction of economic development via the Jordanian Development Board[87] and to establish a currency board based in London to regulate the pace of sterling releases to Jordan.[88]

The Arab-Israeli war of 1948 introduced a significant change to the rentier development of Jordan. As a result of the subsequent annexation of the West Bank, the country, officially renamed the Hashemite Kingdom of Jordan, increased in size by about one-third, while its population expanded from around 375,000 to 1,185,000.[89] Of the new subjects, approximately 460,000 were resident on the West Bank, of whom between 100,000[90] and 160,000[91] were separated from their productive lands or from their employment in coastal Palestine, due to effects of the new borders. Furthermore, the East Bank had to absorb around 350,000 refugees from the fighting.

Following the 1948 Arab-Israeli war and Jordanian independence, two new donors became involved in Jordan: the USA and UNRWA. Until 1949, the British had been responsible for 100% of the external economic assistance to Jordan. This dominance came to an end with the commencement of operations in 1950 by UNRWA, which was established by the UN to assist the Palestinian refugees in the various Arab countries to which they had fled. Indeed Brand argues "UNRWA was a lifeline for Jordan: it provided shelter, food, educational facilities, and monetary support for one-third of the Kingdom's residents."[92] In the first year of operations UNRWA assistance of JD3m became more important than British assistance, although British assistance regained its dominance the following year.

British priorities changed following independence, with investment focusing on gradually developing the infrastructure and agriculture. The first British development loan, amounting to £1m, was offered in late 1949.[93] In spring 1951, Jordan came under the British development programme in the Middle East run by the British Middle East Office. The following autumn, in response to a request for a loan of £14m, the UK granted a second loan of £1.5m.[94] The loan was contingent on the formation of the Jordanian Development Board, the purpose of which was to attempt to co-ordinate development efforts of the UK, USA, UNRWA and the Jordanian government. Further development loans followed until 1956.

By the mid-1950s Jordan had moved from being a relatively inconsequential part of Britain's jigsaw in the Middle East to "the most reliable link in the chain of British bases between Suez and the Persian Gulf."[95] In 1956, the British subsidy had reached £12.5m,[96] of which, in round figures, £9m was for the Arab Legion,[97] £2m for development and £1m for budget support.[98] The British concern with stability both regionally and domestically resulted in the Arab Legion remaining fully subsidised by Britain until 1957. The importance of the support for the Arab Legion can be seen in the proportion of the budget: in 1951 the Arab Legion budget was

£4.898m out of a total government budget of £9.763m, and in 1957 the figures were
£12.272m and £23.181m, respectively.[99] Nevertheless, two errors of judgement by
the British signalled the end of British dominance in Jordanian affairs. The first
move was initiated by the fear of the spread of Communism, which led Britain to
attempt to persuade Jordan to join the Baghdad Pact,[100] a move interpreted by Arab
nationalists as another example of imperialism. Although King Hussein had
originally agreed to join the pact,[101] local sentiment forced him to rethink. The
ramifications included the 'Arabisation' of the Arab Legion on the 1st March 1956
when General Glubb Pasha and eleven other top-ranking British officers were given
two hours to leave the country.

The second error was the Suez War that resulted in Jordan cutting ties with
France on the 1st November 1956 but not immediately with Britain, as King
Hussein was still dependent on the annual subsidy. However, when the 1957 Arab
Solidarity Pact was signed, the 1948 Anglo-Jordanian Treaty was abrogated and
British dominance of the financial affairs of Jordan ended, while simultaneously
resulting in the first significant Arab financial involvement. Egypt, Saudi Arabia and
Syria had promised "to replace the various annual grants paid by the British
government ... for the armed forces,"[102] providing Jordan did not sign the Baghdad
pact. The three countries signed the Arab Solidarity Pact on 19 January 1957, in
which they agreed to provide a total of £E12.5m pa for a period of ten years, at the
end of which the agreement could be re-negotiated.[103] However, the move by King
Hussein in 1957 to establish political control quickly removed Jordan from the Arab
camp into the USA camp.

The USA initially became involved in Jordan through the United States
Operation Mission (commonly known as Point Four), which was "based on the idea
of the transfer and demonstration of technology."[104] Point Four in Jordan started
out on a low-key basis but funding increased rapidly to JD2.73m in 1955, 18% of
aid. By 1954 the Point Four programme employed 1500 Jordanians at higher salaries
than were available locally, weakening the administration of the nascent government.
Kingston argues that the size of the US programme overwhelmed local capabilities,
and when assistance was cut in 1956, from JD2.73m to only JD0.47m,[105] the
withdrawal led to chaos in the development agenda.[106] The Point Four officials were
also concerned about the British domination of the development agenda in Jordan,
resulting in a battle between the UK, the USA, the UN and the Jordanian state,
which itself was divided between supporters of the regime and the nationalists.[107]

The internal political crisis, which had been simmering since the early 1950s,
came to a head in April 1957 when King Hussein moved decisively to gain control
by ousting the government of Nabulsi. The democratically elected parliament was
dissolved, political parties and trade unions banned, the constitution suspended and
martial law imposed. On the 24th April Hussein had requested American support in
the event of Israel or the USSR taking advantage of his forthcoming implementation
of Martial Law. Although the USA had previously declined to increase assistance,
the following day it proposed "an open-ended offer of support and aid, which led to
a long-term economic aid programme that became something of a sacred cow for
the US government very quickly."[108] On the 29th April, an agreement was signed to
grant Jordan US$10m of economic assistance. Satloff calls this agreement "the most
quickly negotiated in history."[109] The USA also tried to pressure Iraq and Saudi
Arabia to increase support but both refused the latter claiming that its obligation

under the Arab Solidarity Pact was sufficient. The initial grant by Washington of US$10m (JD3.57m) was followed by a further US$10m for the army and also US$10m for budgetary support.[110]

The 1967 war once again changed the flows of aid with, on this occasion, the USA stopping its funding in retaliation for Jordan's attack on Israel as part of the war. However, the Arab states at the Khartoum summit in August to September 1967 agreed to fill the breach. Saudi Arabia, Libya and Kuwait promised Jordan either US$112m pa or US$96m pa, depending on the source used.[111] In addition, emergency grants of US$55m[112] or US$58m[113] were pledged.[114] Arab bilateral assistance grew from zero in 1969 to US$35.4m in 1970. However, the move against the PLO in 1970 destroyed the new 'front-line state' policy with the result that both Kuwait and Libya stopped payments, although according to a number of commentators Saudi Arabia continued to pay its share. However, the Saudi contribution does not seem to be recorded in the OECD figures as the level of Arab bilateral assistance shrank to only US$1.5m in 1971 and US$2m in 1972.

Figure 3.2   **Main Donors, 1950-1972**

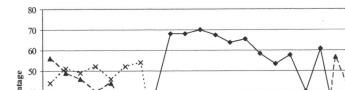

Sources: Adapted by author. 1950-59, Brand, L.A., (1988), *Palestinians in the Arab World: Institution Building and the Search for the State*, (New York: Columbia University Press), table 9.5, the figures of which have been converted to dinars at the official exchange rate of US$2.8:JD1 IMF, (various), *International Financial Statistics Yearbook*, (Washington: IMF) and 1960-1972 OECD, *International Development Statistics*, CD ROM 2000 edition, (Paris: OECD).

Although Jordan's reactions to the domestic and regional instability resulted in donor countries stopping their financial support, the major change in the global political ideology following the end of the Second World War allowed it to replace these donors. Although the end of the First World War brought forth calls for the end of imperialism, the mandate system in the Middle East could be seen as an attempt to maintain the global position of the European powers. By contrast, with the end of the Second World War, the major European powers were no longer in a position to maintain their territorial imperialist approach. The post-war dominance of the world by the superpowers replaced the era of territorial imperialism with an era of economic and geo-strategic imperialism. This change allowed Jordan to attempt to play-off major regional actors such as the USA, the USSR and the richer Arab states against each other in order to maintain levels of aid (see figure 3.2).

A second major change in ideology was again influenced from Europe, where Keynesian thinking was to prove a major factor in dominating economic planning. Until the economic recession of the 1930s the dominant economic paradigm was that of liberalism, which essentially favoured a market solution with the state only providing internal and external security to allow business to flourish. The recession of the 1930s forced a re-think, with the provision of welfare policies and state intervention in the economy becoming the accepted norm. For example, in Britain, the Second World War was followed by the introduction of the Beveridge social welfare plan, a national health service and a social welfare safety net. The commanding heights of the economy, i.e. the major industries such as steel, shipbuilding and mining were nationalised, along with key parts of the infrastructure, such as the railways. Thus the state became the focus of development, not just in the West but in the developing countries as well.

Figure 3.3   **Aid and Annual Change, 1950-1972**

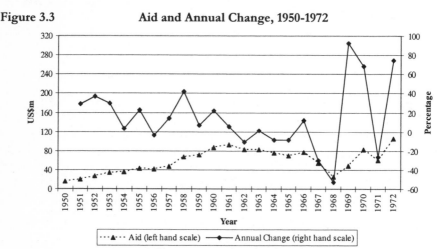

Sources: Adapted by author. 1950-59, Brand, L.A., (1988), *Palestinians in the Arab World: Institution Building and the Search for the State*, (New York: Columbia University Press), table 9.5, the figures of which have been converted to dinars at the official exchange rate of US$2.8:JD1 IMF, (various), *International Financial Statistics Yearbook*, (Washington: IMF) and 1960-1972, OECD, *International Development Statistics*, CD ROM 2000 edition, (Paris: OECD).

During the period, the Keynesian motivation for aid as a basis for economic development was affected by the security environment. As a result three distinct periods for gross aid during the period 1950 to 1972 can be distinguished: 1950 to 1961 in which there were increasing levels of aid; declining levels of aid from 1961 to 1968; and more sharply increasing rates from 1968 to 1972 (figure 3.3). In the first period, a sharp increase of over 40% in the levels is found between 1957 and 1958, with the USA becoming the major donor to Jordan for the first time. In the second period, the levels slumped between 1966 and 1968 (30.4% between 1966 and 1967 and 52.7% the following year) as a result of Jordan's involvement in the 1967 Arab-Israeli War. The adoption of Jordan as a 'front-line state' by the Arab League resulted in levels increasing by 92.5% between 1968 and 1969, and again by 68.1% between 1969 and 1970. However, the outbreak of the Civil War in 1970 saw a drop of 26.6% from 1970 to 1971.

THE RISE, FALL AND RE-EMERGENCE
OF THE INDUCED RENTIER STATE ECONOMY

Having established the changing patterns of aid (remittances were insignificant during the entire period), the analysis now turns to discovering the degree of the induced rentier state economy using the six measures discussed earlier. These measures, which are represented in figures 3.4 and 3.5, not surprisingly mirror the pattern of aid from the early 1950s to 1972: gradually increasing levels of the induced rentier state economy until 1961; falling levels of the induced rentier state economy to 1968; then a further period of increasing levels of induced rentier state economy to 1972. The majority of measures peaked in 1960 or 1961, by which time the economy could be described as a high-level induced rentier state economy.

Figure 3.4: Indicators of an Induced Rentier State Economy, 1952-1972

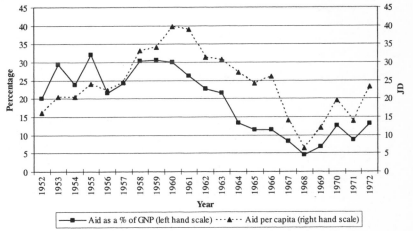

Sources: Adapted by author. As figure 3.2 plus GNP 1952-1959, UN ESCWA and Department of Statistics, (1978), *National Accounts in Jordan 1952-1976*, (Amman: Department of Statistics Press) and 1960-1972, CBJ, (various), *Monthly Statistical Bulletin*, (Amman: CBJ), and CBJ, (various), Quarterly Statistical Bulletin, (Amman: CBJ). Population 1954-59, Winckler, O., (1997), *Population Growth and Migration in Jordan, 1950-1994*, (Brighton: Sussex Academic Press) and 1960-1972, CBJ, (various), *Monthly Statistical Bulletin*, (Amman: CBJ), and CBJ, (various), *Quarterly Statistical Bulletin*, (Amman: CBJ).

As the economy grew and levels of aid declined in the 1960s, so the level of induced rentier state economy as indicated by the six measures declined to a low in 1968. All the measures, with the exception of aid as a percentage of the budget deficit fell consistently during the period to previously unrecorded levels. The measure of the budget deficit actually fluctuated in an upward direction from 1960 to 1967 but did record a low in 1968. By 1968, the level of the induced rentier state economy was low. The problems caused by the 1967 war and the subsequent civil war, along with the changing priorities of the different donors, resulted in an increased level of the induced rentier state economy. By 1972, induced rentier state economy had again increased, but on all measures, with the exception of per capita aid, remained below the levels experienced at the beginning of the 1950s. Overall, the economy could be characterised as one in which the degree of the induced rentier state economy had declined from the end of the Second World War, although, at 1972 Jordan could still be classified as a medium-level induced rentier state economy.

Figure 3.5: Indicators of an Induced Rentier State Economy, 1952-1972

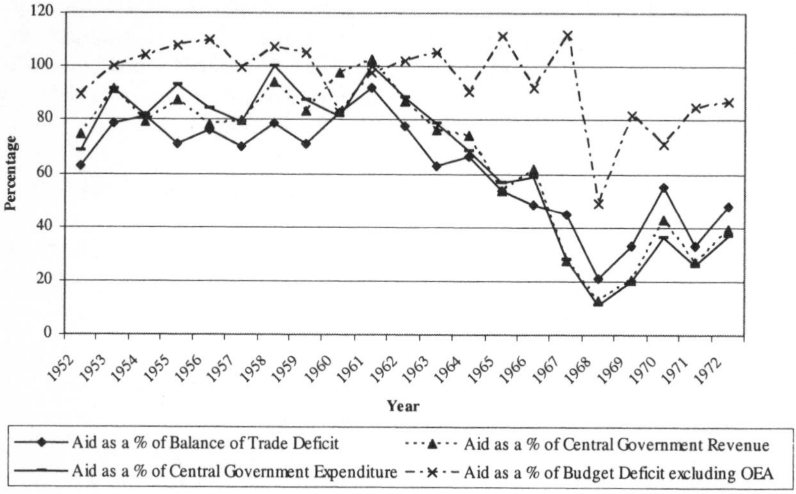

Sources: Adapted by author. As figure 3.2 plus Department of Statistics, (various), *Statistical Yearbook*, (Amman: Department of Statistics), CBJ, (various), *Monthly Statistical Bulletin*, (Amman: CBJ), and CBJ, (various), *Quarterly Statistical Bulletin*, (Amman: CBJ).

ECONOMIC INSTABILITY: THE EARLY 1970s TO 1989

The main factor affecting the changing patterns of aid and therefore the degree of induced rentier state economy until the early 1970s was political instability, both domestically and regionally. From the early 1970s, economic factors became the major determinant of the levels of rent accruing in the economy. The period commenced with the 'years of plenty', which were followed in the 1980s by the 'years of lean'.

During the years of plenty, the degree of rent in the economy was increased by a number of events. The global boom in raw material prices contributed significantly to growth in both aid and remittances. The Arab oil-exporting states were now in a position to promise large sums of aid. Domestically, the civil war ended allowing the state to readjust the focus back to development and also to help attract Arab aid.

Regionally, the Rabat Arab League meeting of 1974 and the Camp David talks and agreement in 1978 to 1979 both helped increase the levels of aid.

The major catalyst for change was the two oil price booms of the 1970s. The consequences of the price rise were to fundamentally affect the level of rent in the Jordanian economy. The first change was the huge increase in employment opportunities, at all levels of skills, for Jordanian nationals in the Arab oil-producing countries. The numbers of expatriate workers rose from a mere 5% of the labour force in 1968 to at least 30% by 1980, and of these 86% were employed in the Gulf States, of which 85% were employed in Saudi Arabia and Kuwait.[115] These workers were able to remit significant sums back to Jordan, increasing from less than JD15m in 1973 to JD381.9m in 1982, almost 23% of GDP.[116] However, the reliance of the labour market on Saudi Arabia and Kuwait was to have profound negative effects as the oil price fell in the 1980s and later during the Second Gulf War.

Secondly, the oil exporting states were now in a position to use the huge increases gained in oil revenues to fund wide-ranging development programmes, through both bilateral and multilateral channels.[117] The forum for developing countries, UNCTAD, of which the Arab OPEC states were members, had pressured OPEC to instigate a policy to assist those developing countries most affected by the oil price rises. Eleven multilateral Arab aid institutions were created in the five years from 1973 to 1978. In addition, the Arab oil states contributed significantly to International Fund for Agricultural Development (1976) and were also encouraged to assist the IMF in funding two facilities for countries affected by the oil price rise: the Oil Facility and the Supplementary Facility. Arab funding of the former was 44.3% and was approximately 32% of the latter.[118] Furthermore, institutional bilateral Arab assistance, which commenced with the creation by Kuwait of the Kuwait Fund for Arab Economic Development on 31 December 1961, exploded. The Abu Dhabi Fund, the Saudi Fund for Development and the Iraqi Fund for External Development were established, while Algeria, Libya, Qatar, and the UAE also granted bilateral aid. In addition, despite the existence of formal bilateral institutions, Kuwait, Saudi Arabia, Iraq and the UAE still granted economic assistance direct from their national accounts. This inter-state funding has often been informal, with the result that the sums are excluded from the OECD figures. Indeed, Brand argues that as much as 90% of Saudi developmental assistance bypasses the bilateral fund.[119]

In the early 1970s, Jordan's regional position was one of virtual political exclusion from the Arab community. The military action by the Hashemite regime against the PLO, the continued claim to the West Bank and the marginal contribution to the Arab cause in the October War against Israel all mitigated regional acceptance.

Only after King Hussein's recognition of the PLO as the sole representatives of the Palestinian people at the October 1974 Rabat Arab League meeting was Jordan able to return to the Arab fold. Importantly, the renewed acceptance allowed Jordan access to the considerable sums of economic assistance available from the oil-producing Arab states, especially those of the Gulf. Promises of Arab aid of US$300m annually were forthcoming at Rabat.[120] However, Arab assistance was not just restricted to the promises at Rabat; Saudi Arabia, for example, promised a further US$216m in support for the 1976 to 1980 Development Plan.[121] The return to the Arab fold resulted in formal Arab bilateral assistance increasing from only

US$2m in 1972 to US$342.1m by 1976, which accounted for virtually the total increase in gross aid from 1972 ($105.1m) to 1976 ($489.9m). Thus the USA lost its predominant position as the supplier of economic assistance to Jordan. The decision also had a negative, although not major, consequence for Jordan, as the PLO now became the official conduit for Arab economic assistance to the Palestinians on the West Bank. Countries such as Libya and Kuwait in late 1970 transferred their aid from Jordan to the PLO.

Jordan's return to the Arab fold was reinforced by the Kingdom's stance during the 1978 Camp David talks and the subsequent US pressure on Jordan[122] to join the treaty signed between Egypt and Israel. In the months prior to the signing of the agreement, both the Americans and the Arab side courted Jordan. When Egypt entered into negotiations with Israel following Sadat's visit to Jerusalem in November 1977, the Arab states agreed to grant Jordan US$1.25m annually for its support under the terms of the Baghdad agreement of 1978. At the summit a US$8.35bn fund was established to provide assistance to the frontline states: US$5bn to Egypt, US$1.8bn to Syria, US$1.25bn to Jordan, the PLO US$150m and the Occupied Territories US$150m. The division of the payments to Jordan on an annual basis was to be: Saudi Arabia US$350m, Iraq US$200m, Kuwait US$200m, UAE US$150m, Libya US$150m, Algeria US$100m and Qatar US$80m.[123] A significant qualitative difference in Arab aid to Jordan followed the 1978 Baghdad Agreement. Gross aid to Jordan jumped from US$445m in 1978 to US$1,317m in 1979; an increase of almost 200%.

The oil boom also contributed to the collapse of Keynesianism, the dominant economic ideology and practice adhered to by the donor countries since the early 1950s. The knock-on effect of the oil price rise (along with that of other raw materials) was a global combination of high unemployment and high inflation. The phenomenon of stagflation was previously presumed to be impossible under the demand management practice of Keynesianism. By the beginning of the 1980s, the Chicago School of Monetarists had become the dominant theory of economics. In turn, the practices of the members of the donor community adopted, to varying degrees, the new ideas. The change of ideology and practice was to play an important role in the 1980s and into the 1990s.

The start of the 'years of lean' coincided with the end of both the oil price boom and the dominance of Keynesian economic development practice. In addition, the Jordanian economy was profoundly affected by the Iran-Iraq war. At the global level, the oil earnings of the OPEC countries slumped, caused by a combination of reduced demand, which resulted in output dropping from about 31m barrels per day in 1979 to less than 17m barrels per day in 1983[124] and lower prices, from a high of around US$33.5 per barrel in 1981 to a low of approximately US$13 per barrel in 1986.[125] The lower revenues contributed to the curtailment of economic assistance by almost 50% in three years, from a peak of US$9,585.7m in 1980 to US$4,798.3m in 1983. By 1989, the levels had declined further to only US$1,486.6m.[126] Secondly, the donor community was placing a growing emphasis on economic liberalism as the main method of attaining economic development in the recipient countries. Thus attempts were made to reduce the role of the state by either placing conditions on the granting of soft loans or attempting to by-pass the state by providing assistance direct to the private sector.

The Iran-Iraq war, which started in September 1980, initially boosted the induced rentier state economy, as Iraq turned on a charm offensive with its closest neighbour. In 1980, President Saddam Hussein, who had already been instrumental in establishing the 1978 Baghdad agreement, agreed to a soft loan of US$189.2m, along with grants of US$58.3m. The funds were mostly used to improve the port at Aqaba (a major conduit for Iraqi trade) and the road between Aqaba and Iraq. In the longer term, however, the close ties were both to exacerbate the recession and to create difficulties in addressing the problems facing the economy in the 1980s. Firstly, Iraq was virtually bankrupted by the war, and therefore stopped assistance to Jordan. Secondly, the threat of instability as a result of the Iraq-Iran war increased defence spending in the Gulf States, which feared invasion from Iran. Kuwait's military expenditure increased to US$535m in 1980/81, US$712m in 1981/82, and US$833m in 1982/83, the largest increases in thirty years.[127] These expenses, in conjunction with the declining oil revenues, meant that fewer funds became available for economic assistance.

Despite the promises made at Baghdad (1978) and Amman (1980), bilateral Arab assistance fell annually from the peak in 1979. Once again conflicting estimates exist for the actual payments received by Jordan, although al-Madfai, in his carefully researched book, produces a set of figures that appear realistic (tables 3.3 and 3.4). According to the figures, Libya failed to make any payments, while Algeria only met the instalments for the first year. The Libyan and Algerian promises were divided between the remaining countries at a conference in Amman in 1980. However, once again these payments were made only for a short time. Only Saudi Arabia met its original commitment in full, resulting in less than 60% of the promised total being received.

Table 3.3: Payments Made by Country in Accordance with Baghdad Summit of 1978 and Amman Summit of 1980

Country	Baghdad Summit			Amman Summit		
	Funds Agreed US$	Paid US$	% Paid	Funds Agreed US$	Paid US$	% Paid
Saudi Arabia	3,571,430	3,571,431	100.0	1,026,280	145,496	14.2
Libya	1,964,280	0	0.0	N/A	N/A	N/A
Kuwait	1,964,290	1,315,390	67.0	563,608	39,988	7.1
Iraq	1,857,140	778,134	41.9	532,764	147,882	27.8
UAE	1,428,570	840,000	58.9	410,702	29,100	7.1
Algeria	892,860	89,290	10.0	N/A	N/A	N/A
Qatar	821,430	342,572	41.7	234,500	41,000	17.5
Total	**12,500,000**	**6,936,817**	**55.5**	**2,767,854**	**403,466**	**14.6**

Source: Adapted by author. al-Madfai, M.R., (1993), *Jordan, the United States and the Middle East Peace Process, 1974-1991*, (Cambridge: Cambridge University Press), Appendix D, pp.233-234. Note the figure given by al-Madfai for the total paid by Kuwait is JD7,781,340. This figure is obviously a misprint. Calculating the yearly figures gives a total of JD778,134, which corresponds with the cross-summation of the other totals.

Table 3.4   **Annual Instalments Received in Accordance with**
Baghdad Summit of 1978 and Amman Summit of 1980 (US$)

Year	Baghdad	Amman	Total
1979	1,053,218	196,336	1,249,554
1980	963,928	152,105	1,116,033
1981	963,928	55,205	1,019,133
1982	874,642	0	874,642
1983	563,572	0	563,572
1984	517,381	0	517,381
1985	461,143	0	461,143
1986	447,143	0	447,143
1987	463,321	0	463,321
1988	462,059	0	462,059
1989	166,482	0	166,482
Total	**6,936,817**	**403,466**	**7,340,283**

Source: Adapted by author. al-Madfai, M.R., (1993), *Jordan, the United States and the Middle East Peace Process, 1974-1991*, (Cambridge: Cambridge University Press), Appendix D, pp.233-234.

As is discussed in detail in chapter five, the Jordanian state failed to recognise (or at least failed to change its economic policies in response to) the changing conditions, believing that the shortfall in aid would be made up at a later date. The failure to change economic direction resulted in the IMF becoming deeply involved in the economy and economic policy-making from 1989.

CHANGING PATTERNS OF RENT: THE EARLY 1970s TO 1989

These changing patterns of economic conditions and ideology impacted significantly on the flows of rent into the Jordanian economy. While Western aid up to the early 1970s had helped "stave off economic privation and maintain a certain controlled level of development, Arab aid was of a completely different magnitude."[128] Arab assistance was not only on a significantly larger scale, but it was seldom tied, allowing for development of infrastructure projects, defence spending and consumer purchases, to which the Jordanian economy quickly became addicted. In addition, the funding was often in the form of grants rather than cheap loans. Rent also started to accrue to the economy in the form of remittances.

Gross aid exploded in the 1970s with annual growth rates as high as an incredible 196% in 1979 following the 1978 Baghdad agreement (figure 3.6). The result was an increase from only US$105.1m in 1972 to a peak of US$1,317m in 1979. Thereafter the pattern was one of decline until 1989, by which stage the level finally dropped below that recorded in 1978.

The high level of grants, generally over 80% of gross aid, reflected the dominance of the Arab states contribution to gross aid during the period (figure 3.7). In 1972, the USA accounted for 72.3% of gross aid and Arab states only 1.9%; in contrast, by 1979 the year after the signing of 1978 Baghdad agreement, the relative shares had changed to 88.7% for the Arab states and only 3.2% by the USA. This change was driven by the size of growth of Arab assistance, from US$2m in 1972 to

US$1,168m in 1979, rather then the decline in American funding from US$76m in 1972 to US$42m in 1979. From 1979 to 1985 Arab aid remained at over 82% of total assistance, thereafter the percentage fell annually to a low of 50.5% in 1989.

Figure 3.6   **Aid and Annual Change, 1973-1989**

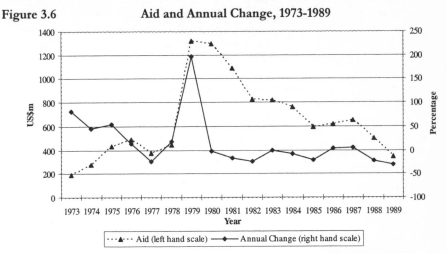

Source: Adapted by author. OECD, *International Development Statistics*, CD ROM 2000 edition, (Paris: OECD).

Figure 3.7   **Main Donors, 1973-1989**

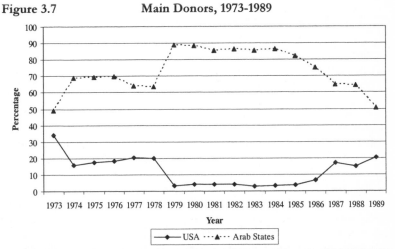

Source: Adapted by author. OECD, *International Development Statistics*, CD ROM 2000 edition, (Paris: OECD).

American economic assistance to Jordan continued to be predicated on the former's policy towards the Cold War and the Middle East as a region, with the position of Israel dictating the agenda. Thus, following Jordan's refusal to be drawn into the Camp David agreement, USA assistance dropped from US$88m in 1979 to US$22m in 1984. As Arab assistance fell, the American share increased to 20.2% in

1989, although the actual level of funding in 1989 was actually only US$70m, still less than the 1978 level.

Meanwhile remittances grew at an average of almost 100% pa over the next five years from just less than JD5m in 1971 to JD136.4m in 1976 (figure 3.8). The rate of increase slowed dramatically towards the end of the decade before a further burst in 1980 and 1981. The end of the oil boom did not stop remittances increasing annually until 1984, when the sums peaked at JD475m, before fluctuating downwards to JD358.3m in 1989.

Figure 3.8   Remittances and Annual Change, 1973-1989

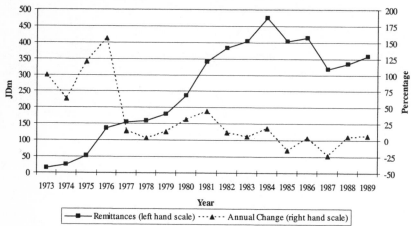

Source: Adapted by author. CBJ, (various), *Monthly Statistical Bulletin*, (Amman: CBJ), and CBJ, (various), *Annual Report*, (Amman: CBJ).

FROM INDUCED RENTIER STATE ECONOMY
TO PRIVATE SECTOR RENTIER ECONOMY

The following section discusses how the changing patterns of aid and remittances between the early 1970s and 1989 affected the changing type of rentier economy in Jordan. From the measures of the induced rentier state economy portrayed in figures 3.9, 3.10 and 3.11, four different phases can be adduced: 1) 1973-1975/76: increasing to a high-level induced rentier state economy; 2) 1975/76-1978: decreasing to a mid-level induced rentier state economy; 3) 1978-1979: dramatic increase to a high-level induced rentier state economy; and 4) 1979-1989: long decline to a relatively low-level induced rentier state economy. As with the period from 1952 to 1972, the measure against the budget deficit diverges from the main pattern. However, of the other five measures all, with the exception of aid per capita, finish the period recording lower levels of induced rentier state economy than was the case in 1973.

Figure 3.9: Indicators of an Induced Rentier State Economy, 1973-1989

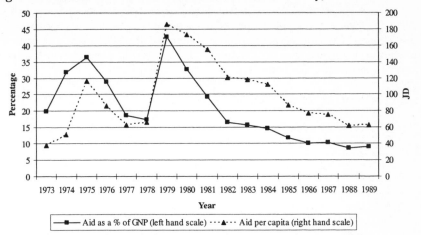

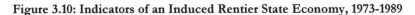

Sources: Adapted by author. CBJ, (various), *Annual Report*, (Amman: CBJ); IMF, (various), *International Financial Statistics*, (Washington: IMF); OECD, *International Development Statistics*, CD ROM 2000 edition, (Paris: OECD).

Figure 3.10: Indicators of an Induced Rentier State Economy, 1973-1989

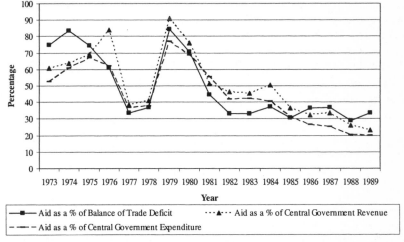

Sources: Adapted by author. CBJ, (various), *Annual Report*, (Amman: CBJ); IMF, (various), *International Financial Statistics*, (Washington: IMF); OECD, *International Development Statistics*, CD ROM 2000 edition, (Paris: OECD).

In the same period, all four measures of remittances, as highlighted in figures 3.12 and 3.13, indicate an overall increase in the level of private sector rentier economy. However, the measures show a degree of conflict. Between 1973 and 1976/77, all the measures indicate increasing level of the private sector rentier economy. Thereafter, in the period to 1983, the levels remain rather static, with the exception of remittances as a percentage of GNP, which shows a decline from its

1976 level of 48.8%. This measure continues to fall until 1987, after which it remains static at around 17%. Remittances as a percentage of trade deficit and of aid fluctuate upwards from 1983, while the final measure per capita initially fluctuates upward after 1983 but finish the period at around the 1983 level. Overall, the amount of remittances entering Jordan by 1989 resulted in a relatively high level of private sector rentier economy.

Figure 3.11: Aid as a Percentage of Budget Deficit excluding Aid, 1973-1989

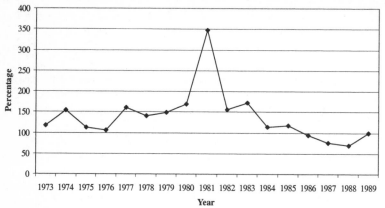

Sources: Adapted by author. CBJ, (various), *Annual Report*, (Amman: CBJ); IMF, (various), *International Financial Statistics*, (Washington: IMF); OECD, *International Development Statistics*, CD ROM 2000 edition, (Paris: OECD).

Figure 3.12: Indicators of a Private Sector Rentier Economy, 1973-1989

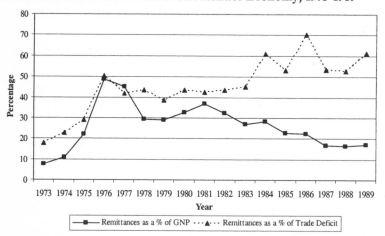

Sources: Adapted by author. CBJ, (various), *Monthly Statistical Bulletin*, (Amman: CBJ), and CBJ, (various), *Annual Report*, (Amman: CBJ).

Figure 3.13: Indicators of a Private Sector Rentier Economy, 1973-1989

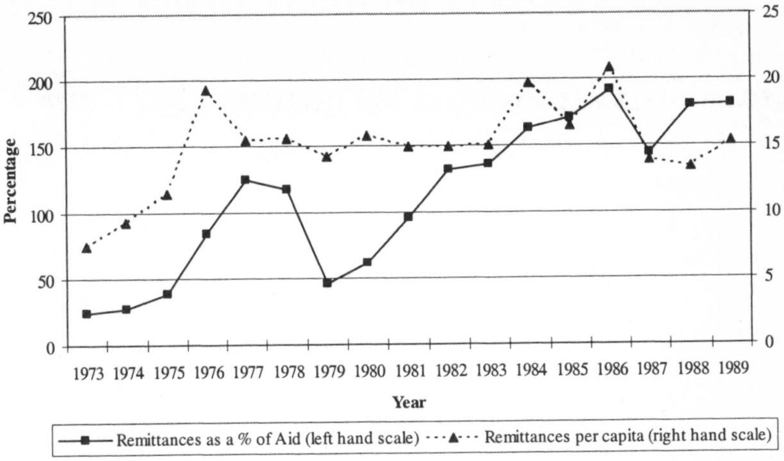

Sources: Adapted by author.   CBJ, (various), *Monthly Statistical Bulletin*, (Amman: CBJ), and CBJ, (various), *Annual Report*, (Amman: CBJ).

SUMMARY

The analysis in this chapter has shown the fluctuating nature of rent in Jordan, driven by different factors in different time frames.   During the Mandate (1921-1946) the level of aid was dependent purely on the British view of the strategic importance of Transjordan.   The discovery of oil in nearby Iraq and the building of the pipeline from Kirkuk to Haifa, and shortly thereafter the Second World War, were important elements in increasing the importance of Transjordan for the UK. Consequently, in 1936/37 the levels of aid increased dramatically, resulting in Transjordan becoming a high-level induced rentier state economy.   Domestic and regional instability informed the levels of aid from independence until the early 1970s, by which time Jordan had once more become a mid-level induced rentier state economy, after passing through periods of high-level and low-level induced rentier state economy.

The 1970s witnessed a dramatic change in the type of economy in Jordan.   The increased revenues of the Gulf States allowed the state to benefit from economic assistance but at the same time remittances enabled citizens to improve their standards of living considerably.   By 1976 the measures indicated high levels of both induced rentier state economy and private sector rentier economy.   Since 1979 the level of induced rentier state economy has declined to a relatively low level, while private sector rentier economy has continued at a high level.   The following chapter discusses the effects of the changes in the induced rentier state economy and the private sector rentier economy between 1921 and 1989 on the nature of the state and the private sector and the relationship between the two.

4

State-Private Sector Relations: 1921-1989

INTRODUCTION

This chapter assesses how the nature of the state and the private sector, and the development of the relationship between the two evolved between 1921 and 1989. The threefold aims are to: assess the depth of the state's involvement in the economy; establish to what degree the outcome was the result of the changing patterns of rent discussed in the previous chapter; and assess the nature of the state and the private sector and the relationship between the two prior to the involvement of the IMF. The conclusions will form the basis for the analysis for the rest of the study.

Following the pattern of the previous chapter the period 1921 to 1989 is divided into the same four overlapping eras: the early 1920s to the mid-1940s; the late 1940s to the early 1970s; the early 1970s to the early 1980s; and the early to the late 1980s. In these four phases, the state's economic involvement underwent a number of changes. In the first period, it adopted a *laissez-faire* approach. By contrast, the second period saw the commencement of state involvement through infrastructure provision and large-scale industrial projects. The third time-span witnessed an era of state domination of the economy, while the fourth stage witnessed the first attempts to reduce the economic role of the state.

The historical development of the private sector differs from that of the state, with only three phases being apparent. The first coincides with the period of the Mandate, during which the priority of the ruling élite was to enforce, stabilise and legitimise their authority. When allied to the British belief in an economic *laissez-faire* approach, the private sector was able to develop autonomously from the state. Indeed, commentators, such as Sha'sha, argue that the private sector exerted a strong influence over the government.[129] Significantly, due to the undeveloped nature of the economy, the private sector remained small, and concentrated in the agricultural sector. The second period lasted until the early 1970s. During these four decades, the private sector and the state gradually became more interdependent. In the final period, the approach of the state was one of planned economic development, with the private sector's role in planning being by way of invitation. By 1989 the private sector, in general, had evolved into a parasite feeding on the body of the state.

In each of the periods, the background context of the changing international and domestic economic factors is discussed. Thereafter, the depth of state's involvement in the economy is measured using the state-market continuum model, which is introduced below. Finally, the position of the state, the private sector and state-private sector relationship is assessed against the characteristics of induced state rentierism and private sector rentierism highlighted in chapter two.

Two factors highlighted in chapter two must be borne in mind in the following discussion. Firstly, the distinction between the state and the private sector became increasingly more blurred, making comparison and analysis less easy. For example, companies in which the government has a shareholding are regularly listed in official statistics as private sector companies. The result is that official figures tend to over-state the value of the private sector and by extension understate the role of the public sector. In addition, neither the state nor the private sector can be treated as monolithic.

THE STATE-MARKET CONTINUUM MODEL

The model is based along five continua, namely: contribution to the national economy; involvement in planning; institutional development; support for the private sector; and government ownership of productive assets. The changes in these five measures are used to help to assess the level of the role of the state in the economy.

The analysis of the contribution to national economy studies the ratio of government expenditure and revenue to GDP in order to assess the changes between the contribution of the public and private sectors. This ratio highlights the current balance between the private and public sectors; in contrast the ratio of public and private contributions to gross fixed capital formation[130] (GFCF) measures investment levels, which affect future trends. In a productive economy such as the UK more than 70% of GFCF is undertaken by businesses, while the rest is accounted for by government investment and personal sector investment in dwellings,[131] whereas in an induced rentier state economy, the state dominates the share of GFCF.

The next field of analysis concerns government planning. This aspect is mainly analysed through the series of official development plans that commenced in 1962. By assessing the projected levels of investment between the private and public sectors, the commitment of the state in involving the private sector in future development can be analysed. As infrastructural development by the state may be of benefit to the private sector, e.g. better port facilities assist exporters, the analysis where possible dissects investment into social and services, infrastructural and productive.[132] The study also discusses the context and outcome of the plans, as well as the level of private sector involvement in the planning process. The planned incentives to the private sector are also highlighted.

Next, the model assesses the impact of the various state and semi-state institutions created to assess their intended role in the economy, whether aimed at assisting the private or public sector. Allied to the budget and planning is the level of state support given to the private sector through financial assistance and legislation. Support is analysed by studying incentives, subsidies, protection, equity investment and the funding of large-scale surveys. Given the propensity for regulations to produce unintended consequences the regulations are analysed to assess not only the intended impact but also the outcome.

State owned enterprises (SOEs) in Jordan can be divided into three categories. These categories are pure state enterprises that are owned and operated by the state; autonomous or semi-autonomous enterprises that are fully owned by the state but operated (at least theoretically) on a market basis; and finally mixed enterprises consisting of both public and private investment and operating on a market basis.

TRANSJORDAN

Virtually all studies concerning Jordan, whether political, economic or strategic, stress two aspects as major influences on its development: the artificiality of the creation of Transjordan and the lack of economic viability.[133] However, all states are "artificial creations of individuals or groups pursuing political ends."[134] Furthermore, a number of states, such as Korea and Japan, which could have been termed as not being viable at the beginning of the 1920s, were able to become economically self-sufficient within the next fifty years. As Tal argues "[w]hat makes Jordan unique are the constraints on its freedom of action."[135] The constraints, which existed at the beginning of the 1920s, were the lack of resources, along with British financial and political control.

In terms of resources "[t]he country had a population of less than 0.5m,[136] limited agricultural land (located primarily in the Jordan Valley and the North), and limited natural resources (only phosphates and potash)."[137] To these limitations can also be added the lack of water, technology, finance, a physical infrastructure (such as roads and electricity), and an institutional framework. In addition, there was only 19km of coastline with only the one undeveloped port, Aqaba, inconveniently situated for the export of goods to the rich markets of Europe.

The British control had two effects. First, the primary concern of the British was to create political stability via the establishment of an effective local administration. Therefore, the concerns were political and geo-strategic rather than emphasising economic development. As Khairy argues, the rationale of the British subsidy was not economic but to create "a political power capable of asserting itself in the area."[138] A British memo of 1922 supports this view when the argument propounded was:

> [w]e regard Trans-Jordan more as a buffer to Palestine than as a country
> capable of development in itself, and at present at any rate, money spent
> in that territory is only justified by the fact that it reduces what might
> otherwise have been spent on military measures in Palestine.[139]

Secondly, Britain was committed to the prevailing orthodoxy of economic liberalism. This approach dictated that government budgets ought to be balanced, trade was to be free, and industrialisation and economic development were not concerns of the state. Furthermore, the idea of the welfare state had yet to evolve. All of these resulted in only a token effort being made to develop the economy, with no protection available to allow indigenous industry to evolve.

The private sector in Mandate Transjordan was based primarily in the agriculture sector due to the undeveloped nature of the economy. Despite only 3% of the area being under cultivation,[140] Transjordan was self-sufficient in food with the exception of tea, coffee and sugar. Furthermore, Konikoff estimated that agriculture accounted for more than 90% of exports in the pre-World War II period.[141] However, a major problem for the accumulation of capital necessary to boost the private sector was the periodic droughts that regularly affected agricultural output. Private sector industry was mostly limited to small-scale flourmills linked to agricultural products.[142] By 1944 the number of factories was still limited, partly due to the lack of electricity (which was confined to Amman and Zarqa). Trade was also limited. In the Ottoman period, the orientation of what little trade existed tended to be focused from north to south along the pilgrimage route. With the British influence in Palestine and Iraq and the building of the Iraqi Petroleum Company pipeline from Kirkuk to Haifa, via Transjordan, the axis of trade rotated ninety degrees to an east-west line.

How the small-scale agriculturally-inclined private sector and the limited economic capability of the state were influenced by the infusion of rent is discussed next. However, a caveat is necessary. The lack of data in the period reduces the scope of the analysis. Therefore, the conclusions are more tentative than in the later sections of the chapter.

MEASURES ON THE STATE-MARKET CONTINUUM

Budget figures for the Mandate period highlight a gradual increase in expenditure[143] from £P274,868 in 1924/25 to £P462,710 in 1937/38. Thereafter, spending increases dramatically due to the building of the Iraqi Petroleum Company road and the Second World War, reaching a peak of £P2,619,757 in 1943/44 (see table 4.1). The available budget figures indicate that prior to the building of the Iraqi Petroleum Company road, expenditure on administration, finance, police and defence (largely non-productive) accounted for between 56% and 61% of the annual spend.[144] Thereafter the figures are too distorted by the war to be of any relevance.

The state increased, albeit slowly, the physical infrastructure of the country. In 1934 only 77km of the total of 1438km of roads were suitable for all weathers, but by 1944 599.2km of the 2000+km of roads were. However, the Transjordanian section of the Haifa to Baghdad road, which was not built for the economic development of Transjordan but "primarily because of imperial interests and considerations,"[145] accounted for 340km of the total. The railway network had actually diminished since the Ottoman administration, as the section south of Ma'an had never been repaired following damage sustained in the First World War. The total track was 363.9km in 1945, but was little used, with losses being incurred in its operation.[146] The port at Aqaba remained undeveloped.

In the regulatory field, two acts in the early years of the administration can be seen as the start of the state's involvement in the market. The first was the promulgation of the Law of the Chamber of Commerce in 1924, and the second was the establishment of the Higher Economic Committee in the same year, with the

Prime Minister as chairman. Branches of the committee were established in seven cities and villages.[147] The only other significant move was the reform of the taxation system in 1933,[148] with the introduction of an income tax and a land tax, the main instrument for direct taxation.[149]

Table 4.1: Summary of Central Government Budget, 1924/25-1943/44 (£P)

Year	Revenue		Expenditure	
	Total	Annual Average	Total	Annual Average
1924/25 – 1937/38	4,864,236	347,445.4	4,859,644	347,117.4
1938/39 – 1943/44	8,375,516	1,395,919.3	8,615,645	1,435,940.8
Total	**13,239,752**	**661,987.6**	**13,475,289**	**673,764.5**

Sources: Adapted by author. For years 1924/25 to 1933/34 Naval Intelligence Division, (1943), *Palestine and Transjordan*, (no place of publication: Naval Intelligence Division), p.500. For years 1934/35 to 1943/44, Konikoff, A. (1946), *Transjordan: An Economic Survey*, (Jerusalem: Economic Research Institute of the Jewish Agency for Palestine), p.95.

From the limited data available, the evidence tentatively points to an economy that was at the market end of the state-market continuum, with a barely perceptible move towards the state end in the latter years of the mandate. The next section assesses the degree of induced state rentierism exhibited at the end of the mandate period.

LAISSEZ-FAIRE STATE, WEAK BUT AUTONOMOUS PRIVATE SECTOR

None of the five characteristics of an economy associated with induced state rentierism (dependency on aid, a chronic balance of trade deficit, a continual budget deficit, service sector predominance, and high levels of consumption) was present at the end of the mandate period. In addition, the state had not yet adopted a policy aimed at accessing and controlling rent. The British control of the finances ensured that aid was granted in the British interest rather than the regime's interest. However, the need for Emir Abdullah to garner local political legitimacy did result in the limited use of an expenditure policy by the regime. The private sector also failed to exhibit any of the signs of induced state rentierism (relatively homogenised outlook, dependency on the state, and service orientation). Finally, the blurred relationship between the state and private sector had also failed to materialise. Thus by the mid-1940s, although the economy had been a high-level induced rentier state economy for almost a decade, the characteristics associated with induced state rentierism were not present to any degree.

This apparent paradox was due to three main reasons. Firstly, the rentier aspects of the state had only recently become consolidated. Secondly, the private sector was largely self-sufficient and restricted to the agricultural sector, and thus autonomous of the state. Finally, and perhaps the main reason, was the importance of external and domestic factors.

At the birth of Transjordan, the ideological leanings of economic liberalism and colonialism collided to create a state that was controlled financially by the British government. The result was a 'hands-off' approach in both the economy and the market of the nascent state. During the two and a half decades of the mandate, the role of the government gradually increased but was restricted to very small-scale infrastructure projects, limited welfare outlays (boosted mainly as a result of the depression of the 1930s and a series of local droughts)[150] and the provision of employment, especially in later years with army recruitment. No state involvement in industrial development or in the workings of the market was apparent. Despite the space provided by the lack of state involvement in the economy, the private sector failed to develop, particularly industrially, due to the lack of infrastructure, natural resources, capital accumulation and skills.

INDEPENDENCE TO THE OIL-BOOM

The significant factors in this period, which affected economic development, were independence, the 1948 Arab-Israeli War, the annexation of the West Bank, the 1967 Arab-Israeli War and the Civil War of 1970-71. Additionally, at the ideological level, the move towards Keynesianism, with the focus on the state in terms of welfare provision and economic development, resulted in the state, rather than the private sector, being seen as the key actor in the economic development of the less-developed countries.

Independence allowed the Jordanians to regain a degree of financial control over government expenditure. Within the constraints of raising finance, this control enabled more funding to be diverted towards economic development than occurred in the Mandate era.

"The economic crisis created by the 1948 war was staggering."[151] The need to absorb refugees,[152] a process made more difficult by the lack of international assistance in terms of speed and finances,[153] resulted in a move towards welfarism by the state as education, employment, health and housing had to be provided. The budget was also strained by the need to increase military spending in response to the continuing regional instability. The private sector was also badly affected, as the war not only cut off the main Palestinian market for which new markets had to be found[154] but also the port of Haifa, through which the majority of exports were shipped. The result was shipping costs increased, as exports were re-routed via Aqaba or Damascus and Beirut. Finally, investment in the private sector was curtailed by the continued instability.

One of the outcomes of the war was the military control of the West Bank by Jordanian forces. On the 24th May 1950 King Abdullah announced the annexation of the West Bank: a move recognised only by the UK and Pakistan. The annexation "unequivocally altered not only the history of the country but also its political, social, and economic structure."[155] The West Bankers, due in part to the British Mandate policy, were on the whole more economically developed than their East Bank counterparts. The result was a boost to the private sector, with the introduction of an entrepreneurial middle class, an increase in 'modern' skills and a huge injection of capital of £P20m, probably greater than the money supply in Jordan at the time.[156] This influx gave an impetus to the change from an agricultural to a service-based economy. In addition, a new private sector élite, comprising "landlords, financiers, wealthy merchants and real estate owners,"[157] was in place by the beginning of King Hussein's reign in 1952. Over the next decade and a half the private sector "played an important role in the development of industry and agriculture and its efforts were responsible for the establishment of the phosphates and cement industries and the oil refinery."[158]

The next major turning point was the 1967 Arab-Israeli war, which resulted in the physical loss of the West Bank: an event Bannerman claims lost Jordan the chance to become economically self-sufficient,[159] although other analysts are more circumspect.[160] Apart from the physical loss of capacity, the state-private sector relationship was affected in ways similar to those experienced during the 1948 Arab-Israeli War. The state budget was once more pressurised by a flood of between 250,000 to 400,000[161] refugees arriving in one week,[162] and increased military spending.[163] The effects of the refugee crisis were not offset on this occasion by the gain of assets, but were exacerbated by the loss of the productive assets on the West Bank.

The problems created by the continuing regional instability were aggravated in Jordan by the civil war of 1970 to 1971. Industry throughout the Kingdom virtually ground to a halt, while agriculture in the Jordan Valley was brought to a standstill. Furthermore, trade was severely disrupted by the actions of neighbouring Arab states. Saudi Arabia closed the TAPline[164] from May 1970 to January 1971. The Syrian border, which after 1967 had become the gateway to Europe following the closure of the Suez Canal, was closed. Restrictions were gradually eased from February 1972 and by December the border was completely re-opened. The effects of the Syrian border closure were made worse by the closure of the Syrian-Lebanese border from May to August 1972. The less important Iraqi borders were closed from the 18th July to the 20th October 1971, with normal trade relations not being resumed until February 1972.[165] In addition, Libya and Kuwait, both of whom had agreed to grant assistance to Jordan following the Khartoum Arab League Conference in 1967, cut the promised funding of US$64m annually. Piro cites one further problem; that of capital flight,[166] i.e. divestment from rather than investment in the private sector.

MEASURES ON THE STATE-MARKET CONTINUUM

The contribution of the government in terms of revenue and expenditure to national income tended to fluctuate around the 30% mark from 1952 until 1963. Although, the expenditure figures do show an increase from 28.0% in 1957 to 39.7% in 1960, the years immediately following King Hussein's regain of political control. A sharp dip is apparent in years 1964 to 1966 but the 1967 war reversed the trend, with both figures settling around the 35% mark from 1968 to 1973 (figure 4.1).

Private GFCF increased by more than fourfold in the period 1954 to 1959, compared with a doubling of public GFCF.[167] Thereafter private GFCF stagnated from 1959 to 1968, before growing again from 1969 to 1973, despite the instability. Public GFCF was also stagnant from 1959, but from 1964 the figures climbed to JD16.6m in 1969. The Civil War saw a steep drop to JD9.5m in 1970, before climbing to JD22.1m in 1973 (figure 4.2). In figure 4.3, the closing of the gap between the public and private sectors from 1959 to 1973 is apparent, although the trend is not uniform. Although, private sector levels remained more important on average than the public sector GFCF, the gap closed to less than 14 percentage points by 1973, from almost 45 percentage points in 1959; a definite move to the state end of the continuum.

Figure 4.1 Revenue and Expenditure as a Percentage of GDP, 1952-1973

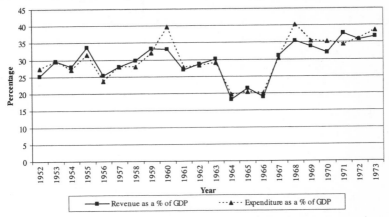

Sources: Adapted by author. CBJ, (various), *Monthly Statistical Bulletin*, (Amman: CBJ); CBJ, (various), *Quarterly Statistical Bulletin*, (Amman: CBJ); Department of Statistics, (1994), *National Accounts 1952-1992*, (no place: Department of Statistics); and UN ESCWA and Department of Statistics, (1978), *National Accounts in Jordan 1952-1976*, (Amman: Department of Statistics Press).

Figure 4.2   Gross Fixed Capital Formation, 1959-1973

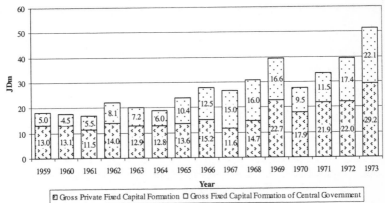

Sources: Adapted by author. CBJ, (various), *Monthly Statistical Bulletin*, (Amman: CBJ) and CBJ, (various), *Quarterly Statistical Bulletin*, (Amman: CBJ).

Government involvement in planning commenced in Jordan following the creation of the Jordan Development Board in 1951. The British sought to use the Board to co-ordinate the development efforts of the British, the Americans and the

UN, as well as the Jordanian state.[168] As a result of US dissatisfaction, the Jordan Development Board was reconstituted in 1957, before mutating into the National Planning Council in 1971, under the Planning Law no. 68 of 1971. Representatives from the private sector, as well as government officials, were included in both organisations. The concerns of these organisations were focused initially on project investment before taking on a more wide-ranging approach to economic and social planning.

Figure 4.3   Share of Gross Fixed Capital Formation, 1959-1973

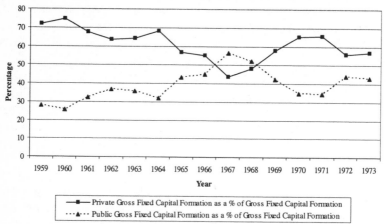

Sources: Adapted by author. CBJ, (various), *Monthly Statistical Bulletin*, (Amman: CBJ) and CBJ, (various), *Quarterly Statistical Bulletin*, (Amman: CBJ).

The first official plan (1962-67), produced by a twelve-man team including five representatives from the private sector, was published in 1961. The private sector was consulted in the early stages of the planning process and again after the first draft of the five-year programme was drawn up. However, the controlling agenda was in the hands of the planning committee of the Jordan Development Board, as were the later stages of the planning process.

> Partly because of a lack of aggregate economic data, the plan was limited
> to proposals for investment projects and fiscal and administrative reforms,
> without much attempt to design an overall strategy or to make aggregative
> projections for the economy as a whole.[169]

The costing of the plan was envisaged at JD127m, of which JD47m was to come from the private sector, JD21m from domestic government sources and JD59m from foreign sources.[170] The plan contained no specific proposals for attracting the JD47m of private sector funding, apart from a change in the tax law "to allow greater retention of earnings by corporations and thus greater investment in industry."[171]

The assumptions behind the plan quickly became out of date "as a result of reductions in the levels of budget support, particularly from the United States of America, and that a corresponding revision of the program was necessary."[172] The plan was replaced by the 1964 to 1970 seven-year plan, which was prepared with the help of the Ford Foundation and the World Bank. Not officially adopted until approved by the Cabinet on 22 December 1965, this plan was cancelled in 1967 as a result of the war. The 1964 to 1970 plan was ambitious and highly implausible.[173] Although the plan stated that the preparation "involved the participation of a great number of government officials, businessmen, agriculturalists, technical experts and others,"[174] the government set the goals prior to the planning process being implemented. The private sector seems to have had little overall input. The estimated levels of GFCF over the seven years were JD260m, which was to be shared almost 50:50 between the state and the private sector. By way of comparison, in 1963 the private sector had contributed 68.2% of GFCF. In terms of total investment the plan was therefore advocating a move towards the state end of the continuum.

The hiatus caused by the 1967 War and the 1970-71 Civil War resulted in economic planning being ignored for approximately five years. An interim plan for 1973 to 1975, the first to be formulated under the 1971 Planning Law was issued at the end of the Civil War. The plan acknowledged that "[i]t is also evident that the relative contribution of the public sector to GFCF is on the increase."[175] The development strategy outlined indicated that "[a]ll possible means are to be used to encourage and induce private initiative, and the private sector will be given priority in carrying out feasible projects."[176] Although the emphasis was on the private sector investment, the public sector was expected to provide 55.6% of the JD179.0m total investment.[177]

In each of the three plans, the private sector was expected to contribute less than 50% of the total investment. However, on closer inspection, in each case the majority of public sector investment was to be spent on infrastructural development, which in theory ought to assist with private sector expansion. The majority of planned investment in the productive sector was to be provided through the private sector, although the ratio between the private and public sectors in the productive sector declined from 8.5:1 in the first plan to only 1.6:1 by 1973-75 (table 4.2).

Table 4.2: Planned Investment by Sectors, 1962-67, 1964-70 and 1973-75 (JDm)

Sector	1962-67		1964-70		1973-75	
	Private	Public	Private	Public	Private	Public
Social and Services	7.53	19.56	67.00	17.06	37.23	27.74
Infrastructure	22.32	43.77	15.13	90.49	17.80	57.09
Productive	30.55	3.58	47.07	12.31	24.39	14.75
Total	**60.40**	**66.91**	**129.20**	**130.86**	**79.42**	**99.58**

Sources: Adapted by author. Jordan Development Board, (1961), *The Hashemite Kingdom of Jordan Five Year Program for Economic Development 1962-1967*, (Amman: Jordan Development Board, 1961), p.360; Jordan Development Board, (undated), *The Seven Year Program for Economic Development of Jordan: 1964-70*, (Amman: Jordan Development Board), pp.37-38 and National Planning Council, *The Hashemite Kingdom of Jordan Three Year Development Plan, 1973-1975*, (undated: a), (Amman: National Planning Council), p.36.

The growing government involvement in the economy was manifested in the creation of a plethora of state and semi-state institutions with the aim of boosting economic development through the private sector. Five specialised credit organisations, which were intended to provide loans to both the public and private sector, were created in the post-Mandate period. Four of the institutions, the Agricultural Credit Corporation[178] (1959), the Cities and Village Development Bank (1966), the Housing and Urban Development Corporation (1966), and the Jordan Co-operative Organisation (1968) were in public ownership. One private-public capital organisation, the Industrial Development Bank (IDB) (1965), which had previously been the Industrial Development Fund (1957), was also established. By 1973, the total lending portfolio of these credit organisations was JD17.5m.

Among the other institutions established in the period to the early 1970s were: Jordan Investment Corporation (JIC) (1953), which had the aim of attracting private investment; the CBJ (1964), which replaced the British-established Jordan Monetary Board, the functions of which "had been limited to currency issue and reserve management"[179]; Jordan Investment Promotion Office (1967), which was established "to provide assistance to the private sector, particularly to Arab and foreign private enterprises in establishing new industries and implementing other economic projects and expanding existing ones"[180]; the Royal Scientific Society (1970), which was created as a think tank for research and development under the sponsorship of HRH Prince Hassan; and the Jordan Commercial Centres Corporation (1972), which is owned equally by the Ministry of Industry and Trade, the Jordan Federation of Chambers of Commerce (FJCC) and the Amman Chamber of Industry (ACI),[181] was established under Law no. 21 for 1972 to assist with export development.

One further institution created in this period was the Economic Security Council. The remit of the Council, which was established by the 1971 Planning Law in the wake of the 1967 war, was "to address economic problems created by the occupation of the West Bank."[182] The Council was composed of the Prime Minister, ministers from the Finance and National Economy ministries, along with the Governor of the CBJ, two members of the National Planning Council and the Director of the Budget Department in the Ministry of Finance.[183] Brand argues that as political repression expanded the role of the Economic Security Council increased, with few decisions being made public. Furthermore, the decisions tended to benefit a specific group of individuals, companies and banks.[184] These members of the private sector became dependent on this decision-making process for their prosperity.

Government assistance to the private sector was also provided through infrastructural projects. Progress was apparent in the area of transport and communications, the port at Aqaba was modernised (to the extent that exports through the port increased from a mere 4000 tonnes in 1953 to 657,000 tonnes in 1966),[185] a national airline was formed, an international airport was built, a programme of road building was implemented, and electric power was introduced to wide areas of the country.

In the post-Mandate period the government used increasingly used protection from imports for newly-established local industries.[186] Import controls, domestic price-fixing, and "the use of licences as an effective means of favouring and rewarding special distributional interest groups"[187] were among the policies adopted. Mazur adds that until the early 1970s the "licensing of new industrial investments was commonly used to restrict the numbers of enterprises established."[188] Thereafter, nearly all licences were approved, with control being implemented through tax incentives under the Encouragement of Investment Law 1972, which replaced the Encouragement of Investment Law 1967. The reason for the change of approach was a change of emphasis by the government in an attempt to adopt an export-based approach, as the domestic market was already saturated.

Government involvement in four of the 'big five'[189] companies began in the 1950s. Table 4.3 details the initial level of state ownership in Jordan Cement Factory Company (JCFC), Jordan Phosphate Mines Company (JPMC), Jordan Petroleum Refinery Company (JPRC), and Arab Potash Company (APC). However, these figures do not tell the whole story: for instance in the case of the JCFC only 10% of the private sector allocation of capital was actually subscribed. The government share in all companies increased in stages until the 1990s; by which time, the government share in JPMC had reached 90%. In addition, the government took an active role in appointing the boards of directors of these companies. As Piro points out, the appointments have been regularly used as a reward for political support.[190] Another example of the role of the state in these companies includes the granting of monopolies. The JPRC was granted the monopoly on production and distribution, while the APC was granted a one hundred percent concession to exploit the minerals in the Dead Sea.

Table 4.3: Details of the Formation of the Main State Owned Enterprises

Company	Date of Formation	Authorised Capital at Date of Formation	Initial Government Share of Authorised Capital
JCFC	1951	JD1.0m	50.00%
JPMC	1953	JD3.0m	25.00%
JPRC	1956	JD4.0m	6.25%
APC	1956	JD4.5m	53.00%

Source: Adapted by author. Piro, T.J., (1998), *The Political Economy of Market Reform in Jordan*, (Lanham: Rowman & Littlefield Publishers Inc.), pp.50-51.

In conclusion, during this period the state, on all measures, took a significant step towards the state end of the state-market continuum. The governmental share of both national income and GFCF was higher prior to the oil boom than after independence, as the newly-independent state threw off the shackles of the British financial straightjacket, and turned its attention to industrialisation, social welfare and defence. Total planned investment levels tended to be split equally, but the public sector was expected to concentrate on infrastructural spending and the private sector on the productive sector. In addition, the government became involved in a number of large-scale industrial projects, such as the phosphates sector, injecting large-scale capital in return for a shareholding. The National Planning Council argues that in the period 1948 to 1961 the public sector concentrated on "creating and strengthening the development infrastructure."[191] Thereafter, from 1962 to 1966, the "emphasis [was] on the development and expansion of productive capacity through the completion of existing productive projects such as the East Ghor Canal, the expansion of phosphate production and the exploitation and export of other mineral resources."[192]

STATE AS FACILITATOR, PRIVATE SECTOR AS INITIATOR

In this period, the degree of the induced rentier state economy climbed to a peak in 1960/61, before dropping to a low point in 1968, followed by a recovery to mid-level by the early 1970s. Despite the overall fall in the degree of induced rentier state economy, the state-private sector continuum model highlights a significant move towards the state end of the economy. This section concludes by assessing what aspects of induced state rentierism were present by the early 1970s.

Four of the five macro-economic measures of induced state rentierism (dependency on aid; continual trade deficits; continual budget deficits; and high levels of consumption) were all strongly in evidence by the early 1970s. The fifth measure, a service-oriented economy, was beginning to grow, accounting for around 25% of GDP in 1973.[193] Furthermore, as was evident in 1956 to 1957 and again in 1967, the state had adopted a policy of maintaining access to aid. In 1970, however, the threat to the Hashemite regime by the PLO meant that for a time the regime's survival became more important than maintaining access to Arab aid. The expenditure side of the two-dimensional state policy had also grown in terms of infrastructure development, state-controlled or state-supported enterprises and support for favoured businesses. However, subsidies of basic necessities remained low at this point. Another characteristic of induced state rentierism is the ability of the state to create and destroy classes. However, the formation of the new private sector élite, which was in place by the early 1950s, was more as a result of gaining control of the West Bank, than because of induced state rentierism. Finally, the private sector had become relatively homogenised in outlook and service-sector oriented, but as yet it was not dependent on the state.

The relationship between the state and the private sector up to 1967 is best described by the development plans, along with the institutional and infrastructure development. These features were in line with the change in the role of the state *vis-à-vis* the private sector, from one of *laissez-faire* to one where the state acted as a facilitator to the private sector. The private sector was still considered to be the main engine for leadership, initiative and investment.[194] In addition, the political and economic élites were still separate entities. However, the relationship altered dramatically in the years after 1967. Four years of instability, during which the private sector was badly affected, resulted in a hardening of attitudes towards economic development. The internal threats to the political élite and the external threats to the Kingdom persuaded the regime that economic development should be based in the hands of the state. According to Sha'sha, the increase in "government intervention came through the invitation and insistence of the private sector."[195] While the statement may be true, the intervention was driven more by the political and security nature of the years immediately following 1967. The private sector, although independent and nominally seen by the decision-makers as the leader of economic development, was too weak to be able to dictate the development agenda.

Overall, in the years from independence to the early 1970s Jordan took a significant step towards the state end of the state-market continuum and was showing increased signs of induced state rentierism. Many of those interviewed by the author were at pains to point out that Jordan became a state-centred economy by default, arguing that ideologically the desire was for a market-based economy. Brand supports this thesis, arguing that Jordan "never...joined in the Arab-socialist or state-capitalist experiments of the 1950s and 1960s of a number of its neighbours."[196] The thesis is often advanced on the grounds that the state in Jordan did not resort to the process of nationalisation. However, unlike in Latin America or certain Middle Eastern countries such as Egypt, a distinct lack of targets existed for nationalisation. The structural problems facing a late-industrialising economy, in combination with the need for national and regime security, and the dominant economic development ideology were the reasons that the Jordanian economy became state-centred. The need to create an economy based on industry and services rather than on agriculture required the injection of large capital sums. This capital was not readily available from private domestic sources, leaving two options available: a state-centred approach based on aid or by attracting private foreign investment. The former option was chosen initially through the strange coincidence of the dominant ideology of state-centred economic development, the Arab nationalist desire to create an independent (from the West) industrial economy through a policy of big-push, state-centred industrialisation and the ability of the state to attract rent. Once the path had been laid, various elements linked to the domestic security of the élite and the external security of the state ensured that the policy did not deviate. The Arab-Israeli Wars of 1948, 1956 and 1967 created an atmosphere of instability in the region, resulting in attempts to push economic development in the direction of industrial modernisation as a means of creating a viable, self-sustaining, independent economy.

THE OIL-BOOM YEARS

The state-private sector relationship altered significantly during this period. A major factor was the relative political and security stability following the end of the Civil War, and the 1973 Arab-Israeli War. Other events of importance were the Rabat Arab League meeting of 1974, the outbreak of the Lebanese Civil War in 1975, the Baghdad agreement of 1978, and finally the outbreak of the Iran-Iraq war in 1980. In addition, the global boom in raw material prices, particularly oil and to a lesser extent phosphates,[197] contributed significantly to the growing dependence of the private sector on the state.

The end of the Civil War paved the way for industrial output to be re-started and enabled agriculture to return to the Jordan Valley. In addition, with the defeat of the PLO the domestic political situation entered a period of relative stability that continued until the 1980s drew to a close. The political stability allowed the regime to turn its attention from political survival to strengthening the economic development of the country. This new emphasis was reflected in a series of social and economic development plans covering the periods 1973-75, 1976-80 and 1980-85.

The oil-boom, which allowed the Arab states to agree to economic assistance packages at the 1974 Rabat Conference and the 1978 Baghdad Conference, boosted the state's power *vis-à-vis* the private sector. The huge sums of Arab economic assistance permitted the state to address its security concerns and thereafter to monopolise the agenda concerning the development of the economy. In addition, the money allowed the state not only to become the "owner of major projects"[198] but also to move seriously into the productive sector. Thus by 1982 the state was responsible for 40% of the GNP, almost 50% of GFCF and almost 50% of the workforce.[199] The oil-boom did have a positive effect on the private sector through the increase in remittances from JD15m in 1973 to JD381.9m in 1982.[200] In theory, the remittances should have increased the funds available for investment, but much of the money was spent on consumption of imported goods or on non-productive assets such as housing.

Following the outbreak of the Lebanese Civil War, 80,000 refugees, along with their capital, moved to Amman, where hopes existed of replacing Beirut as the financial centre of the region. However, within six months, the majority of the businessmen left, as Amman's infrastructure was not sufficiently developed to meet their needs.[201] This loss further focused the minds of the decision-makers within the state on improving the infrastructure. This departure was a blow to the chances of developing an independent private sector.

The Iran-Iraq War boosted the profits of the private sector as Iraq turned to its neighbour for many industrial products, as well as for a port of entry for its own imports, thereby increasing transit trade. The two countries established the Jordan-Iraq Committee for Economic Co-ordination in August 1980, which in turn created the Jordan-Iraqi Overland Transport Company. Exports to Iraq jumped from JD28.35m (23.6% of total exports) in 1980 to JD63.47m (37.6%) in the following year. However, as trade was co-ordinated by the Jordan-Iraq Committee for Economic Co-ordination, the private sector effectively relied on the government for access to the export market of Iraq. As the war progressed, Iraq became mired in debt. In order to maintain the level of trade, an export credit scheme was established, which was controlled by the two states: again increasing private-sector dependency. As Piro argues "[a] number of economic groups...became tied to Iraq's economy, including the cement and pharmaceutical industries and the banking sector."[202]

After the ravages of the Civil War the private sector entered the oil boom era in a weakened position. Capital accumulation still remained low, while the focus of the private sector continued to evolve away from agriculture. Services continued to dominate the economy accounting for around two-thirds of GDP, while the importance of agriculture continued to decline slowly. Manufacturing had jumped from 6.6% of GDP in 1952 to 12.6% in 1973.[203] On the other hand the state commenced the era with renewed confidence after expelling the PLO and suffering little damage in the 1973 Arab-Israeli War. How the relationship between the state and the private sector developed during the oil-boom years with reference to the continuum model is discussed in the next section.

MEASURES ON THE STATE-MARKET CONTINUUM

The trend lines in figure 4.4 highlight the overall drop in importance of the state's contribution to GDP in terms of expenditure and revenue. Thus despite the increase in rent available to the state, on this measure the move was towards the market end of the continuum.

Actual investment by the private sector during the 1973-75 plan was JD67m compared with public investment of JD75m.[204] During the following plan, from 1976-80, the levels of investment were JD721.5m (59% of total) for the private sector and JD500.4m for the public.[205]   However, if private sector investment in housing (a largely non-productive asset in Jordan where no mortgage market existed) is discounted, then the private sector contribution fell to JD471.3m.   In percentage terms the private sector contribution rose steeply from 43.6% in 1977 to almost three-quarters of total GFCF in 1984.   Again the evidence points to a move towards the market end of the continuum (figures 4.5 and 4.6).

Figure 4.4 Revenue and Expenditure as a Percentage of GDP, 1973-1984

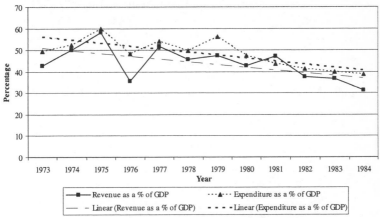

Source: Adapted by author. CBJ, (various), *Annual Report*, (Amman: CBJ).

Figure 4.5   Gross Fixed Capital Formation, 1977-1984

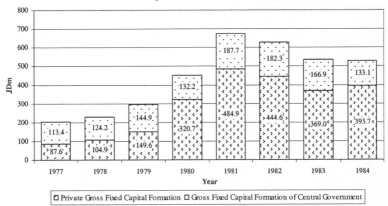

Source: Adapted by author.   IMF, (various), *International Financial Statistics Yearbook*, (Washington: IMF).

Three plans were issued in this period: the plan for 1973 to 1975, the plan for 1976 to 1980 (the first prepared in the oil-boom era), and the 1981 to 1985 plan. The 1973-1975 plan was produced shortly after the end of the Civil War and was essentially designed for short-term recovery.   The objective was to "relieve the economic recession and the crisis of confidence in the Jordanian economy among foreign investors."[206]   One of the basic assumptions of the plan was that "[t]he private sector should assume an active and ever-increasing role in the development effort."[207] The contribution of the private sector was to be achieved by reducing the ratio of private consumption to income from 87.9% in 1972 to 86.8% in 1975.[208] No indication was given in the plan as to how this reduction was to be achieved. The total level of investment forecast was JD179m,[209] with the private sector contributing 44.4%. In the event, private sector investment outperformed the plan by 60%.[210]

Figure 4.6   Share of Gross Fixed Capital Formation, 1977-1984

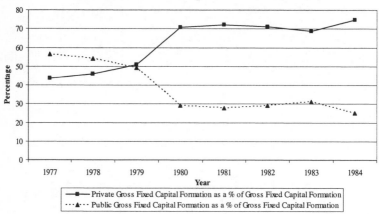

Source: Adapted by author.   IMF, (various), *International Financial Statistics Yearbook*, (Washington: IMF).

The 1976 to 1980 plan was prepared against a background of tight labour markets, inflation, rampant land speculation and unprecedented levels of foreign aid caused by the initial effects of the oil boom. The plan was the first to take on "longer term goals related to phosphates, fertilisers and potash plants, road networks, sewage, communications and water networks."[211] The large volumes of economic assistance permitted the government to implement a strategy of large-scale project investment, with eight projects accounting for 31.8% of the planned investment.[212] In addition, the plan was a:

> blueprint for creating a basic and suitable institutional framework, modernising and improving the performance of the government system, providing a suitable base for the private sector, emphasising manpower training and adopting suitable economic policies to augment the absorbtive capacity of the national economy.[213]

The 1976 to 1980 plan recognised that the "private sector has a basic role in the successful implementation of the plan."[214] As with the previous plan the decision-makers hoped to reduce the level of private consumption, thereby increasing the levels of savings that could be invested. On this occasion the target was to decrease from 74% of GNP in 1975 to 61% in 1980.[215] The plan discussed increasing interest rates on savings and the need to "set up a programme aimed at encouraging savings."[216] Among the fiscal policy measures highlighted in the plan was the creation of incentives to encourage private investment, both domestically and from abroad.[217] Monetary measures included extending sufficient credit facilities through the banking system to encourage the level of private sector investment.[218]

The anticipated level of investment was JD765.0m, of which JD580.4m was expected to be in the productive and infrastructure sectors, while the remaining JD184.6m was in the social sector. The breakdown between public and private was 49.9% and 50.1% respectively.[219] As with the previous plan, the private sector outperformed the target with total investment of JD843.7m, of which the share was 59%.[220] However, the total hides the fact that the private sector under-performed in the productive and infrastructure sectors, investing only JD362.5m against the planned amount of JD408.4m. The private sector share in the productive sector was planned at 88.8%, but the outcome was only 71.4%.[221] However, this level of private sector investment is still significant.

The 1981 to 1985 plan was prepared against the backdrop of explosive economic growth, a result of which was an envisaged real annual growth rate of GDP of 11% at factor cost.[222] The outturn was only 4.2% annually. A major assumption of the plan was:

> that Jordan will continue to pursue a policy of free enterprise, with increased opportunities for private initiative and closer co-operation between the public and private sectors in the process of development.[223]

The plan also argued that the "private sector will continue to respond favourably to developmental efforts and assume an increasingly important role in attaining its objectives."[224] In addition, the government's view of the relationship between the public and private sector was spelled out:

> The concept of public sector participation in economic projects particularly the larger ones, stems from the desire to propagate, support and ensure their proper financing and implementation with the purpose of activating the socio-economic sectors. On this principle, the public sector extends to the private sector the opportunity to contribute a larger share of the capital and the management of these projects on a purely commercial basis.[225]

Thus by the beginning of the 1980s the relationship become the antithesis of the early 1950s, when the public sector was expected to respond to the needs of the private sector, to one where the private sector was to respond to the needs of the public sector.

The continuing flow of economic assistance was once again expected to fund large-scale investment. The planned investment levels were for JD3,300m, of which the mixed sector share was to be only 39%[226] (i.e. the private share was to be lower than this). Khader and Badran argue that despite the high planned levels of state investment the aim was:

> the maintenance of a mixed economy with a strong private sector, the public sector's role being to create the basic infrastructure for private business and to promote the larger-scale productive projects too great to be supported by private investment alone.[227]

Among the fiscal policies, which were expected to promote the private sector, the government sought to revise the Encouragement of Investment Law and to revise customs duties to ensure the growth of local industries.   GFCF exceeded expectations in the first two plans, but thereafter the recession led to a decline. Government investment of JD1,279.5m in the five years accounted for 54.7% of the total investments of JD2,341.1m at 1980 prices: 92.9% of the planned level.[228]

Throughout the period the plans continued to call for the private sector to lead the economic development of the country.   Although the decision-makers' arguments were strong the actual figures in the plans tended to anticipate investment to be the responsibility of the public sector.   A comparison of the planned investment levels in the 1973-75 and 1981-85 plans[229] suggests that the majority of the public sector expenditure was to be spent on infrastructure.   Private sector investment, on the other hand, was planned to be in the productive sector (table 4.4).   The planned private-public investment ratio widened dramatically from 1:1.25 to 1:1.56, the highest of any of the plans up to that time.

The specialised credit institutions, which had been established in the previous period, gained in strength during the 1970s.   A new credit organisation, the Housing Bank, was created in 1974 with a mixed public-private sector capital base.   Total outstanding loans by the six credit institutions rose from JD16.3m in 1972 to JD375.1m in 1984, a factor increase in excess of twenty-three while in the same period their total assets increased from JD20.6m to JD591.1m, a factor increase of more than twenty-eight.   Both measures outperformed the growth of eight and one half times in GDP.   The public sector share of the outstanding loans provided by the credit institutions commenced at 31.3% in 1972, fell to a low of 20.9% in 1980, before increasing to 27.6% in 1982.   The provision of credit allowed for private sector expansion, but at the same time added to the dependency of the private sector on the state.

Table 4.4: Planned Investment by Sector, 1973-1975 and 1981-1985 (JDm)

Sector	1973-75		1981-85	
	Private	**Public**	**Private**	**Public**
Social and Services	37.23	27.74	111.9	549.3
Infrastructure	17.80	57.09	276.2	1369.3
Productive	24.39	14.75	898.7	94.6
Total	**79.42**	**99.58**	**1286.8**	**2013.2**

Sources: Adapted by author.   National Planning Council, *The Hashemite Kingdom of Jordan Three Year Development Plan, 1973-1975*, (undated: a), (Amman: National Planning Council), p.36 and National Planning Council, (undated: b), *The Hashemite Kingdom of Jordan Five Year Plan for Economic and Social Development, 1981-1985*, (Amman: National Planning Council), p.59.

The state also created two public vehicles for investment in this period.   The Pension Fund was established on the 1st January 1977, by the Provisional Law no. 6 for 1976.   The Board of Directors was drawn from the government departments; the Chairman was the Minister of Finance, the Deputy Chairman was the Governor of the CBJ, other members were the Director of the National Planning Council, the Director-General of the Budget Department, and the Director of the Pension Fund along with two other cabinet-appointed members.   The investment objectives of the fund were "taking into consideration the elements of security and profit, [to give] priority ... to investment in productive projects included in development plans."[230] The total assets of the Pension Fund, which is attached to the Ministry of Finance, rose rapidly to JD58.5m by the end of 1984. The second investment vehicle was the Social Security Corporation (SSC), which was established in 1980. By the end of 1984 this institution had total assets of JD99.9m.

In an attempt to boost the economy the state introduced the concept of Free Zones and Industrial Estates in this period. The Free Zones Corporation was created in 1976 to oversee the Free Zones. The Corporation operates under the Free Zones Corporation Law no. 32 for the year 1984, which grants it "independent and administrative status."[231] However, the Corporation was responsible to the Minister of Finance. According to Article 6 of the law, all board members were to be drawn from government ministries and the CBJ.[232] In addition, the Director-General, who was responsible for the management, was "appointed, and his appointment terminated, by decision of the Cabinet, provided such decision has been endorsed by Royal Decree."[233] Even if companies met the qualifying criteria for the zones, their establishment still required permission from the board of directors. Furthermore, the Cabinet had the final say as to which industries were to be allowed access to the benefits of the zones.[234] Finally, the Corporation was "to enjoy all exemptions and privileges accorded to Government ministries and departments."[235] As the Corporation continues to argue:

> The inspiration behind the Free Zones is that it is one of the State tools in development through the allocation of specific geographical sites or areas where special laws and regulations are applied different than those applied in the remaining part of the State and characterized by exemptions and facilities that qualify them to become an investment attraction areas [sic] for the development of export industries, international trade exchanges and transit trade.[236]

The objective of the Free Zones Corporation was to undertake the expansion in establishing and developing free zones as well as placing them in the service of the national economy.[237] Although its aim was to attract industrial, trading, investment and service projects through exemptions from taxes, import fees, customs duty, and licence fees, as well as other benefits, the Corporation was in the main unsuccessful. The first Free Zone had been established at Aqaba Port in 1973 to develop the international trade exchanges and to serve the transit trade. However, the potential benefits were restricted by competition in the region, particularly from the Jebel Ali Free Zone in the UAE.[238] By 1989 only one further zone had been created. In common with the Aqaba zone, this zone at Zarqa was almost totally dedicated to tax-exempt warehousing

The Jordan Industrial Estates Company was established in 1980 to provide an efficient and organised management approach to the growing manufacturing industry. The company is regulated by Law no. 59 of 1985, at which time the capital of JD18m was subscribed to by the government (67.5%), the Housing Bank (8.3%), the SSC (15%) and the IDB (8.3%) (i.e. there was no independent private sector involvement). The Minister of Industry and Trade was appointed chairman, with six other board members representing the government, along with one from each of the IDB, the Housing Bank and the ACI, the Director-General of the Corporation and one representative from industry. The latter two were appointed by the Cabinet. In contrast to the Free Zones Corporation, which focused its assistance on trade, the Jordan Industrial Estates Company was concerned with building an industrial base. The first site, the Abdullah II bin Al-Hussein Industrial Estate, was developed at Sahab near Amman. The second site was not commenced till 1989. Both the Free Zones Corporation and Jordan Industrial Estates Company were unsuccessful in achieving their remit of expanding the private sector industrial base of the economy.

Among the other institutional changes in the period were the establishment of the Jordan Valley Development Authority, the objective of which was to form a comprehensive plan to develop the valley. The Ministry of Labour was created in 1976 in response to the sudden shortfall in the supply of labour caused by the migration to the Gulf States. Part of its remit was to bring women into the economy. This move created a need for domestic workers from Sri Lanka and the Philippines. Other institutions established included the Postal Savings Fund, the Water Supply Corporation, the Public Transport Corporation (PTC), the Jordan Geographic Centre, and the Water and Sewage Authority for Amman.[239] The creation of the Amman Financial Market (i.e. the stock exchange) was an important institutional development in attempting to encourage private sector investment, albeit primarily domestic due to the restrictive nature of the laws governing foreign investment.

During the oil-boom years, the state became more deeply involved in the market, through subsidies, setting prices and monopolising imports of certain goods, as well as establishing shops for government employees. The boom in the early 1970s resulted in inflation increasing rapidly, from 4.7% in 1971 to 19.2% in 1974. Prices of basic goods rapidly outgrew government salaries, with the result that further subsidies were introduced. A brief mutiny by the army in February 1974 resulted in the creation of the Ministry of Supply, whose objective was "providing essential foodstuffs in reasonable quantity and good quality and at reasonable prices."[240] A monopoly was established over imports of wheat, flour, sugar, rice, meat, poultry and olive oil. The Ministry of Supply also fixed the wholesale and retail prices of these goods. Thereafter, "on the grounds of consumer protection,"[241] fixed prices for many locally produced and imported goods were gradually added to a portfolio of around forty items.[242] Milk was added in 1980.[243] In a related move, the Civil Consumer Corporation, under the control of the Ministry of Supply, was established in 1975 "to provide civil servants [and military personnel] with durable and non-durable consumer goods at cost price, duty free in respect of imported items."[244]

Government policies towards industrialisation in general included import protection, fiscal and credit incentives, government shareholdings (later), and direct regulation. In order to promote traditional industries and crafts the partly publicly owned IDB established the Small Industries and Handicrafts Loan Fund in 1975.

At the beginning of the period the government held capital of JD9.4m out of the total of JD28.9m in 26[245] local companies.[246] This figure excludes the holdings of the Pension Fund and the SSC. According to al-Quaryoty, SOEs accounted for 61.3% of GDP by 1985.[247] Government stakes in the 'big five' increased in this period with the establishment of Jordan Fertiliser Industries Company in March 1975. The government took an outright stake of 26%, but also invested via its partly owned company, the JPMC, a further stake of 25%. The following year the government shareholding was raised by a further 25.1%.

DICTATOR STATE, PRIVATE SECTOR DEPENDENCY

The oil-boom era, a period of increasing degrees of both induced rentier state economy and private sector rentier economy, witnessed a move towards the market end of the continuum as measured by investment and contribution to the national income. However, on all other measures the state became more deeply enmeshed in the economy. Despite these measures, Owen argues that the emphasis continued to be on a market economy. His argument is based on an analysis of the policies on trade and payments, the banking and monetary system, manipulation of tariffs and taxes, and representation of the private sector on the National Petroleum Company and national consultative council.[248] He states:

> "[e]conomic policy is ... largely a matter of bargaining and compromise. While the state is given free rein to set the country's main economic targets, to identify growth sectors and to take the lead in providing assistance for the larger projects, other goals have to be pursued more circumspectly."[249]

Although the intention may have been to maintain a market economy, the policies created an economy in which the private sector became dependent on the state. Given these changes, what characteristics of induced state rentierism and private sector rentierism were present in Jordan by the end of the oil boom?

Again, continuous deficits were experienced in the budget and the balance of trade, and the bias was towards services and high levels of consumption. However, by the end of the oil-boom the economy had become dependent on aid. The state was now vigorously pursuing a two-dimensional policy towards attracting aid and using expenditure for political purposes. In the latter case, the use of subsidies to the population in general had extended the benefits of this policy beyond those close to the regime. In addition, the levels of aid had funded a huge increase in numbers employed by the state in the bureaucracy, creating a class dependent on the state "for their existence and influence within the economy."[250] Furthermore, the service-oriented private sector had become homogenised in outlook and was now dependent on the state. The blurred relationship between the public and private sectors was now apparent, with signs that the rentier élite was now in place. Other signs of induced state rentierism were also present, with élite circulation, capture of the private sector by the state, informal rather than formal contacts and accusations of corruption all present.[251] Although high levels of private sector rentier economy based on remittances were noted, the characteristics of private sector rentierism were not apparent (state policy, heterogeneous and independent private sector, separate political and economic elites, and a formal relationship between the private and public sectors).

The reasons behind the development of induced state rentierism rather than private sector rentierism can be attributed to the historical development prior to the oil-boom. The increased revenues allowed the state to intervene at a previously unrecorded level. The drive for industrialisation and a modern infrastructure was not pursued by the weakened private sector, at least partly due to the lack of investment capital (the capital available from remittances tended to be used for consumption or invested in non-productive assets). Among the incentives for the state-led development was the lack of stability in both the region and domestically, which provoked the view that, for security purpose, the commanding heights of the economy should be in state hands. In addition, the failure of Amman to replace Beirut as the financial centre for the Middle East following the outbreak of the Lebanese Civil War due to its lack of modern infrastructure further emphasised the need to build a modern infrastructure. Finally, the dominant development ideology was still one of state-led development, although from the beginning of the 1980s cracks were beginning to appear in the consensus. Thus external events and internal security concerns, as well as the lack of a vibrant private sector, drove the move to a political economy of induced state rentierism.

THE RECESSION YEARS

Five main factors affected the development of the economy from the early 1980s to 1989: the slump in oil revenues; the continuing Iran-Iraq War; the outbreak of the *intifada* in the Occupied Territories; an inappropriate economic response to the impending crisis; and the rise of monetarism as the economic orthodoxy. The latter point resulted in an increased emphasis on the private sector as the key element in economic development. The effects of the drop in earnings of the OPEC countries took time to work through to the Jordanian economy. The drop in the level of remittances affected the private sector as a cutback in employment forced 15,000 expatriate workers to return to Jordan between 1982 and 1984.[252]   In addition, higher prices in the oil-producing countries resulted in the migrants having fewer funds to remit. As well as the slump in remittances, the oil-producing countries were also no longer able to provide economic assistance, thus further reducing the spending power of the state. However, as discussed previously, the government tried to maintain spending levels by borrowing commercially.

A major factor in the developing crisis was that the decision-makers initially disregarded the downturn, or at least considered it to be only temporary. In addition, despite the evidence to the contrary, the planners based their assumptions on the premise that the economic assistance agreed under the Baghdad agreement of 1978 would be met in full. The decision-makers adopted a:

> two-pronged strategy of (1) providing all forms of incentives and support to private capital, especially the large financial and commercial bourgeoisie; and (2) borrowing abroad until Arab money began to flow in again to avoid a painful, more thorough going economic restructuring.[253]

The growing emphasis on economic liberalisation and economic conditionality by the donor community resulted in Jordan adopting (at least rhetorically) a new economic posture from 1985. The need to borrow US$63m from the IMF in 1985,[254] as well as from other sources including commercial banks, meant that the country had to be seen to adopt a reformist approach to its economic policies. The appointment of Zaid al-Rifa'i as Prime Minister in April 1985 was the first signal of the new direction based on export promotion, privatisation and the encouragement of investment. These moves were supposed to set the scene for the retreat of the state.

The continuation of the Iran-Iraq War created problems for both the private sector and the state. Economic assistance from Iraq dried up and indeed Iraq was actually deeply in debt to Jordan by the end of the 1980s. Exporters, particularly the industrial sector, also suffered as trade between the countries slumped despite a barter agreement and an export credit guarantee scheme, which collapsed through mal-administration, if not outright fraud.

The final nail in the coffin was the outbreak of the *intifada*[255] (which started in the West Bank in late 1987) along with the continued cost of supporting the West Bank. The result was King Hussein, on the 31st July 1988, formally severed all legal and administrative ties with the West Bank. Although this action saved the Jordanian economy the cost of salaries and development projects,[256] the uncertainty regarding the role of the dinar in the West Bank and the position of Palestinians in Jordan led to a capital outflow of US$250m.[257]

The private sector was badly hit by the recession, with a number of private companies folding and others experiencing a steep decline in profit levels. In 1985 "twenty of ninety public shareholding companies suffered losses."[258] Thus the private sector entered the last half of the decade in a position of dependency on the state, with profits falling dramatically.

MEASURES ON THE STATE-MARKET CONTINUUM

Figure 4.7: Revenue and Expenditure as a Percentage of GDP, 1981-1989

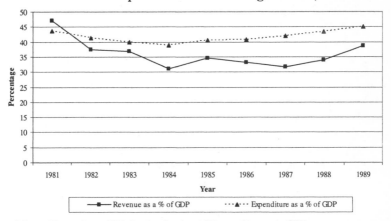

Source: Adapted by author. CBJ, (various), *Annual Report*, (Amman: CBJ).

As the economy entered a period of retrenchment, expenditure as a percentage of the GDP fell from 1982 to 1985, before climbing to 1989. In the latter period, the government attempted the Keynesian approach of increased spending to offset the effects of the recession. Revenue to GDP shows a decline for most of the period to 1987 before climbing to 1989 (figure 4.7). The effects of the recession are reflected in the GFCF. Private sector GFCF almost halved between 1981 and 1985, before recovering to 1989, when the figure was still less than 1981. Government GFCF, although not affected to the same degree, followed a similar pattern (figure 4.8). In terms of relative importance, the private sector's share fell from almost three-quarters in 1984 to two-thirds in 1989: a move towards the state end of the continuum, despite the fall in the induced rentier state economy (figure 4.9).

Figure 4.8   **Gross Fixed Capital Formation, 1981-1989**

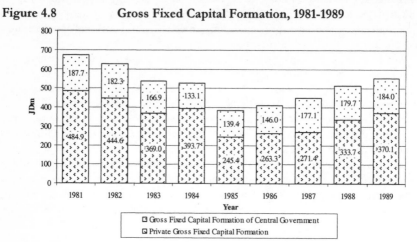

Source: Adapted by author.   IMF, (various), *International Financial Statistics Yearbook*, (Washington: IMF).

Figure 4.9   **Share of Gross Fixed Capital Formation, 1981-1989**

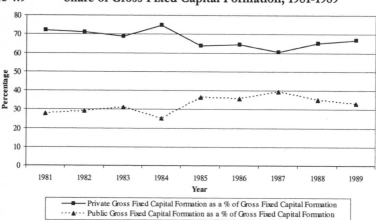

Source: Adapted by author.   IMF, (various), *International Financial Statistics Yearbook*, (Washington: IMF).

The development plan for 1981 to 1985, which had been drawn up prior to the collapse in oil revenues, quickly became inappropriate for the new economic reality. The National Planning Council, which was responsible for the development plans, was revamped into the Ministry of Planning in 1984 with the remit to use local input via sectoral groups and the governates for future plans. The Ministry's development plan for 1986 to 1990, based on the United States Agency for International Development's (USAID) 1984 Rural Development Strategy, was a reflection of the attempt to overcome regional disparities. Unfortunately the constraints, usually financial, meant that national priorities overcame local needs.[259] However, for the first time, the plan involved "a lengthy and conspicuous process of consultation."[260]

A 500-member general assembly was involved, representing most economic and social constituencies.[261]

Significantly, in view of the 1986 privatisation announcement, the plan contained no mention of privatisation. Indeed, one of the aims of the plan was "a continuation of public sector activity while defining its role as a catalyst and complement to the private sector."[262] The plan also acknowledges that "the private sector's role in the development process within the framework of the interaction of market forces are [sic] of particular importance to Jordan's development drive."[263] To this end total central government and autonomous institutions investment was anticipated to be JD1,633.4m, leaving private sector investment at 47.6% of the total planned investment of JD3,115.5m.[264] Table 4.5 highlights the sector breakdown of the planned investments. The plan was predicated on the assumption that the global recession would continue, and that foreign economic assistance could no longer be relied upon. In the event, the position became worse than anticipated, with the result that a number of development projects, including the West Bank Development Plan, were cancelled or curtailed. As with many previous plans events overtook the process, with the result that the plan was eventually discarded.

Table 4.5   **Planned Sectoral Investment, 1986-1990**

Sector	Private Sector		Public Sector		Total Investment
	Amount	Share	Amount	Share	
Social & Services	JD580.0m	46.8%	JD658.0m	53.2%	JD1238.0m
Infrastructure	JD350.8m	29.5%	JD839.7m	70.5%	JD1190.5m
Productive	JD551.2m	80.3%	JD135.7m	19.7%	JD687.0m
Total	**JD1482.0m**	**47.6%**	**JD1633.4m**	**52.4%**	**JD3115.5m**

Source: National Planning Council, (undated: d), *The Hashemite Kingdom of Jordan Five Year Plan for Economic and Social Development, 1986-1990*, (Amman: Royal Scientific Society Press), p.95.

The growth of both the specialised credit institutions and the investment vehicles continued to outperform the growth of GDP. The total loan portfolio of the credit institutions grew by 112.7%, from JD255.1m in 1982 to JD542.7m in 1989, of which the public sector share increased from 21.2% in 1981 to 35.2% in 1989. In addition, the combined assets of the investment vehicles increased by just over 400% in the eight years. Rather than crowding out private sector investment Brand argues that the SSC has proved "an effective way of mobilising private income for investment in productive enterprises."[265]

On the 13th September 1986, a Higher Economic Advisory Council (or Economic Consultative Council) composed of leading representatives of the public and private sectors, including the Chambers of Industry and Commerce, was established "at the behest of [Amman Chamber of Commerce] ACC president Hamdi Tabba [Taba'a]."[266] Its objective was:

to study economic conditions and to make proposals and recommendations aimed at: 1) co-ordinating economic, financial, and monetary policies at the time of their drafting and implementation; 2) developing policies to encourage savings and investment and to channel local and foreign investment; 3) organising and developing the financial markets; and 4) deepening co-ordination between the public and private sectors in implementing the development plan.[267]

The first meeting was held on 12 April 1987, but thereafter only two further meetings were held.[268] Throughout the years, the Council was one of a number of failures to formalise public-private co-operation.

Two other institutional developments were initiated. In spring 1987, the Jordan Marketing Organisation was created to "undertake research and advise the government on marketing and pricing policies."[269] In December 1988, the IDB began offering risk capital loans to entrepreneurs to encourage local participation in industrial and tourism development projects.

By the mid-1980s, three ministries were important players in the state-market relationship: the Ministry of Supply, which used subsidies and price regulation to offset (at least theoretically) poverty; the Ministry of Planning, which invested in infrastructure and capital-intensive projects to help promote the economy and the private sector; and the Ministry of Industry and Trade, which controlled access to trade to a considerable extent. Imports were organised through quotas, duties and state monopolies on certain agricultural inputs. In addition, the Ministry of Industry and Trade was responsible for negotiating bilateral trade treaties with other sovereign states through joint economic committees. The private sector then had to apply to the state, via the Jordan Commercial Centres Corporation, for a share in the agreement. Bureaucratic procedures, which the private sector as a whole was unable to influence mainly due a lack of organisation, were responsible to a degree for blocking an increase in trade.

In the trade sector "the government has maintained its overall commitment to free trade but holds that protectionism is essential if home industries are to develop."[270] Various changes were announced throughout the period, such as lifting and then re-imposing restrictions on imports depending on the economic situation. Overall, the tendency was to lift restrictions on inputs and basic foodstuffs, whereas restrictions on luxury goods were initially lifted but as the recession deepened were re-instated. Exports were encouraged through new regulations in 1986 that included income tax exemptions.

In April 1985, Prime Minister Zaid al-Rifa'i set about lifting restrictions on the private sector, including prices and hours of business. In August 1986, the cabinet approved a five-point privatisation programme, which was intended to alter private-public sector relations in favour of the former.[271] The programme included the increased involvement of the private sector in public sector companies, through ownership and management. In addition, the public sector companies were expected to operate on a commercial basis. A paper on privatisation, together with the 1986 to 1990 development plan, was presented to the Jordan Development Conference, held between the 8th and 10th November. Two areas of action were approved: firstly, the promotion of the private sector through incentives, policies and the legal environment. Secondly, advocating the transformation of the public sector through the sale of shares in mixed companies, the transfer of autonomous enterprises to the private sector, the establishment of private sector universities and the leasing of public land to the private sector.[272] Despite the announcement no progress was made before the crisis of 1988 to 1989 broke.

The companies approved for privatisation by the Cabinet on the 26th August 1986[273] were RJ, the PTC, and the Telecommunications Corporation (TCC). According to Anani and Khalaf, the original proposals also included Aqaba Port but the company "appeared to offer less potential given current industrial and economic conditions."[274]

Table 4.6   State Owned Enterprises According to IMF

Non-Financial Institutions		
Aqaba Railway Corporation	Hotels Corporation	Jordan Phosphate Mines Company
Arab Potash Company	Housing Corporation	Jordan Tourism & Mineral Water Company (Spa)
Civil Aviation Authority	Jordan Broadcasting & Television	Ports Corporation
Civil Employees Consumption Corporation	Jordan Cement Company	Posts Public Corporation
Free Zones Corporation	Jordan Electricity Authority	Public Mines Company
General Transportation Corporation	Jordan Glass Factories	Royal Jordanian Airlines
Himmeh Hot Springs Company	Jordan Hijaz Railway	Telecommunications Corporation
Holy Land Hotels Corporation	Jordan Hotels and Tourism Company	Water Authority
Financial Institutions		
Bank Markazi (CBJ)	Industrial Development Bank.	Pension Fund (JIC)
Agricultural Credit Corporation	Jordan Co-operative Organisation	Postal Savings Fund
Housing Bank	Municipal and Village Development Bank	Public Institution for Social Security Fund

Sources: IMF, (1988), *Government Financial Statistics Yearbook, 1988*, vol. XII, (Washington: IMF), p.567 and IMF, (1989), *Government Financial Statistics Yearbook, 1989*, vol. XIII, (Washington: IMF), p.374.

Other policies aimed at increasing private sector involvement in the economy included: lifting of import restrictions on rice and flour to allow the private sector to import a limited quota;[275] banning the imports of a number goods to protect domestic industry;[276] reducing custom duties on various industrial inputs;[277] lifting major curbs on Arab investment in January 1986;[278] introducing new regulations to boost exports, including exemption from income tax;[279] abolishing the requirement for licensing of new projects;[280] initiating a series of conferences to be held in

Amman to attract expatriate investment;[281] and outlining a new monetary policy to encourage economic activity in a joint memo by the CBJ and the Ministries of Finance and Industry and Trade, which included "increasing the Kingdom's reliance on domestic products and manpower, increasing government investments, turning financial companies into investment banks and attracting more foreign investors and capital."[282]

Direct state involvement in the market increased when government subsidies were extended in 1985 to include frozen chicken. By 1989 the range of subsidies included, among others, wheat, meat, sugar, cooking and fuel oils, and cement.[283] In addition fodder subsidies were available via the co-operative organisations established by the state to assist private-sector farmers. In general, from 1983 the government had moved from fixing prices to higher subsidies of electricity, petroleum derivatives and essential foodstuffs.[284]

The figures for government ownership are clouded by a lack of transparency and the adoption of different definitions of state ownership. However, Piro claims that by 1989 government ownership of the big four amounted to 78% in APC, 90.1% in JPMC, 56% in JCFC and 24% in JPRC. Anani and Khalaf state that central government ownership amounted to 32.2% of the subscribed capital in thirty-one domestic companies with a par value capitalisation of JD90.7m. In addition, the central government also had shares in a number of pan-Arab joint ventures. Of the autonomous investment organisations, the JIC had equity of JD37.2m in forty-eight companies, and the SSC owned approximately JD25m of investments. The total of these three (i.e. the JIC, the SSC and the government) accounted for 25% of the total shareholding in the country.[285] In terms of sectors, the government owned 58% of the capital in mining, 23.2% in manufacturing of which 87% was in four companies (JCFC, JPRC, Jordan Glass Factory, and Jordan Engineering) and 20.8% in services.[286] In 1989 the IMF listed twenty-four non-financial and nine financial SOEs (table 4.6).[287] However, the list is not comprehensive, as among those excluded are the JPRC and the SSC.

FAILURE TO ROLL BACK THE STATE,
CONTINUED PRIVATE SECTOR DEPENDENCY

Despite the calls from 1985 for the state to retreat, the recession actually saw the state's share of GDP increase. However, on most other measures, the tendency was towards a consolidation of the gains made in the previous decade. As Brand argues, in the last half of the 1980s "the desire to liberalise was clear, although the successes were few."[288]

> Government policy combined attempts to stimulate greater domestic private investment, attract foreign investment, cut inefficiencies through mergers, provide capital to certain industries to enable them to compete more effectively, cut certain subsidies (not including the IMF-triggered explosion), privatise certain public-sector companies, and ease banking regulations, with efforts aimed at protecting developing industries with tariffs and regulations and at easing the unemployment situation through greater regulation of the employment of foreign nationals.[289]

However, the earlier economic development had created a political economy, which displayed the characteristics of induced state rentierism, and that mitigated the withdrawal of the state. Piro terms these as "internal structural factors," namely:

> a domestic coalition more interested in maintaining its standing within the economy than in market reform; a symbiosis between the public and private sectors resulting in an unclear divide between the two; the use of state-owned enterprises for political purposes.[290]

Although Jordan "has followed a free-market ideology combined with import-substitution and latterly (post-1985) an export promotion strategy of development ... outcomes have been deficient."[291] Despite the attempts to promote the private sector, by 1989 it was only contributing 50-60% of GDP[292] but even this was dependent to a considerable extent on the state through contracts, licences, access to bilateral trade agreements, etc.

Significantly, the move towards privatisation was not initiated as a result of private sector pressure, but rather as a pragmatic response by the state to the economic crisis gradually enveloping the country. Indeed the private sector was "neither excited by nor able to carry out this programme and did not exert noticeable pressure to that effect."[293] Although private sector influence on the state decision-making process can be found on an irregular and *ad hoc* basis, the realisation by the successful business élite that:

> part of the reason for their success lies not only in the availability of contracts from the state, but also in the relatively stable domestic climate that the state provided during the years of authoritarian and martial law.[294]

Wilson agrees, arguing that "the private sector has benefited from rather than been damaged by increasing public expenditure."[295] Indeed examples can readily be found of the parts of the private sector successfully lobbying to halt arrangements that would assist other sections of the private sector. In 1987, the state proposed establishing a public company to co-ordinate barter deals for private-sector agricultural output and mineral resources in return for goods and raw materials used by public-sector companies. The move was scrapped after pressure from larger merchants, who gained between 5% and 8% commission on imported goods for the private sector. The company had been expected to boost exports, as well as save on foreign currency reserves.[296]

EXPLAINING PRIVATE SECTOR-STATE RELATIONS AT 1989

According to the theory of rentierism, in an induced rentier state economy such as Jordan, state-private sector relations are predicated on a rentier mentality. Thus the state attempts to control access to the rent that is predominant in the economy, while the private sector's main aim is to gain access to the flow of the rent. The result is a certain set of characteristics (induced state rentierism), all of which were present in Jordan in 1989, namely: a dependency on aid; a high level of imports, which help to create chronic balance of trade deficits; a high level of state expenditure leading to continual budget deficits, which are funded by aid; economic sectoral imbalances in favour of services; a high level of consumption in comparison to GDP; the maintenance of a two-dimensional policy by the state; a private sector that is relatively homogenised in its outlook, dependent on the state and service-oriented; the existence of a rentier élite using élite circulation and overlapping authority; voluntary co-optation or capture of the private sector by the state; and informal contacts between the two sectors. As a consequence of the expenditure element of the two-dimensional state policy a state-based, rather than market-based, economy is formed. The results of this expenditure policy were clearly evident in Jordan in 1989, namely: infrastructure development led through state-controlled development plans; state-controlled or state-influenced enterprises; subsidies, both of basic necessities, such as bread, electricity and water, and those aimed at favoured businesses, such as cheap loans and tax breaks; contracts from the state to favoured businesses; regulations aimed at preferred businesses; 'Royal' favours, such as free land in return for political support; bureaucracy built around allocative, rather than extractive, mechanisms; and the state as a major source of employment. A major part of the policy of the IMF SAP was to reduce these aspects of state involvement in the economy while simultaneously increasing its regulatory role.

As was discussed in chapter two, when an economy based on state rentierism enters a crisis, the state as an institution faces major difficulties in adopting policies of economic liberalisation, due to the existence of the rentier élite, which could be potential losers. By 1989, the rentier élite in Jordan were facing this problem. The amount of aid was declining and in order to gain future support from the donor community the state had to introduce economic liberalisation. In addition, the increasing importance of remittances in the economy exacerbated the pressure on the rentier élite. Different economic policies were required in order to gain access to this flow of rent.

At various times, Jordan has attracted high amounts of both state rent and private-sector rent. However, to conclude that the state-private sector relationship was established purely by rent would be wrong. The private sector had remained independent of the state until after the Civil War, despite a period of high induced rentier state economy from 1938 to 1964. Only after the degree of induced rentier state economy fell did the private sector start to become dependent on the state. The structural weaknesses of the private sector had been exacerbated by four years of war from 1967 to 1971. When the need to rebuild the economy came after the end of the Civil War, the private sector, both domestically and internationally, was unable and/or unwilling to lead the way: as the chances of further instability made investment extremely risky.

Thus the defining period in the construction of the private-sector dependence on the state occurred following a period of declining state rent. Indeed 1968 was the point of lowest relative importance in terms of rent accrual to the state. The foundations of the relationship had been built on the structural problems facing a late-industrialising economy, in combination with the Hashemite regime's need for national and domestic security and the dominant economic development ideology. The strange coincidence of three factors resulted in a state-led approach to economic development: the interests of the dominant ideology of economic development, which advocated a state-centred approach; the nationalist desire of a group of bureaucrats based in the Ministry of National Economy[297] to create an independent (from the West) industrial economy via a policy of big-push state-centred industrialisation; and the presence of aid. The increased volumes of aid available following the oil-boom enabled the regime to reward supporters more readily and to co-opt potential opponents with preferential access to the economy, through a policy of élite rotation and the use of overlapping authority.[298] These latter two elements have a further effect in stopping the building of alternative centres of power to the Hashemite regime within the rentier élite. The state was successfully able to act as an allocator of the rents, while the private sector was able to grow in a generally risk-free environment.

The overlap of state-private sector relations, as at 1989, was manifested in four areas: state involvement in productive companies; state involvement in the market; the use of access to the economy by the state for political purposes; and the institutional structure of the private sector. Partial state ownership was not restricted to the 'big four'[299] but was also achieved in many companies via both the JIC[300] and the SSC. State involvement in productive companies occurred not just in terms of ownership but also in the ability to influence the company and the market in which it operated. For example, the SOEs were granted certain monopolies (e.g. Jordan Cement Factories was granted a monopoly on production and APC was given a one hundred-year concession to exploit all minerals in the Dead Sea). In addition, the government made appointments to the boards of directors (e.g. the elected board of directors of JPMC was dissolved in 1963 and replaced by a government-appointed committee). These appointments were used regularly by the regime as a reward for political support. Furthermore, the SOEs received subsidies on inputs and outputs, as well as guaranteed prices for their products. For instance, loans from the specialised credit institutions may be guaranteed by the state (e.g. Jordan Glass Factories in 1981) or given at below market rates of interest (e.g. APC, JPMC).[301]

The second manifestation of the private-public relationship was the involvement of the state in the market through planning, price controls and subsidies, licences and contracts, import restrictions and exemptions, and through investment and credit institutions. For example, in the agricultural sector, which is essentially private-sector dominated, retail prices of basic outputs of fruit and vegetables were set by the state, as were the prices of a number of important inputs such as animal feed and water. The government also procured grain at a fixed price to encourage domestic production. Furthermore, cheap loans and interest write-offs have been a regular feature in the agricultural sector. Finally, 'cropping pattern' licences had to be obtained, which allowed the state control over the crops grown. In the industrial sector, import restrictions were applied through ever-changing tariff and non-tariff means. Tariff applications included the use of custom duties and quotas, while non-tariff measures included the use of permission licences, import bans, and government monopolies on certain commodities.[302] In addition, the Ministry of Industry and Trade was responsible for negotiating bilateral trade treaties with other sovereign states through joint economic committees. In order to obtain a share in the agreement, the private sector then had to apply for a licence via the Jordan Commercial Centres Corporation, which was established in 1972 as a joint venture by the Ministry of Industry and Trade, FJCC and the ACI. Finally, by the late-1980s, three government ministries (the Ministry of Supply, the Ministry of Planning and the Ministry of Industry and Trade) had become important players in the state-market relationship.

The third manifestation was the politicisation of the economy. The first example was the creation of classes, including the bureaucracy and the rentier elite: both dependent on the status quo. The second element of the politicisation was the ability of the state to use appointments on the boards of state companies as rewards or to co-opt potential opponents (élite circulation). In addition, preferential access to the economy via a plethora of formal arrangements (including licences, contracts, subsidies and incentives) was also used for political purposes, as were informal means such as 'Royal' favours. The final aspect of the politicisation of state-private sector relations was the degree of informal interaction between the two. Throughout the years, several economic committees were established to attempt to formalise procedures whereby the private sector was able to provide input into the decision-making process. However, none of these committees functioned beyond the first few meetings.

Although contacts between the private and public sectors were usually informal, the institutional organisation of the private sector was highly formalised, with state control being implemented through both regulation and the threat or actual use of security measures. Until the mid-1980s, the two main institutions of the private sector in Jordan were the Chamber of Commerce and Chamber of Industry. These two institutions were joined by the Jordanian Businessmen Association (JBA) in 1985.

The annual reports of the FJCC indicate less than twenty formal meetings with the government in fifteen years.[303] Among the subjects discussed were general problems, price violations, and income tax and custom duty concerns. A number of joint committees were proposed but no further reference was made to them, leading Brand to argue "that they had either short or unproductive lives or both."[304] She concludes that prior to 1990: "[i]n general, however, it seems clear that formal meetings were few and effective input quite limited."[305] However, the linkage with the public sector was highlighted in the participation of the FJCC in five public-private organisations: the Jordan Commercial Centres Corporation, the SSC, the Institute of Public Administration, the Investment Committee, and the Amman World Trade Centre.[306] Similarly, the ACI participates on a number of national boards including the Economic Consultative Council, the IDB, the Amman Financial Market, the Jordan Industrial Estates Company and the Jordan Commercial Centres Corporation.[307] Furthermore, representatives from both organisations serve on various government boards and committees, including economic development, vocational training, international trading affairs, labour education and adult literacy and training.[308] The representatives also participate in joint trade delegations and assist with the drafting of trade protocols.

In 1985, members of the rentier élite created the JBA, which immediately became an influential player behind the scenes in the economic decision-making process. The JBA was formed as an independent, non-profit organisation, which operates under Law 33 of 1966. The objective of the association "is to create and maintain a business climate that will enable the private sector to accomplish its role in the sustainable economic and business development in Jordan."[309] The select membership[310] of around four hundred represents the core of the rentier élite which, in the words of the JBA, "qualifies the Association to act as the single unified spokesman for Jordanian businessmen in communications and meetings with similar foreign businessmen associations."[311] In this respect the JBA "runs dialogues with ministries concerned with economic affairs in Jordan to boost the role of the private sector in the economic development in the Kingdom."[312]

The establishment of the JBA can be seen as a defensive measure by the rentier élite against the potential divisiveness of both the economic recession and the new export-oriented economic policy. The new economic direction was by its very nature bound to result in winners and losers among the old guard, while the recession signalled an end to the period of risk-free growth of the 1970s and the early 1980s. Suddenly, there was insufficient pie to go around. In this new competitive era, the FJCC and ACI were often at odds over which policies to support. In this context, a classic example of the differences occurred in August 1988: Hamdi Taba'a, the Minister of Industry, Trade and Supply (who had close links to the trading community via the ACC), replaced a ban on imports, which had been introduced a couple of years earlier, with higher duties. The ban was part of a package of policies aimed at protecting Jordanian industry, but it adversely affected the trading community. Furthermore, as Moore argues, the ACC had failed to develop the institutional level requisite for the new economic climate. For example, the research and information department was not established until 1985. Furthermore, by opening its membership base from 1961, and by shifting voting power away from the élite, the ACC was no longer a monolithic vehicle for the rentier élite.[313]

Figure 4.10   Preferred Outcomes of New Groups in Rentier Élite

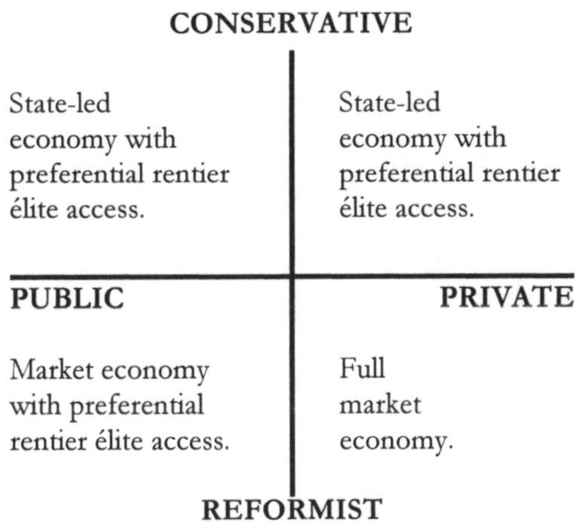

CONSERVATIVE

State-led economy with preferential rentier élite access.	State-led economy with preferential rentier élite access.
PUBLIC	**PRIVATE**
Market economy with preferential rentier élite access.	Full market economy.

REFORMIST

Other institutions exist within the private sector, often as members of the Chambers of Industry and Commerce or the JBA. The Entrepreneurial (or Business) Associations, licensed under Law 33 of 1966, fall under the auspices of the Ministry of the Interior. "Their aim is to provide a suitable climate for the operation of the economic sector to express their views and protect their collective interests."[314] A second sector is the Tradesmen's Associations and Unions, which are regulated under the Jordanian Labour Laws. A final category includes lobbying groups such as the Professional Associations and the Business and Professional Women Club. However, although these groups, particularly the professional associations, have strong informal links with the state over political concerns, they are not as significant as the ACI, the FJCC and the JBA in state-private sector relations.

The recession of the late 1980s, the decline in aid, the increase in the relative importance of remittances and the change of economic direction all combined to create conditions for introducing division within the rentier élite. In the oil-boom era, the state's ease of control of rent and the private sector's ability to gain access to the allocation of the rent allowed the rentier élite to present a homogenous economic and political outlook. From the mid-1980s the beginnings of a battle for control over and access to rent became apparent. Thus, by 1989 the storms of the recession began to erode the comfortable symbiosis that had been built between the private and public sector élites. Differences within the rentier élite very slowly became more apparent. The splits occurred along two axes: private-public sector and reformist-conservative, with three different preferred outcomes (figure 4.10). The potential splits are considered important, if the IMF was to be able to introduce the degree of change wanted.

The next chapter sets the changing context of the economic and rentier development from 1989, before the effects of the IMF-led donor community intervention are discussed in chapters six, seven and eight.

5

The Changing Face of Rentierism: 1989-2002

INTRODUCTION

This chapter is divided into two sections. The first analyses the reasons for the collapse of the economy in the late 1980s, which allowed the Bretton Woods sisters to influence the economic decision-making process from 1989. Thereafter, the main factors that affected the economy throughout the 1990s and into the new century are discussed. The second part of the chapter, using the measures of the induced rentier state economy and the private sector rentier economy, assesses the changes that occurred in the 1990s and early 2000s. The chapter concludes that into the new century the induced rentier state economy was diminishing, although overall rentierism remained strong in the form of the private sector rentier economy.

THE ECONOMY: 1989 TO 2002

THE COLLAPSE

In late 1988, the economy finally collapsed under the weight of inappropriate government policy responses to three events: the oil-revenue slump, the Iran-Iraq War and the renunciation of the claim of sovereignty over the West Bank. As Satloff argues, Jordanian decision-makers ignored "the glaring structural weaknesses in the economy" that were exacerbated by these three events. Instead of introducing tighter fiscal policies, the state embarked on a policy of further borrowing at commercial rates and expansionary policies that reduced the foreign exchange reserves.[315] Furthermore, the revaluation of the dinar at the end of 1987, which was intended to attract more remittances, only created greater pain when the dinar was floated less than a year later.

The effects of the drop in oil earnings of the OPEC countries impacted negatively upon the Jordanian economy. Firstly, the return of migrant labour from the Gulf increased unemployment rates, increased the need for extra welfare spending by the state and reduced the income of the families of the returnees.

Secondly, higher prices in the oil-producing countries resulted in the migrants having fewer funds to repatriate adding to the recession. In addition, the oil-producing countries were no longer able to provide high levels of economic assistance. Finally, exports to Saudi Arabia and Kuwait fell from JD50.3m in 1984 (19.3% of exports) to JD40.7m in 1988 (12.5% of exports).[316]

The economic decision-makers started to borrow commercially at increasingly expensive rates, in the hope that the drop in Arab economic assistance was only temporary, (table 5.1). As Finance Minister Awdah admits:

> [t]his situation was further complicated by the servicing of debts. Jordan had indeed resorted to financial institutions to obtain loans for the purpose of expediting the development process without asking the citizen to share the costs of this servicing.[317]

By 1989, commercial loans accounted for 20% of total indebtedness, up from only 6% in 1985.[318]

Table 5.1   Jordan's Internationally Syndicated Loans, 1983-1989

Date Signed	Size US$m	Maturity	Interest*	Lead Manager
02/1983	225	7 years	1/2	Arab Bank Investment Company
07/1984	150	7 years	1/2	Arab Bank
06/1985	200	8 years	1/2, 5/8	Arab Bank
03/1987	150	7 years	5/8, 3/4	Arab Bank
01/1989	150	7 years	7/8	Gulf International, Arab Banking Corporation, Arab Bank

Source: *MEED*, "Jordan's Hard Times", 24/02/89, pp.2-3.
* percentage above six-month LIBOR.

The outbreak of the Iran-Iraq War initially boosted the Jordanian economy, increasing both economic assistance and the opportunities for trade with Iraq. However, by 1984, the Iraqis had run out of cash due to the costs of the war. In order to maintain trade a barter agreement was established to swap Iraqi oil for Jordanian exports, which had fallen from JD53.5m in 1981 (35% of exports) to JD26.9m (16.8% of exports) in 1983.[319] A further attempt to boost Jordanian-Iraqi trade was the introduction of an export guarantee scheme. Although the two steps allowed Iraq to become Jordan's most important trade partner by 1988 (with almost 20% of exports[320]), a lack of control over the export guarantee scheme triggered the final collapse of the Jordanian economy. Firstly, despite an agreement to the contrary, many of the exports were actually re-exports, which meant that the economy was not benefiting to the extent expected. Secondly, an over-spend of US$240m was discovered in May 1988, resulting in the immediate freezing of the scheme.[321] However, Jordanian exporters already had stocks built up and paid for, placing immediate pressure on this sector. In addition, the size of Iraq's debt[322] to Jordan, allied to increasing dependence of the entire Jordanian economy on Iraq,[323] created further pressure on an already weakening dinar.

The third event was the outbreak of the *intifada* in the West Bank in late 1987 which, along with the continued cost of supporting the West Bank, partly influenced[324] King Hussein to formally sever all legal and administrative ties with the West Bank on the 31st July 1988. While this action saved the Jordanian economy US$60m annually on salaries and development projects,[325] the uncertainty regarding both the role of the dinar in the West Bank and the position of Palestinians in Jordan resulted in a switch from dinars to dollars, and a capital outflow of US$250m.[326] The CBJ unsuccessfully attempted to stabilise the dinar but only succeeded in reducing the level of foreign reserves to less than two weeks cover of imports. On the 15th October 1988 the dinar was floated, and by March 1989, in a series of 'Black Monday' devaluations the official rate was 540 fils to the dollar, a 48% fall.[327] The devaluation dramatically increased the cost of debt-servicing of the foreign loans and subsidies,[328] adding further pressure to the already strained economy.

Between 1987 and 1989 GNP fell from US$6,169m to US$3,673m, GNP per capita fell from US$2,100 to US$1,480 and annual inflation rocketed from 0.2% to 25.8%. Poverty increased from 2% in 1987 to 16% in 1992, while unemployment increased from 4% in 1981 to 20% by 1991. Additionally, government debt climbed from US$1bn in 1981 to US$8.5bn in 1989. The growth of the debt contracted is apparent in table 5.2, with over half the contracted debt being agreed in the three years prior to the collapse of the economy. In addition, the emphasis switched from development loans to military borrowing, with the latter accounting for more than 50% of the loans contracted between 1985 and 1988 (table 5.3). By the beginning of 1989, Jordan had become "one of the most heavily indebted countries in the world."[329] Consequently, debt-servicing rose by over 100% between 1987 and 1988 to US$1277m,[330] around 22% of GDP. In 1989 a negative cash flow of US$794m was recorded, with debt servicing totalling US$1368m and new loans of only US$574m.[331] The upshot was foreign exchange reserves fell from US$425m in 1987 to only US$18.7m by June 1988,[332] and the dinar lost almost 50% of its value between October 1988 and March 1989.

Table 5.2   **Accumulation of Indebtedness to 1988**

Date	Sum of Contracted Debt US$m	% of Total Debt
Before 1977	1,119	9.5
1977-1979	937	8.0
1980	982	8.4
1981-1983	1,540	13.0
1984	(*)1,430	8.9
1985-1988	6,140	52.2
Total	**(**)12,148**	**100.0**

Source: Adapted from speech by P.M. Badran to Parliament on economic strategy reported in *SWB Weekly Economic Report*, Third Series ME/W0110, 09/01/90, pp.A1/4-6.
* Suspect this figure should read US$1,034.6m, which would allow the total to become US$11.752.6.
** Suspect this figure should read US$11,752.6m (which is total in table 4.3) as the percentage in the third column are correct for the revised figure.

Table 5.3   **Use of Loans, 1921-1988 (US$m)**

Type of Use	1921-1985	1985-1988	Total
To Cover Deficit in Budget	192.3	777.7	970.0
Development Loans	2,755.2	1,192.9	3,948.1
Military Loans	1,369.4	3,181.8	4,551.2
Public Security Loans	0.0	155.4	155.4
Development Loans Guaranteed by State	1,300.3	827.6	2,127.9
Total	**5,617.2**	**6,135.4**	**11,752.6**

Source: Adapted from a speech by P.M. Badran to Parliament on economic strategy reported in *SWB Weekly Economic Report,* Third Series ME/W0110, 09/01/90, pp.A1/4-6.

In November 1988, the first austerity programme was unveiled, with a freeze on development projects, an import ban on luxury goods, a rise in fees for foreign workers' permits, an increase in customs duties and the introduction of a tax on hotels and restaurants.[333] Nevertheless, by early February 1989 Jordan was forced to abandon the launch of a seven-year US$150m Euroloan, after asking "to roll over for three months a US$16.6m principal payment on a US$150m syndicated loan due at the end of February."[334] In addition, the EIU reported rumours that discussions on rescheduling overdue American military debt of US$98m were taking place.[335] Although World Bank officials were in Amman in February to discuss a new loan, Prime Minister al-Rifa'i denied that negotiations with the IMF were in progress.[336] However, official confirmation of the seriousness of the situation was finally acknowledged on the 28th February 1989, when the intention to request a stand-by facility from the IMF was officially announced.

FACTORS AFFECTING ECONOMIC DEVELOPMENT: 1989 TO 2002

Following the intervention of the IMF, eight further factors constrained the ability of the state to impose its will on the development of the economy: the advent of political liberalisation; the indebtedness of the Petra Bank and Royal Jordanian (RJ); the Iraqi invasion of Kuwait and the sanctions against the former; the peace process and its subsequent failure; the signing of international economic agreements; the drop in global commodity prices; the recession in Asia; the death of King Hussein; the outbreak of the 2000 *intifada* in Israel and the Occupied Territories; and the US-led 'war-on-terror', following the 11 September 2001 attacks.

The economic crisis precipitated a new era of political liberalisation, with the April 1989 riots drawing forth a promise by the King to reconvene parliament and allow elections in November (the first elections since April 1967). In April 1990, a broadly-based commission[337] appointed by the King was established to formulate a National Charter, which "would govern political life in the country and lay the quasi-constitutional foundations for the democratisation process."[338] The National Charter was ratified in July 1991. Martial Law was completely lifted in March 1992, to be followed by the re-instatement of political parties in late 1992, allowing candidates in the 1993 elections openly to express their political affiliation. Further elections, although less free, were held in 1997, with the next elections scheduled for

November 2001, although these were postponed until June 2003, ostensibly because of the uncertain regional situation. Also, in 1992, the authorities permitted overseas human rights organisations to be established in Jordan: a move which indicated a new degree of political tolerance in the Kingdom. The new political openness (although still limited by Western standards and becoming less free from the mid-1990s) restricted to a degree the ability of the state to implement economic policies, such as the cuts in subsidies demanded by the IMF.

A further constraint for the state was the failure of the Petra Bank, with its potential to undermine the banking system in Jordan, and the debts built up by RJ. The CBJ had to inject US$250m into these two enterprises in the early 1990s when the foreign exchange reserves were already low.[339]

The regional context was extremely fluid in the early years of the 1990s. The invasion of Kuwait by Iraq, and the subsequent US-led action to free Kuwait in January 1991, resulted in Jordan becoming internationally ostracised, since King Hussein's attempts at an Arab solution were interpreted on the international stage as support for Saddam Hussein. The Gulf crisis proved calamitous for the slowly recovering economy in a number of ways. Firstly, 300,000 workers and their families were forced to leave Saudi Arabia and Kuwait reducing the flow of remittance but also increasing government spending as only 10% were said to be reasonably well off, the rest were in "dire need".[340] In September 1991, Planning Minister Ziad Fariz estimated that over the next three to five years the cost would be US$4,500m, of which US$3,700m was for capital investment in housing, health, transport, water, sewerage, and education, while the remainder would be used for recurrent costs.[341] Secondly, a flood of short-term refugees, particularly from Asian countries passed through the Kingdom, costing US$40m.[342] In addition, the closure of the Iraqi market following the imposition of sanctions negatively impacted on exports and industrial production; around 25% of Jordan's exports[343] and 70% of the industrial capability was geared to Iraq.[344] Furthermore, the loss of economic relations with the Gulf states put the final nail in the coffin for Arab aid, cut a major export market and a loss of labour market. Fifthly, the cost of imported oil soared from US$14.75 pb in July 1990 to US$36 pb by September.[345] Sixthly, entrepôt trade to Iraq and Kuwait was cut: approximately 70% of the cargo handled at Aqaba had been bound for Iraq before the War.[346] Seventhly, the effective closure of the port at Aqaba, due to sanctions inspections, cost Jordan US$14m annually.[347] Finally, the important tourist sector was hit hard. In total the estimated loss to the Jordanian economy in the twelve months following the outbreak of the War was at least US$1,200m (the World Bank) and as high as US$2,144m (the Minister of Finance Jardaneh).[348]

However, on the positive side, increased pledges of funding from Japan, Germany and the EU potentially offset the loss of aid from the Gulf States and the USA. By March 1991, pledges of special support, channelled through the Gulf Financial Crisis Group, totalled US$1,230m, of which US$470m had reportedly been received.[349] The economy also received a short-term boost from the money repatriated by the returnees, which was spent mainly in the construction sector creating a short-term economic boom. Jordanian's were estimated to have spent US$600-700m on housing in 1992 and US$50-150m on industrial and commercial building. [350]

The new pre-eminence of the USA in the Middle East following the ousting of the Iraqi troops from Kuwait, resulted in all sides involved in the Palestinian dispute being pressurised into peace negotiations, commencing in Madrid in October 1991. Jordan's strategic importance to the dispute paved the way for its international rehabilitation, although relations with the Gulf States took considerably longer to repair. Following the signing of the Oslo Accords between the PLO and Israel in September 1993, Jordan and Israel signed a Common Agenda for Peace a day later, followed by the Washington Declaration[351] on the 25th July 1994 and the signing of the Peace Treaty in the October.

The Arab-Israeli conflict had long been recognised as a major stumbling block to the development of the Jordanian economy. However, with the signing of the peace treaties the regional situation was expected to improve dramatically, bringing a significant peace dividend to the economy of Jordan. The Peace Treaty paved the way for a series of agreements between the two countries in areas such as tourism, transport, air service, environmental protection and trade. In accordance with the Treaty, in July 1995, Jordan repealed the Israeli Boycott Laws of 1953 (banning trade with Israel), of 1958 (boycotting Israel) and of 1973 (banning the sale of land to Israel or Israelis). Furthermore, the peace process was expected to open up the markets of the Palestinian National Authority, to which the Israelis controlled access.[352] To this end, a "wide ranging economic co-operation agreement" was signed between Jordan and the Palestinian National Authority on the 7th January 1994, with the hope of gaining up to US$500m trade annually.[353]

Part of the international efforts to 'normalise' the peace involved the establishment of Middle East and North Africa annual economic summits: the first was held in Casablanca at the end of October 1994, the second in Amman one year later, Cairo in 1996 and a fourth in Doha in 1997.[354] These conferences increasingly emphasised the need for private sector, rather than government-led, economic development. At the first conference, the World Bank emphasised the regional nature of economic growth, suggesting that "growth prospects would be enhanced by the development of productive trans-national partnerships, both among countries in the region and between Middle East and North Africa countries and external partners."[355] One example of the transnational approach following the peace treaty was the joint Jordan-Israel proposed initiative for developing the Jordan Rift Valley for which the World Bank assisted with the preparation of the preliminary report.

A further international development was the start of the EU-Mediterranean dialogue in Barcelona in November 1995, with the aim of creating a Free Trade Zone between the EU and eight Arab countries, including Jordan, by the year 2010. Jordan entered into the Euro-Med agreement in 1997. The Jordanians also acceded to membership of the World Trade Organisation (WTO) in December 1999. Both these agreements moved the country firmly in the direction of an open economy and acceptance of the global norms of economic decision-making, thereby reducing the economic options available to the state.

Despite the problems caused by the Second Gulf War, the injection of returnees' capital created a mini-boom that lasted until the mid-1990s, with annual real GDP growth averaging almost 9% between 1992 and 1995.[356] The growth petered out by 1996 due to a number of factors including: the end of the short-term boost given to the construction sector of the economy by the returnees; the lack of progress in the peace process; the continuing sanctions on Iraq; the decline in oil prices; and the slowdown in East Asia. Each factor negatively impacted on the export market and on the potential for foreign and domestic investment: two of the main problem areas that the SAP was attempting to address.

The 1996 recession was followed by a global financial crisis in 1997 to 1998, which seriously hit foreign direct investment (FDI) in developing countries as Western investment was returned to the home countries. Unfortunately, this crisis proved to be badly-timed for Jordan, which had just embarked seriously on a privatisation process that required foreign funding to succeed. Commodity prices also fell as demand slackened, hitting Jordan's main export of phosphates.

In July 1998, the Royal Court announced that King Hussein had been diagnosed with lymphoma. His treatment, which was predicted to be lengthy, required to be undertaken abroad. His triumphant return in January 1999, apparently having recovered, was quickly overshadowed by complications. He died a few days later in Amman, having earlier appointed his son, Abdullah, as Crown Prince, in preference to his brother, Hassan, who had been the designated heir for over thirty years. The move came as a shock, particularly in light of the lack of experience of the new king in the political sphere. However, King Abdullah moved swiftly to appoint his own men in positions of power, without upsetting the fragile political balance in Jordan. The accession progressed smoothly, despite initial fears to the contrary.

The new king initially attempted to build on the sympathy evoked by the death of his father by setting out on a tour of the Gulf States to gain economic assistance. By April, however, in an interview with the newspaper *al-Quds al-Arabi*, he stated he understood the Gulf States'

> present circumstances, and that's why we did not ask for assistance or financial grants, but look forward to close economic cooperation that ensures the interests of both sides, like opening the doors to Jordanian workers and opening markets to Jordanian produce.[357]

Furthermore, in May he travelled around the capitals of the Western creditor countries attempting to obtain debt relief of 50%.[358] Despite the backing of President Clinton, the world tour was a failure, with the proposal receiving a lukewarm reception from most countries. The King quickly realised the world had changed. Despite the initial promises of new aid[359] (and even with the strong support of the USA) economic assistance was a thing of the past. In a statement to the Lower House in June 1999 Prime Minister Rawabdeh stated that "up till this moment Jordan has not received one dinar of the financial aid...we don't expect help from anyone."[360] As a result the new king has adopted a pragmatic position echoing the 'Washington Consensus', emphasising the need to role back the state and encourage the private sector. He has been particularly interested in pursing an export-based policy built around the IT sector.

Unfortunately, in September 2000, the vulnerability of the Jordan economy to external events was once again highlighted with the outbreak of the *intifada* in Israel and the Occupied Territories. The impact of the final collapse of the peace process and the rising level of violence, with Israeli incursions into Palestinian areas using tanks and helicopter gunships and regular use of suicide bombings by Palestinians, was exacerbated by the US-led 'war-on-terror', which commenced 12 months later. These events once again reinforced the image of inherent regional instability, immediately negatively impacting on the number of tourists entering the country.

Trade and investment were also curtailed by the regional problems. However, the gradual decline in the volume of aid was reversed as due to Washington's perception of the Hashemites as an important ally and Jordan as an oasis of stability in a region of apparent inherent stability.

RENTIERISM: 1989 TO 2002

Building on the changing global, regional and domestic environment highlighted in the previous section, this section analyses the changes in the induced rentier state economy, along with the changes in the private sector rentier economy.

MEASURES OF THE INDUCED RENTIER STATE ECONOMY:
1989 TO 2002

As with the previous eras, the volumes of aid fluctuated considerably throughout the period. The onset of the economic crisis resulted in aid leaping by over 180% in 1990, before falling to a low in 1993; however, the signing of the peace treaty with Israel witnessed an increase of almost 85% between 1993 and 1994 before the gradual decline set in to 1999. Following the death of King Hussein along with the onset of increased regional instability with the outbreak of the *intifada* in 2000 and the US-led war on terrorism in 2001, all of which undermined the chances of an economic recovery, levels of aid increased to US$642.4m in 2002 (figures 5.1 and 5.2).

Figure 5.1   **Aid, 1989-2002**

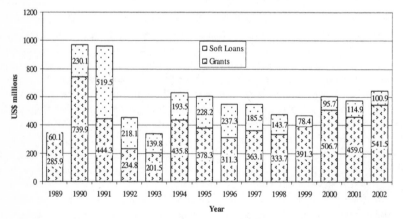

Sources: Adapted by author from OECD, (2000), *International Development Statistics*, CD-ROM 2000 edition, (Paris: OECD) and OECD website, www.oecd.org.

How then have these changes in volume been reflected in the measures of induced rentier state economy? The first measure used is aid as a percentage of GNP (figure 5.3). Although the percentage was relatively high in 1990 and 1991 at around 25%, by 1999 it reached an all-time low of only 5.8%. Even the recovery in absolute levels of aid following the turn of the century only saw aid as a percentage of GDP at 6.8% in 2002. Similar results are found with aid per capita, although the figure for 2002 is above the level of 1989.

Figure 5.2   Annual Percentage Change in Aid, 1989-2002

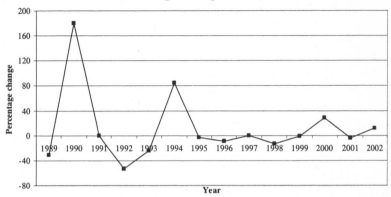

Sources: Adapted by author from OECD, (2000), *International Development Statistics*, CD-ROM 2000 edition, (Paris: OECD) and OECD website, www.oecd.org.

Figure 5.3   Aid as a Percentage of GNP and per capita, 1989-2002

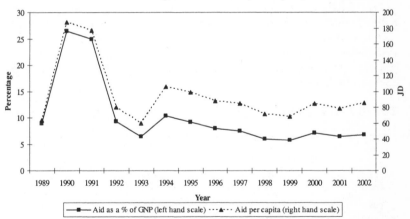

Sources: Adapted by author from OECD, (2000), *International Development Statistics*, CD-ROM 2000 edition (Paris: OECD), *OECD website*, www.oecd.org and CBJ, (various), *Monthly Statistical Bulletin*, (Amman: CBJ).

Three other measures of the induced rentier state economy, aid as a percentage of trade deficit, of government revenue, and of government expenditure, follow the same pattern of peaking in 1990 and 1991, before dropping to 1993, then showing a slight recovery in 1994 before gradually declining to the end of the 1990s and then climbing slightly in the century (figure 5.4). However, on each of measure the low point occurs in 1993, rather than in 1999 as with the first two measures.

Nevertheless, the degree of the induced rentier state economy was far below that of the late 1980s.

Figure 5.4: Measures of an Induced Rentier State Economy, 1989-2002

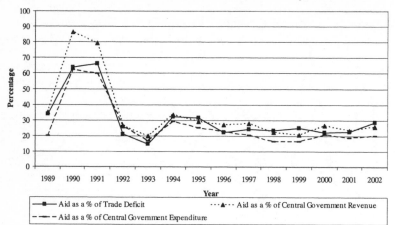

Sources: Adapted by author from OECD, (2000), *International Development Statistics*, CD-ROM 2000 edition (Paris: OECD), *OECD website*, www.oecd.org and CBJ, (various), *Monthly Statistical Bulletin*, (Amman: CBJ).

The final measure, gross aid as a percentage of budget deficit excluding aid, follows a different pattern (table 5.4). The percentage climbs to a peak of almost 3500% in 1992 from only 46.2% in 1989, thereafter, the figure drops to 60.6% in 1998, before recovering to 96.2% in 2000. A small decline is then evidenced in 2001 and 2002. On this measure, the induced rentier state economy has actually increased by the end of the period.

Table 5.4: Aid as a Percentage of Budget Deficit excluding Aid, 1989-2002

Year	Aid as % of Budget Deficit excluding Aid	Year	Aid as % of Budget Deficit excluding Aid
1989	46.2	1996	135.4
1990	222.6	1997	76.1
1991	242.3	1998	60.6
1992	3498.7	1999	78.9
1993	106.3	2000	96.2
1994	222.3	2001	85.9
1995	168.6	2002	83.9

Sources: Adapted by author from OECD, (2000), *International Development Statistics*, CD-ROM 2000 edition (Paris: OECD), *OECD website*, www.oecd.org and CBJ, (various), *Monthly Statistical Bulletin*, (Amman: CBJ).

Although the measure of the budget deficit differs from the norm, the figures indicate powerfully that the era of the induced rentier state economy had ended by 2002. The years 1990 and 1991 can be considered merely the last gasp of this dying phenomenon. Was a similar story apparent in the case of the private sector rentier economy?

MEASURES OF THE PRIVATE SECTOR RENTIER ECONOMY: 1989 TO 2002

As can be seen from figure 4.5, remittances increased dramatically between the start of the period and 1999 (JD1179.8m), despite a drop from 1989 (JD358.3m) to 1991 (JD306.3m): ironically these were the same years that the induced rentier state economy was experiencing its final flourish. Although the trend of remittances has been positive, the annual change indicates that the path has been far from smooth (figure 5.5).

Figure 5.5   Remittances and Annual Change, 1989-2002

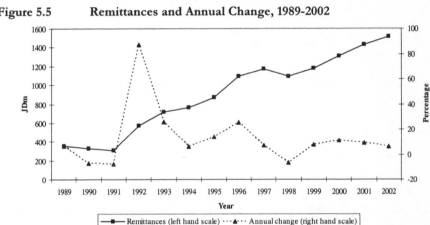

Sources: Adapted by author from OECD, (2000), *International Development Statistics*, CD-ROM 2000 edition (Paris: OECD), *OECD website*, www.oecd.org and CBJ, (various), *Monthly Statistical Bulletin*, (Amman: CBJ).

Remittances as a percentage of GNP fell from 1989 to 1991, thereafter, the figure climbed to a peak in 1997. Following a decline in 1998 the figure has gradually increased to 2002 (figure 5.6). The next measure as a percentage of trade deficit also increased by 2002, despite an initial slump between 1989 and 1991, when the lowest figure since 1975 was recorded However, in 2002 the percentage stood at 95.7%, an all-time high (figure 5.6).

Remittances per capita fell between 1989 and 1991, before recovering to 2002, indicating the increasing importance of remittances to the economy (figure 5.7). The final measure used by the study remittances as a percentage of aid had climbed from around 20% in 1972 to more than 180% in 1989; however between 1989 and 1991 the trend reversed, with the figure falling to 46.7% (figure 5.7). Thereafter, another U-turn was experienced, so that by 2002 the amount was in excess of 320%.

Figure 5.6   **Indicators of a Private Sector Rentier Economy, 1989-2002**

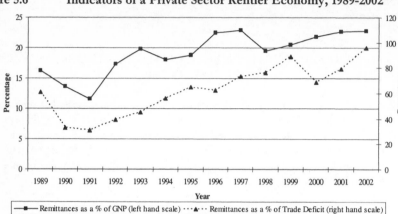

Sources: Adapted by author from OECD, (2000), *International Development Statistics*, CD-ROM 2000 edition (Paris: OECD), *OECD website*, www.oecd.org and CBJ, (various), *Monthly Statistical Bulletin*, (Amman: CBJ).

Figure 5.7   **Indicators of a Private Sector Rentier Economy, 1989-2002**

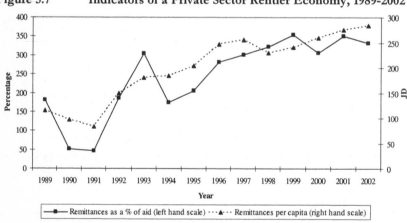

Sources: Adapted by author from OECD, (2000), *International Development Statistics*, CD-ROM 2000 edition (Paris: OECD), *OECD website*, www.oecd.org and CBJ, (various), *Monthly Statistical Bulletin*, (Amman: CBJ).

INDUCED RENTIER STATE ECONOMY VERSUS
PRIVATE SECTOR RENTIER ECONOMY

Prior to the 1990s, perceived and actual threats of global, regional and domestic instability had helped Jordan become addicted to aid. However, since 1992, despite continued instability in the form of the Arab-Israeli dispute and the situation in Iraq, Jordan was no longer able to get its 'fix'. Three changes contributed to the situation: the end of the Cold War; the end of the large dollar surpluses of the Arab oil-exporting countries; and the consolidation of the orthodoxy of economic liberalisation. Indebted states such as Jordan were now expected to follow the policies of financial restraint with borrowing restricted to uses associated with the SAPs. In addition, the new orthodoxy regarded aid as inherently destabilising for the recipient's economy.

Thus, the measures of the induced rentier state economy and the private sector rentier economy have highlighted that the trend of the 1980s (the move from the former to the latter) continued into the 2000s, with the exception of 1990 and 1991, which can be considered the last hurrah of the induced rentier state economy. Table 5.5 illustrates the pattern of declining induced rentier state economy, while simultaneously remittances have filled the gap to push Jordan into private sector rentier economy.

Table 5.5: **Induced Rentier State Economy vs Private Sector Rentier Economy, 1989-2002**

Measure	Induced Rentier State Economy			Private Sector Rentier Economy		
	1989	1990/1	2002	1989	1990/1	2002
Aid (JDm)	197.4	656.2	455.5	N.A.	N.A.	N.A.
Remittances (JDm)	N.A.	N.A.	N.A.	358.3	306.3	1513.7
Per capita (JD)	63.4	187.3	85.5	115.2	82.8	284.0
% of GNP	8.9	26.5	6.8	16.2	11.6	22.8
% of Trade Deficit	33.7	66.0	28.8	61.2	30.8	95.7
Aid as % of Remittances	55.1	214.2	30.1	N.A.	N.A.	N.A.
Remittances as % of Aid	N.A.	N.A.	N.A.	181.6	46.7	332.3

Sources: Adapted by author from OECD, (2000), *International Development Statistics*, CD-ROM 2000 edition (Paris: OECD), *OECD website*, www.oecd.org and CBJ, (various), *Monthly Statistical Bulletin*, (Amman: CBJ).

The introduction of the IMF into the equation coincided with the end of the Cold War, which heralded the apparent victory of market economics over state economics. The change in the international arena gave confidence to the Bretton Woods sisters that the policies of economic liberalisation were now the correct solution to the problems of the indebted countries. This newly-found confidence encouraged the IMF and the World Bank to apply stricter and more intrusive conditions to the countries in which they became involved, resulting in fewer options being available for the domestic governments. The next chapter analyses the outcome of the new era of conditionality on the donor community and its relationship with the regime in Jordan. Thereafter, chapter seven turns to the question of how the rentier élite adapted to the need to re-address the balance between the public and private sectors imposed by the IMF and the World Bank in return for their continued assistance.

6

Donor Community Involvement: 1989-2002

INTRODUCTION

This chapter explores the donor community's involvement in Jordan between 1989 and 2002. Throughout the 1980s, the impact of the troika of the Cold War, Keynesian development practices and the large dollar surpluses of the Arab oil-exporting countries, upon which a rentier mentality had evolved, had been gradually eroded. These changes resulted in an overall reduction in the global levels of aid since the 1980s. In addition, the transition states of the ex-Soviet empire were given precedence in the field of economic assistance, particularly by two of the main donors, the USA and Europe. Furthermore the primacy of the economic orthodoxy based on the monetarist school of thought resulted in assistance being granted only with strict conditions attached. Countries such as Jordan were not only less able to attract aid but also the recipients had to adopt new economic policies to attract further aid. As indicated in previous chapters, from independence, and in particular from the early 1970s, the state as an institution attempted to offset economic problems by rent-seeking, rather than by attempting to build a self-sustaining economy. Given the changes in the international environment in the late 1980s and the changing patterns of global aid in the 1990s, could the state as an institution continue to attract *and also* control access to rent? The evidence in the previous chapter indicates that aid continued to decline during the period to under 7% of GNP. Was this trend an indication of the success of the conditionality of the donor community in weaning the economy away from rent, or has the state as an institution continued to try, but ultimately failed due to the changing patterns of global aid, to retain control over rent by adopting a policy of economic liberalisation? This set of policies has been espoused by the major actors in the donor community, with increasing stridency since the 1980s, in return for continued financial support.

The first section assesses the relative importance of the various donors to the government in terms of their level of funding and also through the leverage each donor is able to exert. The next section discusses the role of the Bretton Woods institutions (BWIs) and their perceptions of the government's responses by focusing first on the IMF, and secondly on the World Bank. Thereafter, discussion turns to the debt negotiations conducted by the government, to assess the impact of debt rescheduling and debt retiral on the government's approach to the process of economic liberalisation. The penultimate section analyses the roles of the major bilateral and multilateral donors, in the relationship between state, economic liberalisation and rent. The analysis is set against the background of the new constraints on the state's ability to adopt economic policies of its own choosing and the change in the patterns of rent discussed in the previous chapter. The changing relationship between the donor community, the state and economic liberalisation established in this chapter, then sets the context for chapter seven, which assesses the reaction of the state as an institution and as an arena of contestation to the new circumstances.

RELATIVE VALUES OF THE DONOR COMMUNITY

Table 6.1   Donor Community Involvement, 1989-2002 (US$m)

Year	IMF	World Bank	Debt Relief	Total of IMF, World Bank & Debt Relief	Total Aid	Grants
1989	84.9	223.0	0.0	307.9	346.0	285.9
1990	0.0	0.0	0.0	0.0	970.0	739.9
1991	0.0	10.0	0.0	10.0	982.4	463.0
1992	30.1	0.0	0.0	30.1	453.0	234.9
1993	15.2	135.0	0.0	150.2	343.5	201.7
1994	93.9	86.6	184.0	365.4	633.0	436.4
1995	115.0	140.0	200.2	455.2	609.3	379.0
1996	119.3	180.0	184.2	483.5	550.5	311.7
1997	133.0	62.0	148.0	403.0	550.5	364.8
1998	32.1	5.0	115.0	187.1	481.3	333.7
1999	75.8	210.0	94.8	345.6	462.9	393.5
2000	17.2	34.7	60.3	112.2	601.8	506.1
2001	38.8	120.0	80.4	239.2	573.9	459.0
2002	92.7	125.0	84.5	351.4	642.3	541.4
Total	**848.0**	**1331.3**	**1151.4**	**3330.7**	**8200.4**	**5651.0**

Sources: Figures for IMF adapted from IMF, "Jordan: Transactions with the Fund from January 01, 1984 to December 31, 2003," *IMF website*, www.imf.org/np/tre/tad/extrans1. cfm?memberKey1=530&ndDate=2000%2D10%2D31%2000%3A00%3A00, using exchange rates given in "International Financial Statistics" *IMF website*, www.ifs.apdi.net. Figures for World Bank from World Bank, (various), *The World Bank Annual Report*, (Washington: The World Bank). Figures for debt rescheduling for 1994 to 2002 from CBJ, (various), *Monthly Statistical Bulletin*, (Amman: CBJ). Figures for Total Aid and Grants from OECD, *OECD website*, www.oecd.org/scripts/ede/DoQuery.asp.

Table 6.1 indicates the level of disbursements by the donor community in the period 1989 to 2002. In terms of value to the Jordanian economy, total aid was just under 2.5 times as valuable as the assistance from the IMF, the World Bank and debt relief.

In addition, 68.9% of the total of aid was in the form of grants, thereby increasing the value to the economy. The grants themselves, from 1994, included the debt relief granted by Jordan's external creditors.

Importantly, as discussed previously, the IMF and World Bank loans can not be considered as pure aid, as the interest charged is at market rates.[361] Nevertheless, the role of the BWIs is integral within the donor community. Although the World Bank has provided more loans than the IMF, the latter organisation has taken the lead in the SAP process: not until the IMF loan conditions/agreements have been met does the World Bank agree to lend further sums. In addition the BWIs set the tone for the conditions of the involvement of other members of the donor community. Despite the supposedly non-political nature of the IMF and the World Bank, the gap in funding from 1990 to 1992 coincided with Jordan's status as *persona non grata* on the international stage, following the Iraqi invasion of Kuwait.

BRETTON WOODS INSTITUTIONS

IMF INVOLVEMENT

Table 6.2   **Agreements with the IMF, 1989-2002 (SDRm)**

SAP	Facility	Date of Arrangement	Date of Expiry	Amount Agreed	Amount Drawn
I	Standby Ordinary	14/07/89	13/01/91	60.00	26.80
II	Standby Ordinary	26/02/92	25/02/94	44.40	44.40
	Extended Fund Ordinary	25/05/94[362]	09/02/96	189.30	130.32
	Extended Fund Ordinary	09/02/96[363]	08/02/99	238.04	202.52
III	Extended Fund Ordinary	15/04/99	14/04/02	127.88	127.88
	Compensatory and Contingency Financing	15/04/99	14/04/02	34.10	34.10
IV	Standby Ordinary	03/07/02	02/07/04	85.28	10.66
Total				**789.00**	**576.68**

Sources: Adapted by author. IMF, "Jordan: History of Lending Arrangements as of December 31, 2003", *IMF website*, www.imf.org/np/tre/tad/extarr2.cfm?memberKey1=530& date1key=2000%2D12%2D31%2000%3A00%3A00 and IMF, "IMF approves Augmentation of EFF Credit to Jordan", Press Release no. 99/13, 16/04/99, *IMF website*, www.imf.org/ external/np/sec/pr/1997/PR9708.HTM.

On the 9th March 1989 the government officially requested assistance from the IMF and a 5-year US$125m stand-by facility was approved on the 14th July 1989 to become the first of four SAPs. A loan of up to US$150m over the following eighteen to twenty-four months was subsequently agreed with the World Bank. SAP I was overtaken by the events of the Second Gulf War. Thereafter a seven-year agreement, SAP II, was approved in February 1992 that eventually comprised of three facilities. The economic downturn from the mid-1990s necessitated the approval of SAP III, in April 1999, while a fourth (and it is hoped final) agreement was implemented in June 2002 (table 6.2). From table 6.3 the fluctuating nature of the IMF disbursements is apparent. Immediate assistance of SDR66m (US$84.9m) was forthcoming in 1989, but significant further levels of assistance were not forthcoming until the mid-1990s, peaking at SDR96.6m (US$133.0m) in 1997, as the economic downturn took hold. High disbursements were recorded in both 1999 and 2002.

Table 6.3   **Transactions with IMF, 1989-2003 (SDR)**

Year	Disbursements	Repayments	Charges Paid	Principal O/S
1989	66,235,000	28,700,000	3,428,589	73,410,000
1990	0	7,175,000	6,429,856	66,235,000
1991	0	0	5,688,025	66,235,000
1992	22,200,000	7,241,875	5,481,049	81,193,125
1993	11,100,000	33,117,500	4,562,212	59,175,625
1994	65,590,000	25,875,625	3,259,148	98,890,000
1995	75,830,000	5,550,000	6,608,282	169,170,000
1996	82,200,000	15,262,500	8,431,857	236,107,500
1997	96,660,000	16,187,500	12,033,711	316,580,000
1998	23,660,000	6,831,667	15,101,537	333,408,333
1999	55,420,000	25,965,834	14,000,900	362,862,499
2000	15,220,000	23,803,333	18,318,904	354,279,166
2001	30,450,000	40,233,334	16,066,609	344,495,832
2002	71,550,000	61,040,835	10,438,741	355,004,997
2003	0	71,440,001	6,135,781	283,564,996
Total	**626,115,000**	**368,425,004**	**135,985,201**	**283,564,996**

Sources: Adapted by author. IMF, "Jordan: Transactions with the Fund from January 01, 1984 to December 31, 2003", *IMF website*, www.imf.org/external/np/tre/tad/extrans1.cfm?memberKey1=530&endDate=2003%2D12%2D31%2003%3A00%3A00 and IMF, "Jordan: IMF Credit Outstanding as of December 31, 2003", *IMF website*, www.imf.org/external/np/tre/tad/exportal.cfm?memberKey1=530&date1key=2003%2D12%2D31%2003%3A00%3A00&category=EXC

Although the Jordanian economy has been extremely susceptible to factors outside the control of the state, the IMF argued, "economic performance was ... handicapped by policy-induced structural weaknesses in various sectors."[364] The weaknesses identified included an inefficient tax system, high military expenditure, extensive subsidy programmes, external debt-servicing and impediments to trade, which adversely affected both exports and the industrial sector. Furthermore, government involvement resulted in inefficiencies in the agriculture and energy sectors, while the financial sector was considered to be insufficiently developed for a modern market economy.[365] Based on the perception of these structural weaknesses, SAP I was designed to:

> focus on effecting a reduction in the state budget through reducing and controlling government expenditure, increasing domestic revenues, improving their collection and rescheduling the repayment of foreign

loans. These elements also centre on enriching the investment climate to increase savings, investment and exports; to rationalise consumption; to control exports; to control inflation rates; and to enhance the pioneering role being played by the private sector in the realms of investment, production and exportation.[366]

To enable the programme to be successful, six targets were set: reduction of the budget deficit (excluding external grants) from 24% of GDP in 1988 to 10% in 1990, or 6% if external grants were included; reform of the tax system, with steps to introduce a VAT system by 1991; a tight credit policy to be maintained; a more prudent debt management and borrowing policy to be adopted; inflation to be cut from the official estimate of 14% in 1989 to 7% by 1993; and the current account deficit of 6% GDP in 1988 to be balanced by 1993.[367] These targets were supposed to allow the following three macro-economic objectives to be achieved:

1) to maintain the stability of the exchange rate of the dinar with its current value, which was viewed as realistic and suitable by the IMF delegation; 2) to realise real growth rates in the GNP in order to make the growth rate reach 4% at the end of the five year programme; and 3) to rely on self-potentials in the realm of the state budget and the balance of payments.[368]

Before the loan could be disbursed, the state was required to raise the prices of certain subsidised goods with the aim of boosting government revenue by JD39m.[369] Despite significant pressure from the IMF,[370] the government was able to retain subsidies on a number of basic foodstuffs,[371] a politically important success, which allowed the state, rather than the IMF, to be seen by the domestic constituency as dictating economic policy.

These increases were the first major attempt to address the rentier aspects of the economy. The result was an outbreak of rioting, which started in Ma'an on the 18th April involving around 2000 people.[372] Ma'an, which was a major centre for the trucking industry, was already under severe economic pressure because of the downturn in the Iraqi transit trade. The fuel price increases were seen as the last straw for a community that normally was perceived to be a solid supporter of the Hashemite regime. The rioting spread to other towns and villages in the evening, and over the following days spread northwards. By the time full control had been re-established, at least 11 people were dead and scores injured. The situation stabilised with the formation of a new government under PM Sharif Zeid bin Shakir, the King's cousin, although the final curfew in Ma'an was not lifted until early May. The threat of instability undoubtedly affected future attempts by the state and the IMF to address issues, such as subsidies and employment that were potentially socially divisive.

Even before SAP I was finally approved in July, by the middle of May the IMF was already praising Jordan's performance as "courageous and comprehensive,"[373] though the support was probably for political purposes to offset further domestic instability. However, within the year Middle East Economic Digest reported that the annual review was cut short because the IMF was unhappy with: the budget for 1990, which was believed to underestimate government expenditure;[374] the continuation of food subsidies; and the armaments fund, which was excluded from the budget.[375]

The failure to achieve a satisfactory review would have had a knock-on effect on undisbursed funds by the IMF and the World Bank, which had only released US$30m of the US$150m agreement, while Japan was reported to be re-considering its position for a new loan of US$150m.[376] In addition, further debt rescheduling with the Paris[377] and London[378] Clubs, as well as other creditors, would be put in jeopardy. The position was resolved at a further meeting held between the 31st March and the 4th April. Nevertheless, the IMF expressed concern about both the implementation and effectiveness of the SAP. The result was that the final tranche of US$33m was to be further split into three tranches of US$11m, allowing the IMF to increase the pressure for policy change on the government. The aspects of concern raised were the lack of control on the budget, including high military spending and subsidies, and a lack of commitment to introducing a VAT system and to restructuring customs tariffs. Despite these criticisms, the IMF, in a later report, considered that the economic and financial performance had been "encouraging"[379] during the year the SAP had been in progress.

> All policy actions contemplated in the program were implemented which,
> in combination with debt relief and bilateral grants by donors, enabled
> Jordan to meet all the quantitative performance criteria in 1989.[380]

Further moves towards implementation of the SAP were abruptly halted when Iraqi forces invaded Kuwait on the 2nd August 1990. The Iraqi invasion resulted "in a sharp rise in unemployment, disruption of trade, loss of remittances and stoppage of aid flows from regional countries."[381] To this list must be added the loss of US aid, although the EU and Japan were quick to fill the gap. The completion of the restructuring programme was initially postponed from 1993 to 1995, while the disbursements due in September and December were cancelled. In addition, a disbursement of US$75m from the World Bank was also cancelled and the rescheduling talks with the Paris and London Clubs were put on hold.[382] However, in December the London Club did agree to roll over outstanding principal for another three months.[383] Shortly after the start of the Gulf War, Jordan stopped repayment of all bilateral foreign debts, except to Arab countries.[384]

The IMF did not visit Jordan to discuss the new economic situation until May 1991, by which time both sides recognised that the targets under SAP I were impossible to achieve. At the time, the team agreed that, as the situation following the Gulf War had not yet been clarified, any further agreement would be postponed until later in the year.[385] In October, a 7-year growth-oriented economic adjustment programme was agreed in principle. However, the government's reluctance to raise fuel prices by as much as 30% delayed final approval by the IMF board until the 26th February 1992.[386] The broad objectives of the 1992 to 1994 phase were to:

> 1) Achieve a significant reduction in the macroeconomic imbalances; 2)
> Continue the process of structural reform; and 3) Achieve balance of
> payments viability by 1998 while attaining satisfactory growth
> performance in the context of stable domestic prices with an increased
> role for the private sector in the economy.[387]

The key policy elements designed to achieve these objectives were to:

1) reduce the fiscal deficit substantially, through revenue enhancements and containment of current expenditures; 2) contain credit expansion consistent with the external and inflation objectives and with achieving interest rates that were positive in real terms; 3) continue a flexible exchange rate management, with a view to ensuring competitiveness of exports; 4) carry forward the process of structural reforms initiated in 1989, particularly the second phase of tariff reform and the reform of the indirect tax system through the introduction of a general sales tax (GST); and 5) prepare a plan of action for reform of the agriculture and water and energy sectors for implementation over 1992-94.[388]

The key macroeconomic targets of the SAP, according the *Jordan Economic Monitor*, are presented in table 6.4.[389] Commentators, such as the EIU, argue that the IMF recognised the difficult social and political situation faced by the state in Jordan caused by the increase in population of 300,000 refugees, the need to maintain food subsidies for social reasons and finally the political sensitivity of the renewed peace process.[390] Consequently, the terms and conditions associated with SAP II were less onerous than those associated with the previous SAP.

Table 6.4   Targets of the 1991-1998 IMF Agreement

Measure	1991	1998
Budget Deficit (before grants) as % of GDP	18.0%	5.0%
Public expenditure as % of GDP	44.4%	5.0%
Domestic revenue as % of GDP	26.5%	30.0%
Real Economic Growth	1.0%	Over 4.0%
Consumption as % of GDP	100.9%	79.5%
Inflation	10.0%	4.5%
Foreign and Domestic Borrowing as % of GDP*	10.6%	3.5%
Current Account Deficit as % of GDP	24.0%	0.0%
Foreign Currency Reserves, Months of Imports	2 months	3 months

Source: Adapted by author. Quoted in EIU, (1992a), *Jordan: Country Report*, no. 1, (London: EIU), p.15. Figure as quoted but should be considerably higher.

At the first consultation, in May 1992, discussion centred round a reduction in military expenditure, an increase in the consumption tax and the implementation of a sales tax as a first step towards VAT.[391] The implementation of the sales tax was to become a long-running saga. The IMF report, issued in mid-June 1992, acknowledged that Jordan had broadly met most targets and went as far as to commend the authorities for pursuing policies in favour of economic growth. However, Jordan was criticised for its preparations for structural reform, especially concerning the implementation of the sales tax. In response, the government promised in the Letter of Intent of June 1992 to implement sales tax by the following January.[392] When the IMF extended the agreement by a further year, in July 1993, the sales tax remained unimplemented, due in part to significant pressure from the private sector, which saw the sales tax as both an unnecessary degree of bureaucracy and a threat to profits.

A three-year SDR127.8m (US$181m) Extended Fund Facility (EFF) was approved on the 25th May 1994, with the government reiterating its commitment to restructuring, including ensuring that the Jordan Electricity Authority (JEA) became self-financing by 1995, and agreeing to implement the sales tax on the 1st July 1994.[393] The EFF was subsequently augmented twice: on the first occasion by SDR25m (US$37m) on the 14th September 1994 and then by SDR36.5m (US$54m) on the 13th February 1995.[394] These additional loans can be taken as a measure of the approval of the IMF for Jordan's commitment to the policy reform programme and success in achieving the macro-economic targets.

At this stage, the IMF was holding up Jordan as an example for other third world countries to follow. Nonetheless, the IMF remained concerned that restructuring in the water and power sectors, in terms of tariffs, administrative reform and greater privatisation, was lagging.[395] Even so, in June 1995, Paul Chabrier, Director of IMF's Middle East Department, said the decision-makers in Jordan:

> probably have greater vision of where they want to go and how to go about it. They are establishing the indispensable basis to move forward with their structural reforms and I think it is where the focus has to be.[396]

A report made public in September 1995 again praised the state of the economy and the economic adjustment programme, although the IMF continued to express concern over the privatisation policy (including a bloated public sector), the level of charges for water and electricity, subsidies and basic rate of sales tax.

The Staff Country Report of October 1995 acknowledged that progress of the macroeconomic performance during 1992 to 1994 had been "remarkable,"[397] but also cautioned that the "external position still remains weak and vulnerable."[398] Real growth, inflation, fiscal adjustment, and balance of payments adjustment all exceeded the targets, but official reserves remained weak at about five weeks of imports by the end of 1994. In addition, "significant progress was made in normalizing payments relating with external creditors."[399] The 1995 report also indicates forthcoming structural reforms. In the fiscal area, the report identifies the need for "further decisive efforts to enhance revenue elasticity and efficiency of the tax system and reduce dependence on non-tax revenues."[400] On the expenditure side the necessity to contain civilian and military wages, and food subsidies are highlighted.[401] The key policy considerations, at this stage, were: reform of the GST system, by increasing the rate and the base; tariff reform, including the simplification of procedures, a reduction in the number of bands, a reduction of non-tariff barriers, and a reduction in the maximum rate by increasing excise duties; income tax reform, including the elimination of tax holidays (except for less developed areas) and the rationalisation of corporation income tax rates; and reduction of food subsidies by improved targeting, or through charging the full price to all consumers, while protecting low-income households through direct cash transfers.[402]

In February 1996 both sides agreed to extend the programme to 1998 with the provision of an SDR200.8m (US$295m) EFF. The medium-term programme aimed to:

> 1) achieve an average annual real GDP growth rate of at least 6 percent in order to sustain improved living standards and expand employment opportunities; 2) maintain low inflation rates in line with those of

industrialised countries; 3) narrow the external current account deficit to below 3 percent of GDP on average, which would lower the debt and debt service burden over the medium term; and 4) build up gross official reserves to the equivalent of about three months of imports.[403]

To achieve the objectives, the government was committed to fiscal restraint, a tight monetary policy and flexible interest rates geared to maintaining the relative attractiveness of dinar-denominated deposits. It was expected to accelerate the structural reforms in tax, budgetary expenditure, the regulatory framework, the financial system and the trade system.[404] Significantly, the IMF wanted a more determined effort to:

> promote the role of the private sector in the economy through an overhaul of the regulatory framework, a comprehensive reform of public sector enterprises, an intensified action plan for privatization, and, for the first time, an undertaking for the divestment of government holdings in the productive sectors.[405]

Throughout 1996 and 1997 the IMF issued a series of public statements praising the Jordanian efforts at implementing economic reform. Following the February agreement, Dr. Mohammed al-Erian, Acting Director of the IMF's Middle East Department, commented "[t]he programme further deepens the authorities structural reform efforts, most importantly in the areas of government finances, the regulatory framework and the trade system."[406] In May, Michel Camdessus, the Managing Director of the IMF stated that its efforts made Jordan one of three countries whose progress was "particularly noteworthy," highlighting the strong, broad-based growth and the substantial reduction in unemployment.[407] However, critics in Jordan were concerned about the assumptions of the government and the IMF, especially concerning inflation and unemployment. The official figures for the former were 3-4% but were unofficially estimated to be at least in double figures, while the latter was estimated to be considerably higher than the official 15% level.

The praise continued in a press release issued following a Consultative Group Meeting in July 1996. The IMF representative, Paul Chabrier, outlined Jordan's impressive record of stabilisation and adjustment and indicated that the reform programme "deserves the continued support of the international community."[408] However, during the meeting he noted that:

> despite strong economic stabilization and reform achievements, generous debt reschedulings, two previous CG [consultative group] meetings and major external assistance (particularly from Japan), Jordan's balance of payments position was still vulnerable to factors outside its control.[409]

The factors referred to included the dinar circulating in the West Bank and Gaza, the peace process and the situation in Iraq.

Following a meeting in August, which resulted in the release of the second tranche of US$60m of the EFF facility, Dr al-Erian stated:

> Jordan continues to make impressive progress under its structural adjustment and reform program. Reflecting the implementation of appropriate macroeconomic and structural reform policies, the Jordanian

economy has registered a high rate of economic growth, low inflation, and increasing foreign exchange reserves.[410]

In February 1997, the IMF announced an augmentation to the EFF of a further SDR37.24m ($51.8m),[411] commenting that:

> on the basis of steadfast implementation of adjustment and structural reforms by the authorities and the strength of Jordan's economic program for 1997, the IMF's Executive Board … decided to approve Jordan's request for an augmentation of the EFF credit.[412]

However, the IMF's 1997 Annual Report, which was generally complementary, considered that progress in privatisation was slow, although it acknowledges that the institutions for implementing the policy had been established. In addition, the directors commented on the need for further budgetary reform, an intensification of structural reforms, and the reform of the public pension system and the civil service.[413]

In early 1998, the Planning Ministry was confidently predicting that when the IMF agreement ended in February the following year, Jordan would not need to renew the facility. However, they confirmed Jordan's commitment to the continuance of economic reform through a one-year programme, which contained the principal objectives of privatising government companies: creating the proper atmosphere for attracting investment, and addressing the structural imbalance caused by poverty and unemployment.[414] The commitment to economic liberalisation could be interpreted as a method to retain the support of the donor community, thus maintaining access to and control of future rents. However, by September, the government publicly acknowledged the reality of the situation with the announcement that talks were well advanced to extend the IMF reform programme by a further year.[415] These negotiations took place against a background of economic slowdown, with the World Bank forecasting a shrinkage in the economy of 1% in 1998, following on growth of only 0.7% in 1997. Real wages were estimated to have fallen 20% since the implementation of the first agreement with the IMF in 1989. Reserves had declined from US$1700m at end of 1997 to US$1400m by the end of August the following year.[416]

In April 1999 the IMF approved SAP III, which was valued at SDR161.98m (US$220m), and was:

> in support of the nation's economic adjustment and structural reform program for the period 1999-2001, and to help offset the impact of a temporary shortfall in exports of goods and services.[417]

The funds were divided between a three-year EFF of SDR127.88m and a Compensatory and Contingency Financing Facility (CCFF) of SDR34.1m. Despite its earlier lavish public praise, the IMF acknowledged that between 1996 and 1998, economic performance "fell short of goals targeted under Jordan's previous EFF-supported program."[418] The press release highlights success in maintaining low inflation and building up foreign reserves, but stressed the failure to achieve real GDP growth and the widening of the fiscal deficit to about 10% of GDP. On the structural reform front important progress was considered to have been achieved, especially during 1997, in financial market development, trade liberalisation and tax reform, but progress was thought to have slackened towards the end of the programme.[419]

The new facility was designed to stabilise the economy and set the stage for sustained recovery over the next two years, with a gradual recovery in the growth rate of real GDP to 3-4%, the maintenance of low inflation and a substantial strengthening in official foreign exchange reserves.[420]   The macroeconomic objectives were to be achieved through fiscal consolidation, prudent monetary policy aimed at a stable dinar and bolstering foreign reserves, and wide-ranging structural reforms. The latter reform agenda emphasises "the areas of taxes, social security, financial sector, trade, and public enterprise reform and privatization."[421]   In the field of privatisation, the government was expected to take:

> significant steps ... to improve the management of the Water Authority of Jordan, restructure and privatize the Royal Jordanian airline and the National Electric Power Company, and develop a privatization plan for the Jordan Telecommunications Corporation.[422]

The government was also expected to continue its efforts to protect the vulnerable social groups and to promote employment regeneration. The macroeconomic targets agreed are highlighted in table 6.5.

Table 6.5   **Macroeconomic Targets under 1999-2001 EFF**

Target	1999	2000	2001
Real GDP at market prices % change	2.0	2.5	3.5
Consumer Price Index (annual average) % change	1.9	2.8	2.4
Fiscal Deficit, excluding grants % of GDP	7.9	5.5	4.0
Fiscal Deficit, including grants % of GDP	4.2	2.9	1.4
Government Debt as a % of GDP	132.6	128.6	124.4
Current Account Deficit incl. grants % of GDP	0.7	1.7	1.8
Current Account Deficit excl. grants % of GDP	5.5	5.4	5.3
Merchandise Exports % change	4.2	5.2	5.9
Merchandise Imports % change	4.0	5.1	6.2

Source: Adapted by author. IMF, "IMF Approves EFF and CCFF Credits for Jordan", Press Release no. 99/13, 16/04/99, *IMF website*, www.imf.org/external/np/sec/pr/1999/pr 9913.htm.

The IMF approved a withdrawal of SDR10.66m (US$15M) in October 1999. In the accompanying news brief the directors "welcomed the improvement in economic conditions and confidence ... [which] reflected the authorities' renewed commitment to both macroeconomic stabilization and structural reforms."[423] However, the government was "encouraged" to exercise expenditure restraint and reform the tax system, specifically introducing VAT by early 2000, modifying income tax, and reducing external tariffs.[424] The IMF also "urged the authorities to move forward vigorously with structural reform, in particular with the restructuring and privatization of public enterprises."[425] Finally, "concern" was expressed about the "misreporting of fiscal and national accounts data in 1996-98."[426] However, the directors welcomed the improvements in the compilation of statistics and monitoring of fiscal accounts.[427]

The second review of the EFF in mid-2000 ended with the release of a further SDR15.22m (US$20m). Following the review, Stanley Fischer, First Deputy Managing Director and Acting Chairman, acknowledged the improvement in Jordan's economic conditions since the beginning of 1999, which he attributed to "restrained macroeconomic policies and the implementation of a number of important structural measures, especially in the areas of privatization and trade reform."[428] The areas of disappointment raised by the IMF included the level of economic growth, which was needed to raise per capita incomes and improve welfare. To achieve the growth required, the emphasis was to remain on reducing the fiscal deficit and on continued structural reform.

In its July 2000 Memorandum on Economic Financial Policies (previously Letter of Intent) the government agreed to a number of conditions including: sales tax to be converted into a fully-fledged VAT by 2001, and the number of exemptions to be reduced; income tax to be rationalised, tax rates simplified, and the tax base broadened; fuel prices to be revised in the second half of 2000, following a technical study by the IMF; public pension system to be revised with the ultimate goal of bringing public sector employees within the framework of the SSC; and public sector services, especially health and education, to be improved.[429]

The conversion of the sales tax to VAT was implemented on 1 January 2001, while a start was made on reforming the tax system, reforming the pension system and restructuring public sector services and adjusting fuel prices towards a market system. In the August 2001 Memorandum on Economic Financial Policies the government continued to promise to address the issues highlighted in the 2000 memorandum. In addition to submitting to a number of short-term performance criteria including increasing foreign exchange reserves, reducing the budget deficit, and reducing foreign indebtedness through debt swaps. Following the third review associated with the Memorandum a disbursement of SDR30.45m (US$39m) was released. The news brief acknowledged that "Jordan's economic performance has` been commendable in most respects"[430] but stressed the need to address the question of fiscal deficit, through reform of the pension system, broadening the tax base, adjusting petroleum prices.

The 3-year SAP III was due to conclude in April 2002, by which time the unstable regional situation (the outbreak of the *intifada* in the Israel and the Occupied Territories in September 2000 and the US-led war on terror following the events of 11 September 2001) had impacted significantly on the Jordanian economy. The instability was used as an excuse by the government for not achieving the short term targets agreed in August 2001. Nevertheless following the fourth and fifth reviews, in April 2002, the IMF sanctioned the release for remaining SDR60.89m (US$77m) under SAP III. At the time the IMF praised Jordan for its move to extend the GST, to increase the petroleum prices and reduce other subsidies. Nevertheless, the need to address pension reform, to broaden the tax base and to increase petroleum product prices was again raised.[431]

The problems caused by the regional instability, which negatively impacted on the Jordanian economy, resulted in a further agreement being concluded with the IMF. On 3 July 2002 a two-year stand-by facility for SDR85.28m (US$113m) was announced, with DSR10.66m (US$14m) being available for immediate drawdown. Among the issues to be address in the new programme were reducing pension liabilities in net present value terms by 30% over the next 50 years; broadening and improving the tax system; and accelerating the privatisation process.[432]

WORLD BANK INVOLVEMENT

Prior to the economic crisis, the World Bank had been providing around US$100m annually for infrastructure improvement throughout the 1980s.[433] From 1989, the emphasis switched to SALs in support of the IMF SAP. At the time, the World Bank perceived its role to be "to restore growth and reduce the economic imbalances" in a complementary operation to the macro-economic stabilisation programme supported by the IMF agreement.[434] The main objective of the adjustment programme was to "create an enabling environment for long-run sustainable growth by improving efficiency and competitiveness of the economy"[435] through the promotion of the private sector at the expense of the public sector.

The World Bank sought to achieve this objective through a number of methods. The most obvious method was through conditional lending, often as co-financiers with other members of the donor community. In order to encourage the necessary growth of the economy, projects and programmes supported by the loans sought to either develop or restructure different sectors considered important but which were deemed to be underdeveloped or incorrectly structured. Invariably, the restructuring involved attempting to reduce the role of the state, while simultaneously promoting the role of the private sector. Other involvement was achieved by acting as: technical advisor on sectoral restructuring and privatisation, including the preparation of a report on the private sector in Jordan; co-ordinator with other donors; sponsor of meetings to attract further pledges of support; administrator of grants donated by other donors; guarantor for lending on the bond market; and propagator of new development practices, such as micro-finance or micro-enterprise schemes.

The role of technical advisor was apparent in various sectors, such as health, energy, agriculture, water, the private sector, and trade. In each case the emphasis was on increasing the role of the private sector in the long term. For example, a government plan to turn Aqaba region into a free trade area received considerable technical assistance from the World Bank.[436] Furthermore, in 1994, the World Bank prepared a project to raise the efficiency of the construction sector by: privatising the production activities of the Housing and Urban Development Corporation; activating the role of the private sector by providing incentives to build houses for low-income groups; encouraging competition in the medium- to long-term financing market through the creation of a secondary mortgage market mechanism; rationalising support for the housing sector to create efficiency; and investing in infrastructure in areas with inferior services.[437]

Also, during FY1995 the World Bank prepared an assessment of the private sector,[438] following a World Bank mission to Jordan in November and December 1994. The mission was at the behest of the state.[439] The report, which was issued in August 1995, after discussions with the government and the private sector, concluded that its focus should be on:

the changing role of the government as a regulator and owner/operator of enterprises; the regulatory constraints faced by the private sector and how to relax them to encourage private investment and business expansion; and The improvements needed in the financial sector to support these activities.[440]

The report argues that "[a]lthough the private sector in Jordan is freer than in several other Middle-Eastern countries, it is still unduly constrained by the extensive presence of the public sector in the economy and by a restrictive regulatory framework."[441] Therefore, the World Bank recommended that the public sector should "focus on providing those public goods and services that can only be provided on a collective basis and leave competitive activities to the private sector which can perform them much more efficiently."[442] The change was to be achieved through:

the divestiture/privatisation of public enterprises over time; the provision of adequate public goods and services (such as public administration and legal machinery); and regulatory reform."[443]

The government's role to assist private sector development required to ensure: macroeconomic stability and policy credibility; competitive markets, in goods, services, financial and factor markets; adequate infrastructure, support services and ancillary activities, all of which should have private sector participation; and the institutional setting allows firms to respond to competitive pressures. In the early years of the SAPs the emphasis had been on macroeconomic reform. The development of the private sector did not receive strong backing until the mid-1990s.

The Bank was also heavily involved with the issue of privatisation. For example, in August 1996 it consulted with JIC and JCFC on the best methods for divesting the former's 49.5% stake in the latter.[444] Furthermore, the World Bank was a major partner in the preparation of other entities for privatisation, such as RJ.

The World Bank also undertook the role of co-ordinating between the many donor groups involved in Jordan. However, the success of this role seems to have been extremely limited, with many interviewees questioning whether overall co-ordination had been achieved,[445] although a number argue that limited sectoral co-ordination had occurred.[446] The role also involved arranging donors' meetings in an attempt to increase the volume of funding available. During the Gulf Crisis, the World Bank was instrumental in establishing a fund to assist with the costs associated with the refugees and returnees. Subsequently it signed an agreement for a loan of US$10m, while countries, including Switzerland, Sweden, Canada and Luxembourg, also contributed.[447] In addition, the Bank also organised a financing tour of the donor community in April 1992. Although the response was generally positive, Jordan's medium-term financing requirements were not met.[448] A further example occurred when 24 states and organisations attended a World Bank-organised meeting, from the 28th and 29th January 1993, which was successful in raising pledges to cover the balance of payments needs for 1993 and 1994 (around US$380m).[449] However, one year later, because of the political difficulties of implementing the restructuring programmes, only US$175m had been used.[450] A further meeting was arranged on the 17th May 1994, during which US$200m was pledged to restructure the water, agriculture, health and electricity sectors.[451] In Paris on the 10th July 1996, at the Third Consultative Group meeting,[452] donor nations pledged almost US$1bn, of which approximately US$600m was promised for 1996, with the remainder over the following two years. The pledged funds were to be used to support trade liberalisation, private sector development, privatisation, and physical infrastructure development.[453]

In addition, the World Bank also administered grants donated by other countries. For example, in 1993 Switzerland granted US$5m, part of which the Bank used to promote local products on the international market through Jordan Export Development and Commercial Centers Corporation.[454] Another element of the World Bank's role was to guarantee facilities, such as the US$50m Eurobond issued in December 1994, which was raised to fund expansion of the TCC.[455] According to the World Bank, the guarantee was the first granted to a Middle East and North African government bond issue on the international market.[456]

Finally, two subsidiaries of the World Bank, the IDA (the soft loan component) and the IFC (loans specifically to boost the private sector) were also present in Jordan. The IDA had made fifteen loans prior to the crisis but did not assist in the period of the study, while the IFC had made ten investments in Jordan with gross commitment of US$97m, prior to 1989. Between 1989 and 1995 no further involvement occurred, but between 1995 and 2000 the IFC assisted in fourteen projects. The IFC had also issued advice on a number of issues, including opening the economy to foreign investment.[457]

For analytical purposes, the lending by the World Bank can be divided into three types: 1) social: concerned with alleviating the effects of the adjustment programme on the most vulnerable groups in society; 2) balance of payments: associated directly with the SALs of the IMF and is usually for balance of payment support; restructuring: and 3) restructuring or developing particular sectors of the economy. In reality, the restructuring loans often contained an element of social provision. Each of the three categories of lending involved conditions being set by the World Bank and agreed to by the Jordanian government. In addition, the loans were usually part of a package involving grants and/or soft loans from other donor sources, not only states but also bilateral institutions, such as the Arab Fund for Economic and Social Development, and multilateral organisations, such as the Islamic Development Bank. The following paragraphs give a brief description of the conditionality attached to a number of the loans.

Table 6.6   World Bank Social Loans, 1989-2002 (US$m)

Date	Loan Title	Amount	Co-Financiers
21/03/91	Emergency Recovery Refugees	10.0	Yes
21/08/97	Community Infrastructure Project	30.0	Yes

Source: Adapted by author.   World Bank, (various), *The World Bank Annual Report*, (Washington: The World Bank).

The social welfare component of World Bank lending was late in arriving, with no lending to Jordan until 1997[458] (despite the Bank's acceptance, from the late 1980s, of the problem of the adverse impact of the SAPs on the poorer elements of society)[459] (table 6.6). Indeed, social lending has only comprised 2.9% of total lending, while restructuring has accounted for 44.7% and balance of payments 52.3%. (figure 6.1).

Figure 6.1   World Bank Lending by Category, 1989-2002

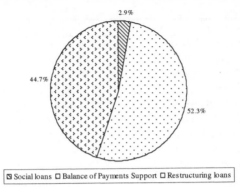

Source: Adapted by author.   World Bank, (various), *The World Bank Annual Report*, (Washington: The World Bank).

In March 1997, World Bank Vice-President for Middle East and North Africa, Kamal Darwish, acknowledged that a decline in living standards had followed the sectoral reform. Consequently, programmes to tackle unemployment and poverty would receive World Bank money. At the time, the government was in the course of implementing a JD400m ($284m) social safety net programme, called the Social Productivity Programme.[460] The Programme had the long-term objective of lifting all households above the poverty line, through training and micro-finance schemes and better targeting of public cash transfers.[461] Darwish's promise of new funding was followed in June by a report that the World Bank was to lend US$60m towards the social security package.[462] However, in September, the loan for the Community Infrastructure Project, part of the Social Productivity Programme, was approved for only US$30m. The Community Infrastructure Project loan was aimed at providing:

> basic physical and social infrastructure for up to about 1.6 million people living in the country's poorest municipal areas and villages. The project, which represents the pilot phase of the wider government Social Productivity Program, will also test the potential for supporting income-generating activities and, possibly, microenterprise development in Jordan's poorest communities.[463]

To date, this loan has been the only one specifically aimed at offsetting the social cost of the various SAPs.

As highlighted in table 6.7, six loans have been granted in support of government finance. These loans are more closely related to the short-term stabilisation policies of the IMF, than to the longer-term structural adjustment undertaken by the World Bank. The first balance of payments support loan for US$150m was approved in December 1989, after the IMF agreement earlier in the year. The loan conditions were designed to help deepen reforms in industry and trade and to restructure public expenditures. The measures, which Jordan was expected to undertake in return for the facility, were divided into three policy areas: stabilisation; growth of industry and diversification of exports; and impact of adjustment on the economically disadvantaged.

Table 6.7: World Bank Loans for Government Finance Support, 1989-2002

Date	Loan Title	Details	US$m
14/12/89	Industry and Trade Policy Adjustment Loan	Repayment over 17 years, including 5 years' grace	150.0
24/10/95	First Economic Reform and Development Loan (ERDL I)	Repayment over 20 years, including 5 years' grace	80.0
11/12/96	Second Economic Reform and Development Loan (ERDL II)	Repayment over 17 years, including 4 years' grace	120.0
01/06/99	Third Economic Reform and Development Loan (ERDL III)	Repayment over 17 years, including 4 years' grace	120.0
21/06/01	Public Sector Reform Adjustment Loan (PSRL I)	Repayment over 17 years, including 5 years' grace	120.0
02/07/02	Public Sector Reform Adjustment Loan (PSRL II)	Repayment over 17 years, including 5 years' grace	120.0

Source: Adapted by author. World Bank, (various), *The World Bank Annual Report*, (Washington: The World Bank).

Under stabilisation, the state was required to achieve a unified exchange rate by March 1990; to take further action to reduce the budget deficit by enhancing revenues and restraining expenditures; and to finalise a public expenditure programme based on discussions with the Bank before the release of the second tranche. The growth of industry and diversification of exports required the government to: restructure import tariff rates by reducing the maximum to 60% and increasing the minimum to 5%; combine the multiple rates of import taxes into a single rate; replace the system of investment incentives with a simplified version in order to increase exports; increase the effectiveness of the CBJ's export rediscounting facility; prepare a study on export development and investment promotion; complete proposals for building institutional capacity; and prepare specifications to improve industrial standards.[464] Prior to the release of the second tranche "the Bank would carry out an overall assessment of the progress on macroeconomic policies, as well as other actions supported by the loan."[465] In the event, the release of the second tranche of the loan was interrupted, not by the failure to meet the conditions but by the Gulf Crisis of 1990 to 1991, thus highlighting the political element in donor support.

The Bank's strategy, as outlined in the agreement, was

tailored to help the Government respond to the fall in oil prices and the resulting slowdown in the regional economies by: 1) accelerating growth in the medium term, while maintaining a viable budgetary and balance of payments position; 2) minimising the emerging unemployment problem; and 3) dealing with two critical long-term constraints to future growth, a rapidly growing population and the increasing scarcity of water.[466]

As the temporary boom following the Gulf War petered out, the World Bank lent a further US$80m, in October 1995, to be repaid over 20 years, including five years' grace. In keeping with the "soft glove"[467] approach, these terms were less onerous than those of the 1989 SAL. The loan was to be matched by Japan, and supported by a further US$20m from Italy. The full amount of the Economic and Reform Development Loan (ERDL I) was to be used to provide for balance of payments support and to boost reserves. The conditions sought by the World Bank included new legislation to reduce customs duties, and an increase in sales tax to 10%. Other areas in which progress was to be made before further facilities could be sought included measures on intellectual property rights, reform of the stock exchange, and the implementation of a comprehensive privatisation process.[468]

A further balance of payments support loan was agreed, in late 1996, for US$120m, repayable over seventeen years, including four years' grace. The repayment terms were tougher than those of ERDL I. ERDL II was designed "to promote enhanced private sector participation in the wider world economy." The loan was closely tied to the Free Trade Agreement (FTA) with the European Community, but also supported investment, savings, and the development of the banking and financial sectors.[469] The conditions attached to ERDL II were similar to the areas in which progress had been expected at the time of granting ERDL I. These conditions included reform of the Amman Financial Market; new legislation including intellectual property rights and leasing; reduction of tariffs; and streamlining of trade.[470] The loan was granted in support of the IMF's EFF with the aim to back "reforms that target[ed] increased competition and exports, a modern financial system, best-practice business laws, and privatisation."[471]

In November 1997, discussion on the ERDL III for US$75m was initiated with a projected approval date of the 18th February 1999. However, due to the economic downturn, ERDL III was finally approved for US$120m in June 1999. According to the loan terms, the "government policy actions will focus first on liberalizing the regulatory framework affecting business entry, operation (including pricing policy), and exit; as well as separating policy, regulatory, and business operation functions."[472] The key objective of ERDL III was "to support the Government's reform program which is aimed at sustaining high growth with exports playing a major role."[473] The policy changes were to include the removal of the remaining trade and investment barriers, an Association Agreement on trade relations with the EU; and accession to the WTO.[474] The loan was, in turn, supported by grants from the Bank's International Development Fund, Japan and the USA for technical assistance in the areas of privatisation, freeports, legal reform and financial sector reform.[475]

In June 2001 the first in a proposed series of three loans to enable reform of the public sector was agreed for US$120m. The second loan for a similar amount was agreed in July the following year. The loans were to be used

> to provide external financing to met anticipated financial gaps while supporting fundamental structural changes in the core public sector to strengthen institutional capacity and the quality of public services.[476]

From the outset of the IMF involvement following the economic crisis until the outbreak of the Gulf War, only one loan aimed at the long-term restructuring of the economy was signed: a loan of US$73m in June 1989 aimed at the education sector (table 6.8). Not until 1993, were further restructuring loans agreed. In that year, three loans were implemented, which aimed at restructuring the transport, health and the energy sectors. The US$80m energy loan, which was matched by an equal loan from Japan, focused on undertaking key structural reforms in the sector in order to ease the burden on state finances. These conditional reforms included the phasing-out of energy subsidies in order to attract the private sector into power generation and distribution.[477] Furthermore, the loan could not be drawn down until increases in electricity and other selected prices had been implemented.

In 1994, a loan for US$80m was agreed, co-financed by a DM30m loan from Germany. The objective was to restructure the agricultural sector, along the line suggested in a report drafted in part by the UN Food and Agriculture Organisation. The loan was supported by a smaller World Bank Agricultural Sector Technical Assistance Programme loan of US$6.6m and a DM4m technical co-operation grant from Germany, which were to be used "to mitigate the social effects of the necessary adjustment process in agriculture."[478] According to the CBJ the aims were to: promote a more efficient use of and conservation of natural resources, especially water and land, including the phasing out of the control of cropping patterns; liberalise the agricultural markets; and enable the private sector to invest, produce and trade.[479]

The water element of the agreement sought to achieve efficiency and conservation through the restructuring of Jordan's institutions associated with water, the implementation of demand management policies for water, the prioritisation of government investment in water and the abolition of subsidies.[480] The structural changes to the agricultural sector sought to improve productivity and increase exports through the reduction of food subsidies and the revamping of the institutions associated with agriculture, such as the Jordanian Co-operatives Organisation and the Agricultural Credit Corporation.[481] The Ministry of Agriculture, which was responsible for agricultural policy and development, was expected to address three key issues: to adapt the structure and staffing to a new more limited role; to implement privatisation, commercialisation and other forms of decentralisation; and to make public services more productive and better managed.[482] The public sector role in the agricultural sector was envisaged, in the long run, to be no more than one of regulator and co-ordinator.[483]

The World Bank's view of the agricultural sector in 1994 was outlined in the Technical Annex to the Agriculture Sector Technical Support Project. The World Bank argued that although agriculture was small in relation to the overall economy, the sector was relatively important in the production of tradable goods. On a narrow definition, agriculture contributed about 7% of GDP, but if upstream and downstream linkages were taken into consideration, the figure increased to 28%. Furthermore, on the broad definition, agriculture had accounted for more than half the growth of GDP in the early 1990s. The sector employed around 10% of the workforce and accounted for 15% of exports. The major constraints identified in the Technical annex were water scarcity, weak producer services and vulnerable markets. The importance of the relationship between water and agriculture was emphasised by agriculture's consumption of almost 75% of total water usage, while the pumping of groundwater exceeded renewable levels. Furthermore, the use of irrigated water was considered to have a low efficiency. Prior to the Second Gulf War, 88% of total exports of fresh fruit and vegetables were to the Gulf States, while other Arab states took 11% and Europe only 1%. The Gulf War considerably eroded the Gulf States market, leaving an oversupply of agricultural produce in Jordan.[484]

Table 6.8   World Bank Restructuring Loans, 1989-2002

Date of Approval	Loan	Sector	US$m	Co-Financiers
29/06/89	Human Resources Development Sector Investment Loan	Education	73.0	Japan, UK
20/02/90	Integrated Phosphate Project	Mineral	25.0	
11/03/93	Third Transport Project	Transport	35.0	EIB
16/03/93	Health Management Project	Health	20.0	Finland, EC, USA, France, Germany, UK
07/10/93	Energy Sector Adjustment Loan	Energy	80.0	Japan
08/12/94	Agriculture Sector Adjustment Operation	Agriculture	80.0	Germany
08/12/94	Agriculture Sector Technical Support Project	Agriculture	6.6	GTZ, KfW
30/03/95	Second Human Resources Development Investment Loan	Education	60.0	Yes
28/03/96	Export Development Project	Exports	40.0	Private Sector
25/06/96	Urban Development	Housing	20.0	N/A
31/07/97	Second Tourism Development Project	Tourism	32.0	N/A
19/05/98	Training and Employment Support Project	Education	5.0	UNDP
16/03/99	Amman Water and Sanitation Management Project	Water	55.0	EIB, Italy
25/03/99	Health Sector Reform Project	Health	35.0	No
29/02/00	Higher Education Development	Education	34.7	N/A
27/06/02	Horticulture Exports Promotion and Technology Transfer Learning and Innovation Loan	Agriculture	5.0	No

Source: Adapted by author.   World Bank, (various), *The World Bank Annual Report,* (Washington: The World Bank).

Further loans followed, including a US$60m loan for education reform in April 1995. This loan, apart from helping to restructure the education system, was designed to help share economic growth throughout the population by enhancing "the quality and further expand[ing] access to basic schooling."[485] In 1996, the World Bank signed three agreements with Jordan, including loans for US$20m to the housing sector (March),[486] US$40m for export development (March),[487] and a grant of US$2.7m for controlling pollution at Aqaba (June).[488]

The principal objective of the Export Development Loan was to support the government-conceived Export Sector Development Programme, which was designed to:

> 1) reduce transaction costs to firms through simplification of import and export procedures, including customs operations; 2) increase the level of investment flows, in particular, FDI; 3) facilitate the use of specialised consulting and other support services, to enable firms to raise their product standards and quality, and penetrate new markets; and 4) improve access of private firms to medium-to-longer term finance for productive capacity development or expansion.[489]

The overall objective was to enhance the:

> international competitiveness of Jordanian exports and increasing export revenues. The immediate objective of the project is to help private firms expand their productive capacity through a credit line for term lending.[490]

Approximately 80 firms were expected to benefit from the funding provided jointly by the World Bank, USAID, the EU and Deutsche Gesellschaft für Technische Zusammenarbeit (GTZ), with the provision of an expected one thousand jobs.[491]

The World Bank appraisal of the project points out the difficulties faced in the export sector in Jordan, namely: a narrow base of exports; the small size of domestic firms (98% of firms employed less than 20 workers); high tariff and transaction costs; institutional and regulatory rigidities; weak enterprise support systems; and limited term finance. In addition, a major factor was the use of bilateral governmental trade protocols, which curtailed the development of an understanding of what to produce for and how to sell in global markets.[492]

When signing the Housing Finance and Urban Sector Reform loan of US$20m, in 1996, the government agreed "to shift responsibility to the private sector for developing land and housing for lower income households, and to implement measures to mobilize increased longer-term, market based financing for mortgage lending."[493] In the longer-term, public sector activities would be reduced to policy, planning and research and basic upgrading works,[494] with the private sector filling the void. The reforms were based on the 1994 project to raise the efficiency of the construction sector.

In August 1997, a US$32m loan to assist with developing the tourist sector was announced, to create the conditions for sustainable and environmentally sound tourism at Petra, Wadi Rum, Jerash, and Kerak, and to provide income-generating opportunities for the local population, including the Bedouin women.[495] The May 1998 US$5m loan for Training and Employment was to fund a pilot project aimed at linking public funded training with the requirements of the business community.[496] In November 1998, a loan of US$35m was approved to support a Health Sector

Reform Project, based on the joint government/World Bank study published in April 1997. The state was expected to contribute a further US$13.9m. The project focused on three key areas:

1) containing growth in health expenditures; 2) assuring the efficient utilization of physical facilities; and 3) improving the delivery and quality of health care services.[497]

The five components supporting the first phase of reform were:

1) rationalizing Jordan's health delivery system; 2) developing and implementing health information systems; 3) improving hospital financing and management; 4) reforming the pharmaceutical sector; and 5) continuing the reform process.[498]

In March 1999, the World Bank announced the approval of a US$55m loan to improve the efficiency, management, operation and delivery of water and wastewater services for the Amman Service Area, which covered about two million people. Importantly, the project supported the involvement of a private sector operator. The cost was estimated at US$136m, with additional funding from the European Investment Bank (EIB) (US$44m), Italy (US$20m) and Jordan (US$17m).[499]

At the end of 1999, detailed discussions were held between the government, the World Bank and "other stakeholders in the country"[500] concerning the Country Assistance Strategy[501] for the period 2000-2002. The Bank's assistance in the period was forecast to focus on:

1) reviving, maintaining, and accelerating *economic growth*, emphasizing higher levels of private investment, export development, and tourism; 2) promoting *human development*, including *social protection*; 3) undertaking *public sector reforms*; and 4) improving *water resources* management and the environment.[502]

The World Bank involvement for the three years was expected to average US$100-150m pa, in addition to a total of US$200m in guarantees for private sector infrastructure investments. The lending would cover projects in higher education, agriculture exports, vocational education, tourism, social protection, water and public sector reforms.[503] The first loan of US$34.7m for a higher education development project under the Country Assistance Strategy was announced in February 2000,[504] with a US$5m agricultural sector loan granted in June 2002.

Despite the continual stress on water scarcity as a significant constraint on economic growth, the sector has only received US$55m of the total of US$606.3m lending between 1989 and 2002 (figure 6.2). The importance of education to economic growth and poverty alleviation has been addressed with this sector receiving the highest percentage of funding, followed by agriculture, energy, and health.

As with the IMF, the political nature of World Bank lending can be noticed from figure 6.3. King Hussein's position of attempting to seek an Arab solution to the Second Gulf War was interpreted by the USA as a pro-Saddam stance. The USA cut off aid to Jordan and was able to influence both the IMF and the World Bank to withdraw their support until the cessation of hostilities. The result was a slump in lending in FY1991 and FY1992, at a time when the economy most needed assistance. However, the requirement for increased loans was recognised as the economy entered a downturn in the mid- to late-1990s. Given the close relationship between the IMF and the World Bank, the pattern of lending closely followed that of the IMF. As discussed previously, new loans were only approved after receiving IMF confirmation that the conditions of the SAP were being met.

Figure 6.2   World Bank Restructuring Loans by Sector, 1989-2002

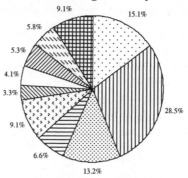

Source: Adapted by author. World Bank, (various), *The World Bank Annual Report*, (Washington: The World Bank).

Figure 6.3   World Bank Lending, 1989-2002

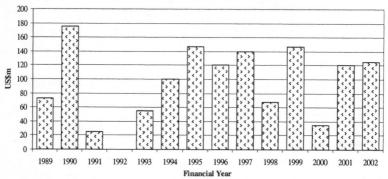

Source: Adapted by author. World Bank, (various), *The World Bank Annual Report*, (Washington: The World Bank).

World Bank Assessment of Government Policy

By August 1992, the World Bank was expressing confidence in the government policies, following a review by a team led by Caio Koch-Weser, Vice-President responsible for Near East and North African Affairs. At the time, the team planned to return to Amman in September, once the situation following the end of the Gulf War had become clearer, to revamp policies on agriculture, power and water tariffs.[505] The 1993 World Bank Annual Report stresses the need for Jordan to undertake civil service reforms and raises the possibility of requiring "special forms of debt relief."[506] A more optimistic note was sounded in the 1994 report, which highlights the broad base of the economic growth achieved in 1993, the implementation of stabilisation policies, and the occurrence of encouraging signs that private sector activity was picking up.[507]

The 1995 Annual Report emphasises the necessity to achieve rapid economic growth. This rapid growth could only be achieved by moving away from the state-centred development strategies to "a 'new paradigm' for prosperity, based on unleashing the energies of the private sector as the engine of growth."[508] The Report acknowledges that developing the private sector was a "complex task, involving a wide range of policy actions,"[509] adding that Jordan had been successful to date in implementing its reform programme.[510]

Following agreement of ERDL I, in October 1995, World Bank vice-president for Middle East and North Africa, Caio Koch-Weser stated "[w]e are very satisfied with the government's economic performance in the past two-three years," adding that the country was deserving of strong donor support.[511]

At the Third Consultative Group meeting in 1996 the World Bank representative praised the Government's accomplishments in stabilisation and adjustment, while noting that progress was still required in four key aspects of reform: trade liberalisation and export development; financial sector strengthening and deepening; regulatory reform to improve the investment climate; and privatisation. The representative also stressed the need for a sound infrastructure to encourage private investment in export production and tourism. The major infrastructural challenge was deemed to be water, followed by road and rail development. Furthermore, he pledged the Bank's continued support for improvements in education and health.[512] Following the meeting the press release states that "Jordan is one of the leaders in the region in transforming its economy."[513]

At the same meeting, the IFC praised the improved climate for private investment. The example of the reform in the telecom sector had allowed the IFC to assist in the launching of Jordan's first cellular telephone company. Future investment could be expected in the phosphate sector, quality hotels, cement production, leasing, micro-finance enterprise, an equity fund set up jointly with the Overseas Private Investment Corporation, and a credit reference agency (in association with the Arab Monetary Fund).[514]

In March 1997, World Bank Vice-President for Middle East and North Africa, Kamal Darwish, said that the bank was highly satisfied with Jordan's efforts to streamline its economy. As a result, he anticipated lending a further US$1bn over the next five years in support of economic restructuring. However, he suggested that Jordan needed to think seriously about reform in the water, power, energy and transport sectors. Furthermore, the 1997 Report argues that the reform of the education sector backed by World Bank funding was beginning to pay off.[515] According to the 1998 Annual Report: "[s]ince the late 1980s the Bank's support has increasingly featured policy-based lending for comprehensive private sector-oriented economic reform."[516]

The relationship with the World Bank soured to an extent in June 1998 when Darwish expressed concern about the state's estimates for economic growth in 1996 and 1997. The estimates had been around 6% for both years, but following the statement were immediately reduced by the state to 1% for 1996 and 2.5%-3% for

1997. The forecast for 1998 was similarly revised downwards from 6% to 3.2%.[517] Despite having been heavily involved in restructuring the economy, the World Bank quickly and publicly absolved itself from any blame about the accuracy of the figures. In a statement to the Jordan Times, the World Bank points out that it relied on the government to produce accurate figures. However, the statement did include praise for the economic reform and development agenda and acknowledges the need to address growth in order to offset the effects of poverty and unemployment.[518] In September, John Page, World Bank Chief Economist for the Middle East and North Africa region argued that although the investment rate in Jordan was favourable when compared regionally, the bulk was focused on housing projects. He stressed the need to invest for exports.[519]

Following the death of King Hussein in February 1999, World Bank President, James D. Wolfensohn, was quick to announce continued "full support to King Abdullah and to the people of Jordan."[520] The Annual Report for 2000 praises the privatisation programme as one of the most successful in the region, with thirty-three of the targeted forty companies having been privatised.[521] The laudatory nature of public statements by World Bank has continued into the new century. In July 2003, Charles Humphreys, Task Manager, commented "We are impressed by the Government's commitment and effort to create a more accountable, performance-oriented public sector that is on a par with the any country in the world."[522]

THE BRETTON WOODS INSTITUTIONS, THE STATE AND ECONOMIC LIBERALISATION

The importance of the position of the IMF in Jordan's relationship with other members of the donor community was pivotal during the period 1989 to 2002. Firstly, the World Bank's contribution to the SAP was dependent on an initial agreement being reached with the IMF and then adherence to the conditions of the programme. By issuing loan funds in tranches, implementation of the conditions agreed between the donor and the recipient can more easily be achieved. Secondly, the creditor nations and banks through the Paris and London Clubs would not even begin negotiating on debt-rescheduling until the relevant IMF agreement was in place. Finally, a number of the important donor nations, such as the USA, switched funding from developmental projects into restructuring programmes associated with the SAP.

The reaction of the IMF to the government's policy of prevarication throughout the majority of the period depended to a considerable extent on the political situation in the region. The conditions attached to SAP I were more onerous than those attached to SAP II, at which stage the importance of Jordan to the peace process and maintaining sanctions on Iraq was paramount. By the late 1990s, when SAP III was 'negotiated', the regional situation had changed. The peace process had stagnated, the international reaction to the death of King Hussein indicated a perception that Jordan could no longer play an important role in unlocking the peace process, and sanctions on Iraq no longer received the full backing of the international community: thus, reducing the strategic importance of Jordan. Thus, the worsening economic position in Jordan took precedence over the regional political situation. By the time negotiations on SAP IV commenced in 2002 Jordan's strategic importance had once become paramount, given the regional instability, resulting in less onerous terms being applied.

Throughout the period, the IMF seems to have adopted a public 'carrot' and private 'stick' approach to the delays by the state in implementing the agreed conditions. The public demonstrations of support by the IMF could be seen as boosting the stability of the regime, in the face of public unrest expressed in the riots in 1989 and 1996. Furthermore, the praise also helped the supporters of change among the rentier élite in the face of considerable opposition to the economic reform process (from the street, in parliament, and the bureaucracy, as well as from other members of the rentier élite). In common with the IMF, throughout the period the World Bank issued a series of laudatory comments concerning the government's policy on economic restructuring. Regularly, these statements contained a 'but' clause indicating that further progress was needed to be achieved on certain fronts: a signpost for future areas of concern to be addressed by the state to ensure World Bank support continued.

DEBT RESCHEDULING

As discussed previously, the volume of external debt rocketed during the 1980s, so that by 1989 external debt stood at US$8.5bn (JD5.41bn), almost 250% of GDP. However, the problem of debt was further exacerbated by the 50% devaluation in the dinar. Repayment of the debt was contracted in dollars, thus with devaluation more dinars were required to purchase the dollars necessary for repayment. Consequently, the cost of debt-servicing reached 37.9% of exports of goods and services. The need to address the problem of debt through a variety of methods, including write-offs, swaps, buy-backs,[523] and reschedulings, was deemed vital for the future performance of the economy. This section assesses the impact of the negotiations with the various representatives of the debtors, which also form part of the donor community. The outcome of the negotiations between Jordan and the creditors allows an analysis of how the non-BWI members of the donor community impacted on the rentier élite.

The sudden willingness of the creditor nations, from 1994, to allow debt write-offs and swaps rather than rescheduling created a new type of indirect rent. In the case of write-offs state expenditure allocated for debt-servicing was freed up, potentially increasing the funds available on the rent circuit. With equity swaps, foreign debt is converted into FDI in an existing or new Jordanian company. The local companies then receive not only investment but also foreign technology and expertise, which give them advantages over their local rivals. Although usually a one-off exercise, and given the limited volumes available, in the short term access to the rent of debt-for-equity can be an important element in creating rent-seeking competition within the rentier élite. In the longer term, two possible outcomes are possible. If the debt for equity swap has resulted in a new company, the business will be less likely to be dependent on the state, resulting in a desire to separate the private and public spheres. If, however, the investment is in an existing company with close ties to the state, the blurring of private and public sectors will remain unchanged. Consequently, the investment will enable continuing access to any rent controlled by the state.

Importantly for Jordan's perilous finances, the 1989 agreement with the IMF allowed debt-rescheduling arrangements to be initiated with both the Paris and London Clubs of debtors.[524] Around half the external debt was owed to members of the Paris Club, with a further 15% to non-Paris Club official creditors, such as the Arab countries and the former Soviet Union; commercial debt accounted for another 15%.[525] Finance Minister Basil Jardaneh opened negotiations with the Paris and London Clubs, requesting that US$650m of debt be rescheduled. The figure covered approximately 65% of the total of debt repayments due in 1989 to external creditors. The remaining 35% was to be financed by new multilateral loans and Arab donors.[526] In the event, the Paris Club signed an agreement on the 19th July 1989 covering part of the debt of US$1.213bn[527] due in 1989 and of US$1.278bn[528] in 1990.[529] Taking into account the need for currency to pay for imports of goods and services and to increase reserves, "the gap needing exceptional foreign currency finances through the rescheduling amounts to US$656m for 1989 and US$622m for 1990."[530] Accordingly, the Paris Club agreed to reschedule US$696m for 1989 and US$676m for 1990, with repayment over ten years, including a period of five years' grace (table 6.9).[531]

Table 6.9   **Paris Club Agreements, 1989-2002**

Date of Agreement	Period Covered Start	End	Amount US$m	Details
07/89	1/89	12/90	1,372	10 years, including 5 years' grace
02/92	1/92	6/93*	1,400	20 years, including 10 years' grace
10/94	7/94	6/97	1,215	20 years, including 10 years' grace
10/96	7/96	5/97	308	15 years, including 3 years' grace
06/97	6/97	2/99	450	22 years, including 5 years' grace
05/99	3/99	4/02	787	20 years**
07/02	7/02	12/07	1,170	20 years, including 10 years' grace

* Extended, in July 1993, to include debt repayments due until February 1994.
** Details of the grace period not released.

On the 11th September, the London Club committee, with a total debt of US$1.2bn, agreed in principle to reschedule debts over an eleven-year period with five years' grace on US$575m of debt falling between January 1989 and June 1991. Under the agreement, Jordan was required to meet its interest of US$82m in full in 1989.[532] However, the Jordanian cabinet rejected the deal as not being sufficiently favourable. In November, agreement in principle to release US$50m in loans (from previously undisbursed funds) was forthcoming, but the London Club refused to drop the interest rate from 0.8125% to 0.625% over Libor.[533] However, the banks did cut their management fee to 0.125% from 0.375%.[534] The loan was contingent on the payment of outstanding interest. By the time of the invasion of Kuwait, the agreement remained incomplete, mainly due to differences regarding Jordan's request to include a debt buy-back option.[535]

Immediately prior to the invasion of Kuwait by Iraq, Finance Minister Jardaneh announced a three-pronged policy for dealing with foreign commercial debt: using idle industrial capacity as a basis for debt-export exchanges; encouraging new investment through debt equity swaps; and buying-back debt via concessionary loans from the World Bank and other international agencies.   The World Bank was reported to be happy with the third prong of the strategy as "long as they [the government] have adopted a sound, medium-term economic policy."   Commercial debt at that stage could be purchased at 50-70% of its face value.[536]

As the Soviet Union was not a member of the Paris Club, separate negotiations began on the 7th August 1989. After protracted negotiations, an agreement, which was highly favourable to Jordan, was reached in February 1990 on US$214m worth of repayments due in 1989 and 1990. US$42m of the debt, representing interest due in 1989 and 1990, along with the bulk of arrears, was to be bartered for exports. A US$4m interest payment was to be made in cash before the 15th March, with the remaining US$168m rescheduled over twelve years with six years' grace at a fixed interest of 5%.[537]   In addition, official debt from Brazil was purchased at a large discount.[538]

The collapse of the economy and the debt negotiations following the Gulf War resulted in overdue obligations increasing to almost US$800m by the end of 1991, with an estimated debt-servicing for 1992 of US$1bn,[539] around 40% of exports of goods and services. The approval of the IMF standby agreement in February 1992 was followed in the same month by a second rescheduling agreement with the Paris Club. Debt relief was obtained on:

> all interest and amortization on account of pre-cutoff date which would be
> falling due during an 18-month period beginning on January 1, 1992 and
> all amortization arrears and 50 percent of interest accumulated up to end-
> 1991.[540]

The terms were softer than under the 1989 agreement.[541]   The agreement was extended in July 1993 in line with the standby arrangement to the end of February 1994. The agreement provided for selling or exchange of debt, debt for aid, debt for equity swaps or other local currency swaps.[542]

The commercial banks took a pragmatic view of Jordan's situation, realising that even with generous debt-rescheduling, debt service ratios would remain threateningly high. As reserves strengthened following the repatriation of savings by the returnees, the government was able to buy-back debt at a considerable discount. For example, in early 1993 the authorities were able to buy debt totalling about US$600m for US$115m.[543]   Agreement in principle with the London Club was finally reached on the 30th June 1993 and formalised on the 23rd December 1993. The agreement covered principal of US$736m and around US$121m of interest. As a result of the reschedulings, the stock of arrears fell from a peak of US$780m by the end of 1991 to about US$120m at the end of 1992, and only US$11m one year later.[544]

Following the approval of the EFF facility in May 1994, a further rescheduling agreement was negotiated with the Paris Club.   The sum of US$1215m, corresponding to all debt due for three years from the 1st July 1994, including debts of US$322m previously rescheduled in 1989, was rescheduled over twenty years, with a ten year grace period.[545] In recognition of the attempts to implement policy reform, the terms concluded were more favourable than the standard terms applied to other debtors, which were for fifteen years with seven to eight years' grace. The

IMF estimated that total debt relief by the Paris Club during the consolidation period from the 1st July 1994 to the 31st December 1997 was US$1.2bn.[546]

A further agreement was negotiated with the Paris Club in autumn 1996. Principal of US$250m and interest of US$58m due for repayment between July 1996 and May 1997 was rescheduled over fifteen years, with repayments commencing in June 1999.[547] The shorter time-scale was an indicator of the perceived recovery of the economy. By May 1997, Jordan was again in discussions with the Paris Club members over rescheduling debts. On this occasion, the government was hoping to reschedule US$520m worth of debt, falling due between the 1st June 1997 and the end of the SAP agreement in February 1999.[548] Agreement was reached in June for US$450m worth of bilateral debt and export credits. The former was rescheduled over twenty-two years, with a ten-year grace period, while the latter was over twenty years, with a moratorium of five years.[549] The sixth Paris Club agreement in the period was concluded in May 1999, following the new IMF package agreed earlier in the year. The agreement rescheduled US$787m of debt, amounting to US$397 in principal and US$390m in interest[550] due between the 31st March 1999 and the 30th April 2002, over twenty years. The agreement also allowed the government to conduct debt swaps of US$106m with Germany, France and Spain at a discount rate of 50%.[551] At the same time, an agreement was concluded to reschedule between US$200m[552] and US$350m[553] in non-Paris Club official debt. The agreement reduced debt-servicing for 2000 by around 30% from 14.2% of GDP to 8.6% of GDP.[554]

In July 2002, a further agreement confirmed the Jordan's improved relationship with the donor community, driven to a degree by international concerns about the unstable regional situation. Uniquely, the Paris Club granted a debt rescheduling agreement covering a period beyond the relevant IMF SAP. The agreement allowed for rescheduling of 100% of debt maturing between July 2002 and June 2004 (the period of SAP IV) was agreed, 90% of maturities falling between July 2004 and December 2005, 80% of maturities falling due in 2006 and 70% of maturities falling due in 2007. Debt swaps were also permitted under the arrangement. In return the government committed itself not to seek further rescheduling programmes.

The bilateral arrangements under the Paris Club agreements resulted in different styles of dealing with the problem of debt, including a number of outright write-offs. Significantly, the political realities of the Middle East imposed considerably on the methods of dealing with the debt. Prior to the invasion of Kuwait, the sole approach by the creditor nations was to offer simple rescheduling. During the actual crisis, although a number of the creditor countries promised and delivered economic assistance in the form of grants to cope with the humanitarian aspects of the war, the same countries did not consider writing-off any of the outstanding debts. This stance was probably due to the position of King Hussein in seeking an Arab, rather than international, solution to the invasion. Indeed, negotiations on rescheduling were put on the back burner during the war.

With its rehabilitation into the world community following the start of the peace process in Madrid in 1991, and in particular after the signing of the peace agreement with Israel, Jordan was in a stronger position to negotiate various forms of debt-retiral, rather than rescheduling, which merely postpones the day of reckoning. By the end of 1993, Jordan was actively seeking debt write-offs from Washington. In July 1994, on his return from the USA King Hussein stated that his talks explored "a formula to lift or cancel the debts."[555]   He acknowledged that the American administration was willing to assist Jordan, but the support was conditional on participation in the peace process and a meeting between King Hussein and the Prime Minister of Israel, Yitzak Rabin. The King was quoted as saying that "if the meeting between me and the Israeli Prime Minister is a price to change the picture of this country, I will not hesitate at all and consider it a service for my country."[556] On the day of the signing of the Peace Treaty between Israel and Jordan, President Clinton promised "to assist Jordan in dealing with its burden of debt and its defence requirements…I am working with Congress to achieve rapid action on both these matters."[557]   Shortly after the signing, Congress approved a bill allowing the first tranche of debt to be written-off. The US was expected to cut US$696m of the US$950m debt in three stages in 1994 ($190m), 1995 ($252m) and 1996 ($254m).[558] When the agreement was signed, the US Ambassador to Jordan, Wesley Egan, stated "[t]he US government will support those who take risks for peace."[559] Again the idea of the tranches was to ensure that Jordan remained onside in the peace process. Later in the same month President Clinton wrote a public letter asking the leaders of the Paris Club to take urgent action to relieve Jordan's debts.[560] At the same time, the UK announced that £60m (US$92m) of debt would be converted to grants (i.e. effectively a write-off).[561]

The influence of political developments within the donor countries was evident in the debt write-off from America. Congress first permitted debt forgiveness up to US$220m in the Conference Report on FY1995 Foreign Operations Appropriation Bill (H.Rept. 103-633, August 1st, 1994) but the Report added that to obtain further debt relief Jordan should sign a final peace agreement with Israel, abrogate the Arab economic boycott, and comply with sanctions against Iraq.   In March 1995, Congress initially refused to sanction the US$252m write off scheduled for 1995, offering, instead US$50m. On the 29th July, the House of Representatives agreed that the full amount should be written-off, but only US$50m prior to October 1995; the remainder thereafter.[562] Within six months, the US promised to cancel all the outstanding debts (US$488m),[563] the agreement being signed on the 25th September. As a *quid pro quo* the promise was swiftly followed by the cancellation of a series of Jordanian laws banning economic contact with Israel.

Other methods of debt reduction were also forthcoming. In November 1993, an agreement had been signed in which Switzerland wrote-off JD16.5m, in return for Jordan financing development projects to the tune of JD4.5m.[564] The following year, Germany reduced its debt by DM50m, in exchange for Jordan committing 50% of the funds against environmental projects.[565] The Jordanian Cabinet approved the first debt for equity swap in April 1996. The UK was to sell £35m (US$53m) of debt at 50% of its face value to companies wishing to invest in Jordan. In addition, ACCOR of France was given approval to use the agreement to cover its US$5.5m equity stake in the Arab European Company for Tourism and Hotel Management.[566] A further debt-equity swap with France was approved in July.[567] Debt swaps have continued to be a feature of Jordan's debt management programme.

DEBT, THE STATE AND ECONOMIC LIBERALISATION

Although Jordan has been successful in obtaining debt rescheduling, debt buy-backs, debt write-offs, debt swaps and debt for equity swaps,[568] due in considerable part to the pressure imposed on the bilateral donor community by the USA after 1993, the overhang of debt still inhibits domestic and foreign private sector investment, as well as threatening economic growth. As can be seen from figure 6.4, the levels of external debt have actually increased since 1993, while the percentage of external debt to GDP after a initial dramatic fall (from 245.2% in 1989 to 115.8% in 1993) decreased only slowly thereafter, before increasing in 1999 to 90.6% and dropping to 75.2% in 2001. One notable exception in the support for debt reduction has been the main debtor, Japan. In line with its philosophy for aid, Japan emphasises the need for self-help, which has resulted in a less sympathetic attitude to the question of debt write-offs.

Figure 6.4   **External Debt, 1989-2002**

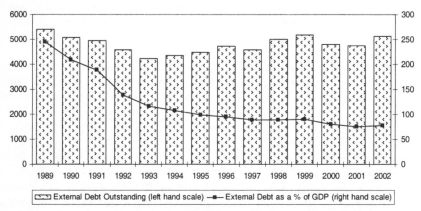

Source: Adapted by author. CBJ, (various), *Monthly Statistical Bulletin*, (Amman: CBJ).

The case of the debt rescheduling highlights the considerable influence of geo-political factors on the ability of the state to continue a policy of rent-seeking. While rescheduling can only be considered a very short term form of rent-seeking, other forms of retiring debt, such as write-offs and swaps can potentially be a major one-off source of rent. Early attempts at retiring debt were constrained by the conditionality of the IMF programme, then by the Second Gulf War. However, the international rehabilitation, in particular after 1994, allowed the state to adopt rent-seeking on a more pro-active basis. Despite America's efforts to encourage the donor community to undertake large-scale debt write-offs,[569] these peaked at just over US$200m in 1995, before falling annually to US$60.3m in 2000. The international community's perception of the renewed importance of Jordan following the outbreak of the intifada and the 'war-on-terror' witnessed an increase in debt-write offs in 2001 and 2002. Thus, significantly, although debt rescheduling arrangements have been closely linked with IMF policies, the more important debt write-offs, such as those by the USA, have tended to be political in nature. The political aspect has encouraged the state as an institution to continue to adopt a rentier mentality in this field.

THE AID COMMUNITY

In terms of actual funding, bilateral aid has been significantly more important than multilateral aid, accounting for almost 75% of the total (table 6.10). However, the figures are distorted considerably in 1990 when only US$32.9m of the total of US$970.0 was provided by the multilateral agencies. In the later years, bilateral assistance tended to account for around two-thirds of the total aid. Two bilateral donors have dominated the scene in Jordan, Japan and the USA, followed by Germany and the Arab countries (although since the Gulf War the Arab aid contribution has virtually disappeared). Other donors of lesser importance have been France, Italy and the UK (despite the latter's close historical links). In the multilateral field, the EU has become an increasingly important donor, outperforming Germany in the last few years. Since 1992, the UNRWA has been the most consistent donor, averaging just over US$74m annually.

Table 6.10   **Total Aid and Grants, 1989-2002 (US$m)**

	1989	1990	1991	1992	1993	1994	1995	1996
			Aid					
Total Bilateral	322.1	937.2	714.5	329.9	194.3	466.0	449.2	355.5
of which								
USA	70.0	66.0	38.0	64.0	57.0	259.0	152.0	49.0
Japan	14.3	165.9	443.1	126.4	45.5	106.7	184.2	123.7
Germany	29.5	174.7	128.0	64.0	29.2	35.3	36.4	73.7
Arab Countries	174.7	456.1	4.4	2.0	0.1	0.5	0.0	0.1
Total Multilateral	23.9	32.9	249.2	123.0	146.9	163.3	157.3	193.1
of which								
EC/EU	4.2	6.6	193.2	40.8	43.7	57.6	61.9	120.1
UNRWA	0.0	0.0	0.0	63.2	63.3	71.4	77.3	65.2
Arab Agencies	5.6	4.2	23.3	3.9	28.5	24.8	5.5	0.0
Total ODA	346.0	970.0	963.8	452.9	341.3	629.3	606.5	548.6
			GRANTS					
Total Bilateral	268.4	714.5	222.6	120.2	96.1	307.9	251.7	151.4
of which								
USA	63.0	61.0	36.0	44.0	32.0	243.0	138.0	30.0
Germany	15.9	141.8	105.8	20.6	19.9	18.2	25.7	35.6
Arab Countries	159.8	440.5	1.0	2.0	0.1	0.5	0.0	0.1
Japan	7.4	8.5	6.7	5.1	7.9	11.2	42.5	46.4
Total Multilateral	17.6	25.4	221.7	114.6	105.3	127.9	126.7	159.9
of which								
UNRWA	0.0	0.0	0.0	63.2	63.3	71.4	77.3	65.2
EC/EU	3.8	6.5	193.2	39.9	30.7	47.3	37.1	88.5
Total Grants	285.9	739.9	444.3	234.8	201.5	435.8	378.3	311.3

Table 6.10 (cont.)   **Total Aid and Grants, 1989-2002 (US$m)**

	1997	1998	1999	2000	2001	2002	Total
		Aid					
Total Bilateral	**365.3**	**333.9**	**350.5**	**384.5**	**289.5**	**371.1**	**5863.5**
of which							
USA	132.0	140.0	170.2	187.8	155.9	286.8	1827.7
Japan	143.8	54.8	76.9	104.7	42.7	0.0	1632.7
Germany	35.7	58.6	64.1	44.3	59.7	51.1	884.3
Arab Countries	0.0	0.0	0.0	0.0	0.0	0.0	637.9
Total Multilateral	**183.3**	**143.4**	**119.1**	**168.0**	**133.1**	**163.2**	**1999.7**
of which							
EC/EU	93.2	56.6	21.7	84.0	44.6	76.3	904.5
UNRWA	76.8	76.0	83.0	79.3	79.8	80.0	815.3
Arab Agencies	0.0	0.7	2.8	2.6	0.7	1.9	104.5
Total ODA	**548.6**	**477.4**	**469.6**	**552.5**	**432.6**	**534.3**	**7873.4**
		GRANTS					
Total Bilateral	**214.4**	**238.2**	**289.4**	**334.0**	**353.6**	**400.5**	**3962.9**
of which							
USA	106.0	122.6	170.2	187.8	158.8	291.2	1683.6
Germany	20.8	24.8	27.5	22.0	104.5	49.9	633.0
Arab Countries	0.0	0.0	0.0	0.0	0.4	0.2	604.6
Japan	49.3	29.2	63.8	85.0	63.9	32.6	459.5
Total Multilateral	**148.7**	**95.5**	**101.9**	**172.1**	**105.4**	**141.0**	**1663.7**
of which							
UNRWA	76.8	76.0	83.0	79.3	79.8	80.0	815.3
EC/EU	59.9	11.4	11.0	85.9	18.1	52.8	686.1
Total Grants	**363.1**	**333.7**	**391.3**	**506.1**	**459.0**	**541.5**	**5626.5**

Source: Adapted, for 1989 to 1998 inclusive OECD, (2000), *International Development Statistics*, CD ROM 2000 edition (Paris: OECD) and for 1999 OECD, "International Development Statistics: Online Databases", *OECD website*, www.oecd.org/dac/htm/online.htm#dac/o. Totals may not agree due to rounding. Total ODA figures for 2000-2002 are the net position.

Multilateral aid has also been important, in that 83.2% of multilateral funding has been in the form of grants, compared with less than 68% of bilateral funding. All the UNRWA funding has been in grants, as has over 75% of EU funding. In the bilateral field, the figures are distorted by the Arab countries, which in the early years of the period gave the majority of the funding in the form of grants. The difference between the Japanese and American assistance is apparent when the level of grants is analysed. Only 28.1% of Japanese assistance has been in grants, whereas 92.1% of US funding has been in this form. Indeed, Japan is behind both Germany and the Arab countries as to the level of grants.

The time series also shows the importance of donors' national interests on the flow of aid, resulting in fluctuations in the flow. The reactions of the various donors to the Gulf War are a prime example. Arab and American assistance virtually dried up, as both sides interpreted the Jordanian position as pro-Saddam Hussein. By contrast, in 1991 Japan, which is reliant on Middle Eastern oil supplies and consequently needs regional stability, provided over 27% of its total assistance for the period. The American involvement has fluctuated dependent on the changes of Washington's perception of Jordan's role in the stability of the region, particularly towards the peace process. The opening of the Madrid Peace Conference paved the way for increased levels of US aid. The signing of the Peace Treaty with Israel coincided with the peak in US assistance followed by a slump as the situation in the Arab-Israeli peace process stagnated. In recent years, as the US has attempted to move the peace forward, Jordan has again benefited from assistance. Economic assistance has also been boosted, particularly from Washington, in the aftermath of 11 September 2001 and the subsequent US-led 'war-on-terror'.

BILATERAL DONORS

This section briefly analyses the bilateral involvement of the USA, Japan, Germany and the UK, bearing in mind that each country has a different structure for and national interest in providing aid to Jordan. In addition to the bilateral funding, each donor also contributes to multilateral organisations, such as the EU, the UN, the IMF and the World Bank.

United States of America

The USA[570] has been providing economic aid since 1951 and military aid since 1957.[571] Total aid to 1990 was almost US$3.5bn, of which US$1.9bn (54.3%) was in the form of economic assistance. From 1990 to 2002 total aid was US$3.46bn, with US$1.08n (31.3%) in the form of economic assistance (table 6.11). Four overlapping periods of American assistance to Jordan can be discerned, with the focus of each preceding time-span being carried forward to the next era. 1) Budgetary assistance and basic infrastructure provision, from 1951: the focus of the infrastructure provision centred mainly around transport networks, and basic physical infrastructure in social welfare, such as health, education. 2) Institution building, from the early 1970s: the emphasis switched from physical infrastructure to a developmental focus on the provision of the 'basic needs' of water, housing, health and education. 3) Private sector and NGO building, from the mid-1980s: local Non-Governmental Organisations (NGOs) were boosted by grants to Bani Hamida, Queen Alia Fund, Jordan River Design and Noor al-Hussein Foundation,[572] while the private sector was assisted through the establishment of the Jordan Trade Association and other export-oriented project drives; the launching of small and medium sized enterprises (SMEs) initiatives; and an equipment financing programme. 4) Expansion of USAID, from 1997: The expansion allowed renewed emphasis on budgetary support, infrastructure provision, institution building and private sector development on a hitherto, unprecedented scale, adding depth to scale.

Following the invasion of Kuwait by Iraq, the Bush administration placed a hold on the disbursement of both economic and military assistance. Indeed, in March 1991 the US Congress approved a bill cutting off aid, which was frozen the previous month, in response to the King's televised statement on the 6th February when he

asserted that the Americans were trying to assert a regional hegemony.[573]   A
spokesperson for USAID stated that if the payments were to resume then they
would be used "to provide financial and technical support to the private sector as
the main engine for growth and employment generation."[574]   The sums involved
were US$57.2m for 1991 and US$50m in undisbursed aid for 1990. Congress then
suspended FY1991[575] funds under emergency legislation (P.L. 102-27, April 10,
1993, section 502):

> unless the President certified and reported to appropriate congressional
> committees that the Government of Jordan has taken steps to advance the
> peace process in the Middle East, or that furnishing assistance to Jordan
> would be beneficial to the peace process in the Middle East.[576]

In addition, Section 586D of P.L. 101-513 prohibited the use of aid funds to
countries not in compliance with the UN Security Council sanctions against Iraq.
The President could over-ride this legislation if the actions were deemed to be in the
national interest of the USA. President Bush waived the suspension of economic
assistance in July 1991 and military assistance in September. However, following
discussions between the White House and Congress, an informal hold was
maintained on FY1991 disbursements, with the exception of US$1.245m
International Military Education and Training funding. The Foreign Assistance
Appropriation Act for FY1993 (P.L. 102-391, October 6, 1992) retained the ban on
assistance to Jordan, even strengthening the conditions needed for the Presidential
waiver. The President had to ensure that: Jordan had taken steps to advance the
peace process in the Middle East; Jordan complied with UN Security Council
sanctions against Iraq; and (ironically) the assistance given to Jordan was in the
national interest of the USA.

Not until early 1993, following consultations with the congressional committees
did the Bush administration begin to release FY1991 funds. By late July 1993, all the
FY1991 and FY1992 funds had been disbursed. Following the signing of the
Jordan-Israeli agreement to a bilateral agenda on the 17th September 1993, the
President signed the waiver. The Foreign Assistance Appropriation Act for FY1994
(P.L. 103-87, September 30, 1993), which was drawn up prior to the bilateral
agreement, maintained a strong line against assistance to Jordan, with the President
once more waiving the restrictions on the 13th January 1994. The Acts for the
following years did not contain any stipulations on assistance to Jordan, but
continued to stress the need for any country to comply with the UN sanctions
against Iraq.   The battles of Presidents Bush and Clinton against Congress
concerning assistance to Jordan were a reflection of the position on debt write-offs
in 1994 and 1995 discussed in the earlier section. By November 1996, relations
between the two countries had improved to the position whereby Jordan was
decreed a 'major non-NATO ally', entitling the Kingdom to priority military aid.

US economic assistance to Jordan took off following a visit by King Hussein to
Washington in November 1997 in response to the worsening economic situation.
Prior to the visit, the talk within USAID had been that Jordan was about to turned
into a "limited presence country."[577] King Hussein was able to build on a number of
factors, which allowed for increased US-Jordanian co-operation. Two groups of
American politicians, both with members of the Appropriations Committee of their
respective Houses, had visited Jordan prior to King Hussein's Washington visit. The

Jordanian presentations to these politicians were extremely persuasive. The King's response, both verbally and in allowing the allies access to Kamal Hussein, President Saddam Hussein's son-in-law, further increased Jordan's standing. In addition, King Hussein was credited with playing a major part in pushing through the Hebron agreement between the Palestinian National Authority and Israel in January 1997.[578] Finally, on the 17th June 1997, President Clinton had highlighted the importance of providing extra assistance for countries supporting the peace process. Following the visit, the level of American funding increased dramatically, from a budget of US$7m in FY1996 to US$200 in FY1999,[579] at a time when the overall US aid budget was being cut. This expansion of USAID activities from 1997 added depth to the already agreed 1997-2001 programme. Indeed over 25% of total US assistance over the 50 years of the relationship was provided in the years from 1997 to 2000. However, the USAID/Jordan Mission Director, Lewis Lucke, gave two notes of warning. At a meeting of the Rotary Club in Amman on the 31st August 1999, he stated that:

> these funding levels are extraordinarily high … . They cannot and will not last forever. They do, however provide Jordan with an important 'window of opportunity', offering valuable support for a more long-term economic restructuring process that can and must take place.[580]

Later in the speech he emphasised that Jordan should not rely on foreign assistance for its development strategy, as "over the long-term, it is private capital, not government funds, which will truly transform Jordan."[581]

What, then, has been the focus of USAID in Jordan since 1989? As early as 1987 USAID was attempting to raise the profile of the private sector in Jordan. In the Congressional Presentation for FY1988,[582] four constraints on the growth of the private sector are highlighted for action: market entry restrictions caused by government controls; inadequate incentive structure caused by pricing controls, taxes and exchange rates; controls of financial markets which tend to work against private sector investment and the ability to raise working capital; and government ownership. Interestingly, the Presentation argues that "given the high level of interest of Jordanian officials in the subject [of privatisation], it is possible that significant progress can be made in this area."[583] Based on these and other constraints the Presentation proposes a series of policy initiatives, which include: influencing government policy, to establish a policy framework which was conducive to private sector growth through specific initiatives, including studies on the above-mentioned constraints; an analysis of revenue collection and its impact on private sector investment; training for policy-makers concerned with the private sector; and funding for the development of private sector advocacy groups such as a Consumers' Association, a Manufacturers' Association, and a Private Sector Association; assisting with privatisation, through helping create a viable privatisation policy, and assisting SOEs to develop a privatisation programme; overcoming financial constraints, through the transfer of technology and encouraging institutional development; establishing or strengthening private sector business organisations, including the Jordanian Business Forum, a Manufacturers' Association, and an Exporters' Association; and overcoming the lack of marketing skills and investment opportunities.[584] The emphasis on the need for private sector investment to improve, expand and sustain productive capacity and employment remained a key feature of the successive annual congressional presentations.

The prescription of the private sector as the medicine to cure the ills of the economy was underlined when the IMF and World Bank became involved, dispensing a similar prescription. USAID issued a '*Strategy for Sustainable Development*' in March 1994 that had five objectives: the protection of the environment; the building of democracy; the stabilisation of world population growth and the protection of human health; the encouragement of broad-based economic growth; and the provision of humanitarian assistance and aiding post-crisis transition.[585] Noticeably, despite the new emphasis on poverty in the global development ideology, the USAID objectives did not address this particular aspect directly: indeed there was little on human development. Simultaneously, USAID began targeting its policy in Jordan through a number of Strategic Objectives (SOs) all within the overall objective of achieving broad-based economic growth. Two of these SOs have been consistent: water, and health and population. The third has evolved with time from 'increasing foreign exchange earnings from selected export industries and services' from FY1996, to 'enhanced private-sector opportunities' in FY1998, to the more broad-based 'increased economic opportunities for Jordanians' in FY 1999. The USAID/Jordan strategy for the period from 1997, which was approved in June of that year, had three objectives: improved water resources management; increased economic opportunities for Jordanians;[586] and improved access to and quality of reproductive and primary health care.[587] The second SO concerning economic opportunities had three sub-objectives, namely: increased access to business services; more effective identification and implementation of policy reform; and improved environment for sustained policy reform. The second and third sub-measures were concerned with the government's role in the SAP. The first measure was aimed directly at the private sector and based on the USAID funded private-sector needs assessment, which was completed in March 1997. The report identifies lack of access to financial services as the single most important constraint facing SMEs (including micro-enterprises). The other constraints highlighted included technology transfer, marketing and management.[588]

The need to concentrate on policy reform was based on the assumption that while policy reform legislation is relatively easily enacted, implementation is often weak. Drawing on experience gained in other countries, USAID identified a number of constraints to effective policy implementation, including:[589] the failure of mid-level officials to understand fully the technical aspects of the policy reform; the lack of an obvious constituency to galvanise a reform effort; an inability to explain properly the reasons for reform to the broader public; and the lack of effective feedback systems to inform policymakers about what is and what is not working. USAID decided to concentrate its efforts on making the Investment Promotion Corporation effective and efficient, to the extent that nearly 17,000 new jobs and over US$4.5bn of new investment would be forthcoming. In addition, assistance was planned to help the Customs Department show a 37% improvement in efficiency over the five years, the major constraints to WTO membership were to be removed or significantly reduced, an Intellectual Property Rights bill consistent with WTO membership was to be passed, and impediments to businesses were to be significantly reduced in the economy.

Table 6.11   **USA Assistance to Jordan, 1990-2002 (US$m)**

Fiscal Year	Economic Assistance		GSM*	Military**		TDA
	DA	ESF		FMF	IMET	
1990	0.0	3.7	137.0	67.8	2.1	0.0
1991	0.0	31.1	30.0	20.0	1.1	0.0
1992	0.0	0.0	30.0	20.0	0.6	0.0
1993	0.0	65.0	0.0	9.0	0.5	0.0
1994	4.0	24.0	35.0	9.0	0.8	0.0
1995	5.0	7.2	15.0	7.3	1.0	0.5
1996	0.0	7.2	40.0	100.0	1.2	0.4
1997	6.0	120.0	40.0	30.0	1.6	1.4
1998	0.0	140.0	40.0	50.0	1.6	0.0
1999	0.0	150.0	60.0	45.0	1.6	0.0
2000	0.0	150.0	60.0	45.0	1.6	0.0
2001	0.0	150.0	60.0	45.0	1.6	0.0
2002	0.0	235.0	75.0	120.0	2.0	1.5
Total	**15.0**	**1083.2**	**622.0**	**568.1**	**17.3**	**3.8**
% of Total	**0.43**	**31.28**	**17.96**	**16.40**	**0.50**	**0.11**

Fiscal Year	PL 480	Debt Forgiveness	Export Guarantees	Section 416b	Total
1990	0.0	0.0	0.0	13.3	**223.8**
1991	0.0	0.0	0.0	22.9	**105.1**
1992	20.0	0.0	0.0	9.1	**79.8**
1993	30.0	0.0	0.0	0.0	**104.5**
1994	15.0	219.9	0.0	0.0	**307.7**
1995	21.0	417.2	0.0	0.0	**474.2**
1996	15.0	0.0	0.0	0.0	**163.8**
1997	21.0	63.5	200.0	0.0	**483.5**
1998	15.0	0.0	0.0	0.0	**246.6**
1999	0.0	0.0	0.0	15.0	**271.6**
2000	0.0	0.0	0.0	15.0	**271.6**
2001	0.0	0.0	0.0	15.0	**271.6**
2002	0.0	0.0	0.0	26.0	**459.5**
Total	**137.0**	**700.6**	**200.0**	**116.3**	**3463.3**
% of Total	**3.96**	**20.23**	**5.77**	**3.36**	**100.0**

Source: *USAID files*. Notes: Totals may not add up due to rounding. * GSM for FY 1999 includes US$20m for the private sector. ** In FY 1996 a transfer of US$100m in military equipment was made. Abbreviations: DA: Development Assistance, grants to promote sustainable development. ESF: Economic Support Fund, grants to advance economic and social development. GSM: Soft loans to import food commodities. FMF: Foreign Military Fund, grant for military assistance. IMET: International Military Education and Training, grant assistance. TDA: Trade Development Agency, grant assistance to conduct feasibility studies in promoting bilateral trade. PL 480: Public Law 480, soft loan to purchase agricultural commodities from the US Department of Agriculture. Section 416b: donation of US agricultural commodities that are sold in the local markets.

The third sub-measure was to assist in improving the environment for sustained policy reform.[590] USAID intended to further develop on trade and investment reform, financial and legal sector reform, and to increase public sector efficiency. Among the aims of trade and investment reform were accession to the WTO, rationalisation and consolidation of tariffs, and reduction of costs of imports related to customs administration. The financial and legal sector reforms were to include the introduction of modern commercial laws and regulations, more efficient financial intermediation through central banking law, strengthened banking supervision, and regulated and efficient capital markets. To this end, a cash transfer of US$50m was disbursed in September 1997 with the aim of improving the environment for sustained policy reform. This transfer was associated with the new Companies Law (May 1997), the new Securities Law (May 1997), and the abolishing of the remaining foreign exchange controls (June 1997).

The use of targets as a measure of the success of USAID's economic objective SO became explicit in the Congressional Presentation FY1999 when the targets set were: 25,000 micro-finance borrowers to be active by 2001; investments facilitated by the Investment Promotion Corporation to have created 17,000 new jobs and investment of US$4.5bn by 2001; three micro-finance institutions to have met best practice principles by 2001; two major privatisations by 1999, with a further three by 2001; and accession to the WTO[591] to have been achieved by 2000.[592]

The assumption behind the SO, subtitled 'Increased Economic Opportunities for Jordanians', was that with export growth and increased foreign exchange earnings the problem was no longer one of accumulation but now one of sustaining and distributing the benefits at a time when the benefits of growth were perceived to be narrowly distributed.[593]

The Access to Micro-finance and Improved Implementation of Policy Reform (AMIR) programme was one of the new institutional developments funded by the increased levels of American aid. AMIR is a four-year project, which was launched in March 1998. The project has two broad objectives: transforming Jordan's business environment to stimulate greater investment to meet the challenges of economic globalisation; and increasing economic growth with equity through sustainable micro-finance initiatives. The programme, which is directed by Chemonics International Inc., a USA development firm with a team of Jordanian and US-based sub-contractors, has three primary initiatives: sustainable micro-finance based on best practices;[594] improved implementation of policy reform; and the development of Business Associations.[595] The first of these initiatives falls under the sub-objective 'increased access to business services', while the second and third are related to 'improved identification and implementation of policy reform'.

The micro-finance project, which is run through the AMIR Program, is a four-year US$13.4m programme funded entirely by USAID. The aim is to develop a sustainable micro-finance industry, based on commercial funding and sound business practices. To ensure that 'best practices' are followed, AMIR sponsored a banker's workshop on the necessary methodologies in July 1998. According to USAID, these practices, if followed, result in a profitable diversified portfolio of low risk loans. The first of the new generation of micro-finance schemes (i.e. based on sustainability and best practice) commenced in 1994, when the Save the Children Fund established a Group Guaranteed Lending and Savings pilot in two of the Amman refugee camps, Mahatta and Natheef. The programme proved to be successful and has been rolled out in the north from late 1996, through a local NGO, the Jordanian Women's Development Society, which was specifically created for the purpose.[596] The Co-operative Housing Foundation, in co-ordination with the Jordan River Foundation, initiated a second sustainable microfinance project in the south of Jordan. The third project, established in October 1999, was the Jordan Micro Credit Company. The company is an offshoot of the Noor Hussein Foundation, and was grant-funded to the extent of US$1.73m. The medium-term aim of the micro-finance project is to involve the private sector on the supply side, as a result of which Jordan National Bank, the Bank of Jordan and the Cairo-Amman Bank are all becoming actively involved.[597]

The AMIR programme's focus on the business associations (the third primary initiative) has been notable in creating new institutions to offset the power of the established organisations of the Chambers of Commerce and Industry and the JBA. These organisations are seen to be "charter corrupted," allowing for a limited-scale democracy, which ensures that power remains in the hands of the few.[598] Thus AMIR has concentrated on the more democratic, flexible organisations of the Young Entrepreneurs Association,[599] the Amman World Trade Centre, and the Jordan Trade Association. These associations have usually been established by the younger, Western-educated generation of the rentier élite. Thus the split is not so much by those outside the élite but a generation split within the élite. The younger generation, unlike the older élite, does not see its profits coming from a liaison with the government but from a market-oriented economy. This erosion of the rentier mentality has been assisted by the continuing 'education' process of the donor community, with programmes of discussions,[600] lectures,[601] seminars,[602] workshops,[603] conferences,[604] training courses[605] and media intervention.[606]

The programme has funded consultants from the Center for International Private Enterprise to work with various business associations[607] "to perform diagnostic reviews and assist in the preparation of three year strategic plans."[608] The major areas of emphasis were management, advocacy, membership development, human resource development, and stakeholder management. A further goal was the establishment of an informal alliance of the business associations that would help promote advocacy to create a strong private sector in Jordan.

The Jordan-United States Business Partnership (JUSBP), which came into existence in January 1999, was initially funded by a grant of US$15m, signed on the 27th October 1998. The grant enables the International Executive Agency for International Development, an association of American corporate executives, to provide on-site, hands-on management expertise. Lewis Reade, a former director of USAID in Jordan, was appointed the CEO of the JUSBP.[609] The four-year programme, which aims to become self-sustaining, has three main purposes: to provide technical assistance and other consulting services to SMEs; to provide similar assistance to the trade associations, to enable them to pass on the expertise to their members and, importantly, improve their awareness and skills in advocacy; and to provide technical assistance to the Industrial Development Directorate of the Ministry of Industry and Trade, to enable them to improve the services offered to the private sector.[610]

Institutionally, a joint committee comprising members of USAID, the JUSBP and Ministry of Industry and Trade agree the objectives, with the latter having identified the possible projects, providing they fall within the USAID's strategic objectives. According to JUSBP, the programme itself is demand driven, with awareness being raised regionally in the media.[611]

Within the first seven months of operation four associations[612] had already signed agreements with JUSBP.[613] The initial target for the private sector was to assist three hundred and fifty companies by the end of the period. Assistance to the companies is usually on a fifty-fifty cost-sharing basis, although as the relationship develops the companies have to increase their share of the costs. Having identified a number of problems (such as price, quality, management skills and marketing as weak or non-existent), which affected the level of competitiveness, the JUSBP programme was designed around these failings. Interestingly, USAID found access to financial resources was only a problem at the micro-level of enterprise.[614]

The Jordan Vision 2020 (JV2020)[615] was another project implemented with USAID funding. JV2020 was set up through the YEA, who invited other business associations to become involved in setting out a path for the economic development of Jordan by the year 2020. "The intent is to play a catalytic role in a process in which Jordan can emerge as a leader rather than as a follower in terms of its role in the regional as well as global marketplace."[616]

Japan

In the last decade, despite its own economic crisis, Japan has been Jordan's second largest contributor of soft loans. Aid has also been provided by way of grants, the first of which was issued in 1993 for health and medicine, with a second in 1994 for structural adjustment and technical assistance. Japan issued an Aid Charter in 1992, stating that its philosophy is to "support the self-help efforts of developing countries" and stressing the importance of the environment and human rights. This philosophy, Kohama argues, made the situation difficult when Jordan had to continually seek further debt rescheduling programmes, particularly at a time when Japanese aid was under the twin pressures of its own economic downturn and the need to provide assistance towards the crisis countries in East Asia.[617] Japanese aid to Jordan is predicated on three factors: Jordan's active commitment to the Middle East peace process, coupled with Jordan's stability as being integral to peace in the Middle East; Jordan's active promotion of democratisation and economic reform; and the good relationship between the two countries, including their royal families.[618]

Following the signing of the Peace Treaty between Israel and Jordan, the Japanese government established a committee to study Japan's aid to Jordan. The Committee on the Country Study for Japan's Official Development Assistance to the Hashemite Kingdom of Jordan, under the auspices of the Japan International Cooperation Agency (JICA), issued their report in March 1996. The report answers two main questions: 'why give assistance to Jordan?' and 'what kind of assistance is most appropriate?' In answer to the first question the committee argues that

> assistance to Jordan is integral to support for the Middle East peace process and coincides with Japan's national interests in terms of pursuit of security and stability throughout the world, including in the Middle East. Japan ought also to take into account, of course, that Jordan is striving to

become more democratic and economically independent; more fundamentally, assistance for Jordan has strategic importance to sustain the process of regional conflict resolution.[619]

Japan considers that its assistance to Jordan helps to promote Jordan's political and economic stability and the regional economy's development, bearing in mind the Palestinian question. With these points in mind the committee's report argues that three basic aid orientations should be considered:

1) laying the foundations for economic stability and development; 2) supporting the stability and sustainable development of Jordan's domestic communities; and 3) assisting the Jordanian economy to become a more active entrepôt site in prospect of the regional economies take-off.[620]

In each of these orientations the report lists a number of priority areas for Japanese aid, including support for structural adjustment through small grants for 'safety net' assistance, for economic infrastructure (including power and transportation), and for the promotion of industry (particularly small-scale business, tourism, Qualifying Industrial Zones (QIZs), and the development of Aqaba region). The report further stresses the need for these priorities to comply with "the stipulations of the aid charter, [and] stress on self-help efforts" among other aspects.[621] The emphasis on the self-help aspect is reinforced later in the report, which stresses that Jordan must be informed at every opportunity that continued support depends on the government making "independent efforts to end its financial and economic dependence on other countries."[622]

The Committee was not optimistic that in the short-term (i.e. by 1999) Jordan could complete its SAP, arguing that "Jordan is still far from being fully equipped with large-scale infrastructure and from receiving appreciable foreign investments."[623] The analysis highlights three types of assistance: short-term, medium and long-term, based on the assumptions that the Arab-Israeli dispute would move forward, spreading tangible economic benefits and the situation in Iraq would normalise, allowing trade with Jordan to recover. Short-term assistance should be designed to permit the following:

1) to facilitate the various reforms now under way; 2) to foster Jordan's industry to give its economy a strong foundation; 3) to make it possible for Jordanians to recognise tangible peace dividends; and 4) to provide backing for the various schemes for establishing co-operative ties between Jordan and other countries in the Middle East and give an economic underpinning to the political (Middle East peace) process.[624]

According to the report, medium-term Japanese aid should aim:

1) to foster industry and better establish Jordanian institutions to activate the economy effectively; 2) to facilitate regional economic co-operation within the Eastern [sic] countries and building of infrastructure; and 3) to meet basic human needs (BHN) and achieve social development.[625]

In the long-term (10 years), the Report argues that Jordan will have to be more economically independent, but that problems with a growing population could create an increased economic and social burden. To overcome these difficulties, long-term aid should build the foundations for investment tailored to regional economic development and direct attention at improving economic and social infrastructures to make sustainable development possible.[626]

Following the publication of the report, discussions were held with the Jordanian government, after which the Japanese priorities became: the improvement of basic necessities of life, such as water, food, health and education; the promotion of industry, through tourism and transit trade infrastructure, and human resource development; and environmental protection.   To this end, a three-year policy advisory co-operation agreement was signed in September 1996. The agreement was based on the need for a close relationship of trust between the people and the government, with the latter sharing information with the population. The objectives of the programme were: the creation of a vision on industrial development and a formulation of coherent policies; the improvement of communication between the public and private sectors; the strengthening of long-term financing facilities for industry; and the strengthening of the management capabilities of the private sector.[627]

Unlike other members of the donor community, the Japanese have not stressed the need to adopt Washington consensus-style economic liberalisation. They do not want to amputate companies from the body of the public sector and attach them to the private sector. JICA argues that the way forward is to help the formation of a small, vibrant independent private sector. Thereafter, parts of the public sector would automatically move over to the private sector. JICA's future role, therefore, will be to assess which sectors of the economy to develop. However, the Japanese are not optimistic about the private sector's will or ability to grow independently of the public sector. Consequently, current projects are aimed at attempting to vitalise the private sector.[628]

One such project, the Jordanian-Japan Industrial Co-operation Programme, funded by the Japanese, is run under the auspices of the Higher Council for Science and Technology. The programme has four objectives: creating a vision for industrial development in Jordan; improving access to long-term finance; enhancing communications between the private and public sectors; and improving the managerial capacity of the private sector.[629]

Others

German aid[630] has been "based on a country concept developed by the Federal Ministry for Economic Co-operation and Development."[631]   The country concept identifies structural deficits specific to the country, and aid is then used to overcome them.   Two agencies are used to dispense the assistance: Kreditanstalt für Wiederaufbau (KfW) and the GTZ.   As at 1998, the assistance was concentrated in the water and sewerage sector, the agricultural sector, social infrastructure, and the promotion of the private sector, with environmental projects gaining in importance.

Promotion of the private sector has largely been through assistance to SMEs via the IDB, although this type of funding has recently decreased because the funds by-pass the Jordanian government.[632]   Although not explicitly stated, the implicit assumption was that the Germans did not seek the reduction, offering an example of the state attempting to maintain control of access to rent.   By September 1998, a total of DM73m had been committed to the IDB in a series of loans. The seventh such loan, for DM20m, was used in sixty-four sub-loans to finance, up to a maximum of 30%, plant and equipment and raw material purchases by privately-owned SMEs for civilian needs. The ninth loan, of DM5m, was used to finance investments in environmental protection. This loan was part of a move to take into account environmental factors in assisting the private sector. Future plans for the private sector revolve around the idea of a Public-Private Partnership, but at present these are still on the drawing board.[633]

According to Dr Hasse, Team Leader, GTZ in Amman, over the last fifteen years the German Government has started to question the wisdom of funding aid through the recipient government. Although the majority of aid still follows this path the change in thinking has been brought about by three factors: the German perception that funding through the Ministry of Planning is not reaching the target audience; the ideological change, in that government was deemed to be trying and failing to do everything, i.e. aid was propping up a bad system; and the realisation for the need for partnership between the donor and the recipient—no longer a case of telling and doing by the donor but watching and listening.[634]

The KfW director in Jordan, Richard Avédikian, argues that KfW do not pressure Jordan to privatise or take certain courses of action. They are concerned, however, with trying to increase co-ordination within the donor community.[635] These two factors are often not mutually compatible as the main movers in the donor community are seeking to have government adopt certain courses of action.

The German bilateral assistance agreement follows a laid-out path. First, the Germans advise the level of funding, and then the Jordanians submit a three to four page document of ideas for funding. The Germans pick the ideas most in line with their country programme. The ideas are then discussed over two meetings, before the Germans undertake a feasibility study of the projects.[636]

British aid is dispensed through the Department for International Development, (previously the Overseas Development Administration). For the first half of the 1990s, the British priority was on education, water and telecommunications.[637] By the end of the decade, the focus had switched to economic reform/privatisation, education and poverty-reduction. The majority of the funding is on a government-to-government basis but a small amount is channelled directly to local NGOs, via a Small Grants Scheme: in the period 1990 to 1998, the UK provided £1.08m to one hundred and fifty-two different projects.[638] Among the projects, in which the UK was involved at the end of the period was a Capital Markets Development Project aimed at transforming the Amman Financial Market into three new organisations: the Jordan Securities Commission; the Jordan Securities Exchange; and the Securities Deposit Centre. Future involvement was planned to include providing technical assistance to the Executive Privatisation Unit and the Sales Tax Reform Project. Department for International Development had previously been heavily involved with the restructuring and privatisation of Jordan Telecommunications Company (JTC).[639]

At one of the occasional donor community meetings, the Third Consultative Group Meeting in July 1996, the importance of different sectors in the Jordanian economy to the different donors was highlighted. The German representative, after commending Jordan's ambitious adjustment programme, emphasised his country's support for the water sector, the environment, and for public sector decentralisation via local representation and privatisation. In addition, he stressed the need for a better social safety net, in which NGOs would play a greater role, greater participation in civil society and improved human rights.[640] The Germans promised that "Jordan would continue to stand in the top ranks of recipients in per capita terms, based on its commitment to economic and social development and peace in the region."[641] At the same meeting, the Japanese representative expressed support for Jordan's role in the peace process and for its structural adjustment efforts. He urged Jordan to follow the "export or death" model followed by post-war Japan. The required policies included linking import liberalisation to the needs of exporters, promoting exports and tourism, and forging closer government-business co-operation. He stressed his support for the IMF and World Bank programmes but stated that Japanese support would "reflect the views of Japan's Government and taxpayers."[642]

The Swiss were keen to stress the need to ratify the Jordan-EU Business partnership, which would help Jordan's exports immediately. The UK representative was concerned with the balance of payment deficit, debt, and the build-up of reserves. UK assistance focused on economic reform and the social sectors, including privatisation, capacity-building in the social sectors and fiscal reform. Italy's representative stressed the importance of the EU agreement, as well as regional economic integration. The Italians were concerned also about the abolition of food subsidies, as was The Netherlands' representative. Canadian support was to focus on management of water, environment and private sector participation; social resources development; and facilitating the peace process, particularly in assisting refugees. In addition, a number of countries, such as Italy, Switzerland, France and the UK promised to assist with debt rescheduling.[643] The importance of Jordan to the US regional interests was emphasised by the latter's call "on donors to give Jordan unequivocal support." The representative supported the trade reform efforts, but called for greater intellectual and financial property protection for foreign investors.[644]

An important element in the meeting was the call by many of the donors for better co-ordination mechanisms, with the Chairman proposing not only that the donor group meet regularly, but that specific task forces be set up for the water sector and social safety net issues.[645] Despite the rhetoric, no serious attempts have been made to increase co-ordination. Indeed, since the increase in their levels of aid, the Americans have tended to move away from the idea of co-ordination.

MULTILATERAL DONORS

A number of concerns were raised during the Third Consultative Group Meeting in July 1996 by the multilateral organisations present. The Islamic Development Bank representative was concerned, among other things, with how the public investment programme would support private sector development, especially in potash and phosphates where no private investment existed. The Islamic Development Bank planned to commit US$150-200m over the next three years, with around 50% for mineral-based manufacturing activities at the Dead Sea Complex, 25% for agriculture, integrated rural development and infrastructure, 10% for human resources development and the remainder to finance exports to Islamic

Development Bank members and supporting the Social Development Fund. The Arab Monetary Fund joined other voices in calling for deeper reforms in the civil service and privatisation. EU assistance was directed to budget support, technical assistance and grant to UNRWA, in addition to the Association Agreement to develop the FTA between Jordan and the EU. The EIB[646] expected to become more involved in Jordan with the post-1996 Facility for Mediterranean Region Activities and identified a number of attractive propositions in the state's public investment programme, including water, electricity, tourism, transport and SME development. The Arab Fund for Economic and Social Development, after praising Jordan for having one of the best project implementation records in the region, as well as being one of the most effective partners, stated that efforts over the next two years would be concentrated on the water sector. The UNDP, after congratulating the government's efforts, promised to maintain support for the country's progress. However, the representative raised a number of concerns on the long-term sustainability of the recovery, given the pressures of the population on income distribution and employment. Furthermore, he argued that "growth does not automatically trickle down or lead to human development: policies to ensure this must be deliberate and be integrated into the public investment program." Future UNDP support would aim at improving revenue collection, strengthening the social safety net and improving environmental protection. The social safety net was believed to be deficient in important areas such as microfinance provision.[647]

The UNDP

The UNDP has been assisting Jordan to build its institutions and to enhance the competitiveness of both the government and private sectors. Private sector assistance was directed at helping Jordan to achieve competitiveness in manufacturing, and in industrial extension services to foster industrial growth, focusing mainly on smaller enterprises.[648] The focus on small enterprises is a deliberate policy, bearing in mind that in 1996 89% of the 18,592 industrial firms and 96% of the 35,935 trading firms employed no more than five workers.[649] In 1992, the Vocational Training Corporation initiated a programme offering industrial extension services.[650] The programme was supported by the UNDP (which provided technical assistance), the International Labour Organisation (which provided its global expertise in small business development) and the government (which provided in-kind assistance). The Corporation visited business premises and offered seminars and workshops, which tackled management and technical issues, with follow-up visits to ensure that the teachings were being applied correctly. The UNDP argues that the project initially did not meet with much enthusiasm, as this sector was not used to working with the public sector. Indeed, arguably the small businessman associates the public sector with tax collection and unnecessary bureaucracy. However, nearly five years into the project, "the psychological barrier between small enterprises and the Vocational Training Corporation has begun to crumble."[651] The news release points out that no longer do the Vocational Training Corporation officers have to knock on doors, but that small businesses are actively seeking its assistance.

Further UNDP support was aimed at building the state's capacity to integrate into the global economy, especially in investment and trade. To this end, the UNDP assisted the government in the WTO negotiations, through a US$300,000 technical assistance programme. This funding helped develop technical and mediation skills for the negotiations phase and prepared the grounds for the trans-national period, leading up to the final integration process into the WTO.[652]

The fourth country programme (1988-1992) saw the UNDP concentrate on four major areas, namely: human resources development; support to the productive sectors; macro-economic management; and science and technology.[653]

In the fifth country programme (1992-1996) the major areas were identical, except that 'science and technology' was replaced by 'Natural resources management'.[654] The programme, which was designed following 'dialogue'[655] between the UNDP, the government and other organisations of the UN system, was:

> formulated to reflect the Government's views as to how best utilize UNDP's cooperation in support of the achievement of select national development objectives within the overall adjustment process and circumstances following the Persian Gulf crisis.[656]

In the fifth programme, the support to the productive sector focused on industrial development and trade promotion and agriculture. In the industrial sector support would aim to:

> assist the industrial sector to diversify and promote industrial production and exports, identify new investments and employment opportunities, increase and upgrade industrial productivity, and promote and encourage private sector initiatives, specifically those regarding medium- and small-sized enterprises.[657]

The emphasis on the private sector had not appeared in the fourth country programme, which commenced before the collapse of the economy and the subsequent adoption of the IMF and World Bank philosophy of development. Although the fifth programme had assumed a core contribution by the UNDP of US$7.091m, with a further US$3.0m from the state, the outturn was just over 50% of the core funding, while the government's share proved to be unrealistic. The result was the curtailment or cancellation of projects.[658]

Country Co-operation Frameworks replaced the UNDP country programmes in the late 1990s. The first such framework for Jordan covered the years 1998 to 2002, inclusive. The framework notes that the progress witnessed up to 1996 may not be sustainable in the medium- to long-term, for a number of reasons, including the fact that much of the recent growth (i.e. up to 1996) had occurred in areas highly protected against international competition. Once the WTO membership was agreed and the Euro-Mediterranean agreement signed with the EU, many structural changes would be needed which could cause severe dislocation.[659] The framework proposes that the UNDP interventions should aim "to strengthen the sustainability of Jordan's recent economic and social progress."[660] The areas of concentration were to be: governance, with special emphasis on capacity-building in the public sector; poverty reduction, with special emphasis on social integration; and protection of the environment, with special emphasis on conservation of natural resources.

Within the scope of capacity-building in the public sector the framework included a suggestion that given sufficient funding the UNDP programme could cover support for the government's privatisation efforts, thereby "ensuring that optimal benefits will accrue to the country and the Government from the divestiture of public assets."[661] The support was to include the expertise of the UN system to facilitate Jordan's integration into the global economy, especially concerning trade facilitation, intellectual property protection and WTO membership.[662] In 1999 assistance was forthcoming through UNDP's project 'Support for Jordan's Integration into the Global Economy', in which UNCTAD provided technical support for the private sector in preparing for membership of the WTO and the implementation of the EU-Med agreement.[663] Furthermore, assistance was to be provided to Jordan Investment Promotion Corporation in "articulating a long-term investment promotion strategy."[664]

The EU

The EU involvement in Jordan started on a bilateral basis on the 1st January 1979 with a series of financial protocols, each larger than its predecessor.[665] These bilateral protocols have now been replaced by MEDA,[666] which acts regionally. Jordan, therefore, has to compete with other regional countries and the PNA for access to the pot. However, the EU looks favourably on Jordan due to the political situation related to Iraq, refugees, Syria, Saudi Arabia, and the peace process, where the issuing of passports to Palestinians and the severing of control over the West Bank have gained Jordan credibility. Other factors which have positively influenced the EU perception of Jordan include the Kingdom's relatively open economic and political situation, the severe water problems and the lack of self-sufficiency in food.[667] EU funding has not been imposed with conditions, but does support the IMF SAPs, thus effectively creating indirect conditionality. Under MEDA, the EU has attempted to by-pass the Ministry of Planning and directly fund civil society.

EU-private sector interaction can be assessed at three levels: 1) MEDA: the regional level, where funding is for general priorities with the aim of increasing regional integration; 2) a long-term strategy paper for each country: the priorities for Jordan include SAP, water, the environment and support to the private sector; and an annual identification of needs.

As political integration has strengthened, the EU has become more deeply involved in Jordan, based on the perception that the country is integral to peace and stability in the region. However, as with other donors, the EU stands accused of pursuing its own interests at the expense of the recipient country. According to Dr Mohammed Smadi, Director-General of the ACI, the EU merely implements its plans without dialogue. He argues that the previous bilateral agreements were better than the new EU-Med partnership, citing the case of Tunisia where the implementation of the EU-Med partnership has resulted in 35% of industries being lost. Furthermore, the private sector in the countries that signed the agreement were initially offered ECU5.5bn, but this sum was later reduced to ECU4.6bn on a first-come first-served basis. Although Jordan was one of the first countries to sign, no funding has reached the private sector.[668] Ghalia Alul, Executive Co-ordinator, proposed a further critique of the EU-Mediterranean 'dialogue' forward YEA, arguing the example of Spain's refusal to accept the terms of the agreement on tomato imports from Jordan. Rather than sticking to the tenor of the agreement, the government allowed itself to be 'bribed' with promises of extra economic assistance.[669] The EU assistance has been subject to criticisms of in-fighting between the different nationalities, often resulting in slow and inefficient dispensing of the funds or technical assistance.[670]

Arab Agencies

The Iraqi invasion of Kuwait proved to be a watershed for the Arab development agencies, whether bilateral or multilateral. Jordan was already suffering from the loss of oil revenues when the stance by King Hussein over the Gulf crisis was interpreted by the major Arab donors as being pro-Iraqi. Consequently, funding from the Arab agencies virtually dried up in the early 1990s. For example, the Arab Monetary fund did not lend from 1990 to 1993, inclusive, while the OPEC Fund for International Development had a gap of five years from 1989. Based on the figures for Arab aid given by the CBJ, informal bilateral assistance (which bypasses the OECD figures) seems to have continued.

AID, THE STATE AND ECONOMIC LIBERALISATION

A lack of coherence between the objectives of each of the aid donors to Jordan is apparent at the bilateral level. These differences occur because of differing national interests and differing economic philosophies. The two main donors have both diluted the efforts to implement a policy of economic liberalisation. The national interest of the USA to impose a regional order in the Middle East (based on ending the Arab-Israeli dispute, whilst maintaining sanctions on Iraq throughout the 1990s and regime change and the 'war-on terror' after 11 September 2001), pitched Jordan into a key strategic position from the early 1990s. As a result, from the start of the Madrid conference the USA was able to convince the IMF and the World Bank to adopt the soft glove approach, contrary to their normal global approach. The USA encouragement of rent-seeking through increased aid (including debt write-offs) increased with the signing of the Jordan-Israel peace treaty. However, the Jordanian government has been unhappy with the level of assistance in comparison to the amounts received by Egypt and Israel following the Camp David agreement. The Japanese philosophy of development differed from the hegemonic Washington consensus. Based on their own experiences, they believe the state has a significant role to play and that the way forward was through new private sector growth rather than through privatisation of older companies. In addition, the Japanese desire for regional stability, based around the Hashemite regime, allowed Jordan to continue rent-seeking during the Second Gulf War, when other donors pulled out. The funding by Japan has allowed the state to procrastinate to a degree on adopting the policies of the Washington consensus.

Overall, the policies followed by the bilateral donors have reduced the pressure on the state as an institution to adopt policies of economic liberalisation, while allowing the rentier élite to continue to rent-seek. On the other hand, the multilateral agencies, including the UN family, have tended to emphasis the policies of the BWIs. Although the levels of rent provided by the EU are relatively small, the signing of the EU-Med agreement has increased the pressure on Jordan to adopt policies of economic liberalisation.

At the level of the pluralist state, the bilateral donors, in particular the USA and Japan, have embraced a policy aimed at creating a new vibrant private sector, to bypass the captured old guard. Policies adopted by the donors have included training, seminars, workshops, conferences and media campaigns to encourage an enterprise culture. Funding of new enterprises has been encouraged at the grassroots level by micro-finance, while larger companies have been encouraged through loans administered by the IDB. The emphasis by the donor community on support institutions, particularly in the field of advocacy for private sector organisations such as the Young Entrepreneurs Association, has allowed the divide between the private and public sector to become more defined, and helped to swing the balance of power in favour of the reformist-private sector camp. Although the aim is to create a market mentality, the policy of using aid maintains a degree of rentier mentality, with businesses and support organisations fighting for access to the aid rent. However, with the donor emphasis on sustainability, the funding is usually on a one-off basis, in order to focus long-term efforts on the market-based solution.

DONOR COMMUNITY HETEROGENEITY

Since 1989, three factors have dominated Jordan's economic relations with the outside world: the need for loans from the IMF and World Bank; the need to address the problem of debt; and the need for aid. The countries and institutions, which could fulfil these requirements, form what this study terms 'the donor community', whose price for providing assistance has been to extract promises for a change of economic direction by the Jordanian state. The pressure for change has not only emanated from the IMF SAP but also from international agreements to liberalise trade (including with the WTO, the Jordan-EU Med agreement, and the European Free Trade Association agreement), as well as numerous bilateral treaties including the FTA with the US. In a related move, the USA also pushed Jordan to adopt the global norms of the advanced industrialised countries by placing the Kingdom on the intellectual property rights 'watchlist'.[671] The eventual 'reward' for implementing legislation on intellectual property rights was the signing of an FTA between the two countries.[672]

The major players identified within the donor community are the IMF, the World Bank, USA and Japan, while included among the less influential players are the EU, Germany and the UN. For a brief time at the beginning of the 1990s the Arab bilateral and multilateral organisations were important, but following the outbreak of the Second Gulf War this group became virtually invisible. In terms of influence, the role of the IMF has been found to be pivotal in the donor community, setting the agenda for the relationship between the state and the donor community at the economic level. However, for its own political reasons, the USA persuaded the BWIs to adopt a soft glove approach to conditionality from around 1992. The result has been to slow down the move from a rentier mentality to a market mentality at the level of both the state as an institution and the pluralist state.

Initially in 1989, three of the four major players, the IMF, the World Bank and USA, adopted a strong version of the Washington consensus requiring a series of conditions to be met, in order to ensure future access to funding. The government was usually willing to meet the performance criteria of the IMF, such as reduced budget deficits, credit expansion, and debt reduction. Other aspects such as the reduction of customs duties, hitherto the main source of domestic revenue raising, and privatisation were being forced on the government.[673]

America's perception of the need to restore regional stability following the end of the Second Gulf War, through sanctions on Iraq and the renewed emphasis on the Arab-Israeli peace process, changed the political environment. The US increasingly saw Jordan as a key player in the new era, hence the stability of the regime was seen as vital. The initial SAP had created tension within Jordan, inducing rioting in Ma'an—an area associated with the regime's bedrock supporters. SAP II was negotiated with the need to maintain political stability, rather than economic change, in mind.[674] While individuals within the donor community are committed to the development policy of the Washington consensus, the overall policy from 1992 has been to maintain the stability of the regime, despite the lack of real growth in the economy.

Despite the attempts by the IMF to implement strict economic conditionality, the political and security situation in the Middle East has allowed Jordan not only to access aid beyond the level normally associated with a developing country with as high a GDP per capita, but also to be able to delay the restructuring policies. In May 1999, the author was told off the record by one of the bilateral donors, of the pressure exerted by the "heavyweights of the USA and the World Bank to continue funding in Jordan." This pressure has enabled the state as an institution to continue to seek access to and to retain control over rent. Simultaneously, USAID has maintained a degree of pressure on the state as an institution by adopting conditionality on its disbursements. In the FY2000 Congressional Presentation USAID argues that the disbursement of US$50m for FY1999:

> will require that significant progress toward WTO accession be made and further streamlining of trade and investment policies and procedures has been completed (e.g. reducing company registration time and licensing requirements).[675]

The donor community has never addressed to any major degree the problem of bypassing the state in terms of funding. Jordanian legislation requires that all foreign funding must either be passed through the Ministry of Planning or receive permission from it before the recipient organisation can receive the funds. Consequently, the majority of aid continues to be both received and dispensed by the state.

Incentives for rent-seeking have been provided by the lack of coherence within the donor community, particularly concerning which policies to adopt. The BWIs adopted a soft glove version of the Washington consensus between 1992 and 1999, (following further regional instability starting with the outbreak of the intifada in September 2000 a renewed soft approach has been in evidence) of the including the reduction in government expenditure, while the UN family, along with other donors, have stressed the importance of allocating extra government expenditure for social safety nets. As discussed earlier, the US has allowed Jordan considerable latitude because of its role in the Arab-Israeli peace process. In contrast, the Japanese have continually questioned the philosophy behind reducing the role of the state which, based on their experience, is considered vital for development. However, although donors may have their individual perception of what is best for Jordan within the context of the donor's national interest the overall tendency has been to support the IMF's attempts to change the economic direction. Even the UN family, which has as its emphasis human development rather than economic development, has accepted the IMF's conditionality.[676]

The state has been able to influence the coherence of the donor community by actively not seeking donor group meetings. The impression is that the state can improve its bargaining position through a policy of divide and conquer.[677] The lack of co-ordination is increased by the approaches of the individual members of the donor community. Japan, for example, has a different outlook on aid, with the emphasis on self-help and regional stability, along with a desire for state involvement in the process, and therefore has not been active in promoting co-ordination. The USAID approach has also veered away from seeking co-ordination since 1997 with the advent of increased amounts of aid.[678] Firas Gharaibeh, Senior Programme Assistant with the UNDP, argues that donor co-ordination is only possible if a well-defined area, such as water, is present, otherwise too many conflicting interests appear. He adds that as the Ministry of Planning is aware of the specific interests of each of the donor community it can target the donor directly for assistance.[679] Co-ordination also is difficult because of institutional problems. The BWIs are not represented locally, making day-to-day co-ordination difficult. Furthermore, different donors are involved in different sectors. For example, the World Bank is concerned at the macro-economic level with stabilisation and restructuring, while the UN family is more focused at the micro-level.

Finally, by playing on the fears of the international community, in particular the USA, concerning the domestic stability of Jordan, the state has been able to use the threat of the opposition within Jordan to the conditionality to increase rent-seeking, or at least ensure that the opportunities for rent-seeking are not as limited as the economic position would have justified. However, when necessary the IMF has been able to force the state to implement change that was potentially destabilising, as in the case of the bread price rises in August 1996. In that case the population was 'prepared' for these rises as a result of debate in the media and parliament, as was not the case prior to the riots in 1989.

The situation has changed with the death of King Hussein, which coincided with the worsening economic situation and the expiry of SAP II. The almost inevitable first reaction of his successor was to attempt to benefit from the plethora of promises of support by the international community in the days after the death. A tour of the Arab capitals to seek increased aid, followed by a world tour of the creditor nations, with the aim of gaining a 50% debt write-off, met with many promises, but with little in the way of actual success. This early failure seems to have convinced King Abdullah to change direction from his father's policy of regime stability based on rent-seeking to a policy of regime stability based on the Washington consensus version of economic development. This change of emphasis has been supported by the terms of SAP III, which are harsher than those associated with SAP II. The ability to rent-seek, via aid, has narrowed considerably for the state, although seemingly with the support of those at the very top of the regime, with the new king as a driving force behind the new approach. At the Davos Forum in January 2000, he spelled out his government's commitment to an enhanced private sector. The Dead Sea meeting in the following November, initiated by the King, produced a thirteen-page blueprint for socio-economic reform via economic modernisation, greater privatisation, legislative and bureaucratic reform, and a redefinition of educational objectives at the heart of the programme. The participants wanted the government to withdraw from the mining (previously a taboo area due to its 'strategic' nature) and transport sectors and to strengthen regulatory bodies governing the privatised companies. A twenty-member Economic Consultative Council (ECC), drawn from both the private and public sectors, was established to monitor progress of reforms. Unlike previous attempts to implement private-public decision-making bodies, the ECC has to date been extremely active and successful in not only producing but also implementing ideas.

This chapter has focused on the relationship between the donor community and the state, treating the state primarily as a single entity. The analysis has shown that the state has been able to use divisions within the donor community to continue its attempt at gaining access to rent. However, the constraints imposed by the international, regional and domestic environment (chapter 5) have reduced the state's scope for manoeuvre to gain access to aid. The next chapter, using three case studies, assesses how the state, both as an institution and as an area of pluralist contestation, has coped with the new environment in which the relationship between the donors and state has evolved.

7

State, Rentier Élite and Conditionality: 1989 to 2002

INTRODUCTION

In the previous chapter, the analysis highlighted the relationship between the state as an institution and the donor community, and how the differing interests within the donor community allowed the former to continue to seek rent despite the declining levels of aid. This chapter concentrates on the reaction of the state to the conditions sought by the donor community in general, and the IMF in particular. However, as argued in chapter two, the state cannot always be analysed as a monolithic entity. Thus the discussion now focuses on the rentier élite as the driving force of economic and political decision-making, although constrained by the changes in the international, regional and domestic environment (chapter 5), along with the changing patterns of rentierism (chapter 5) and the increased ability of the donor community to intervene in the economy (chapter 6). This élite came to prominence in Jordan in the early 1970s, but the recession in the late 1980s saw cracks beginning to appear within the group (chapter 4). This chapter has three objectives: to assess the degree to which the state as an institution was able to resist or comply with the conditionality of the SAPs; to assess to what extent the rentier élite was able to balance the possible conflicting outcomes, on its economic and political bases, of implementing the conditions sought by the IMF; and to assess the effects of the changes on the homogeneity of the rentier élite.

The analysis uses three case studies to answer these questions: the implementation of the process of privatisation; the implementation of a VAT system; and the withdrawal of subsidies. Each case was highlighted as an area for immediate action in 1989, but over a decade and a half later, privatisation remains incomplete. A full VAT system has still not been introduced, and subsidies continue to be a drain on the government's limited resources.

Privatisation reduces the ability of the state to buy political support as the scope for using the companies to reward supporters through directorships, contracts, etc is narrowed. On the other hand, if the rentier élite choose, they can actually increase their economic base through the acquisition of the privatised companies. Thus the opportunity cost is the loss of a traditional form of political power in return for increased economic power. This is not to say that the political power cannot be enhanced by new methods. The example of the sales tax/VAT illustrates how the rentier élite reacted to a condition that could threaten both its economic and political bases. The imposition of a sales tax would increase prices, affecting levels of sales and therefore profitability, at a time when the private sector was under pressure from the opening of the economy to high-quality, low cost goods. The threat of higher prices was also politically sensitive as the riots in 1989 proved. Finally, as with privatisation, the withdrawal of subsidies was potentially a double-edged sword. The continued drain of subsidies threatened the economic recovery of the economy but at the same time withdrawal removed another pillar of the political advantage of expenditure policy. Furthermore, a number of subsidies, such as assistance for exporters and agriculture and fuel, had a direct bearing on the economic base of the rentier élite. It must be noted that in each case the effects would not be evenly distributed throughout the rentier élite, and implementation would also offer new opportunities.

PRIVATISATION

The process of privatisation has been a hard fought battle, ranging from periods in which the process seemed to be completely bogged down to periods in which considerable progress was made. The discussion is broken into four periods, namely: 1985-1989; 1989-1995/96; 1995/96-1998; and 1998-2002.

1985 TO 1989: THE RHETORIC YEARS

The growing emphasis on economic liberalisation and economic conditionality by both the donor and the commercial lending communities resulted in Jordan adopting (at least rhetorically) a new economic direction nominally based on export promotion, privatisation and the encouragement of investment. The new policy began in April 1985. As mentioned previously, the need to borrow US$63m from the IMF in 1985, as well as from commercial sources, meant the country had to be seen to adopt a reformist approach to its economic policies, including privatisation. Significantly, therefore, the move towards privatisation was not initiated by private sector pressure, but was a response by the state as an institution to enable it to continue accessing rent from the donor community, albeit that borrowing was now on a commercial basis.

As discussed in chapter four, on the 26th August 1986, the Cabinet approved a five-point privatisation programme, which was intended to alter private-public sector relations in favour of the former.[680] The programme sought to increase involvement of the private sector in public sector companies, through ownership and management. In addition, public sector companies were initially expected to operate on a commercial basis: a policy that has become termed 'commercialisation'.[681] Three companies were earmarked for privatisation: RJ, the PTC, and the TCC.

A paper on privatisation, along with the 1986 to 1990 Development Plan, was presented to the Jordan Development Conference, held between the 8th and the 10th November 1986. Significantly, the development plan made no mention of privatisation, indicating the late switch to this policy. Two areas of action were approved at the Conference. The first area was the promotion of an autonomous private sector investment through incentives, policies and the legal environment. The second was the trimming of the public sector through the sale of shares in mixed companies, transferring autonomous enterprises to the private sector, establishing private sector universities and leasing public land to the private sector.[682] Thus prior to the involvement of the IMF Jordan had moved nominally in the direction of privatisation. However, Abu Shair argues that at the time "there was no deep-seated commitment on the part of Jordan's decision-makers to follow the path of privatisation."[683] Dougherty and Wils agree that "in practice the realisation of the program was at best half-hearted."[684]

1989 TO 1995/96: THE LOST YEARS

Although the actual terms of SAP I have not been made public, the emphasis of the package was undoubtedly on the short-term stabilisation of the economy. Although the Finance Minister, Basil Jardaneh,[685] did reveal certain parts of the agreement no specific mention was made of privatisation but the longer-term aim would have almost certainly included the need to move ahead with the policy. In September 1989, Planning Minister Ziad Fariz reaffirmed the country's commitment to privatisation. Once again the three companies mentioned were PTC, TCC and RJ, but, under pressure from the BWIs, he included a new component—that of the sales of shareholdings in the tourist sector held by the JIC. According to Khalaf and Anani, prior to this no thought had been given to selling off government shareholdings in domestic corporations held by the JIC.[686]

Further moves towards privatisation were halted abruptly when Iraqi forces invaded Kuwait in August 1990. The war adversely affected RJ and the tourist sectors permitting a delay in their privatisation. Following the re-opening of relations with the IMF in late 1991, the Lower House, after considerable debate, passed an investment bill lifting certain restrictions on Arab and foreign investment. The bill was a result of IMF pressure to open Jordan's border to external investment in order to assist with the next stages in the privatisation process. However, by 1995 Jordan had done very little in the way of starting the process of transferring state assets to the private sector, with the notable exception of leasing the majority of the bus routes in Amman to the private sector in 1992 for a 15-year period. Indeed the JIC continued to invest in new companies, through minority shareholdings. For example, in 1994 the JIC had been instrumental in establishing new companies for the production of glucose, glass containers and polypropylene bags.[687] In 1996 two new agricultural companies, the Agricultural Marketing and Processing Company and the Agricultural Materials Company, were established with a capital base of JD5m, of which the JIC invested 10%.[688] The major effort in this early period of the privatisation process was opening up the debate about the necessity for privatisation in the media and in parliament.[689]

In their assessment of the private sector report issued in August 1995 the World Bank argues that the reasons that privatisation was less advanced than originally expected were:

1) a lack of political consensus about the desirability of privatisation; 2) fragmented management of privatisation without a strong central direction; and 3) social concerns especially about potential labor redundancies[690] in the overstaffed public enterprise sector.[691]

To accelerate the process, the report recommended several policy and operational steps including:

1) clarifying and announcing its privatisation strategy and a concrete program; 2) improving the management of the program by establishing a small privatization office[692] in the Prime Minister's Office (or the Ministry of Finance) and giving it clear decision making authority, and by developing systematic procedures; 3) enacting an omnibus privatisation law rather than repealing and enacting individual laws; 4) providing adequate anti-monopoly safeguards in competitive sectors and a regulatory framework for non-competitive sectors; and 5) resolving labor redundancy issues early and quickly.[693]

The report also notes that while the privatisation of utilities would be slow because of the need to establish agencies to regulate prices and quality of service, divestment of shares in non-utility firms could be "accomplished at a faster pace."[694]   In addition, the report extends the concept of privatisation to accelerating the private sector provision of infrastructure services in order to make the provision of these services more efficient.[695]

1995/96 TO 1998: THE FOUNDATION YEARS

An increase in the rhetoric of, if not the commitment to, privatisation occurred with the appointment of the King's cousin, Sharif Zeid bin Shakir, as the new Prime Minister in January 1995. The prime minister's policy speech argued for a gradual approach to privatisation, which would "initially target investments in the tourism sector and manufacturing industries. The government will keep its investments in strategic industries."[696]   He added JEA to the three favourites for privatisation, although the JEA would remain in government hands as a commercially operated company. King Hussein had advocated this move in his address to parliament in the previous October.[697] Shakir also confirmed that, as a first step towards privatisation, each of the three other companies would be commercialised while remaining government-owned. In addition, prompted by the IMF, the National Resources Authority was to be transferred to a private oil company, again through a first stage of a commercialised government-owned shareholding company.

As well as privatising companies, the state as an institution began to accept the necessity to commercialise public sector entities. The Investment Promotion Corporation in its 1995 publication 'Business and Investment in Jordan, 1995' suggested thirteen entities which were deemed suitable (table 7.1).

A new era in the privatisation programme was entered following the Cabinet's authorisation in June 1996 for the creation of the Executive Privatisation Unit, within the Prime Ministry: a clear indication of the political importance of the programme. The following month, the state as an institution officially announced its main goals of privatisation, the most important of which were:

1) to raise enterprise efficiency and improve the competitiveness of the economy; 2) to increase private investment in the infrastructure; 3) to develop the domestic capital market, broad base ownership and mobilize long-term private savings; 4) to consolidate the public finance through the proceeds from privatization, so that the government can better address the social agenda and concentrate on its core activities; and 5) to attract foreign investment, technology and know-how.[698]

Table 7.1: Public Sector Entities with Potential for Commercialisation in 1995

Public Sector Entities	No. of Employees
Public Administration Institute	71
Vocational Training Institute	1095
Jordan Investment Corporation	75
Free Zone Corporation	446
Agricultural Marketing Corporation	136
Civilian Consumers Corporation	853
Royal Geographic Centre	270
National Resources Authority	521
Housing and Urban Development Corporation	320
Water Authority	5183
Port Authority	2667
Aqaba Railway Corporation	7[699]
Public Transport Corporation	575

Source: National Information System, "Privatisation in Jordan", *NIS website*, nic.gov.jo/economics/invest/330.html.

In March 1995, the JIC sold two million shares in Jordan Hotels and Tourism Company to Zara Investment Company, reducing its stake from 87.7% to 32.7%:[700] the first significant step in the divestment of shares by the JIC. Simultaneously, the JIC's 32.5% stake in the Amman Marriott Hotel was offered for sale by the 7th June. However, these shares were not sold at this time. JIC General Manager, Muhammed Batayneh, stated that the JIC would sell almost all its public shareholding companies over the next two years, with the exception of investments in strategic assets including potash, phosphates and cement, although the level of the stake in these sectors *could* be reduced.[701] In the event, in March 1996 JIC sold shares in three troubled companies, Jordan Company for Radio, TV and Cinema Production, Jordan Tourism and Spa Company, and Jordan Glass Industry Company.[702] In June the intention to sell the 33.7% share in Jordan Holiday Company was announced[703] with a subsequent sale in August.[704] In September, JIC failed to sell shares in Jordan Tobacco and Cigarettes Company, in Jordan Worsted Mills and in Jordan Paper and Cardboard Factories. These three holdings were placed for sale on two further occasions during 1997, without success. However, the remaining shares in Jordan Hotels and Tourism Company were sold to Zara Investment Company in early 1997. By the end of 1997, JIC had sold all its smaller shareholdings, where it held a less than 5% stake.[705] Other companies were also listed for sale in 1997, including

Jordan Tanning Company (June[706] and October)[707] and Jordan Himmeh Mineral Company (sold in June).[708]

In his Letter of Designation of June 1991 to Tahir al-Masri, the new Prime Minister, King Hussein had apparently cleared the way for the privatisation of RJ when he stated, "the Royal Jordanian Airline should be reinforced and transformed into a joint-stock company in which the government will have a share and Jordanian citizens and others will have another share."[709] Although a number of studies had been commissioned to investigate the privatisation of RJ,[710] and the Cabinet had endorsed "the principle of transforming this state corporation into a public company whose shares are fully owned by the government and [which] is run on a commercial basis as a first step to privatisation,"[711] the only positive action by the government had been to convert around US$49m of debt into equity, raising the capital base to around US$80m in mid-1994. A report issued in 1992 had recommended the raising of the capitalisation to US$100m. In 1994, a report by KMPG Peat Marwick recommended a capital injection of JD130m (US$185m) to improve the equity loan ratio from 13:87 to 40:60. In addition the report recommended axing the long haul routes and concentrating on profitable regional routes.[712] At the same time, the directors were announcing plans to expand routes to south and south east Asia. In 1997, after three years of little or no progress, the new Transport Minister, Bassem al-Saket, announced that the political will to privatise RJ existed, but a major problem was the company's debt burden, which at end of 1997 was US$846m— almost one-tenth of Jordan's entire GDP. A degree of restructuring had taken place within the company, including a series of internal rationalisations, the closure of the long-haul routes to Singapore and Canada and the sale of five ageing Tri-Stars and the leasing of four new Airbuses. In mid-1998 a five-phase plan drafted by the World Bank was adopted, the aim of which was substantive change by 1999, including the sale of a minority stake to a global strategic investor. The plan included the creation of a separate company to operate non-core businesses, which would then be sold off.

In the telecom sector, the government announced, in mid-1993, that its intention was to use public funds to double the number of lines from 300,000.[713] By the end of 1994, legislation had been passed to allow the private sector to invest in peripheral services such as radio pagers and cellular phones. In November, the Minister of Telecommunications and Post, in a statement short on specific details, announced a launch date of June 1995 for the plan for privatising the TCC. In August 1995, the Lower House had passed Communications Law no. 13 for 1995 allowing for the restructuring of the telecom sector, with the policy and regulatory functions being hived off. The new company, JTC was to be registered as a fully owned government company by January 1996. In September, the state announced its intention to sell a 26% stake in the TCC[714] by the end of 1997. By October, the level of the sell-off had increased to 40%.[715] Strategic partner bids were invited in November, and by March 1998 four companies remained in the running for the stake.

In 1995, a Specialised Tourism Transport Regulation was approved to allow the private sector to invest in tourism transport, although the rental prices of the buses continued to be dictated by the transport ministry. The regulations were followed by two private sector transport companies entering the market in the first half of 1995.[716] The following September, Transport Minister Nasser al-Laouzi announced plans for further privatisation of the Amman public bus transport network. The PTC, which then operated around 45% of the public transport operations in Amman, was to be reorganised, downsized and turned into a regulatory body. The plan called for the one hundred and seventy buses to be sold to between three and four private companies, which would take over the PTC routes. The PTC was eventually converted into the regulatory body in autumn 1997,[717] with contracts being signed with three local companies[718] on the 19th November 1998.

Also in the transportation sector, the government was attempting to grant a concession to operate and manage Aqaba Railway Company. The company had debts of JD50m and the cost of modernising the rolling stock was estimated to be JD15m.[719] In January 1996, four technical bids, three of which pre-qualified were received.[720] However, by September the process had been restarted, with consultants invited to submit offers.[721] By July 1998 eight companies had submitted offers to take over the management of the Aqaba Railway Company.[722]

The JEA was dissolved on the 1st September 1996 as a step towards privatisation. National Electric Power Company, the new company with paid-up capital of US$160m and assets of US$190m, remained a monopoly but was to be commercialised. No firm timetable for private sector involvement was set at this stage, although legislation had been passed to allow private sector involvement in the sector. The role of government was to be restricted to strategic decisions concerning the power sector. In an effort to attract private sector interest subsidies were to be phased out, with the consequent raising of the electricity prices. The first such move was announced in July 1996 with price increases of 12%.[723] In addition, the energy sector was to be opened up to the private sector through the building of private power plants following the passing of General Electricity Law no. 10 for 1996.

Although work had started to a limited degree on the privatisation policy, by 1998 no major companies had been privatised. However, JIC had implemented a programme of divestment for companies in which it held a minority stake. At this stage JIC was estimated to hold shares in companies that totalled 40% of the JD3200m capitalisation of the Amman Financial Market,[724] down from around 60% in 1995.[725] The outcome of the debate over privatisation was still unclear, with Prime Minister Majali arguing that privatisation "is neither a process of selling Government shareholdings or enterprises to the local or foreign private sectors, nor an opportunity for foreign capital to infiltrate into the Jordanian economy."[726] In an attempt to overcome domestic opposition to privatisation he added that:

> [t]he privatisation program in Jordan is based upon a redefinition of the roles of the Government and the private sector with the primary responsibility being assigned to the Government for supervision, follow-up and regulation, and to the private sector for investments, trading, export and import, and acquisitions.[727]

However, a few months later, the Economic and Finance Committee of the Lower House of Parliament called for a curb on privatisation.[728]

Nevertheless, in a series of incremental moves, progress was apparent in the legislative field from 1994 onwards. Laws were promulgated on Sales Tax (1994), Income Tax (1995), Investment Promotion (1995 plus subsequent amendments), Telecommunications (1995), Electricity (1996), Labour (1996), Companies (1997),

Securities (1997), the JIC (1997), and Customs Duties (1997 and 1998).[729] A major step was the promulgation of legislation at the end of 1995 that provided for equality of treatment between non-Jordanian and Jordanian investors. By the end of 1997 the 49% ceiling on foreign investment remained only in the construction, retail trading and mining sectors. In addition, the Cabinet had approved the sale of the CBJ holding of 750,000 shares in the Housing Bank, the specialised credit institution, which was being transformed into a commercial bank.[730] Also in response to the World Bank's suggestion, an institutional framework, had been created with the establishment of a higher ministerial committee led by the Prime Minister to implement and supervise privatisation policy. In a move that highlighted the new importance placed on this policy, a technical unit on privatisation was established in the Prime Ministry in 1996. The formation of this institution kick-started the next phase of the privatisation policy by creating, for the first time, the semblance of a centralised co-ordinated approach to the whole issue of privatisation. Previously, individual ministries had been responsible on an *ad hoc* basis for the process. In mid-1997, under pressure from parliament and the media over the issue of privatisation, the state announced its intention to establish a fund with the revenues from privatisation. Debate over the use to which these funds would be put continued over the next few years.

1998 TO 2002: THE ACTION YEARS

Following the death of King Hussein in early 1999, SAP III was quickly concluded with the IMF to replace the previous agreement, which had been allowed to fizzle out. Because of the prevarications of the state concerning previous conditions, the IMF placed stricter conditionality on the new loan. Indeed the agreement could have been seen as a last chance for the Jordanians to retain the support of the donor community. Among the conditions was the requirement to develop a clear strategy for privatisation, including a plan for JTC by the end of June with the aim of effecting a sale by the end of the year. The privatisation of RJ and National Electric Power Company was also highlighted. The state, in its Letter of Intent of the 28th August 1999 stated that privatisation would be extended to new areas, including the postal service and the storage facilities of the former Ministry of Supply.[731] In addition, the state was preparing a privatisation bill to provide "a framework for the treatment of privatisation … ensuring privatisation proceeds are not transmitted into unsustainable increases in government expenditure."[732] At a national seminar on the Five-Year Economic and Social Development Plan (1999-2003) organised by the Ministry of Planning on 17th and 18th June 1999 the government admitted that "progress [on privatisation] has been very slow."[733]

Although the new King is often credited with kick-starting the privatisation process, a major step had already been taken in October 1998 with the sale of a 33% stake in JCFC[734] to the Lafarge Cement Group of France for US$102m.[735] The sale was concluded despite the continuing recession and the faltering of SAP II. In February 2002 the remaining shares were transferred from JIC to SSC at a cost of US$41.3m.[736] As with JTC, the Chairman of the JCFC, Hamdi Taba'a, had been opposed to the idea of introducing a foreign strategic partner, seeking instead local investment.[737] Although these initial steps had been taken, King Abdullah's appointment undoubtedly gave the privatisation process a considerable boost. In his letter of appointment to his first prime minister in March 1999, he stressed that "[p]rivatisation needs to be further institutionalised."[738]

The institutional nature of the privatisation process was upgraded in July 2000 with the endorsement of the Privatisation Law (no. 25 of 2000). The law upgraded the Higher Ministerial Committee to the Privatisation Council and the Executive Privatisation Unit into the Executive Privatisation Commission. The law also established the Privatisation Proceeds Fund (see later).

The death of King Hussein, who many argue had viewed RJ as an important marketing tool for Jordan rather than as a profit-making company, paved the way for the privatisation of the airline. Indeed, in his letter of appointment in 1996 to the new Prime Minister Kabariti, the King had indicated a lack of willingness to privatise the company when he stated that:

> [t]he Royal Jordanian Airlines has undertaken an important role in bearing the bright image of Jordan to the world. It is one of the state institutions of which we are proud. Its merit from us every care and attention, so that it may overcome its difficulties and fulfil its function with the efficacy that we desire.[739]

By October 1999, a legal, financial and technical restructuring[740] of the company had been completed and expressions of interest for the purchase of a strategic 49% stake were being sought. The significant problem of debt had been overcome with a financial restructuring which reduced the airline's debt to an estimated US$150m from an estimated US$1bn.[741] A new law (no. 31 of 2000) was enacted that transformed RJ into a shareholding company wholly-owned by the government. In February 2001, RJ was then registered as a public shareholding company totally owned by the government, as a prelude to finding a strategic investor. Throughout 2000, a number of subsidiaries were established with the aim of selling them as independent companies: these subsidiaries were initially owned by Royal Jordanian Investment Company Ltd. The first, Jordan Airports Duty Free Shops Company, was purchased by Aldeasa of Spain for US$60.1m.[742] 80% of the shares in the Aircraft Catering Centre were sold to Alpha British Company, with RJ retaining the remaining 20%.[743] The third subsidiary, the Royal Jordanian Air Academy, was approved for sale by cabinet on 17 December 2002 to Jordan International Real Estates and Tourist Investment Company at a price of US$5.8m.[744] The other subsidiaries yet to be sold are the Engine Overhauling Centre and the Aircraft Maintenance Centre, each of which has been turned into an independent company. In addition RJ shares in Alia Hosting Company, Alia Hotel and Royal Tours have been transferred to RJ Investment Company.[745] However, the downturn in the aviation industry since the events of September 2001 severely hampered further progress towards privatisation.

Despite inviting bids in November 1997, the JTC privatisation remained in abeyance at the beginning of 1999, as the state seemed unable to make a decision on which strategic partner to select or on what terms the bids should be made. In addition, JTC's Director-General Ali Shukri, who had links with local telecom interests, was strongly opposed to bringing in a strategic foreign investor. His resignation in March 1999, citing intolerable government interference, paved the way for the sale of a 40% stake to a foreign strategic investor. Shukri's replacement was

Jamal Saraireh, who had links to international telecommunication companies. The first attempt to find an investor had failed in October 1998 after Southern Bell withdrew from the bidding leaving only Cable and Wireless in the process. The state, at the behest of the Shukri, had introduced two new conditions for the sale at the last minute. One of the conditions included revising the number of seats on the executive council to which each partner would be entitled, after the end of the period of JTC exclusivity. The second change was the sale of extra shares to the SSC, JTC employees and other local investors.[746] A new plan was unveiled at the beginning of August 1999 for an accelerated programme to sell a 40% stake within three months. Formal expressions of interest were to be lodged by the 21st August, financial offers by the 2nd October and a final decision concluded by the 15th October. Three bids were received by the due date: as two were identical at US$508m the process was delayed. However, on the 23rd January 2000, 40% of JTC was finally sold to a consortium of France Telecom (35.2%) and the local Arab Bank (4.8%). A further 8% was purchased by the local SSC, while 1% was set aside for a staff pension fund. To satisfy opponents of the process the government retained a majority on the board. In deference to the IMF, however, a seven-member 'operation committee', with five people from France Telecom and two from the government, was formed. In October 2002, in a first move of its type in Jordan, a further 10.5% stake was successfully sold by an Initial Public Offering, which attracted 10,000 domestic investors at a time of high regional uncertainty.[747]

At the behest of the IMF, the National Petroleum Company had been established in 1995 with a capital base of JD20m, owned principally by the JIC,[748] with the IDB holding shares to the value of JD10,000.[749] The National Petroleum Company took over the work of the National Resource Authority, including the 50-year prospecting concession in the 8,000 sq km Risheh area. The company was expected to operate as a fully independent company without government interference. However, according to Khadduri, the concession agreement "has given the firm a very narrow and limited mandate within which to operate, thereby impeding any momentum towards a proper take-off."[750] The Minister for Energy and Mineral Rights retained "full technical and financial control over the company's activities, as well as the right to inspect at any time all its records, correspondence and accounts."[751] In August 1999, the company's drilling activities were hived off to a new commercially-operated state-owned company, the Petra Drilling Company. The company was expected to be privatised within the following two years. Also in the field of energy, the Energy Minister announced towards the end of 1999 that "[i]n the next three or four years, the government has to contemplate adopting the principle of competition through the establishment of refineries for the purpose of exporting." However, he added that the interest of the country was a prerequisite in any changes.[752]

Negotiations for managing and operating Aqaba Railway Company started on the 21st November 1998[753] with a consortium led by the Raytheon Corporation and the Wisconsin Central Transportation Corporation of the USA and which also included the local Kawar Group, JPMC and Mitsubishi of Japan. The deal, which was finalised in August 1999, committed the consortium to upgrading the existing railway line, and to investing an estimated US$154m to extend the line at the Shidiyeh mine and at the industrial jetty at Aqaba. 250 of the workers deemed surplus to requirements[754] were found jobs at the JPMC; the rest were absorbed in other government posts or retired,[755] in recognition of the objections of parliament. When it debated the law for privatising the company in December 1998 fifty-seven out of the eighty deputies opposed the law.[756]

At the beginning of 1999 National Electric Power Company was separated into three firms: one for generation, the Central Electricity Generating Company; one for distribution, the Electricity Distribution Company; and one "to own and manage the transmission network and control centers"[757] (a scaled down National Electric Power Company). The new firms for generation and distribution were set for privatisation but transmission, control, buying and selling of power were to be commercialised but remain wholly-owned by the state.[758] Under Jordanian law these companies cannot be privatised until they have produced two annual reports. In addition, the Electricity Law no. 13 for 1999 allows for the establishment of a regulatory body.[759] In September 2000, the Energy and Resources Ministry announced its intentions to privatise both Electricity Distributing Company and Central Electricity Generating Company, and that the state would divest its 70% holding[760] in Irbid Electricity Company.[761] However, the Temporary Electricity Law (no. 64 of 2002), which was endorsed in October 2002, altered the parameters to 100% sale of Electricity Distributing Company, 60% of Central Electricity Generating Company and 55.4% of Irbid Electricity Company.[762] A further indication of the move towards the private sector was the opening of negotiations to construct a 300mw-450mw power plant on a build-operate-own basis. However, the negotiations have progressed at a snail's pace since the announcement in 1998 with the state continually changing its mind on the nature of the arrangement.

The first contract for private operation of wastewater treatment plant was awarded in April 1997.[763] Thereafter, the ministers responsible for water and irrigation maintained pressure to increase private sector involvement in the water sector. The Minister, Dr Mundhir Haddadin, stated in May that if the Water Authority of Jordan was in the private sector it would be bankrupt. In September of the following year the Secretary-General of the Water and Irrigation Ministry, Qusau Qutayshat, called on the private sector to become involved in equipment maintenance, designing, constructing and supervising projects and managing wastewater projects. In addition he specified three projects for private sector involvement, namely: managing Amman's water supply; wastewater treatment projects for the Amman-Zarqa basin under build-operate-transfer arrangements; pumping Disi water to Amman via a build-operate-transfer scheme.

With seemingly little public debate or political opposition, on the 19th April 1999 the operation and management of all water-related services with the Amman region (these represent about 40-50% of the total Water Authority of Jordan operations)[764] was awarded to a French company, Suez Lyonnaise des Eaux, in association with Jordan's Arabtech Jardeneh.[765] During 2000, further moves to involve the private sector included the construction and management through a twenty-five year build-operate-transfer scheme for wastewater facilities at al-Samra, as well as the operation and maintenance of the West Zarka pumping station, the Hashamiya pumping station and the main wastewater pipeline to al-Samra from Ain Ghazal.[766] In September, the Water Authority of Jordan also sought to widen involvement for the management of water and wastewater facilities in the governates of Irbid, Jerash, Ajloun and Mafraq.[767]

A lull in new initiatives occurred in the latter part of Abdul-Ra'uf S. Rawabdeh's premiership. However, the installation of Ali Abul Ragheb in June 2000 as prime minister gave fresh impetus to the process. Moves to privatise the postal sector were reintroduced, having first been raised in July 1998, and approved by Cabinet in January 2000, along with new proposals for the storage facilities of the former Ministry of Supply[768] (first approved the 21st November 1998),[769] the media and the Civil Aviation Authority (including Queen Alia airport, Marka Airport and Aqaba Airport), and Royal Jordanian Aviation Academy. A new postal services law (no. 5 of 2002) was issued on 17 February 2002 transforming the company into a public shareholding company, Jordan Post Company" totally owned by the government with a view to full privatisation in 2004. In addition, a regulatory commission, under the umbrella Telecommunications regulatory commission was created.[770] Progress towards the sale of the storage facilities occurred with the formation of Jordan Silos and Supply General Company in January 2001 as a fully government owned public shareholding company, with the aim of full privatisation in 2004.[771]

A significant change in the culture of the privatisation process occurred at the beginning of 2001, with announcement of the latest candidates for possible privatisation, which included JPMC, APC[772] and Aqaba Port.[773] Previously, the JPMC and APC were considered as strategic assets, which would not be privatised. This move more than other in the privatisation process indicates a shift in power to the reformist camp within the rentier élite. Other candidates which are in the process of being privatised include Customs Department Warehouses and Department of Vehicle Inspection. Furthermore a number of infrastructural projects, including the Amman-Zarqa light railway, the Disi-Amman water conveyor, the Egypt-Jordan gas pipeline, the private power station, which are set to involve the private sector to a greater or lesser degree, have been discussed for a number of years now; however problems of profitability and a lack of decisiveness on the best way forward have haunted implementation of the projects.

JIC continued to divest government shareholdings in mixed investment companies. By the end of 2002 the government's shares in 49 companies, had been sold for a return of around US$151m; of which: 20 were companies with less than 5% government ownership; 12 were companies with 5-10% government ownership; and 17 were companies with more than 10% government ownership.[774] The most significant sale was that of US$30.3m worth of Housing Bank stock, but the semi-autonomous SSC purchased these shares. A number of the JIC's divestments have been of this nature, which has resulted in the shares in SSC's assets increasing by 38% from JD148.4m (12.5% of total assets) in 1998 to JD270.4m (18.6% of total assets) in 1999. However, as the al-Arab al-Yawm columnist Khalid Zubeidi comments: "selling the shares to the SSC is like swimming against the tide and a way of skirting privatisation and its economic and investment indications."[775] In early 1999, the JIC also used a policy of leasing to increase private sector involvement in its activities. The management of the Ma'in Spa Hotel was leased[776] for a period of thirty years to the French company Accor, with Ali Ghandoor as the local partner.[777] The second arrangement was to lease Jordan Poultry Processing and Marketing Company to a local company with an option to buy at the end of the five-year period.[778]

A debate had been simmering since the start of the programme concerning the state's use of the proceeds raised through privatisation. For once, the IMF, along with the rest of the donor community and the street were in agreement that the proceeds should not be wasted on the recurrent spending in the budget. The donor community wanted the entire funds to be used to retire debt; by contrast, the street was looking for the money to be spent on offsetting the negative effects of privatisation, through schemes such as re-training of those made unemployed and improving the welfare infrastructure of the state. The final law balanced the competing pressures by allowing for "up to 15% of the proceeds [of privatisations] for high quality spending on infrastructure and social sectors," taking into account future recurrent costs. The remainder would be invested in financial assets or used to retire public debt.[779] By the end of 2002, privatisation proceeds spent amounted to JD309m (50.1% of the proceeds of JD615.4m[780]), of which JD111.8m was used to buy back debt, JD63.6m to repay RJ debts, and the rest on infrastructure development[781] (with exception of JD2.3m which went to Merill Lynch for fees).[782]

This section has highlighted the changing nature of the state's response to the BWIs' insistence on the implementation of a programme of privatisation. The first moves occurred in 1986 (before the advent of IMF conditionality), with the need to borrow commercially on the international markets. However, at this stage the adoption of the policies was more rhetorical than real. In 1989 IMF conditionality was first imposed, but the outbreak of the Second Gulf War intervened before any change of state policy was evident. From this time, however, the donor community as a whole can be seen as 'educating' the rentier élite, parliament, the street and the opinion-formers in Jordan as to the benefits and necessity of privatisation. The education policy eventually paid off, with an increase in the acceptance from 1995 when a raft of legislation was passed that enabled the next stage of the privatisation to be undertaken. A further increase in the commitment could be seen in the late 1990s as the divestment of government shareholdings was initiated. However, a major boost was received for the IMF policies following the death of King Hussein and the failure of King Abdullah's world tour to increase the levels of aid.

STATE, RENTIER ÉLITE AND PRIVATISATION

Although the analysis has highlighted an increasing commitment to privatisation, the state still continues to prevaricate on a wholehearted pledge to the process (to an extent the unstable regional situation has given a valid excuse since the outbreak of the *intifada* in September 2000). RJ, for example, has been mooted for privatisation since 1986 but, at the time of writing, although parts of the company have been hived-off and some sold, a strategic partner had yet to be found. Opposition can still be raised concerning the highly sensitive issues of the threat of job losses in the newly privatised companies (at a time when unemployment is unofficially estimated at over 25%) and the question of security.[783] Despite the existence of a peace treaty between Israel and Jordan, the lack of progress over the Palestinian track and the continued Israeli aggression worries many Jordanians. Local sentiment fears that uncontrolled opening of the economy to foreign investment could lead to a legitimate Israeli take-over of vital assets, such as the phosphate industry. Nevertheless, the pressure on the state by the donor community to adopt privatisation by promising continued, albeit lesser, volumes of aid—indeed aid is often granted specifically to help with various aspects of privatisation—has been successful to a degree. The state has used a number of defensive policies that can be interpreted by the donor community as assisting with the process of privatisation, although in reality the policies may merely be a form of procrastination. For example, the plethora of legislation promulgated in the mid-1990s, which although in place, may not necessarily be acted upon. Secondly, the commercialisation of SOEs as a prelude to later disposal of shares to the private sector can again be seen as playing for time. In addition, commercialisation allows political advantages of the two-dimensional state policy to be retained. Thirdly, a further method of prevarication has been changing the terms of the sale whilst the process was actually underway—leading to potential investors pulling out. Fourthly, there has been a failure to develop the necessary institutional infrastructure to support the process.[784] Finally, the transfer of assets from the JIC to the SSC is merely swapping ownership from one semi-autonomous government agency to another.

Five types of actual privatisation have been used to date: part sales to strategic foreign investors (JCFC and JTC); sales of minority shareholdings held by JIC to local investors; leasing of operations to consortiums of local and foreign companies (Aqaba Railway Company and Water Authority of Jordan); leasing of operations to local businesses (PTC); and an initial placement offer (JTC). The sales of shares in companies in which JIC held a minority holding were relatively easy to achieve: thus the disposals from 1995. The sale of minority holdings could allow the rentier élite to increase their economic base, while not threatening their political base. The rentier élite have potentially been able to cherry-pick the more attractive holdings, while allowing shares in the more troubled companies, such as Jordan Tobacco and Cigarettes Company, to be retained in the state's possession by transferring them to the SSC. As discussed earlier, the part sale of JTC to a strategic investor was not without difficulty, but it did highlight the lack of unanimity within the rentier élite over the direction of privatisation. However, the state attempted to offset the potential loss of the political advantages caused by the privatisation by retaining a majority of directors on the board. Opposition to the leasing part of privatisation has been muted, despite the potential for loss of employment and the threats to security, perhaps because the rentier élite have been in a position to benefit economically, while not being disadvantaged politically. The first transfer of the PTC's bus-routes was able to take place as early as 1992.

Overall, the state has, by various methods, been able to subvert the process of privatisation, thus retaining much of its ability to use these economic assets for political gain. The rentier élite has been in the position to be able to improve its economic base through the sales of the JIC shareholdings and the leasing arrangements, without losing its political base. However, the process (including that of 'education') has highlighted potential differences within the rentier élite which may be used in the future by the donor community to further its own objectives.

THE SALES TAX

One of the conditions of the first SAP was that the government should introduce a VAT system by 1991. As a first step towards compliance, a consumption tax on a range of imported and locally-produced items was introduced in the 1990 budget. Thereafter, a GST was to be introduced before VAT was fully implemented. After only one year, the IMF was already expressing dissatisfaction with the government's commitment to introducing VAT.[785] The hiatus caused by the Gulf War saw little progress being achieved in the immediate aftermath. Thus, by June 1992, in the Kingdom's Letter of Intent, the government promised to implement a GST by January 1993.[786] Although, the draft law was prepared by November 1992, the government failed to implement the tax as promised. After considerable debate, a watered-down version of the General Sales Tax Law was eventually enacted on the 1st June 1994. The IMF had initially sought a rate of 12% and the government 10% but parliament diluted the rate further, to only 7%. On luxury goods the government had sought 25%, but this rate was reduced to 20%. In addition, a number of exemptions from the tax were granted. Finally, parliament decreed that the government could not commit itself to implementing VAT for five, rather than three years, and also that the change would have to be discussed in parliament first.

The IMF had agreed tacitly to delay the introduction of GST until after the November 1993 elections because of the unpopularity of the tax both on the street and in parliament. However, the major reason for delay was the considerable pressure applied by the private sector, which argued that the economy was not prepared for the tax. Partly in an effort to gain support from the private sector, a joint private-public sector committee was established at the beginning of 1994 to study GST. As a result, certain sections of the private sector were able to gain significant levels of exemptions. Indeed, local economist Dr Fadel Fanek argues that private sector importers and professionals (i.e. those with access to the rent circuit) were able to benefit at the expense of local industry and government revenue.[787] In addition, the private sector had also been able to delay the extension of the tax to the service sector from six to thirty-six months. The private sector was also able to influence the bill through parliament. As Ali Abul Ragheb,[788] Chairman of the Financial Committee of the Lower House (and later Prime Minister), commented (concerning the changes to the bill) that the committee had met with many economic figures "particularly those associated with the Amman Chamber of Industry, the Amman Chamber of Commerce and various professional associations."[789]

Following the promulgation of the law, a committee was established to close the loopholes. The committee comprised the Director-General of the Customs Department, the head of the FJCC, the Chairman of the ACI and the Secretary-General of the Ministry of Industry and Trade. However, rather than expand the base of the tax, pharmaceuticals were also given exemption within two months.[790]

A recurring feature of the state's policy since 1989, particularly in the economic field, has been to allow parliament to water down various proposals, only for the policy to be fully implemented at a later date: often with little protest in parliament or on the street despite the strength of the initial opposition. Thus, sixteen months after sales tax was first introduced the rate was raised from 7% to 10%, albeit at the insistence of the IMF. However, as a *quid pro quo*, the number of goods exempted was raised from fifty-five to seventy-eight.

The conditions attached to SAP III, which was agreed in April 1999, included the agreement to replace GST with VAT. The Memorandum on Economic and Financial Policies, dated the 4th July 2000, acknowledged that the legislation modifying GST to convert it into VAT had not be submitted to parliament before the end of March 2000, as promised. The government blamed the necessity on passing the WTO-related amendments for the failure to process the legislation. A VAT system was eventually implemented at the beginning of 2001, the sales tax rate having been increased from 10% to 13% in mid-1999, with the number of exemptions also being reduced.

STATE, RENTIER ÉLITE AND THE SALES TAX

The case study of the sales tax illustrates the ability of the rentier élite to be able to use the threat of instability to stave-off its implementation, as well as reduce the level (at least temporarily). The imposition of a sales tax was another case of a double-edged sword. The declining levels of rent required new sources of revenue if the state was to be able to maintain any semblance of an expenditure policy. Importantly, the choice of sales tax as the new vehicle for the state to raise its revenue can be seen as part of the continuance of élite control of the decision-making process—an indirect tax, such as the sales tax falls proportionally more heavily on the poor than a progressive direct tax such as income tax élite, which hits the rich harder. Thus revenues were required to be raised to ensure the continuance of the political base of the rentier élite, but the necessary price rises provoked the spectre of renewed social dislocation, as happened in April 1989. However, the tax also directly threatened the economic base of the rentier élite, through reduced sales and therefore reduced profits. These threats help explain the long battle against the implementation and the level of the tax raised. On the question of homogeneity of the rentier élite, certain sectors, the importers and the service industry professionals in particular, were able to benefit by gaining exemptions from the tax, at a direct cost to other parts of the economy.

SUBSIDIES

The question of food subsidies has been even more politicised than that of the imposition of the sales tax. On two occasions, in 1989 and 1996, riots have broken out over the withdrawal of subsidies. Worryingly for the regime, on both occasions the disturbances emanated from amongst what are considered to be the traditional supporters of the Hashemites.

Prior to the involvement of the IMF, the Ministry of Supply set the prices for basic staples, including wheat, bread, sugar, rice, milk, beef, lamb and poultry. By maintaining the price below the market level, the state was forced to meet the shortfall. Before the collapse of the dinar, the cost was approximately JD4m pa.[791] However, with the onset of the recession, the budget for 1989 had initially allocated JD33m for this purpose,[792] but by March the estimates had already grown to JD60m.[793] Despite the growth in the cost, the state reiterated its commitment to subsidies on basic goods as well as continuing "to support the military and civil consumer corporations, which serve about 350,000 employees, military, retired and their families."[794] The eventual cost for 1989 was JD72m[795] and by 1990 subsidies on food reached JD102m (3.9% of GDP).[796] Before the IMF would allow SAP I to be confirmed, the government was forced in April 1989 to implement a series of price increases, including fuel prices, telephone charges, oats and barley. The outbreak of violence in reaction to these increases in non-food items created extra space for the government in later discussions with the IMF, because of the fear within the donor community of political instability.

The IMF was, nevertheless, determined to cut the food subsidy bill through the targeting of the subsidies to those most in need, thereby reducing some of the political concerns of addressing the problem. In March 1990, the IMF was reported to have cut short its annual review because, among other reasons, it felt the government was not serious about addressing the problem of food subsidies,[797] which were expected to cost JD90m in 1990.[798] The refugee crisis of August 1990 helped focus the minds of the decision-makers, with the result that food-rationing coupons were introduced on the 1st September for sugar, rice and powdered milk. A year later, the scheme was extended to include flour.[799] The coupons were available to all families, thus creating a two-tier pricing system, which was expected to reduce the cost of the subsidies by around JD20-30m pa.[800] These changes met with a subdued reaction on the street, in the media and in parliament.

In January 1994, subsidies on sugar, rice, dried milk, frozen chicken and olive oil were restricted to families with an income of less than JD500m per month. Nevertheless, the failure to address the main subsidy, bread, resulted in the cost of the subsidies rising to JD100m in 1995,[801] with the Minister of Supply, Munir Subar, claiming that the cost would be JD150-160m for 1996.[802] The escalating cost was partly due to an increase in the world price of wheat. As a result, Subar announced in early July that bread prices would be increased from 85 fils per kilo to 250 fils per kilo. The proposed increases were condemned in the media, in parliament and on the street. However, the IMF maintained pressure by refusing to accept the Letter of Intent of the 13th June 1996, arguing that Jordan had already promised to deal with the question of subsidies in the Letter of Intent of the 31st December 1995. The regime, in the person of Crown Prince Hassan, was reported to have requested leeway from the IMF in implementing the price rises, but the IMF said that arrangements made with other donors could not be implemented until the subsidies were lifted.[803] Although attempts were made to debate the situation in parliament, the sitting was suspended on the 8th August without the issue being resolved. Eventually, the price was raised to 180 fils per kilo[804] on the thirteenth, with the result that riots broke out on the sixteenth in Karak[805] and spread to Amman the following day.[806]

The coupon system of subsidies on rice, sugar and milk was replaced on the 1st September 1997 by cash for those families with an income of less than JD500m per month. In January 1999, all general cash transfers on food had been replaced by targeted assistance to the needy families through the National Assistance Fund. This system met the requirements of the IMF by targeting welfare spending to the needy. In addition, the prices of fruits and vegetables, along with a number of other consumer commodities, were liberalised.[807] Nevertheless, the price of a number of other commodities, including the important ones of bread, oil derivatives (at the end of 2000, subsidies accounted for 20%-40% of the price),[808] and agricultural inputs such as fodder were still set by the state, which in effect creates a subsidy system for these products. In its letter of intent issued in April 2002, the government agreed to increase the prices of fuel oil, diesel, kerosene and LPG by a weighted average of 10% (a move that would not bring prices in line with market prices). In addition, the government also committed itself to raising the price of bread "gradually at the appropriate time" and to raise the prices of animal feed to market levels.[809] The administrative pricing structure for animal feed was dismantled immediately following the letter. One further indirect method of subsidisation is through the Civil and Military Stores, which supply cut price, if not subsidised, goods to government employees: these stores were opened to the general public in 1998.

STATE, RENTIER ÉLITE AND SUBSIDIES

The subsidies' case study demonstrates that as the levels of state rentierism fall the rentier élite had to adopt different policies in order to continue the legitimacy of their political rule. No longer were they able to buy wholesale political support; the support now required more careful targeting in order to husband the declining resources. However, broad-based subsidies could be continued through controlling the price of basic staples, such as bread, and via the Civil and Military Stores. The riots in 1989 and 1996 in the face of declining state rentierism enabled the rentier élite to gain support from the donor community, which did not wish to see the collapse of the Hashemite regime, fearing this reaction would cause further instability in a region already considered to be inherently unstable.

STATE, RENTIER ÉLITE AND CONDITIONALITY

The three case studies have highlighted the complexity of the relationship between the donor community, the state and the rentier élite. The relationship has not only been affected by the declining levels of aid rent, but also by the changing interests of the central actors. The priority of the economic conditionality of the IMF SAP has been diluted by the political interests of certain members of the donor community. The threat of political instability within Jordan and regionally has allowed the rentier élite greater latitude than would have been expected given the severity of the economic crisis and the structural problems facing the economy. However, over the period, the IMF has managed to exacerbate differences within the rentier élite created by the changing patterns of the rentier economy, thereby reducing the cohesiveness of the latter. This split within the rentier élite has allowed an increasing acceptance of the conditions sought by the donor community. However, a full-blown commitment is not yet possible due to the historic relationship between the rentier élite and society in general. In Jordan considerable opposition to the policies of economic restructuring still exists in parliament, on the street and within the media. The need to preserve the support of certain sectors of society in order to maintain political legitimacy continues to be a major factor in the behaviour of the rentier élite, and in particular the regime.

What, then, has been the relationship between the state, rent and economic liberalisation in relation to the BWIs? Between 1986 and 1989, prior to the involvement of the IMF, plans were made to initiate the process of economic liberalisation. Despite the rhetoric, very little progress was actually made. These 'window dressing' moves were driven by the desire of the state as an institution to continue to maintain access to and control of the rent in the form of loans and grants. The rentier élite at this stage was still relatively homogenous in its agreement on the economic direction, putting little pressure on the state to actually adopt wholesale economic liberalisation.

The three case studies indicate the pressures faced by the state in attempting to implement the change of the economic direction sought by the IMF. The slow and uneven move towards a democratic state following the 1989 riots has resulted in parliament and the media being able to question the state to a greater degree than previously. The state, in turn, has been able to use this opposition as a bargaining chip in the negotiations with the IMF. However, when the IMF has exerted pressure, as with the case of the bread prices in July and August 1996, the state has been able to force through the issue despite opposition in parliament, in the media and on the street.

Following the intervention of the IMF from 1989, a number of phases in the relationship between the state, the BWIs and economic liberalisation can be adduced. From 1989 to 1995, the state was to a large degree able to repel the main thrust of the conditions sought by the BWIs. From 1995 to 1998, the pressure applied by the BWIs began to tell with positive moves, especially in the legislative field, to implement the policies of economic liberalisation. Finally from 1998, came an acceptance by the state of the need to adopt the conditions sought. However, even in this period the degree of support for the process has fluctuated, such as the drop in initiatives towards the end of Rawabdeh's premiership. The ebb and flow can be seen as part of the battle within the rentier élite concerning the desirability of adopting economic liberalisation, and also regarding the most appropriate method of implementation: should the change allow a state-led economy in which the rentier élite dominate or, as sought by the donor community, a market-based economy.

The case studies indicate the increasing internal differences within the rentier élite. The example of the privatisation of JTC is an excellent case, with the Director-General, Ali Shukri, attempting to stop the sale of 40% of the company to a foreign strategic investor, due to his local connections with the telecommunications industry. The sales tax saga also highlights the fight within the rentier élite to continue to access rent, through exemptions from the tax and by delaying its implementation. From 1995, the process can be envisaged as one in which the BWIs have been in the driving seat, trying to reduce the state's dependence on rent. Simultaneously and as a result of the education process, the consensus within the rentier élite concerning economic liberalisation was breaking down. The acceptance of the importance of economic liberalisation by the state as an institution from 1998 is indicative of a change in the balance within the rentier élite between the conservative elements resisting change, and the reformist elements seeking change.

Overall, the rentier élite has shown a willingness to comply with the general principles of the IMF SAPs. However, the support has been watered-down by the need to maintain political legitimacy, and also by short-term, self-interested economic expediency. Major threats, such as the imposition of the sales tax at 13%, were fought bitterly as the tax was perceived to be a major threat to the interests of the majority of the rentier élite. The private sector economic interests of the élite have not sought a fully-fledged free market, but have been increasingly willing to support liberalisation. A complex balancing act has been forced on the state to maintain sufficient support for the IMF policies to ensure the continued support of the rest of the donor community; to maintain the political support of certain segments of society; and to ensure that control and access is maintained to the decreasing volumes of aid rent. This balancing act has been achieved by following the general momentum of the IMF policies, while continually grinding out concessions that are later often diluted, as the educating effects of the donor community win out.

Despite poor economic conditions (during which privatisation can be difficult to implement) in the late 1990s and into the new century, along with the continued security fears over normalisation with Israel (exacerbated by the outbreak of the latest *intifada* in 2000 and the 'war-on-terror'), the majority of the economic élite in Jordan seemed to be convinced of the need to privatise. What swung the balance in favour of reform? A number of reasons can be found to account for the change. Firstly, the debate over privatisation encouraged by the certain sectors of the state and donor community for the previous thirteen years had helped prepare both the street and parliament as to the necessity of the programme, through a continual drip-by-drip approach. Secondly, the donor community aimed considerable resources at helping foster a climate of acceptance for the idea of privatisation. By funding academic seminars, training courses, media advertising, discussions through local and foreign NGOs and the promotion of advocacy groups the donor community was able to slowly build up a groundswell of support for privatisation. Not only was the street and, to a degree, parliament convinced, but more importantly elements of the rentier élite previously opposed now realised that personal gain could be won. Their conversion was not ideological but for reasons of self-interest. However, this new pressure for reform is not only driven from the top of the regime but is also now coming from the private sector. Two private sector initiatives backed by donor funding and expertise have been produced recently. JV2020 is a comprehensive plan to double GDP per capita by the year 2020, and the IT REACH initiative aims to increase exports earnings in the IT sector to US$550m pa by 2004, creating 30,000 new jobs in the process and attracting US$150m in cumulative foreign investment.

This chapter has built on the analysis of the relationship between the donor community and the state (chapter 6) to establish the effects on the rentier élite. The next chapter discusses the effect of these changes on the relationship between the state and the private sector.

8

The State-Market Interface:
Which Political Economy?

INTRODUCTION

The IMF-inspired reform programme has two main objectives: macroeconomic policy adjustment to reduce internal and external imbalances, mainly by reducing the fiscal deficit and maintaining a flexible and competitive exchange rate; and trade liberalisation and industrial policy reforms. It has also one sub-objective: protection of the poor through targeted safety nets. The two main objectives were based on a range of policies that aimed to roll back the state and increase the role of the private sector. The Washington consensus assumes that state intervention in the economy is ultimately counter-productive, while in contrast the engine of growth was the private sector. This assumption is predicated on the notion that the public and private sectors are separate entities, each with their own clear-cut identifiable interests. In virtually any process of change, such as economic liberalisation, winners and losers are created. In an economy with a clear division between the public and private sectors the major problem facing the implementation of economic liberalisation would be to convince the potential losers in the public sector that in the long term their interests would best be met by switching the economy to a market-based one. However, as has been discussed in the earlier chapters, by 1989 in Jordan the public and private sectors were deeply enmeshed, leaving potentially important losers in both camps following the introduction of the reform programme. Thus economic liberalisation is not only an economic process but also, importantly, a political process.

This chapter is set against the background of three important changes in the 1990s: firstly the type and volume of rent entering the economy (chapter 5); secondly the attempts by the donor community to wean the state from the addiction of aid (chapter 6); and thirdly the limited acceptance by certain members of the rentier élite of the need to introduce economic change (chapter 7). In addition, the changing international regional and domestic environment highlighted in chapter five must be borne in mind. Two questions are discussed. The first question raised is: to what degree have these three factors affected the relationship between the public and private sectors? The main thrust of the analysis uses the state-market continuum model.

The second question is: to what degree are the changes highlighted by the model reflected in changes in the rentier aspects of the economy, bearing in mind that the model is not driven solely by changing patterns of rent? As previously discussed, the rentier mentality adopted by both the private and public sectors results in a unique style of economic development, of private and public sector development, and of a relationship between the two based on the evolution of a rentier élite, with public political interests and private economic interests. This question is answered by assessing the degree to which the aspects of rentierism evident by 1989 have been broken down, but bearing in mind that other factors can also influence the measures (i.e. the cause-effect relationship between both the retreat of the state and the fall in the induced rentier state economy and the changes in type of rentierism are not necessarily straight-forward). At the level of the economy, three aspects are of interest: whether the level of government expenditure and consequently the budget deficit has fallen; whether the volume of imports has fallen both in relation to GDP and to exports; and, more importantly, whether the productive sector has gained at the expense of the service sector. In terms of the private sector, the theoretical discussion noted that under induced state rentierism the private sector tended to be relatively homogenous in outlook. Therefore an assessment will be made of this feature. In addition, the analysis concentrates on the response of the private sector (whether homogenous or heterogeneous) to the changes of rent, donor involvement and the reactions of the rentier élite. In terms of the state, the rentier mentality is evidenced by the use of 'expenditure' policies to maintain political support from relevant groups in society. One of the assumptions in chapter two was that in an economy in which rent changed from state to private sector the state would attempt to change policy to maintain control of the new style of rent. The chapter will look at the state's policies in this respect, such as taxation, exchange and interest rates, and maintaining relations with the labour-importing Gulf States. The final aspect to be discussed will be the type of interaction between the two sectors: whether through informal induced state rentierism type relations or formal private sector rentierism type relations.

THE STATE-MARKET CONTINUUM: 1989 TO 2002

As was shown in chapter four, the state continued to dominate the Jordanian economy, despite (or perhaps because of) the recession in the mid- to late-1980s, the change of direction to an export-oriented economic policy and the dominance of the free-market ideology of monetarism. Indeed, the rentier élite, which controlled the major parts of the private sector, actively encouraged the status quo in Jordan. Four main features of the public-private sector relationship were highlighted: the heavy involvement of the state in the productive sector through SOEs (many in liaison with the private sector); state involvement in the market through price controls, subsidies, licences and contracts, input restrictions and investment and credit control; the granting of access to the economy in return for political support; and the institutional structure of the private sector being adapted to allow informal contacts with the political public sector élite. This section measures the changes (if any) on those aspects of the state-public sector relationship from 1989 to the end of 2002, based on the five-continua state-market model.

STATE PROGNOSIS OF THE PRIVATE SECTOR

Throughout the period in question the state has issued a series of official statements indicating its desire to implement economic reform that would involve reducing the role of the state, while simultaneously assisting with the development of the private sector. These statements were forthcoming at the highest levels, with King Hussein repeatedly charging his governments to promote the private sector.[810] The various prime ministers reiterated this message in their statements to parliament on assuming office, and in their speeches in support of the budget. For example, Prime Minister Badran, in February 1990, stated that:

> the economic reform programme is principally based on improving the efficiency of the public sector and reducing it as far as possible; and on increasing, broadening and diversifying the private sector's investment opportunities.[811]

Prime Minister al-Masri in his policy statement to parliament in July 1991 confirmed that he would create a healthy environment for private sector investment.[812] Then at a seminar to the Jordanian Businessmen Club in Amman in August 1993, he confirmed the need to "reassess the relationship between the private and public sectors in a manner that ensures the private sector will have freedom of initiative, action, investment and trading."[813] He added:

> [i]t is no longer reasonable that the public sector should assume the responsibility of running commercial and industrial companies and institutions, or interfere—under jurisdictions that are no longer acceptable—in pricing policies, and confiscate the freedom of the private sector, making decisions on its behalf.[814]

By the middle of the 1990s, the state was still emphasising the need to activate the role of the private sector through creating a suitable environment for investment while maintaining a role for the state which would "continue to develop the infrastructure for the national economy and provide the basic auxiliary services, especially water, electricity, communications and roads."[815] A further two years down the line, the state was anticipating expanding the role of the private sector into the field of infrastructure. King Hussein in his address at the opening of parliament in November 1996 stated that the government sought "to encourage the private sector's participation in national production through the expansion of its role in initiating infrastructure projects, especially in the fields of telecommunications, energy, transport, water and tourism."[816]

In 1998 the struggle to separate the private and public sectors was still in full flow. As discussed in the previous chapter, Prime Minister Majali defined privatisation not as a matter of sell-off shares but more fundamentally as a redistribution of roles between the public and private sectors. The advent of the new king witnessed a continuation of the calls for restructuring the economy so that "the private sector must be allowed to play a vigorous role in this endeavour."[817] By

May 1999, King Abdullah was attempting to reactivate the joint public-private investment board meetings, while stressing the need for the private sector to make decisions jointly with the government.[818] The King continued with this theme in his speech to parliament in November and again in his letter of designation to the new Prime Minister in June 2000. However, the tone of his statements indicated that the process should be a two-way one, in which the state ought to create the legislative and economic environment to allow the private sector to develop. Nonetheless, the private sector was expected to play its role fully in the process of development.[819]

The statements of support for restructuring the economy in favour of the private sector were also issued in the publications of the official state organs, such as the CBJ. In the Annual Report for 1993, the CBJ argues about the necessity of:

> concentrating efforts to activate the role of the private sector and enhancing its participation in the development process, improvement of the incentive and institutional structure of investment within the framework of a clearly defined and applicable strategy.[820]

The report calls on the state to:

> reconsider legislation related to foreign trade and facilitate administrative measures related to investment activities as well as exports, to adopt the international system for specifications and measurements enabling Jordanian exports to compete on the basis of quality, to expand the program for the introduction of production technology, to increase support for potential exporters through providing information on external markets, to promote the use of communication and information technology and to increase efforts on attracting foreign investment especially in joint ventures.[821]

This very brief review of the calls by the state for an increase in the importance of the private sector, and by implication a reduction (or at least a change of direction) for the state, has demonstrated that, publicly at least, there was strong support among the apex of the rentier élite for this policy. The next section discusses how these calls were translated into action by using the state-market continuum model.

CONTRIBUTION TO THE NATIONAL ECONOMY

The government's share of the national income is measured in two ways: government revenues (excluding grants) as a percentage of GDP and government expenditure as a percentage of GDP (figure 8.1). On the first measure, the government's share increased dramatically from 1989 to 1992. The increase was partly due to the continued economic recession, which hindered the growth of the private sector, but mainly because of the improved revenue-collecting abilities of the government; levels of domestic revenue increased by over 100% between 1989 and 1992. Despite this increase, state expenditure as a share of GDP fell sharply in the same period as result of tight fiscal policies, despite a rise in expenditure of 18.6%. Since 1992, government revenue as a percentage of GDP has drifted downwards to less than 27% by 2002, whilst the figure for expenditure has fluctuated downwards to less than 35%. Although the state has increased its share of the economy since 1989 in terms of revenue, it is actually over-performing according to the level of 31% set by the World Bank.[822] In terms of expenditure over the period a clear withdrawal of state is evident, although since 1992 the levels have been relatively stable.

Figure 8.1:   Government Budget in Relation to GDP, 1989-2002

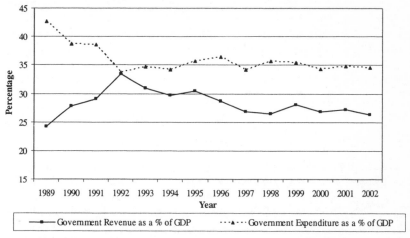

Source: Adapted by author. CBJ, (various), *Monthly Statistical Bulletin*, (Amman: CBJ).

An important aspect of the government expenditure is the changing pattern between recurrent and capital expenditure. Although the level of expenditure has fallen in terms of GDP, the policy has deliberately focused on budget cuts in capital expenditure, allowing high levels of recurrent expenditure. Between the budget for 1989 and the budget for 2002 the state projected current expenditure to increase by almost 170%; in contrast, projected capital expenditure was expected to increase by just below 25%. The budgeted figures are reflected in the actual outcomes, with actual state current spending increasing by almost 150% while capital expenditure increased by 80.7% over the period. The emphasis on recurrent expenditure is particularly important given the need to fund the high level of employment in the state sector. Thus, although the indicators of induced state rentierism have been seen to decline, the state has continued attempting to maintain the rentier policy of garnering political support by economic means, in this case through employment in the public sector.

The need to apply fiscal restraint in the early years of the SAP resulted in the government's share of total consumption falling from 1989 to 1992; thereafter, the share increased and remained consistently in excess of 25% until 1999 (figure 8.2). Thereafter a further decline to just over 22% was experienced. Thus, whereas expenditure to GDP indicates a significant decrease in the government's share of the economy since 1989, the figures record a more gradual fall in the government share of consumption.

Figure 8.2:   **Government Share of Total Consumption, 1989-2001**

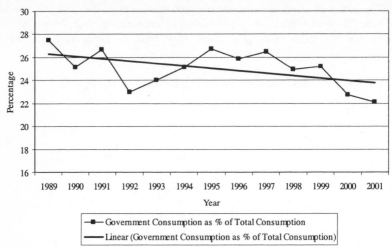

Source: Adapted by author. IMF, (various), *International Financial Statistics Yearbook,* (Washington: IMF) and CBJ, (various), *Monthly Statistical Report,* (Amman: CBJ).

While consumption figures are an indicator of the present condition of the economy, investment figures ought to give an indication of the future path of the economy. The figures for GFCF show, contrary to expectations, how the state's share has increased by the end of the period. The percentage climbed to just over 39% in 1990, before almost falling by 50% by 1993; thereafter, the state's share increased to a high of 45.2% in 1998 as the government tried to overcome the downturn in the economy (figure 8.3). Although the share grew significantly between 1994 and 1998, this change is not due entirely because of increased government spending. The public sector's GFCF increased by 10.5% between 1994 and 1998, while private sector GFCF fell by 28.5% in the same period (figure 8.4). Almost 60% of the public sector GFCF between 1990 and 1998 has been invested in government services; in contrast, in the same time period, no private sector GFCF has been invested in this sector, despite the exhortations of the donor community for the private sector to become involved in service provision. Government services GFCF has accounted for around 21.5% of GDP since 1992, having fallen from 23.2% in 1989. On the other hand, almost three-quarters of the private sector GFCF has been invested in finance, insurance, real estate and business services. The latter is a major indicator of the failure of the policies to move in the direction of an industrial export-oriented economy.

The macroeconomic figures paint a confusing picture of the changing levels of the state involvement in the economy. While the percentage of state expenditure to GDP indicates a withdrawal of the state from the economy, the figures for the state's share of total consumption show a less clear trend. Indeed, the state's share of total GFCF has actually increased considerably between 1989 and 1998.

Figure 8.3:   Public Share of Gross Fixed Capital Formation, 1989-1998

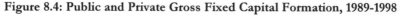

Sources: Adapted by author. Department of Statistics, "Gross Fixed Capital Formation by Kind of Economic Activity for 1990-1993 and 1994-1998", *Department of Statistics website*, www.dos.gov.jo.

Figure 8.4: Public and Private Gross Fixed Capital Formation, 1989-1998

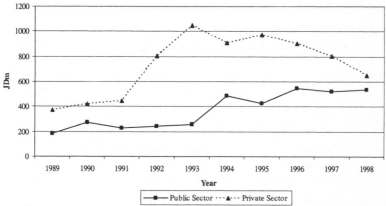

Source: Adapted by author. Department of Statistics, "Gross Fixed Capital Formation by Kind of Economic Activity for 1990-1993 and 1994-1998", *Department of Statistics website*, www.dos.gov.jo.

PLANNING

Following the involvement of the IMF, five-year development planning by the state was no longer considered to be an appropriate response to the problems facing the economy. The IMF believed that SAPs were in effect a plan for economic development, and therefore replaced the need for the five-year plans which had been a feature of the previous decades. However, in an attempt to highlight its independence from the IMF (a move especially important in light of the increasing political liberalisation) the state still sought to produce medium-term plans. Although in November 1990 the King intimated that a plan for 1991 to 1995 was being prepared[823] the next plan that emerged was for the years 1993 to 1997. The plan evolved as the Arab-Israel peace process was beginning to bear fruit, bringing new optimism for economic growth to the region. For example, over US$16bn of Jordanian investment was planned in joint projects with Israel, valued at US$33-42bn. In addition, the stock exchange was booming in anticipation of the peace dividend as Jordan was expected to assume the mantle of moderator between Israel and the Arabs.

As with the previous plan, the 1993-97 one was drawn up in the context of the IMF SAP. In the words of the Ministry of Planning:

> the Plan is not an alternative to the adjustment and economy recovery programme. It complements the programme [SAP II] and enhances its prospects of success by encompassing social aspects and providing decision-makers with a comprehensive view of the socio-economic situation in Jordan.[824]

The state justified the existence of the plan on the grounds that:

> the package of adjustment policies that the programme entails is not sufficient, on its own, to address all imbalances in the economy, nor is it capable of providing an adequate and appropriate social package for solving Jordan's poverty and unemployment problems.[825]

The plan was considered by the Ministry of Planning to be more comprehensive than the IMF SAP, adding the dimensions of unemployment, poverty, administrative reform and an integrated water policy.[826]

The government introduced the plan as a radical departure from the previous process of economic and social planning. The changes included presenting the plan as "a package of integrated economic and social policies,"[827] rather than a list of projects and investment programmes, with the objective of not just attaining economic growth but also of achieving sustainable economic and social growth. In addition, the Ministry claims the new plan "aims at providing a greater role to the private sector in investment, direct production and employment."[828] Previous plans had reflected government control over economic life. In contrast, this plan:

> respects private sector decisions and affirms the sector's need to run its own affairs. It imposes no policies or projects on the private sector but rather seeks to influence its decisions in the direction of conforming with the government's general framework, without prejudice to the principles of economic freedom and private enterprise.[829]

The plan was deemed to be a "testimony to Jordan's new economic approach."[830] Furthermore, for the first time the whole process was to be subject to review and annual updating to reflect changing circumstances and the actual levels of performance.[831]

In line with the thinking of the IMF, the Ministry of Planning admitted that the "public sector [had] emerged as a competing and restraining force *vis-à-vis* the private sector," as indicated by: the government's determination of various prices; the subsidisation of production inputs, of locally-produced commodities, and by supporting inefficient public enterprises; the granting of concessions to certain businesses; the lack of anti-trust and consumer protection legislation; and 0074he involvement of the public sector in production.[832]

The planners listed the main problems facing the private sector in what they termed 'the investment sector', which was deemed to include agriculture, mining, manufacturing, trade and tourism. The problems highlighted, with which the state could assist, can be divided into existing and missing factors. The tariff system, overlapping authority among public enterprises in the field of investment management, and the complexity of registration and licensing procedures were all stressed as major existing problems. In addition, the lack of a comprehensive investment strategy, including a unified source of information, the lack of inadequate incentives provided both by the Income Tax Law and the Investment Promotion Law and the lack of support services for this sector, were deemed to be barriers to development.[833]

The plan was based on a number of important principles, including the liberalisation of the economy. This change was to be implemented in a number of ways, such as enhancing the regulatory and supervisory role of the government; reducing the government's role in direct production, while enhancing the private sector by encouraging investment; increasing the areas in which the private sector could operate; improving the efficiency of public sector institutions and government departments; and encouraging certain industries. Among the other principles highlighted was the need to develop the export sector by opening new markets, expanding existing markets, and improving human resources.[834]

The focus of the plan on the private sector as the engine of growth is confirmed by the planned investment levels during the period (table 8.1). These were expected to total JD5242m, of which almost 50% was to be spent on the social and services sectors, with the remainder divided almost equally between infrastructure and the productive sectors. The private sector was anticipated to provide almost two-thirds of the total investment. Private funding was expected to account for over 85% of the investments in the productive sector, almost 70% in the social and services field and one-third of the infrastructure spending.

Table 8.1   **Planned Sectoral Investment, 1993-1997**

Sector	Public Sector		Private Sector		Total Investment	
	Amount	Share	Amount	Share	Amount	Share
Social and Services	JD810m	31.2%	JD1788m	68.8%	JD2598m	49.6%
Infrastructure	JD890m	66.3%	JD453m	33.7%	JD1343m	25.6%
Productive	JD174m	13.4%	JD1127m	86.6%	JD1301m	24.8%
Total	**JD1874m**	**35.7%**	**JD3368m**	**64.3%**	**JD5242m**	100%

Source: Adapted by author. Ministry of Planning, (undated: a), *Plan for Economic and Social Development: 1993-1997*, (Amman: Ministry of Planning), p.139 and p.197.

The growth rates of total consumption at 1991 constant prices were anticipated to be 2.8% for the period 1993 to 1997, with private consumption increasing by 3.0%, and public consumption increasing by 2.1%. Although the plan aimed at increasing the role of the private sector, over the five years the public sector was expected to provide the majority of the growth in GFCF. However, if the figures for 1993 are removed from the equation then in the last four years the private sector was expected to provide more impetus for growth than the public sector. Thus, after an initial fall of 30.1% in 1993, private GFCF at 1991 constant prices was planned to rise by a total of 8.9% over the last four years of the plan. The public sector figures were expected to grow by a total of 3.4% over the last four years.[835] Overall, the contribution of the private sector in GFCF was expected to rise from 60.2% in 1993 to 64.3% in 1997.[836]

The fiscal policies aimed at achieving the programme were a repetition of the policies sought by the IMF, namely: broadening the tax base; replacing consumption tax with GST as a prelude to the implementation of VAT; reducing and targeting subsidies; pricing government services to ensure cost recovery, specifically regarding electricity, water and sanitation, irrigation water, postal services, and transport fares; and covering a larger portion of the costs in the health and education sectors, whilst taking into account the needs of lower income groups.[837]

Specific polices aimed at assisting the 'investment sector' had the objective of providing "a suitable investment environment conducive to increasing domestic production and exports and to rationalising imports."[838] The policies upon which the plan was predicated included: providing investment information by establishing a central body within the Ministry of Industry and Trade to provide an information database, to simplify registration procedures, particularly for trade licences, tourist related licensing, and to confine all registration and licensing procedures to a single point; encouraging the financial sector to provide investment funding though developing an institution to provide partial guarantees for SMEs; creating an export credit guarantee institution; expanding the remit of the IDB; simplifying custom regulations; granting tax incentives, through the Income Tax Law; amending the Investment Promotion Law to increase investment incentives; upgrading the quality of goods by complying with international standards and building awareness of the necessity for quality; and restoring financial and administrative autonomy to public institutions, and permitting the private sector to provide public services.[839]

The plan argues for "a detailed study to explore the most feasible options for moving towards privatisation on a clear foundation."[840] Three types of companies were envisaged for privatisation: those considered best served by privatisation; those of strategic importance which should remain in the public sector but be run on a "cost-effective basis"; and those to be run on a commercial basis, with privatisation to follow at a later stage.[841] The proposals for privatisation specifically highlighted in the programme were to: convert the PTC and the United Company for Organising Land Transport into public shareholding companies run by the private sector; restructure RJ to make it amenable to gradual and partial privatisation; promote private sector participation in energy and electricity projects; and provide JEA with the financial and administrative autonomy to allow operations on a commercial basis. No mention was made of privatisation efforts in the water and telecommunications sectors.

After a gap of two years, the state produced another five-year social and economic development plan covering the years 1999 to 2003. The process for the new plan was initiated in 1997 but by mid-1999 it was still being debated. During the three-day National Seminar in Social and Economic Development, in July, the King asked for it to be prepared within the next two months.[842] The specific objectives for the plan were drawn up at the Dead Sea retreat in November 1999. Overall the plan is a continuation of the three pillars of the IMF policy from 1989, viz: liberalising the national economy; encouraging the private sector; and attracting Arab[843] and foreign investment.[844] In addition, the need to increase productivity, fight unemployment and poverty, and improve the quality of life through achieving consistency between economic development and human development are highlighted.[845]

Among the general goals of the plan are to: create conditions of sustainable growth in excess of population growth rate; continue the policy of openness in trade and investment; continue to reform the administrative and legislative frameworks that regulate all economic activity, including privatisation; maintain the monetary and fiscal stability, eliminate production and price distortion, increase domestic savings and secure a proper climate for private sector investment; restructure the role of the public sector in economic activities; and enhance the role of the private sector in these activities; and confront corruption and emphasise transparency in both the public and private sectors.[846] The specific economic objectives are: achieving real growth of 4.5% annually; achieving annual growth of 5.2% in exports and 5% in imports; decreasing debt service to 24.2% of the value of exports and reducing the percentage of the general indebtedness to 75% of GDP; maintaining national savings of 30% of GDP; maintaining monetary stability, containing inflation, and maintaining a sufficient [unspecified] level of hard currency; reducing the budget deficit before grants to 1.2% GDP by the last year of the plan; and reinforcing the role of private sector and following up the privatisation programme.[847]

As with the previous plan, the state acknowledged the importance of the private sector to the future of the economy. The aim of a balanced, sustainable and comprehensive development could not be achieved "without the real participation of the private sector. This sector could be encouraged by providing a suitable environment for investment and the removal of all obstacles."[848]

In terms of the public and private contributions to the economy, the plan anticipates that private consumption will increase by on average 7.3% pa, in contrast to a public consumption increase of 2.7% pa.[849] In line with the objective to increase the level of domestic savings, the overall level of consumption is expected to fall from 96.1% of GDP in 1998 to 87.6% in 2003.[850] On the question of investment levels, the plan envisages that the private sector will be investing 80% of total investment by the end of the plan, an increase from less than 75% at the beginning of the plan (table 8.2). In addition, it seeks to change the quality of investment by increasing levels in industry, communication and the financial services and moving away from the construction sector.[851]

Table 8.2   **Planned Capital Expenditure, 1998-2003**

Year	Private Sector Amount JDm	% Share	Public Sector Amount JDm	% Share	Total Amount JDm
1998	979.7	74.8	329.2	25.2	1308.9
1999	1103.7	76.4	341.0	23.6	1444.7
2000	1143.8	75.9	362.4	24.1	1506.2
2001	1500.3	79.4	388.5	20.6	1888.8
2002	1708.1	80.7	409.3	19.3	2117.4
2003	[852]1870.9	80.7	448.3	19.3	2319.2

Source: Adapted by author. Ministry of Planning, (undated: c), *Plan for Economic and Social Development: 1999-2003*, (Amman: Ministry of Planning), Table 1.10.

On privatisation, the plan admitted that a slowdown had occurred.[853] The plan defines privatisation as:

> an organised and methodological process, which aims at preparing a suitable environment that would support sustainable economic growth and which is represented in the re-distribution of roles between the public and the private sectors. This entails that the government restricts its activities to drawing up policies, control, organising, and focusing on activities such as health, security, education, and preserving the environment. The private sector controls the economic activities including public projects which are run on commercial bases.[854]

This broad definition allowed the state to argue that the success/failure of the process could not be measured solely by the divestment of shares in the SOEs. The reasons given for implementing the privatisation process were in line with dominant economic thinking associated the Washington consensus, namely to: enhance and improve productivity and the competitiveness capability through activating market forces, and removing economic distortions; encourage domestic savings and attract investments (domestic, Arab, and foreign) through opening markets and abolishing monopolies; halt the drain in public capital due to loss-making projects and to limit foreign borrowings that are designed to help the loss-making projects; deepen the market for domestic capital and direct investment towards the long term; and facilitate the acquisition of technology and modern managerial means.

Again in line with the Washington consensus concerning privatisation, the plan commits the state to withdrawing from production activities while increasing its enabling, supervisory and regulatory roles both in the process of privatisation and in the subsequent post-privatisation period. The plan lays out the new role for the state as: finding and developing a suitable competitive environment for the market; completing the organisational and legislative frameworks to support privatisation; establishing independent bodies for organising and controlling the privatised areas to monitor quality, issue permits and control monopoly; introducing privatisation gradually; evaluating the value of the companies to be privatised in order to know the value of the project as an initial indicator for the process of privatisation; selecting the ideal method for privatising each project; ensuring transparency and publicity in decision-making relevant to privatisation; and preserving the acquired rights for all parties.[855]

The plan also indicates the priority given by the state to the various sectors in implementing privatisation, namely: the energy sector; transportation: public transportation, railways, air transport (including airports), and ports; communications and post; water; TV and radio; and hotels and rest houses.[856]

The approach to each of the four MENA economic summits is instructive in highlighting the change of emphasis of the state's role in the development of the economy, including areas such as infrastructure provision that were previously considered the sole preserve of the state. At each summit Jordan put forward a list of projects for consideration. The lists for the first two conferences sought investment from the private sector, the state, and mixed ventures.[857] In line with the dominant economic theory of neo-liberalisation, the take-up rate at the two conferences was weak. However, prior to the Cairo conference, the decision-makers realised that in order to succeed the private sector had to become the main engine for growth, particularly if considering external investment. As a consequence, the list of twenty-five schemes,[858] with an estimated value of US$3,700m, was exclusively seeking private investment.[859]

Although the state continued to be involved in the economy through the use of five-year plans, the focus of these plans had changed in number of ways. Firstly, the plans themselves were no longer 'wish lists' but approached development in a more holistic manner. Secondly, they actively encouraged the development of the private sector, which was now seen as the motor of growth. Thirdly, they acknowledged the changing role of the state away from that of the leader in development to that of a facilitator, which involved the state's withdrawal from productive activities to focus on supervision and regulation. This change of role can be considered as a move towards the market end of the continuum.

INSTITUTIONAL DEVELOPMENT

The institutional development related to the process of economic liberalisation in the period 1989 to 2002 can be divided into two types. The first is the creation of joint committees comprising members of the private and public sectors in an attempt to formalise the informal arrangements already existing in the economic decision-making process. If this institutionalisation of state-private sector relations becomes effective it can be seen as an indicator of the declining aspects of state rentierism. The second type of arrangement is the creation or revamping of organisations to assist the promotion of the policies of economic liberalisation, in particular attracting investment and promoting exports. In addition, the section also briefly analyses the evolution of the specialised credit and investment institutions.

In the autumn of 1989, the ECC,[860] which had been established in 1986 and suspended in January 1989 by the Cabinet after only meeting a further twice, was revived.[861] The Council, which was chaired by the Prime Minister, had the aim of co-ordinating private and public sector activity to ensure best use of investment and to facilitate increased output. The scope of the ECC was to discuss "investment legislation, economic and monetary policies, prices and wage policies, privatisation, [and] the contribution of the public and private sectors to economic activities."[862] Also included in the remit were oil and gas exploration; agriculture; employment conditions and training; health; the environment; food and water; and infrastructure and tourism. Private sector representatives were drawn mainly from the commercial, industrial, tourism, banking, insurance and transport sectors.[863] According to the EIU, the private sector initiated the resurrection of the ECC,[864] presumably in response to the threat of the process of economic liberalisation. As with similar previous attempts the formalisation did not prove to be successful, despite further attempts to restructure the Council in 1993. The close web of informal ties between the private and public sectors built up under the induced state rentierism proved resilient to the attempts to formalise the interaction.

On the 13th December 1999, a new ECC was born following a conference at the Dead Sea from the 26th to 27th November initiated by King Abdullah. On this occasion the appointed twenty-member committee was drawn primarily from the private sector (fourteen), thereby emphasising a switch in priorities of the rentier élite.[865] The recommendations that were announced following the retreat also underscored the new priorities. For the first time, the state was recommended to withdraw from the mining sector, an area previously considered sacrosanct due to its 'strategic' nature. Among the other recommendations (the usual list of suspects) were the call for the withdrawal of the state from productive activities, incentives to help the private sector raise standards in health, education and social services, the reshaping of policies to attract local and foreign investment, an increase in the number of build-own-operate/build-operate-transfer schemes in major economic projects and, finally, the placing of more emphasis on the educating process about the benefits of privatisation.[866]   In contrast to the previous ECC, the latest reincarnation has been successful at initiating and implementing change.   For instance, recommendations for the introduction of English and computer studies at first grade level in primary schools, a reduction in telecom charges, increased spending on tourism promotion and an easing of visa procedures have already been implemented.[867]

Two further committees established during the period highlight the desire by the rentier élite to retain control of or access to the rent circuit. The committee established to close the loopholes in the sales tax law was an example of how the rentier élite with private sector economic interests was able to maintain access to the rent circuit. Previously, those with private sector interests had been able to delay the implementation of the tax and also to reduce the tax rate levied. The committee itself allowed further exemptions from the tax to be negotiated rather than to close the loopholes, as had been the intention. A 12-strong Royal Committee for Modernisation and Development, headed by Crown Prince Hassan, was created in August 1994, following a letter by King Hussein to the Crown Prince. In the letter, the King argued that the judicial system, the Audit Bureau and the Bureau of Administrative Control and Security should have modern laws to deal with trade. Furthermore, he added that:

> [a]mong the duties of this committee is to endeavour to establish an economic and investment climate on clear foundations in order to give everybody his right without negligence, disorder or deviation. This should cover both the public and private sectors.[868]

The top priorities were reported to be the establishment of a central purchase system and the drafting of a foreign trade policy.[869] Although the commission comprised of representatives of the private and public sectors, the members were hand-picked by the rentier élite.

A series of institutions was established or revamped from 1992 onwards to assist with improving the climate for investment and the ability to export. Two types of organisation were formed: those directly linked to the state, say, through various ministries and joint public-private limited companies. Among the first type were: 1) JCCC became Jordan Export Development and Commercial Centers Corporation in 1992, with an increased responsibility to implement the government's commitments on all trade protocols; 2) The Investment Promotion Corporation was formed in 1993 as part of the Ministry of Industry and Trade and in 1995 was converted into a separate body with the aim of concentrating "on promoting rather than controlling investment;"[870] 3) The Higher Council for Investment Promotion (1995), under the chairmanship of the Prime Minister, with the Ministers of Industry and Trade, Finance, Planning, Tourism, and Transport, and the Governor of the CBJ, the chairmen of the FJCC and the ACI, and three private sector representatives recommended by the Minister[871] with the goal of the Council was to "create a suitable environment for investment";[872] 4) the investment window (1995)[873] in the Investment Promotion Department as a one-stop shop,[874] with a three-week deadline to approve investments[875] and to deal with investment matters;[876] 5) an industrial development investment unit (1997) was created at the Ministry of Industry and Trade to facilitate further investment after a project has been established; and 6) Jordan Investment Board (2000) was launched as the revamped version of the Investment Promotion Corporation.

Among the jointly-subscribed companies launched were: 1) The Jordan Loan Guarantee Corporation (1995) which has the aim of financing small and medium scale projects by granting guarantees to cover financial borrowing. The company was established with a capital base of JD7m, of which the CBJ provided JD3m by way of a USAID funded grant. Other subscribers were licensed banks, two insurance companies, the SSC, the Cities and Villages Development Bank and the Chambers of Commerce and Industry;[877] 2) The Jordan Export and Finance Bank (1995), which is required, as a condition of its licence, to devote 50% of its resources to export-related activities. The capital (JD20m) was subscribed to by, among others, JPMC, APC, JCFC, members of the Jordan Trade Association, a number of insurance companies, SSC, JIC, and Jordan Export Development and Commercial Centers Corporation: the majority of these are SOEs; and 3) The Jordan Mortgage Refinance Company (1996), which was founded with a capital of JD5m, including JD0.9m from CBJ, also contributions from SSC, HUDC, and Jordan Loan Guarantee Corporation. The objective of the company is to refinance medium- and long-term bonds in the capital market.

In line with the move to an export-oriented private sector, Free Zones in Jordan have undergone a series of reforms during the IMF years. The FZC had two free zones under its auspices by 1989, both primarily focusing on tax-exempt warehousing. Towards the end of 1993, the FZC announced plans to develop two new zones, one at Queen Alia Airport and one in Amman at the Sahab Industrial Estate,[878] both of which are now active. In 1994, a new draft law was prepared granting further incentives and simplifying the procedures for investment. The FZC came under heavy criticism in JICA's 1996 study for restricting its activities virtually entirely to tax-exempt warehousing, without encouraging heavy industry, or providing the free trade zones or transportation routes to other countries.[879] In response, the following year, the concept of Free Zones was extended to the private sector, since when nine further zones have been established.

The JIEC was established in 1980 to manage the industrial zones, the second of which, Al-Hassan Industrial Estate, was initiated in 1989 and operational by 1991. In the mid-1990s the JIEC's remit was extended to include QIZs.[880] The QIZs are a direct result of the Jordan-Israel Peace Treaty and significantly allow duty-free quota-free access for goods into the American market.[881] The first QIZ at the Al-Hassan Industrial Estate was designated as such by the US Trade Representative in March 1998.[882] In late 1999, the private sector also announced its intention to establish a site at Dulayl and a second at Sahab.[883] By the end of 2002 seven QIZs were in operation (table 8.3), of which two are state operated, and a further four were in the process of construction. These QIZs were home to 62 projects employing 18,254 Jordanians (however a similar number of foreign workers are also employed), in which JD383m had been invested.[884] The success of the QIZs can be seen by the growth of exports from the QIZs to the USA from US$25m in 1999 to US$384m in 2002.[885] However, the target of up to 100,000 jobs with exports of US$2,500-3,000m by 2005[886] is unlikely to be achieved, especially given that all duties will be removed from textiles entering the US market as from January 2005 (textiles constitutes over 93% of exports from the QIZs).

Table 8.3   **QIZs in Operation as at 31/12/02**

QIZ	Ownership	No of Projects	Investment JDm	Local Employment
Al-Hassan Industrial Zone	Public	15	98.5	4,890
Al-Karak Industrial Estate	Public	3	40.0	1,701
Al-Dulayl Industrial Park	Private	11	50.0	2,900
Tajamouat Industrial City	Private	25	150.0	6,780
CyberCity	Private	5	20.0	700
Al-Qastal	Private	2	16	713
El Zay	Private	1	7.5	570
Total		**62**	**383.0**	**18,254**

Source: Adapted by author.   Manneh, J., (2003), *Sector Report: Qualifying Industrial Zones*, (Amman: Export and Finance Bank)

The final move in the free zones development was the announcement in mid-2000 of the King's wish to establish a Special Economic Zone (SEZ) in the region of Aqaba. Parliament approved the draft law in July of the same year,[887] with the intention of having the zone functioning at the start of January 2001.[888] The law grants the Aqaba SEZ complete exemption from:

customs duties and any other rates and taxes on imports into the SEZ; and GST or any other tax that replaces sales tax on imports into the SEZ, or on sales of goods and services within the designated SEZ area.[889]

Initial expectations, which seem over-optimistic, are that the zone will attract US$6,000m in investments and create more than 70,000 jobs.[890]

An important institutional development was the abolition of the Ministry of Supply on the 1st November 1998, a move that formally signalled the end of much government involvement in the economy. The Ministry had been responsible for subsidies and price regulation of a number of basic goods, but as these elements were gradually phased-out it became redundant. As a prelude to the scrapping, from August 1996 the private sector was allowed to import wheat, wheat derivatives, sugar and rice, all of which were previously part of the Ministry's monopoly: as recently as 1995 the Ministry had been responsible for JD320m worth of food imports[891] (over 60% of the total food imports).

In the case of privatisation, two main institutional developments were important. The Privatisation Unit was established by a Cabinet agreement on the 6th June 1996, at the recommendation of the World Bank. The Executive Privatisation Unit comprised of a Higher Ministerial Committee, under the supervision of the Prime Minister, to "formulate general policy so that the process of privatisation is conducted in an organised manner, thereby ensuring economic growth and greater productive efficiency."[892] A technical unit to implement the process of privatisation was also formed. This move was the first step in producing a co-ordinated policy towards privatisation. The second step came with the promulgation of Privatisation Law no. 25 for 2000, which replaced the Executive Privatisation Unit with the Executive Privatisation Commission under the supervision of the Higher Ministerial Council for Privatisation. In addition, the law controversially granted the government "a distinct voting power through the 'Gilded/Golden' share, which empowers it to oppose resolutions of a Company's board of directors or general assembly, if the national interest so requires."[893]

The growth of the specialised credit institutions shows mixed results from 1989. The Housing Bank lost its status as a specialised credit institution in 1997 with the promulgation of Law 16, which cancelled the Housing Bank for Trade and Finance Law, no. 4 of 1974. Consequently, the organisation now operates as a normal commercial bank. The loan portfolio of both the IDB and Agricultural Credit Corporation grew dramatically between 1989 and 2000, the former by 160.6% and the latter by 216%. In comparison, GDP grew by 168%. These figures are at odds with the World Bank's 1995 Report,[894] which argued that these institutions were a major constraint on the development of the private sector. However, in the period to 2000 the loan portfolio of the Cities and Villages Development Bank grew by only 9.1%, while the Housing and Urban Development Corporation portfolio actually declined by almost one-quarter. The lack of growth in the loan portfolio of these two institutions supports the tenor of the 1995 Report. The growth of the Agricultural Credit Corporation has been in great part due to the drought conditions, with the packages of cheap loans and roll-overs of existing facilities. In contrast, the growth of the IDB has been primarily due to donor assistance. Generally, though, the importance of these institutions has diminished over the period, with the state encouraging the banking sector to fund private sector development: between 1998 and 2002 licensed bank lending grew by 197%, where as the specialised credit institutions lending actually decreased by 0.5%. In addition, the donor community's concentration on establishing sustainable micro-finance schemes has assisted the funding of the small enterprises in the private sector.

To summarise, the relationship between the private and public sectors became more formalised into the twenty first century. In addition, the creation and revamping of the various institutions associated with the economy have also shown a tendency to move to the private sector end of the continuum. The state organisations have moved from an objective of outright control to one of facilitation of investment and exports, while the joint public-private organisations have as their objective the facilitation of the efficiency of the markets, in particular the financial market. A similar change has been apparent in the development of the Free Zones, the Industrial Estates, the QIZs and the Aqaba Special Economic Zone. The institutionalisation of privatisation has also highlighted a move to the private sector, with state control moving from ownership to regulatory control. Finally, the reduction in the role of the specialised credit institutions is another example of the move away from the state dominance of the economy. Overall, then, the measure of institutional development has moved towards the private sector end of the market continuum.

PRIVATE SECTOR SUPPORT

The main areas of state support for the private sector over the decade had three foci. The first was the continued support for the agricultural sector, driven by internal pressures of the farming lobby. The second and third were new, with a switch to export-oriented companies and the desire for increased investment, whether domestic, Arab or foreign. These latter two foci were initially instigated at the insistence of the donor community.

The agricultural sector remains small, accounting for a maximum of 7% of the GDP, while not contributing significantly to the employment situation. Indeed, as many as half a million migrant labourers are employed in the sector, at a time when in excess of this number are unemployed locally. Furthermore, the sector uses at least 70% of the water consumed annually. Despite the small size of the sector, and considering that Jordan has not been self-sufficient in food since the Second World War, the importance of attempting to maintain food security remains important in the Jordanian psyche, mainly as a result of the unstable security in the region. A second reason for the strength of influence of the agricultural sector is the preponderance of land-owners among the rentier élite. The significance of the sector was reflected in the debate in parliament concerning the WTO agreement. As part of the agreement for accession to the WTO, the state agreed to reduce estimated domestic support and export subsidies by 13.3% over seven years from the date of joining. The WTO allowed the extra time due to the drought conditions over the previous few years.[895] However, debate in parliament expressed concerns about the effects on the agricultural sector, in particular. Farmers were concerned that Jordanian agricultural products would not easily compete in Europe, given the stringent quality standards applied and given the fact that Europe is traditionally protective of its agriculture sector and under pressure from its own influential farming lobbies. Local farmers also fear that they will be threatened in the Jordanian market as well, when high quality agricultural products enter the Kingdom at extremely competitive prices.

At the beginning of the period, the state controlled significant aspects of the sector, including fixing the prices of many inputs and outputs and what could be grown through the use of crop licences, as well as subsidising outputs and inputs including finance and the scarce resource of water. In February 1993, following a report drafted with the assistance of the UN Food and Agriculture Organisation, the state announced that the public sector role would in the future be no more than one of regulator and co-ordinator, with an emphasis on encouraging exports, investments and water conservation.[896] In December 1984, after more than a year of discussions, a World Bank loan of US$80m was approved. The loan was to enable the restructuring of the sector and was aimed at improving productivity and exports, through phasing-out subsidies and price controls, improving water conservation and restructuring the associated institutions (such as the Agricultural Credit Corporation and the Jordanian Co-operatives Organisation). In the twelve months prior to signing the agreement, the sector had been granted exemption from customs duties for all inputs to agricultural production. In addition, exemption had been granted from interest payments at varying rates of between 30% and 100% for small farmers, at a cost to the Treasury of JD11m. Finally, the purchase price set by the state of locally-produced grain was raised to encourage production. The only move to liberalise the market was the abolition of the purchase of tomatoes at fixed prices by the Jordan Agricultural Marketing and Processing Company. The price was now left to market forces.[897] The following year, customs duties were imposed at a flat rate of 30% on imported fruit and vegetables and 10-30% on poultry.[898] In 1996, domestic fodder prices were restructured and a system of direct cash transfer for owners of one hundred or fewer goats and sheep was introduced.[899] The following year, the prices of fruit and vegetables were finally floated. In addition, over the period, the state has consistently rescheduled loans, granted exemptions from interest payments and granted custom duty exemptions on inputs for agricultural production. In April 1999, a new package of assistance (worth JD12-15m) was announced which included the provision of livestock fodder barley at JD75/tonne and bran at JD65/tonne. The package also: exempted 50% of interest on ACC loans and rescheduled the remaining 50%; provided farmers with vaccines and veterinary supplies and transport for using them; continued to purchase field crops from local producers; granted free water for livestock; and provided farmers with pesticides.[900] Part of the WTO agreement was that the state agreed to reduce estimated domestic support and export subsidies to the sector by 13.3% over the following seven years.[901] The prices of livestock feed was finally liberalised in April 2001, but the question of water subsidies remains to be addressed.

The moves to assist the export sector have included: abolishing most trade licences (the number of licences issued had increased from 36,000 to 1000 traders in 1985 to 100,000 licences to 36,000 traders in 1992)[902] and easing trade regulations (1992); allowing exemption from income tax on 70% of net profits accrued from exports (1993); reducing interest rates for export facilities to five points below discount rate (1993); increasing the allowance in commercial bank credit for exporters to JD400m, of which JD335m was set aside for the private sector (1994);[903] abolishing export licences for Jordanian commodities, except to countries with which the Kingdom has payment arrangements (1997);[904] and reducing difficulties in obtaining import licences through Ministry of Industry and Trade regulation no. 1, which makes import licences a formality rather than a barrier (1997).[905]

In the industrial sector, the state has been reducing the level of customs duties[906] in line with the IMF agreements and the need to meet the international agreements with the WTO, the EU, European Free Trade Association, the USA FTA, and other bilateral accords. This move has not been actively sought by the state since the reductions have always met the minimum conditions necessary to meet the various agreements. Despite the agreement to join the WTO, the state has still attempted to protect manufacturers against the increasing global competition. In November 2000, new regulations were passed to increase duties on imports, providing that local manufacturers could prove the damage sustained by their industries. The duties could be imposed for up to four years, and could be extended if the situation remained the same. However, local companies are expected "to enhance efficiency and upgrade their status" according to Minister of Industry and Trade Secretary-General, Samir Tawil.[907]

A series of laws have been implemented to encourage investment, in particular FDI. Initial attempts to allow foreign investment were hampered by the Islamic opposition in parliament. In August 1991, they defeated three articles in the draft bill, on each occasion by 29-28 votes, with twenty-three deputies refraining from voting. The first article would have required any foreign investment to be approved by Cabinet, whereas the deputies were interested in allowing only Arab investment to be approved in this manner. The second article was said to interfere with local labour organisations, while the third would have allowed foreign investors to participate in all tenders and projects provided that they deposited convertible currency to the extent of JD25,000.[908]   A spokesperson for the Muslim Brotherhood, Deputy Mohammed Abu Faris, stated "We are not interested in those investments which aim at ruling us in the future."[909] In 1992, a new law regulating Arab and foreign investments was passed, allowing income tax and social security exemptions from five to seven years in Amman, ten years in the Irbid and Balqa regions and fifteen years elsewhere.[910]   The Law Governing Arab and Foreign Investment, no. 22 of 1992 also allowed for non-Arab foreign investment to be approved by Cabinet. This system did not actually prove to be an incentive for investment: in 1993 approval was granted for US$60m, but the actual investment totalled only US$0.7m, a take-up rate of just over 1%.

A new draft investment law was submitted in 1994 and approved in 1995. The Investment Promotion Law no. 16 of 1995 contained two elements: 1) easing bureaucratic disincentives for businesses, including no longer requiring government approval for projects and investments in the stock market. In addition, the law allows any non-Jordanian investor to own all or part of a project or economic activity in the Kingdom, provided that the capital, the value of the share or the amount of the contribution to the project is transferred to Jordan in convertible foreign currency before the conveyance procedures are finalised; and 2) increasing incentives for businesses, such as reducing corporation tax from 50% to 30% in the banking and insurance sectors, from 40% to 15% in priority sectors (for example tourism and mining), and to 25% in other sectors. The specific details concerning restrictions on investment were covered in Non-Jordanian Investment Promotion Regulation, no. 1 of 1996. The regulation aimed at encouraging foreign investment by opening up certain sectors, such as tourism, in the Amman Stock Exchange (ASE) to foreign investment beyond the 49% ceiling. However, the ceiling remained in construction and contracting, land and air transport, trading and trade services, banking and insurance, telecommunications, mining and agricultural products.[911] In addition, foreign investors were able to buy shares on the ASE for up to 50% of existing companies unless the percentage of the non-Jordanian ownership was more than 50% at the time of closing of subscription in the shares of the public shareholding company, in which case the maximum limit for non-Jordanian ownership was fixed at that percentage.[912]   The minimum level of any foreign investment in ASE was reduced from JD5000 to JD1000. The minimum level of FDI was set at JD100,000 in any one project.[913]

Finance Minister Jardaneh argued that the new law was "a very liberal by-law and the spirit of the by-laws is that foreign and domestic investors will be treated equally with no discrimination."[914] The law also states that "a non-Jordanian investor can repatriate his foreign capital ... and what he has gained in profits or the liquidation or sale of his project or stock without delay and in convertible currency."[915] The law grants customs and GST exemptions (among other incentives) to industry, agriculture, hotels, hospitals, marine transport, railways and "any other sector or sub-sectors the Council of Ministers approve of upon the Council's recommendation."[916] In addition, leisure and recreational compounds and conference and exhibition centres have been added by virtue of the Cabinet's resolution dated 28 October 1997.[917]

In July 1997, the Higher Council for Investments recommended the abolition of the 50% ceiling on foreign investment in the mining, construction contracting, and commercial and commercial services sectors.[918] In September, Regulation no. 1 of 1996 was amended by Regulation no. 39 of 1997. Originally, the intention was to lift all restrictions on foreign ownership in all sectors. Restrictions were lifted in land and air transport, trading and trade services and mining products. However, following pressure from the private sector, the ceiling remained on the three areas recommended for liberalisation by the Higher Council for Investments.[919]   In addition, the law reduced the minimum investment by non-Jordanians in any project from JD100,000 to JD50,000, as well as abolishing the previous minimum of JD1000 in the Amman Financial Market.[920]   In 1999, the Higher Council for Investments again recommended that the 50% ceiling on foreign investment be removed, this time using the banking and insurance sectors as the prime examples.[921] Despite the recommendation, Non-Jordanian Investments Promotion Regulation no. 54 for 2000 maintained the ceiling. However, as a result of the WTO agreement, the state must allow 100% foreign ownership in the eleven service sectors, including construction services, communications, business services, tourism and financial services.[922]

Other steps to improve the regulatory environment for investment included: the Securities Law 1996, which allows dual-listing of Jordanian firms on Amman Financial Market and international exchanges; encourages Jordanian Global Depository Receipts; and for the first time allows the listing of mutual funds on the stock exchange;[923] the Company Law 1996, which among other aspects abolished the state issuing committee which determined the price of new share issues;[924] the Securities Law no. 23 for 1997, which separated supervision from the operation of the Amman Financial Market, through the creation of the Securities and Stock Exchange Commission (a public body), the ASE and the Securities Depository (both private companies);[925] the agreement to establish an Arab Free Trade Zone by 2008, which was reached in Cairo in February 1997; the amendment of 1999 to the 1997 Companies Law, which controversially allows the Trade and Industry Minister to dissolve a company board in the event of any financial irregularity following which the Minister can then appoint members until elections for a new board take place;[926] the EU-Med partnership which was ratified by parliament in September 1999, and activated at the beginning of 2000; the WTO agreement signed on the 27th December 1999, which came into force in March 2000; and the agreement to sign a FTA with the USA,[927] which eliminates all tariffs in four stages over ten years on bilateral trade for goods and services, including textiles, farm goods and other products.[928]

The initial success of the emphasis on gaining FDI,[929] including the privatisation programme, is apparent from the UNCTAD figures, which show that in the five years from 1992 to 1996 average FDI inflows were less than US$8m per year, whereas in the period 1997 to 2000 the average was US$404m. The increase in instability in the region has seen FDI fall to US$100m in 2001 and US$56m in 2002.[930] Foreign investment in all sectors of the stock exchange has also been promoted since 1989, although to varying degrees (table 8.4), with services have shown the most dramatic increase, climbing 23.9 percentage points to 26.8%. However, despite the privatisation programme and other efforts to gain FDI, the share of foreign investment in the Amman Financial Market has fallen since 1998 indicating once more the vulnerability of Jordan's economy to external events. In this case, the effects of the East Asian crisis, which negatively affected investment in the emerging markets in general, and the regional instability, which affected investment in Jordan specifically.

Table 8.4: Foreign Ownership in Amman Financial Market, 1994-2002 (%)

Date	Banks and Finance	Insurance	Services	Industry	All Sectors
1994	46.7	16.0	2.9	23.6	31.1
1995	46.3	15.7	3.3	19.9	31.0
1996	47.7	16.5	7.3	21.8	32.8
1997	53.8	16.0	9.3	26.0	39.1
1998	56.3	15.1	11.6	28.1	43.9
1999	56.7	15.6	11.7	30.6	43.1
2000	55.1	17.9	21.3	30.2	41.7
2001	49.3	17.8	20.0	27.4	38.5
2002	50.2	18.9	26.8	26.3	37.4

Source: Adapted by author. Amman Financial Market, (various), *Annual Report*, (Amman: Amman Financial Market) and Amman Financial Market, (various), *Monthly Report*, (Amman: Amman Financial Market).

The support for the private sector by the state has shown a move on the continuum away from the state end. Although the strength of the agricultural lobby has allowed subsidies and other forms of support to continue, a very gradual liberalisation of the sector has been evident. A greater change has been apparent in the reduction of customs duties (although this change has been at the instigation of the donor community rather than the state). State involvement in the export sector and in the promotion of investments has altered from direct intervention (with the aim of complete control) to indirect control by regulation (with the aim of maintaining as much control as possible).

STATE-OWNED ENTERPRISES

The attempts to privatise the SOEs have been dealt with extensively in the previous chapter. Tables 8.5 and 8.6 give a brief review of the sales by the state. According to the re-named Executive Privatisation Commission, the JIC had divested shares in forty-nine companies by the end of 2002. Twenty of the companies had less than 5% government ownership, 12 between 5% and 10%, and 17 over 10%.[931] The JIC sales have raised US$151m.[932] In theory, therefore, the divestment of the SOEs ought to mean a strong move in the direction of a market economy. However, two factors mitigate this analysis. Firstly, many of the divestments have been to the SSC. Although the organisation is legally and administratively independent, the board of directors is dominated by state officials; the Chairman is the Minister of Labour, and should any legal conflict occur the Minister is considered the representative of the organisation.[933]   Secondly, the JIC has continued to invest in new projects in partnership with the private sector. The JIC still encourages investment promotion activities by identifying investment opportunities, developing feasibility studies for projects and inviting the private sector to invest in these projects, with or without JIC participation. However, the maximum state investment is presently limited to 10%.

Table 8.5   Completed Privatisation Transactions to 31/12/02

Company	Date	Size and Type of Transaction
Ma'in Spa Complex	10/98	30-year lease agreement with consortium led by French company ACCOR.
Public Transport Corporation	11/98	10-year contract with 3 local companies, annual fee of JD0.7m.
Jordan Cement Factories Company	12/98	33% stake to French company Lafarge Group for JD72m (US$102m).
Water Authority of Jordan	04/99	Management agreement to a consortium led by French company Suez Lyonnaise des Eaux.
Aqaba Railway Corporation	08/99	25-year management lease to consortium led by US company Raytheon for JD20m.
Jordan Telecommunications Company	01/00	40% stake to France Telecom and Arab Bank for US$508m. 9% to local parties for US$114m.
Duty Free Shops (RJ)	08/00	100% sale to Spanish company Aldeasa for US$60.1m.
Aircraft Catering Centre	08/01	80% sale to Alpha British Company for US$20m.

Source: Adapted by author. Atlas Investment Group, (April 2001), *Jordan Country Report*, (Amman: Atlas Investment Group), p.42 and Executive Privatization Unit, (various), *Privatization News.*

One of the early suggestions of the ECC had been the enactment of a privatisation law,[934] something the donor community had been actively promoting for a number of years. In the final law, parliament managed to have a 'golden share' clause inserted that allowed the government to veto company policy that it deemed was against the 'national interest'. Interestingly, parliament promoted this clause against the advice of their normally influential Economic and Finance Committee, headed at the time by future Prime Minister Ali Abul Ragheb. The state did not seem to seek this power but the clause was not revoked by the Upper House, a more representative element of the rentier élite. Thus, although privatisation *per se* ought to be a move towards the market economy, the control of the process by the state has allowed the process to be subverted.

One particular change of outlook by the SOEs has been their acceptance of the need to become involved in joint ventures with foreign companies.[935]   JPMC negotiated a US$600m joint venture with Norway's Norsk Hydro, which eventually failed (ostensibly due to an internal restructuring of Norsk Hydro). Two successful joint ventures have been concluded with the Indo-Jordan Chemicals Company (with sales of US$82m in 1998) and the Nippon Jordan Fertiliser Company (with US$40m in the same year). APC has concluded 50:50 venture agreements with Albemarle Holdings of the US for a US$120m bromine project and with Kemira Agro (Finland) for a US$100 potassium nitrate and dicalcium phosphate project. In addition, the APC subsidiary Jodico has signed an US$80m agreement with Monenco Agra (Canada) and Atilla Dogan (Turkey) for the turnkey construction of a magnesium oxide plant. A further thirty-two projects have been identified by Jodico that are suitable for joint ventures.

Table 8.6   **Major Sales by JIC to 31/12/02**

Date	Shareholdings Divested
1995	Jordan Hotels and Tourism Company
1996-97	Jordan Paper and Cardboard Factories; Jordan Tobacco and Cigarettes (100%)
1998	Jordan Cement Factories
1999	The Housing Bank; Cairo Amman Bank; Export and Finance Bank; Jordan Dairy Company; Petra Tourist Transport Company; The Industrial Commercial Agricultural Company; Jordan Electrical Power Company; Jordan Ceramics Industries Company; Jordan Worsted Mills Company; and Jordan Tanning Company (100%)
2000	Arab International Hotels Company; Jordan Poultry Processing & Marketing Company
2001	Jordan Paper and Cardboard Factories Company; Jordan Press Foundation
2002	National Shipping Lines

Source: Adapted by author. ASE, "ASE—Foreign Investment Regulations; Privatisation", *ASE website*, www.ase.com.jo/pages/privatisation_eng.htm.

This measure has again highlighted a move towards the market end of the state-market continuum. However, the move has not been as clear-cut, with continuous delays with the process of privatisation and the insertion of the golden share clause in the privatisation bill. In addition, the key export earner of mining has not yet been privatised, although since the creation of the ECC the state has begun to acknowledge the need to include JPMC and APC in the programme.

THE CHANGING ROLE OF THE STATE

This review of the changing public-private sector relationship has highlighted how certain elements of the rentier élite have been proclaiming the necessity to change the direction of the economy to enable the private sector to become the engine of future development. This approach is in line with the donor community's objectives in introducing the SAP. The successful implementation of the policy would reduce the state's ability to continue with its expenditure policy, while the policy's adoption would result in a move towards the market end of the state-market continuum model on all five measures. The evidence highlighted in this section has not produced any clear-cut result, although overall the tendency has been to move the economy to a more market-based one. Part of the confusion has stemmed from the changing role of state which has latterly been encouraged by the donor community.[936] The involvement of the state in a market-based economy is essentially restricted to the regulatory sphere and the provision of goods/services of a 'common good' nature. In Jordan during the 1990s, a slow withdrawal of the state was evident in the productive sector, with a commensurate increase in the regulatory functions. However, the state still retains its role as facilitator in the economy through investment in infrastructure, the planning process, and institutional support. Thus, the state's role has shifted from direct intervention with the aim of complete control to indirect control by regulation with the aim of maintaining as much control as possible in order to continue access to rent.

What, then, has been the outcome of the changes on the four manifestations of the Jordanian state-market relationship as at 1989? The four features discussed were: state involvement in productive companies; the manipulation of the market by the state; the politicisation of the economy; and the institutional arrangements of the private sector. The first three features are discussed immediately below, while the final feature is discussed in the third section.

Firstly, the state has reduced its share of ownership in the productive sector, although it still dominates the economically and strategically important mining sector. Although in 2003 26% of the shares in APC were sold to the Canadian company, Potash Corporation of Saskatchewan. Furthermore, the scope for the state to influence the SOEs through other means, such as pricing, subsidies and monopoly arrangements, has been reduced by international agreements and pressure from the donor community. However, pricing of phosphates, for example, remains dictated by the state rather than the market. In addition, the composition of the boards of directors of a number of companies, as well as who serves on these boards, is still in the hands of the state.

Secondly, pressure from the international community, along with the economic recession, has resulted in a considerable reduction in the direct manipulation of the market. The abolition of the Ministry of Supply, which used subsidies and price regulation extensively during the 1970s and 1980s, had a major effect on the new direction. In addition, a reduction in the influence of the Ministry of Industry and Trade has been apparent, particularly in the field of external trade. However, the Ministry of Planning has been able to maintain an important influence in the economy by redefining its roles and activities. It has been able to strengthen its role in the economy as the interlocutor between the state and the donor community, as well as retaining its role of dispensing the OEA received and continuing to issue five-year development plans, despite the wishes of the IMF to the contrary.

Thirdly, the politicisation of the economy remains, although the state is less able to grant access to the economy in return for political support due to the twin constraints of the donor community and the economic recession. The appointments by the regime to the influential ECC are an example of the continued politicisation of the economy. In addition, the relative initial success of the ECC when compared with previous attempts indicates the increased acceptance of formal arrangements between the state and the private sector.

Thus to a degree the changes in the state-market continuum are reflected in the changes in the state-market relationship. The next sector analyses how these changes have been mirrored in the changes in the rentier features of Jordan's political economy.

CHANGING CHARACTERISTICS OF THE POLITICAL ECONOMY

In chapter two, the theoretical discussion highlighted an important number of differences between production economies, induced rentier state economies and private sector rentier economies. The main differences are illustrated in table 8.7. At the macro-economic level, private sector rentier economies and induced rentier state economies both display similar aspects of: dependency on rent (albeit of differing types); suffering from chronic balance of trade deficits due to the high levels of imports; showing high levels of consumption in comparison to GDP; and having a tendency towards a service-oriented economy. However, only the induced rentier state economy can afford to run continuous budget deficits as the levels of aid can cover the shortfalls.

Table 8.7: State and Private Sector in Different Types of Economies

Economy Type	State	Private Sector	State-Private Sector Relationship
Induced State Rentier Economy	Rentier mentality results in expenditure policy aimed at control of access to rent.	Relatively homogenous; Dependent on state; Service orientation.	Regime élite; Blurred with élite circulation; Voluntary co-optation; Informal contacts; Corruption.
Private Sector Rentier Economy	Rentier mentality results in policy adapted to gaining access to rent.	Relatively heterogeneous; Independent of state; Service orientation.	Separate; Formal but weak contacts.
Production Economy	Taxation policy to recreate itself.	Heterogeneous; Independent of state; Production orientation.	Separate; Formal but strong institutional contacts.

The following section assesses to what degree and in what direction the political economy of Jordan has moved from that of the induced state rentierism exhibited in 1989. Different outcomes have been possible given the decline in state rent, the increase in private sector rent and the attempts by the donor community to induce the birth of a market economy. Which element has won out? Has the state managed to maintain the political economy of induced state rentierism? Or has the increase in remittances allowed private sector rentierism to be become dominant?

Or has the market economy won over the state-led economy? Or are all three aspects (induced state rentierism, private sector rentierism, and the market economy) now part of the political economy landscape of the new millennium in Jordan?

To recap, the following aspects of induced state rentierism were strongly in evidence in Jordan in 1989. An economy exhibiting a dependency on rent, with consequent imbalances in the budget and balance of trade, a bias towards the service sector and high levels of consumption. Secondly, the private sector was relatively homogenous in its outlook, dependant on the state and service-oriented. Thirdly, the state had adopted a rentier mentality that was manifested in a two-dimensional policy. On the one hand the policy was based on maintaining control of and access to the rent, while on the other hand the expenditure policy allowed the state to buy political legitimacy. Finally, the relationship between the private and public sectors was predicated upon the rentier élite, voluntary co-optation or capture of the private sector by the state and informal contacts between the two sectors. Based on these aspects, the following sections analyse the changes in the political economy of Jordan during the 1990s.

ECONOMY LEVEL ANALYSIS

This section discusses the changes in the macro-economy relevant to the changing rentierism between 1989 and 2002. The first measure is the continuous budget deficit excluding aid, which can be maintained in an induced rentier state economy, but not in a production economy or under private sector rentier economy. The second and third measures are the high levels of imports and bias towards the service sector, both of which are evident in either type of rentier economy, but not in a market economy.

As discussed earlier in the chapter government expenditure as a percentage of GDP has declined over the period as the expenditure policy has been weakened. Initially, the related budget deficit (excluding aid) fell dramatically from in excess of JD425m to under JD10m, but thereafter the deficit climbed until reaching a peak in 2002 of to JD542.6m (figure 8.4). Relating the deficit to the GDP, a similar pattern emerges. However, the percentage of the deficit falls from a peak of over 18% in 1989 to only 8.2% by 2002. Overall, then, the figures indicate a move away from induced state rentierism towards a production economy.

One of the effects of an induced rentier state economy is that higher levels of consumption can be maintained and that this excess of consumption becomes directed towards imports because of the underdeveloped industrial sector.   In normal circumstances, if the induced rentier state economy were being replaced by a successful export-oriented industrial market economy then the relative levels of imports should decrease. Two indicators have been used to assess whether this reduction has taken place in the last decade: imports as a percentage of GDP and imports as a percentage of exports (figure 8.5). The first measure indicates the importance of imports in the economy as a whole. The expected path ought to be downwards as the rentier mentality of high consumption can no longer be maintained. If the economy has successfully moved towards an export-oriented one then a downward curve should also be in evidence in the second measure. As can be seen, both sets of figures follow roughly similar paths. However, although a general decline is evidenced in both cases between 1990 and 1999, between 1989 and 2002 no clear pattern can be traced: the figure for 2002 is higher than in 1989.

Figure 8.5   **Budget Deficit, 1989-2002**

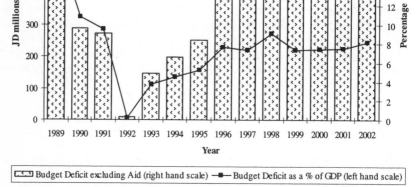

Sources: Adapted by author. CBJ, (various), *Monthly Statistical Bulletin*, (Amman: CBJ) and CBJ, "Monthly Statistical Bulletin", *CBJ website*, www.cbj.gov.jo/docs.

Figure 8.6 Imports as a Percentage of Exports and of GDP, 1989-2002

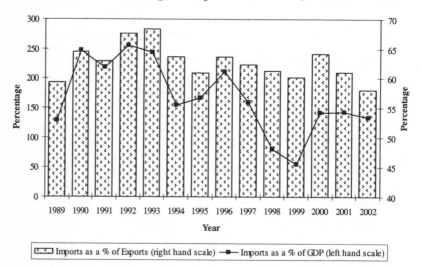

Sources: Adapted by author. CBJ, (various), *Monthly Statistical Bulletin*, (Amman: CBJ) and CBJ, "Monthly Statistical Bulletin", *CBJ website*, www.cbj.gov.jo/docs.

In the relationship between imports and exports the figure for 2002 (180.5%) is the first year that the level has fallen below that of 1989 (192.9%). The problem for the IMF in attempting to reduce the level of imports whilst simultaneously raising exports, is that the constraints facing Jordan, such as the lack of resources and investment, are exacerbated by the fact that the induced rentier state economy has been replaced by the private sector rentier economy: as discussed in chapter two, private sector rentier economy also encourages high levels of consumption, which are directed towards imports. The evidence would seem to suggest a move away from an induced rentier state economy, but in the direction of a private sector rentier economy rather than a production economy.

Table 8.8 Registered Companies and Individual Enterprises, 1989-2002

Year	Registered Companies			Individual Enterprises		
	Number	Capital JDm	Average Capital JD	Number	Capital JDm	Average Capital JD
1989	1871	52.5	28060	7169	24.9	3473
1990	2393	46.2	19306	7919	28.1	3548
1991	4145	94.0	22678	10755	40.0	3719
1992	4556	162.6	35689	11944	61.1	5116
1993	4409	242.5	55001	11119	76.1	6844
1994	4462	408.4	91528	12169	114.6	9417
1995	4456	460.1	103254	12368	103.3	8352
1996	4217	288.1	68319	12174	66.2	5438
1997	4294	206.7	48137	11740	62.2	5298
1998	4097	191.3	46693	11549	51.7	4477
1999	3755	138.6	36911	12710	76.1	5987
2000	4351	145.5	33441	16025	74.9	4674
2001	4943	193.4	39137	15656	74.2	4739
2002	4717	128.4	27223	17512	66.6	3801

Source: Adapted by author. Ministry of Industry and Trade, *Ministry of Trade and Industry website*, www.mit.gov.jo.

As was highlighted in the theoretical chapter, one of the major effects of induced state rentierism is the over-development of the service sector vis-à-vis the industrial sector. Has the decline in state rentierism allowed the balance to be redressed to any degree, especially considering the aim of the donor community to promote industrialisation? This section answers the question by looking at the following statistical data: numbers and capitalisation of registered companies by sector; numbers and capitalisation of individual enterprises by sector; output as percentage of GDP by sector; share of exports by sector; trading volumes and market capitalisation on the ASE by sector; and new issues on the ASE by sector. The difference between the first two measures is that registered companies include all forms of partnerships, limited liability companies and public shareholding companies; by contrast, individual enterprises are owned by a single person. Intuitively, since the registered companies have a larger average capitalisation (table

8.8), they ought to be more likely to have closer contacts with the rentier élite. Therefore, the individual companies lacking the comfort of links to the rentier élite ought to be more responsive to the pressure to adopt a market-oriented approach. As a result, any movement from rentierism to a market economy ought to be more evident in these enterprises.

The dramatic increase in numbers and capitalisation of both types of companies in the early 1990s can be attributed to three factors. Firstly, the boom was driven by returnees' capital after the outbreak of the Gulf War. The second factor was the relaxation by the state of the entry requirements for all types of business, but especially in the manufacturing sector—a move associated with boosting the production economy. Thirdly, the outbreak of optimism following the progress in the peace process helped promote a boom in the registration of new companies.[937] However, the overall number of companies stagnated for the rest of the decade as the boom fuelled by the returnees' capital extinguished itself, the peace process stagnated and the economy again entered a period of recession. Further evidence of the effects of the recession is that although the number of companies has tended to remain static (with the notable exception of the growth in individual enterprises in 2000 and registered companies between 1999 and 2001) the total capital of the companies has fallen significantly since peaking in 1994/95. In the case of registered companies, total capitalisation has fallen from around JD460m in 1995 to just over JD128m in 2002, while the individual enterprises' total capitalisation fell from just under JD115m in 1994 to just under JD67m in 2002.

Table 8.9   **Registered Companies by Sector, 1989-2002[938]**

Date	Industry				Services			
	Number	%	Capital JDm	%	Number	%	Capital JDm	%
1989	370	19.8	19.4	37.0	1490	79.6	32.7	62.3
1990	488	20.4	16.7	36.1	1897	79.3	29.3	63.4
1991	710	17.1	46.5	49.5	3418	82.5	47.1	50.1
1992	813	17.8	101.0	62.1	3724	81.7	60.0	36.9
1993	668	15.2	146.8	60.5	3720	84.4	93.2	38.4
1994	648	14.5	182.3	44.6	3804	85.3	225.6	55.2
1995	533	12.0	155.2	33.7	3919	87.9	300.8	65.4
1996	301	7.1	28.5	9.9	3915	92.8	255.6	88.7
1997	306	7.1	50.1	24.2	3988	92.9	156.6	75.8
1998	387	9.4	24.0	12.5	3710	90.6	167.3	87.5
1999	400	10.7	28.0	20.2	3355	89.3	110.6	79.8
2000	446	10.3	25.3	17.4	3905	89.7	120.2	82.6
2001	517	10.5	23.9	12.4	4416	89.4	167.9	87.0
2002	645	13.7	32.2	25.1	4027	85.4	93.7	72.9

Source: Adapted by author. Ministry of Industry and Trade, *Ministry of Trade and Industry website*, www.mit.gov.jo. The percentages will not add up to 100% as agriculture sector is omitted.

In terms of the numbers of registered companies, the balance between industry and services has swung dramatically in favour of the latter, with the industrial share falling from 20.4% in 1990 to only 13.7% in 2002 (table 8.9). The industrial share had fallen as low as 7.1% in 1996 and 1997 before recovering. The recovery coincides with the strengthening of the move towards economic liberalisation, while the slump covers the period of the repatriation of the returnees' capital which, according to most analysts, was invested mainly in construction. Although a clear picture of a swing to services is evidenced by the numbers of registered companies, a more complex picture emerges when the capitalisation of those companies is analysed. The share of the volume of capital invested in industry increased from 1990 to the end of 1992. The share then collapsed to the end of 1996, before recovering erratically to 2002. However, over the period, the share of capital of industrial companies has fallen by almost 12 percentage points in the period. Overall, between 1989 and 2002 this measure indicates a consolidation of the rentier economy, although since 1996 a move towards the production economy is in evidence.

Turning to the evidence of the individual enterprises, in contrast to the registered companies, the relative numbers of industrial enterprises has fluctuated to a lesser degree, falling from 9.5% in 1989 to 6.1% in 2002 (table 8.10). As with the registered companies, a more complex picture emerges when looking at the capitalisation of the individual enterprises. After an initial decline from almost one-third in 1989, the industrial share increases to a peak of almost 55% in 1994 before declining haphazardly to just over 21% in 2002. As predicated, the shift towards the service sector is less evident than among the registered companies (figure 8.6). Nevertheless, these figures would seem to reflect a failure to promote either an industrial sector or a market economy.

Table 8.10   **Individual Enterprises by Sector, 1989-2002**[939]

Date	Industry				Services			
	Number	%	Capital JDm	%	Number	%	Capital JDm	%
1989	678	9.5	8.0	32.1	6489	90.5	16.8	67.5
1990	727	9.2	7.8	27.8	7186	90.7	20.2	71.9
1991	921	8.6	10.3	25.8	9831	91.4	29.6	74.0
1992	1288	10.8	19.0	31.1	10646	89.1	42.0	68.7
1993	1190	10.7	32.3	42.4	9925	89.3	43.7	57.4
1994	1080	8.9	62.3	54.4	11075	91.0	52.2	45.5
1995	1204	9.7	40.7	39.4	11155	90.2	62.5	60.5
1996	1051	8.6	20.4	30.8	11107	91.2	45.6	68.9
1997	1064	9.1	15.4	24.8	10669	90.9	46.7	75.1
1998	1065	9.2	15.4	29.8	10480	90.7	36.2	70.0
1999	1133	8.9	18.0	23.7	11568	91.0	57.8	76.0
2000	1359	8.5	18.9	25.2	14655	91.4	55.9	74.5
2001	1041	6.6	17.6	23.7	14604	93.3	56.4	76.0
2002	1065	6.1	14.1	21.2	16408	93.7	52.0	78.1

Source: Adapted by author. Ministry of Industry and Trade, *Ministry of Trade and Industry website*, www.mit.gov.jo. The percentages will not add up to 100% as agriculture sector is omitted.

Figure 8.7   **Service Sector Share of Capitalisation, 1989-2002**

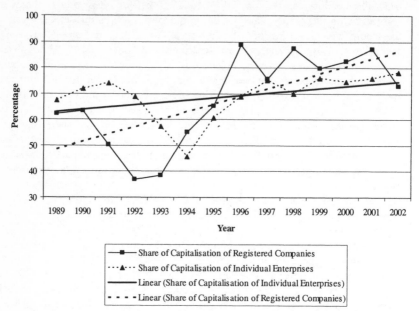

Source: Adapted by author. Ministry of Industry and Trade, *Ministry of Trade and Industry website*, www.mit.gov.jo.

Table 8.11   **Output as Percentage of GDP by Sector, 1989-2002**

Date	Productive Sectors	of which	
		Industry	Service Sectors
1989	35.3	16.9	64.7
1990	35.2	17.3	64.8
1991	35.1	16.1	64.9
1992	37.4	16.1	62.6
1993	35.1	15.4	64.9
1994	36.3	17.7	63.7
1995	35.9	17.8	64.1
1996	34.1	16.2	65.9
1997	31.1	17.7	68.9
1998	31.1	18.5	68.9
1999	30.2	18.9	69.8
2000	29.9	18.7	70.1
2001	30.4	18.8	69.6
2002	31.5	19.8	68.5

Source: Adapted by author. CBJ (various), *Monthly Statistical Bulletin*, (Amman: CBJ).

To date, the analysis has concentrated on the numbers and capitalisation of the registered companies and individual enterprises. However, these figures ignore the overall contribution to the economy of the productive and service sectors. A clearer

picture of the changing balance in favour of the service sector emerges when the
share of GDP is measured between services and the productive sectors. The service
sector has increased its strength relative to the productive sector since 1994, while
industrial output has increased its share to almost 20% by 2002 (table 8.11). As with
the two previous the contribution of services to the GDP has increased over the
period, contrary to the objectives of the SAP.

A major objective of the SAPs has been the promotion of exports. As can be
seen from table 8.12, an impressive swing away from services to the exports of
goods has been experienced. In 1993, goods accounted for 44.2% of total exports
but by 2001 this figure had increased to 60.8%. This move towards increasing
industrial importance is the opposite of that experienced in other measures to date
and has been significantly boosted by the success of the QIZs.

Table 8.12   **Share of Exports by Sector, 1989-2001**

| Date | Goods | | Services | | Total |
	JDm	%	JDm	%	JDm
1989	1109	47.2	1239	52.8	2348
1990	1063	42.4	1447	57.6	2510
1991	1129	45.5	1351	54.5	2480
1992	1218	45.7	1449	54.3	2667
1993	1246	44.2	1573	55.8	2819
1994	1425	47.7	1562	52.3	2987
1995	1770	50.9	1709	49.1	3479
1996	1817	49.6	1846	50.4	3663
1997	1836	51.4	1737	48.6	3573
1998	1802	49.7	1825	50.3	3627
1999	1832	51.8	1702	48.2	3534
2000	1899	53.7	1637	46.3	3536
2001	2294	60.8	1482	39.2	3776

Source: Adapted by author. EIU, (various), *Jordan Country Report*, (London: EIU).

The final set of measures of the changing balance between the productive and
service sector is concerned with the ASE. The stock exchange, to a degree, reflects
the level of investor (both foreign and domestic) confidence in the economy. As can
be seen from figure 8.7, regarding both the service sector share of volume of trade
and the market capitalisation, the figures fluctuate considerably. In the case of
trading volumes, a low of just below 35% was recorded in 1989, with a high of
almost 65% in 2000. The lows and highs for market capitalisation were just under
50% in 1993 to just below 77% in 1998. However, when the trend lines are added, a
clear picture emerges of the strengthening of the service economy over the period,
supporting the case for the strengthening of the rentier economy.

The trading volume and capitalisation on the stock market tend to paint a picture
of investor confidence in the present. In contrast, new issues can be seen as a mark
of investor confidence in the future. New issues tend to be offered when the
business climate is optimistic that economic growth is or will occur in the sector in
which the shares are offered. Therefore, new issues ought to be a good barometer

for judging business optimism in the industrial and services sectors. As can be seen from tables 8.13 and 8.14, the levels of new issues in general have followed the pattern of economic growth in increasing during the first part of the 1990s, before declining as the economy faltered from 1995. Indeed, between 1998 and 2002 inclusive the annual average of new issues was only JD63m: at least partially indicating low business confidence in the long term potential of the economy. In the growth period, industry led the way in the new issues accounting for almost 62% in both numbers and volume, but in the latter part of the decade the service sector took the major share in both numbers (67.7%) and volume (77.4%). Again, the evidence suggests an increase in the strength of the rentier economy.

Figure 8.8 Service Sector Trading Volumes and Capitalisation, 1989-2002

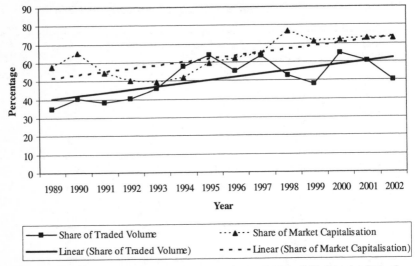

Source: Adapted by author. ASE, "Trading Value at First and Second Markets by Sector", *ASE website*, www.ase.com.jo/pages/hist_english3.htm and Amman Financial Market, (various), *Annual Report*, (Amman: Amman Financial Market).

Overall, the different measures used, with the exception of exports, all paint, to varying degrees, a picture in which the service sector has become more dominant during the period: a move that indicates a consolidation of the rentier economy. A number of the measures highlight a two-stage process, with a turning point around 1996, which coincides with the move towards the implementation of economic liberalisation policies. Even in this latter period, the evidence suggests the growth of the service sector at the expense of the production sector. However, the necessity to provide the market economy with the relevant financial infrastructure has helped boost the changes highlighted. As the 1995 World Bank Private Sector Report argues "[t]he private sector is especially dependent on the efficiency of financial intermediation to fund its investments and business operations."[940] Therefore the development of the banking and insurance sectors has been actively encouraged, helping skew development of the economy in favour of the services sector. Thus, the initial conclusion about the strengthening of rentierism can be questioned, as the services increases could merely be the foundations for building the production economy.

Table 8.13 Primary Market New Issues, Amman Financial Market, 1989-1998

| | | Industry | | Services | | Total |
Date	No.	Value JDm	No.	Value JDm	No.	Value JDm
1989	3	6.3	4	14.6	7	20.9
1990	0	0.0	3	9.4	3	9.4
1991	6	17.5	3	6.7	9	24.2
1992	16	81.0	2	6.0	18	87.0
1993	22	114.1	17	119.9	39	234.0
1994	32	271.3	20	145.8	52	417.1
1989-94	**79**	**490.2**	**49**	**302.4**	**128**	**792.6**
1995	17	88.2	28	252.8	45	341.0
1996	5	21.7	30	178.2	35	199.9
1997	11	80.4	20	257.4	31	337.8
1998	9	19.7	10	32.7	19	52.4
1995-98	**42**	**210.0**	**88**	**721.1**	**130**	**931.1**
Total	**121**	**700.2**	**137**	**1023.5**	**258**	**1723.7**

Source: Adapted by author. Amman Financial Market, (various), *Annual Report*, (Amman: Amman Financial Market) and Amman Financial Market, (various), *Monthly Report*, (Amman: Amman Financial Market).

Table 8.14 Primary Market New Issues, Amman Financial Market, 1989-1998

| | Industry | | Services | |
Date	Number %	Value %	Number %	Value %
1989-94	61.7	61.8	38.3	38.2
1995-98	32.3	22.6	67.7	77.4
Total	**46.9**	**40.6**	**53.1**	**59.4**

Sources: Adapted by author. Amman Financial Market, (various), *Annual Report*, (Amman: Amman Financial Market) and Amman Financial Market, (various), *Monthly Report*, (Amman: Amman Financial Market).

CHANGES IN THE PRIVATE SECTOR CHARACTERISTICS

The private sector under induced state rentierism had become homogenous in its outlook, dependent on the state and service-oriented. The last aspect has already been addressed in the previous section, while the second element is assessed later in the chapter. If the economy was moving towards either private sector rentierism or a market economy, then the private sector ought to be becoming more heterogeneous. This move would be reflected by a change in the institutional structure of the private sector, including an increase in the number of independent business advocacy organisations and the possibility of splits or a reduction in the power of the existing institutions. This element will be analysed in the second part of this section. The first part will study the initiatives and responses of the private sector between 1989 and 2002 to assess to what degree the private sector has changed, and if possible in which direction the sector has moved.

The donor community, in particular USAID and the World Bank, has been a powerful champion of increasing the role of the private sector in the economy through promoting the advocacy skills of the latter. Indeed, one of the objectives of the USAID policy is to encourage:

> [a] vibrant business association community that is effective in identifying and advocating market-oriented policies and practices, including those that support the increased participation of women in all aspects of the economy.[941]

In the present USAID programme, US$3.5m has been set aside to promote this particular aspect through AMIR.[942] The 1995 World Bank Report on the private sector had previously recommended that these organisations required to develop the following functions:

> 1) collecting and disseminating business information ... relating to their own members; 2) carrying out business-related economic and financial analysis to inform their members and to be able to give informed advice to the government; 3) providing a forum for forming collective networks for SMEs; and 4) carrying on an active and regular dialogue with the government on economic and business matters.[943]

In response to these pressures, a change in the pattern of private sector lobbying activities has been in evidence since the mid-1990s. The lobbying has moved from being one that could be described as existing on an *ad hoc* informal basis to one of a more focused formal nature. Paradoxically, on a number of occasions, the emphasis on improved lobbying and advocacy has created problems for both the state as an institution and the donor community, during attempts to introduce new policies concerned with economic liberalisation. Firstly, the private sector was extremely influential in having the sales tax adopted at only 7%, when the IMF was seeking a rate of 12% and the state 10%. However, the victory was short-lived, with the rate being increased to 10% sixteen months later, before being increased further to 13% in mid-1999. Furthermore, the private sector organisations successfully lobbied for the 50% ceiling on non-Arab foreign investment in certain sectors to be retained in the 1995 Investment Law.[944] Once again, in the longer run, the state was able to overcome the private sector resistance. In both cases, the initial outcome was against the wishes of the donor community. Recently, a further example was the ACI's[945] insistence on the imposition of a 5% flat tax on the Aqaba SEZ and offshore income "in order to dissuade industrialists from moving their current operations from other parts of Jordan."[946] The adoption of the sales tax and the opening of the economy to foreign investment threatened the position of the rentier élite. Thus these acts have to be seen in light of the rentier élite with private sector connections attempting to maintain their control over the economy and therefore the rent within the economy.

A major case where the private sector was unsuccessful in challenging the state was the WTO agreement.[947] The WTO agreement was passed by parliament in February 2000 with a "degree of reservation" by a majority of forty-six votes out of the sixty-three cast. Parliament, along with the private sector, was concerned about its impact on the economy, in particular on the agricultural and pharmaceutical sectors. At the time of the debate, Jordan had seventeen registered pharmaceutical manufacturers, four of which had only recently started production. In both 1998 and 1999, pharmaceuticals were the fourth largest contributor[948] to export earnings with an annual value of JD101m (US$140m).[949] Local consumption in 1998 was estimated at US$120m, roughly 60% of which was spent on imported medicine. Only 2% of the Kingdom's production was under licence from foreign companies, with the remainder 'copied' or 'pirated' from both patent and off-patent drugs from countries around the world. A major American pharmaceutical lobby claimed that pharmaceutical piracy in the Kingdom costs US drug manufacturers US$25-50m a year in lost exports. Many Jordanian manufacturers expressed fears that the terms of WTO membership, which compel compliance with the TRIPs (trade related aspects of intellectual property) agreement, would drive the cost of medicines too high for most Jordanians, while the cheaper local substitutes would be forced from the shelves.

The cases discussed to date have been concerned with the private sector responses to state policies. However, in the late 1990s, for the first time since at least the early 1970s, the private sector undertook a couple of high profile initiatives in the form of publicly-issued long-term plans. The REACH Initiative was launched by the Jordan Computer Society in conjunction with AMIR in July 1999 in response to a request by King Abdullah the previous month for a concrete proposal aimed at strengthening Jordan's IT sector. The first plan (REACH) was presented to the King in October 1999, with an updated version (REACH 2.0) published in July 2000 by the newly-formed umbrella organisation, the Information Technology Association, Jordan.[950] The document critically assesses the strengths and weaknesses of the IT sector, with the aim of developing it over a five-year period. The plan outlines a comprehensive framework covering the regulatory environment, the necessary infrastructure, education, capital finance and human resource development. The USAID-funded plan aims to create annual exports of US$550m by the year 2004, up from only US$7.5m in 1999. In addition, the initiative anticipates increasing the number of jobs in the sector from 3,000 in 1999 to 30,000 by the end of 2004.[951] As with other attempts to diversify the Jordanian economy, the REACH initiative has proved optimistic. In 2001 export revenue from the sector totalled only US$38m, while employment was around 5,000. The efforts to improve the position were hit by the global down turn in the sector, while better infrastructure and lower wages in countries such as India reduce the competitiveness of Jordan as an outsourcing IT country. Furthermore although Jordan produces 2,400 IT graduates per year (one of the highest rates per capita in global terms),[952] many of these graduates become the Kingdom's latest labour export.

The second initiative, JV2020, has been co-sponsored by the YEA and the US-funded AMIR programme. The plan was initiated in April 1999 at a meeting with representatives of sixteen of the business associations. By the time JV2020 was launched, twenty-eight business associations, representing over 80% of the economy, were involved. JV2020 aims to double GDP per capita by 2020 through expanding FDI to US$3.5bn pa. The plan lists nearly fifty specific immediate (within twelve months), medium-term (eighteen months) and long-term (twenty-four months) recommendations, along with appropriate benchmarks for implementation.

Although the start date for the recommendations was the 1st January 2000, the plan was not presented to the King until the following year. The recommendations are divided into seven strategic areas: leadership, governance, competitiveness, market access, business environment, infrastructure and human resources. As the YEA argues:

> [t]hese areas are critical to Jordan's modernisation and to its ability to generate jobs of the quality and quantity necessary to meet the expectations of its young and rapidly growing population.[953]

The REACH initiative and JV2020 are important steps forward in the relationship between the private and public sectors. During the 1970s, the private sector had come to rely on the public sector for its continued existence. This reliance ensured that moves towards economic liberalisation and establishing a market-based private sector were not actively sought initially by the majority of the private sector élite. The promotion by the private sector of initiatives related to the process of economic liberalisation, albeit at the prompting of the donor community, represents a significant change of ethos. However, both plans still stress the importance of the government in achieving a successful outcome. One of the six strategic thrusts of REACH 2.0 states that "total commitment and active government leadership is required to stimulate, facilitate and promote the software and IT services sector."[954] Similarly JV2020 acknowledges that an effective private-public partnership is necessary.

The state has responded positively to these moves. In the case of the REACH initiative, a REACH Advisory Council comprising members of the private and public sectors, but headed by the Minster of Information and Telecommunications, was formed at the end of 2000. The objective of the committee is to help with the implementation of the plan. According to the Reach 2.0 final report of the thirty actions suggested, five have been completed, thirteen partially achieved and ten were pending. Of the other two, one remains ongoing, while the other has been revised.[955] One of the participants in JV2020 is the Ministry of Planning's Competitiveness Unit, while the Ministry of Industry and Trade and the Royal Hashemite Court have observer status.

The examples used in this section have highlighted the improved ability of the private sector in being able to use advocacy to respond to threats to its interests, such as the sales tax. However, in the long run the economic recession, backed by the influence of the donor community, has allowed the state as an institution to introduce policies that conflict with the (short-term) private sector interests of the rentier élite. These cases appear to indicate a growing division between the private and public sector élites. The REACH and JV2020 initiatives also imply a division within the rentier élite, on this occasion between the traditional state-dependent private sector and a younger, western-educated group that is less reliant on state contracts. These plans can be taken as a sign of success of the donor policies to create an independent, vibrant private sector. However, given the close ties of this new element with the rentier élite, and given that both plans are predicated on a close partnership between the state and private sector it would seem fair to indicate the continued strength of the rentier élite, albeit in a different format. This difference could be an indicator of a move from induced state rentierism to private sector rentierism, diluted by an increasing production economy.

Inherent in all private sectors are a number of cleavages. In Jordan, in the 1970s and early 1980s the existence of state rent allowed the private sector to develop with few risks. The risk-free environment tended to disguise these cleavages and resulted in a private sector that was relatively homogenous in its relationship with the state. However, with the advent of the economic crisis and the donor community's attempts to introduce economic liberalisation, the comfortable symbiosis between the state and the private sector was threatened, as was the homogeneity of the private sector. As the 1990s wore on, the cleavages along sectoral lines, across space, and also demographically, became more apparent.

One reason for sectoral cleavages is the requirement of different forms of state backing. For example, broadly speaking, industrialists may seek protection from imports through the imposition of customs duties and quotas. On the other hand, those involved in the export/import business do not want these barriers to trade. The case quoted in chapter four is a prime example. In August 1988, Hamdi al-Taba'a, the Minister of Industry, Trade and Supply who had close links to the trading community via the ACC, removed a ban on imports. The ban, which had been introduced a couple of years earlier, was part of a package of policies aimed at protecting Jordanian industry. However, the ban had hit the trading community and was replaced by the introduction of higher customs duties, which had less direct effect on the importers.[956] Other divisions in the private sector can be found spatially, with those businesses outside the Amman-Zarqa conurbation requiring extra infrastructure and grants/incentives. As became apparent in the interviews with the YEA representatives, a relatively new phenomenon in Jordan is the demographic division between the older, established élite, who have prospered under the old policies and the younger more dynamic élite who have a western-style approach to the separation of state and market.[957] Finally, the perception of the Transjordanian-Palestinian divide remains strong with the former being associated with the public sector and supposedly obstructive to the private sector and the latter as the private sector. Although a number of recent studies have challenged the dichotomy,[958] the perception remains powerfully embedded in the minds of many Jordanians and scholars of Jordan.

One arena in which these differences have been exposed is the business associations. Three main business organisations were prominent in Jordan in 1989: the FJCC, the ACI, and the JBA. In addition, a number of other organisations were also in existence, usually catering for specific sectors, such as the Bakery Owners Association. Prior to 1989, the problems of the private sector in maintaining a monolithic outlook were already apparent. As discussed in chapter four, the JBA had been formed in 1985 by the rentier élite as a defensive measure against the differing requirements of the FJCC and ACI. The spatial dimension of the heterogeneity of the private sector surfaced in February 1998 when twenty-three industrialists from Zarqa and Irbid sought to split the ACI into two due to the "power [being] centralised in ACI hands,"[959] with the consequent marginalisation of industrialists outside Amman. The initial response of the ACI was to lobby the Ministry of Industry and Trade to pass a law to establish a Jordan Chambers of Industry, thereby retaining power in Amman. However, later in the year, two new chambers, the Zarqa Chamber of Industry and the Irbid Chamber of Industry, were allowed to be established.[960] The battle for control has been sustained, with the ACI continuing to lobby for a centralised institution while industrialists from the south are seeking to form a fourth chamber.[961]

The donor community's promotion of advocacy as an integral feature of the business associations, with the aim of increasing pressure on the state to promote economic liberalisation and an independent private sector, met with a degree of unresponsiveness from the established organisations. Direct donor influence to overcome this problem could be seen with the registration, in November 1998, of the Young Entrepreneurs Association (YEA) with the assistance of the Friedrich Naumann Foundation.[962] Part of the pressure for creating the YEA came following a survey by the University of Jordan which found that most private sectors companies were family-owned, risk averse and little schooled in modern ways of doing business. The objectives of the YEA are:

> 1) to identify and organise entrepreneurs in Jordan; 2) to change the mindset through the promotion of innovation and creativity; 3) to affect public policy to improve the business environment; 4) to facilitate success of entrepreneurial ideas through provision of relevant training and education; 5) to develop a forum for networking among members and the global business community; and 6) to promote best ethical business practices.[963]

Importantly, although the members of the YEA are usually Western-educated entrepreneurs whose ideological belief is free-market capitalism, many are also the younger relatives of the rentier élite.[964] Over 50% of the eleven members of the latest board of directors, elected in April 2000, are from families in the main circle of the rentier élite.

This section has highlighted the increased fragmentation of the private sector. At first sight, the evidence would seem to support the thesis that the political economy was moving in the direction of becoming market-based. However, as the strength of the JBA and the direction of the YEA would seem to suggest, the rentier élite is adjusting its strategy in the face of the changing economic environment: again, evidence of a move towards private sector rentierism.

CHANGES IN THE STATE CHARACTERISTICS

In the second section of this chapter the state's policies based on the state-market relationship were analysed in light of the declining volumes of aid. The conclusion was that the state had reduced its role in the economy to a limited extent. However, to date the study has not assessed the state's attempts to access the increasing volume of remittances. As has been discussed previously, the state cannot directly access these funds, but has a number of policies that firstly ensure their continuing flow and secondly gain access to the funds through indirect taxation. The maintenance of high interest rates and over-valued exchange rates can be used to attract remittances, but both these measures are detrimental to building an export-oriented private sector. Furthermore, maintaining political relations with the labour-importing countries must be considered a priority. Finally, (as discussed previously) in order to access the rent of remittances the state must use indirect taxation policies. This section briefly reviews these policies.

As mentioned previously, the Gulf War had a dramatic effect on the expatriate workforce of Jordan, when King Hussein's attempt to provide an Arab solution to the conflict was interpreted by the Gulf States as one which supported the Iraqi position. As a consequence of the conflict and the King's stance, around 300,000 people returned to Jordan in a relatively short space of time of time. Around 60% of these had been in Kuwait for more than ten years, and 25% were born there.[965] Remittances, already in decline due to the recession of the 1980s, fell further, from just under JD360m in 1989 to just over JD300m in 1991. Having the constraint of a significant percentage of the population who were Palestinian in origin,[966] the regime was unable to support the American-led coalition. In this case, as Brand argues, the short-term interests of regime stability overrode the need to ensure the flow of remittances.[967] The dramatic increase in remittances in the rest of the decade in excess of JD1500m by 1999 suggests that the policy adopted at the time was correct for the regime. The policies followed since the end of the Second Gulf War have included high interest rates, with discount rate being increased from 6.25% in 1988 to 8.5% in 1990. Although the rate fell to 7.75% in 1997, it increased again to 9% in 1998. The onset of the recession in the late-1990s required the adoption of new policies to boost business, with the result that interest rates were steadily decreased to 4.5% by the end of 2002. By this stage, the stability of the dinar was argued to be sufficient to continue attracting remittances: its value had fallen by around 50% in 1988 to 1989. Nevertheless its value against the dollar continued to fall from an average of US$1.753 to the dinar in 1989 to US$1.41 in 1996. Since then the dinar has been tied to the dollar (which has been a strong currency for the majority of the period). The result has been a dinar that can be considered to be over-valued and thus able to attract remittances.

The invasion of Kuwait by Iraq put pressure on the relations between Jordan and the Gulf States. On the 19th September 1990, the Saudi Arabian Oil Company cut off supplies of oil, then running at 33,000 barrels per day, at only six hours notice—allegedly for non-payment of bills.[968] The situation escalated when the Saudi Government requested that Jordan close the office of its military attaché in Riyadh and also to reduce the numbers of employees at the embassy in Riyadh and the Consulate General in Jeddah.[969] On the 30th of the month the Saudis refused entry to Jordanian lorries.[970] The relationship hit its nadir on the 4th October when Jordan recalled its ambassador; the recall was followed by reciprocal action a couple of days later.[971] No positive moves were made by either side to restore the relationship until June 1992, when King Fahd wished King Hussein a speedy recovery: the latter in his reply expressed the hope that the painful breach with Saudi Arabia would end.[972] However, eighteen months later when King Hussein was on '*umrah*'[973] King Fahd failed to met him.[974] Three years after the outbreak of the War, Kuwait still refused to resume relations. The Kuwaiti Foreign Minister, Shaykh Sabah al-Ahmad, was reported to have said that Kuwait had no objection to resumption of relations with Arab states who supported Iraq, except for Jordan and the PLO.[975] By 1995, relations between Saudi Arabia and Jordan had been regularised with ambassadors being exchanged. However, access to the Saudi job market remained controlled until after the death of King Hussein. Direct trade with Kuwait was not resumed until March 1997,[976] with the first visit of a Jordanian minister, Rima Khalaf, taking place only in July 1998.[977] Relations were finally officially restored in March 1999.[978] Throughout the period, King Hussein made periodic attempts to return relations to normality, not only because of the labour market, but also for other economic reasons, such as trade and aid. However, not until his death were relations able to be restored to previous levels. Indeed one of King Abdullah's initial priorities was to ensure a speedy return to normalisation of relations with Saudi Arabia and Kuwait, with the result that both markets were fully opened to Jordanian workers.

The tax-raising policies of the state have been dictated to a considerable degree by the pressure exerted by the donor community and the signing of various international treaties, such as the WTO agreement. The result has been a move away from tax-raising on imports to a sales tax. The introduction of the latter has allowed the state a wider base of indirect access to the flow of remittances. In this case, the interests of the state as an institution and the donor community have coincided. However, as discussed previously, the slow introduction of the tax was due to the threat faced by the rentier élite with private sector interests.

Apart from the state's attempts to access the remittance rent circuit, the rentier élite also sought other methods of gaining access to rent. The state attempted in February 1998 to introduce a draft Provident Funds Law governing savings funds, which includes company pension funds. The law would have allowed the state to intervene in the management and investment policies of the funds of the professional associations and large private companies. The state was concerned that these funds, estimated to have a value of JD250-300m,[979] lacked effective regulation and consequently claimed that the objective was to protect the small investors from corruption and malpractice. However, the media and a number of deputies were concerned that the policy was merely a ploy to gain access to the funds held by the savings plans. The private sector was unhappy with the draft law to the extent that members of the Arab Bank plan voted to dissolve their fund with assets of JD30m, rather than allow the state to gain access to the assets.[980] A second example is the question of privatisation, which has two elements: the ownership and control of the privatised company, and the use of the privatisation proceeds. In terms of ownership and control, the state has maintained a significant holding in the major privatisations of JCFC and JTC, while also using regulatory measures to maintain control, as with JTC. In the debate over the privatisation proceeds (a form of rent), the state has attempted to maintain control of their usage, despite pressure from parliament and the donor community.

Since 1989, the state as an institution has attempted to access new sources of rent to replace the declining aid. However, other pressures, such as regional instability and international economic demands have constrained its choices. As a result, the state has not only attempted to gain access to the remittance rent circuit but also has looked at internal sources of rent, such as the savings funds. The rentier mentality has continued to drive the actions of the state despite external and, to a lesser degree, internal pressures to the contrary. Again, the evidence suggests a move towards a private sector rentier economy rather than a production economy.

CHANGES IN THE STATE-PRIVATE SECTOR RELATIONSHIP

Since the advent of IMF conditionality, the three main business associations have become progressively more influential in the public debate concerning all aspects of economic liberalisation, as has been discussed previously. Dougherty and Wils argue that a more formal process of negotiation between state officials and private sector associations has been evident from 1990, although they conclude that relations between the economic élites "are as much, or probably more affected by informal processes behind the scenes."[981] The article was written prior to the formation of the ECC in 1999 which, as argued previously, has increased the level of formal relations between the private and public sectors. Overall, the change in the patterns of public-private sector relations and the acceptance of the need to move along the path of economic liberalisation have reduced the ability of the informal network to operate as powerfully as previously—a sign that certain aspects of the rentier state were beginning to be eroded. Nevertheless, the informal relationship still seems to dominate public-private relations, indicating that the donors' wishes to create an independent private sector remain a distant goal. In addition, no clear evidence, anecdotal or otherwise, is apparent that the reformist elements in the private sector are yet fully behind the idea of a market-driven economy, rather than a market economy with preferential access for the rentier élite.

INCREASED PRIVATE SECTOR RENTIERISM AND MARKET ECONOMY, REDUCED INDUCED STATE RENTIERISM

This chapter has sought the answers to two main questions: how have the changes in the 1990s affected state-market relations? and are the changes highlighted by answering the first question reflected in changes in the rentier aspects of the economy that were evident in 1989? The first question was answered by using the five-continua model of the state-market relationship. A number of significant changes have occurred since 1989, namely: in the type and volume of rent entering the economy; in the increased pressure from the donor community to adopt policies of economic liberalisation; and within the rentier élite. Despite these transformations, the evidence of a move towards the market end of the state-market continuum can be described as positive but far from clear-cut. The state has reduced its role in the ownership and control of productive assets and in influencing the market, but continues to politicise the economy. Part of the reason has been the changing role of the state, from direct intervention (with the aim of complete control) to an acceptance of indirect control by regulation (with the aim of controlling as much of the economy as possible). In addition, the flow of remittances has helped the state as an institution to access significant flows of rent via indirect taxation.

The second question was answered by looking at the characteristics of induced state rentierism relating to the economy, the private sector, the state and the state-private sector relationship. In the economy, expenditure had been curtailed which was a move away from the induced state rentierism. The evidence from the changes in volume of imports indicated a move from induced state rentierism to private sector rentierism, while an assessment of the strength of the service sector indicated a possible growing rentierism. The discussion about the aspects of private sector rentierism indicated that splits were becoming more apparent within the rentier élite along two lines: those with public sector interests and those with private sector interests, and, secondly, those with traditional state-dependent relations and those with a more market-based focus. The section concluded that a move away from induced state rentierism had occurred, although the new direction was a mixture of private sector rentierism and a production economy. However, a clearer picture emerged when looking at the state aspects, with a move towards private sector rentierism rather than a production economy. Finally, the strength of informal relations between the sectors remains strong, again indicating a failure to establish a market-based economy.

Although the evidence is extremely confused, the conclusion can be made that while induced state rentierism has weakened (admittedly not dramatically, but sufficiently), private sector rentierism and the market-based economy have both been strengthened to a degree. The rentier élite, although becoming more divided, seems to remain in control of the direction of the economy, despite the pressure from the donor community. On the whole, as Dougherty and Wils argue, "rather than challenging the old private and public sector relationship, the process of privatisation and liberalisation has opened new areas for their co-operation and given the regime new opportunities for patronage."[982]

9

Concluding Comments

INTRODUCTION

This chapter is comprised of three parts. The first section briefly reviews the preceding chapters, while the second part assesses the impact of the study on the debate on rentierism in the Middle East and North African context. The final section turns from the theoretical implications to the practical repercussions for the actors involved.

STUDY REVISITED

The book sets out to understand the effects on the political economy of Jordan (in particular on the state and the private sector and their relationship) of two major changes since 1989, namely: the transformation from an economy primarily based on aid (which tends to be distributed by the state) to one primarily based on remittance income (which tends to be distributed through the private sector); and the increased level of involvement of the donor community, led by the IMF and the World Bank, which has as its stated aim the desire to increase the involvement of the private sector in the economy at the expense of the state. The analysis is conducted through the prism of rentier theory. This theory contends that an economy based primarily on aid creates a different political economy (induced state rentierism) from one based primarily on remittances (private sector rentierism), both of which are different from a 'normal' market economy. The thesis identifies four areas in which the outcomes are differentiated: the natures of the economy, the state and the private sector and the relationship between the state and the private sector.

The third and fourth chapters establish the context for the main analysis. In these chapters the historical investigation illustrates that by 1989 Jordan's economy had moved from one primarily based on aid to a mixture of aid and remittances (with the latter becoming relatively more important). Despite this transformation, which had started in the early 1970s, the characteristics of the political economy were still those of induced state rentierism. These characteristics included: the existence of a rentier élite; state ownership and/or control of productive assets; state involvement in the market; the (ab)use of the economy by the state for political purposes; and the co-optation of the private sector institutions by the state.

In the main analysis, the thesis concludes that by the year 2002 the economy had become a high-level private sector rentier economy, with only a low-level of induced state rentier economy. In addition, the stated intention of the donor community, following the introduction of IMF conditionality from 1989, was to increase the role of the private sector at the expense of the state. The first of these changes ought to have pushed the political economy in the direction of private sector rentierism, while the second aimed to create a market-based political economy. However, the lack of coherence (for political reasons) within the donor community has allowed the state and the rentier élite to maintain a degree of control over the changes. Thus, despite the increasing evidence that the homogeneity of the rentier élite was being eroded, at the end of 2002 both the rentier élite and the state continue to be able to rent-seek, albeit in reduced and different formats.

The conclusion of the analysis in the eighth chapter, using the five-continua state-market model, is that the economy has moved slightly towards the market end of the continuum. However, the role of the state has also altered from one of direct control (e.g. through the ownership of productive assets) to more subtle indirect methods (e.g. using regulatory techniques) in order to attempt to maintain control of the rent flows within the economy. An analysis of the characteristics of the political economy highlights that the features of induced state rentierism have been slightly reduced, while the features not only of the market economy, but also, against the wishes of the donor community, of private sector rentierism (due to the inflows of remittances) have been strengthened.

THEORETICAL IMPLICATIONS

The study has contributed to the existing band of knowledge concerning rentier theory in the Middle East and North Africa in four ways: the clarification of the terms used; the introduction of new terms; the innovation of four models to measure various aspects of rentierism; and the refuting of a number of criticisms of the theory.

Terms, such as 'rentier economy', have been used previously in a conflicting manner. Figure 2.1 expanded as figure 8.1 has helped to clarify the relationship between the various concepts associated with rentierism. Secondly, the new concepts of private sector rentier economy and private sector rentierism have been forged, in order to take account of the effects of remittances on the political economy of the receiving country. The introduction of these terms has allowed an extension of Kiren Chaudhry's pioneering study on remittances (i.e. private sector rent) in Yemen.[983]

The thesis has also initiated the idea of measuring degrees of both the induced state rentier economy and the private sector rentier economy through two separate models. The third innovative model is the five-continua state-market model, which is used to help assess the relationship between the state and the private sector. This model also assisted with the detection of the changing role of the state from one of direct control to indirect control. The final model used measures of the characteristics of induced state rentierism, and allowed an assessment of how these changed during the period studied.

Figure 9.1   Relationship between the Concepts of Rentierism

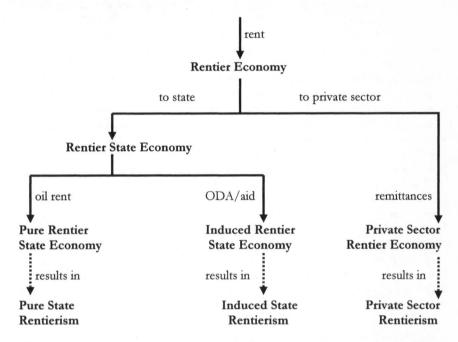

Rentier theory has not been without its critics, the majority of whom raise questions on the theory's inability to account fully for the political economy of the Middle Eastern and North African states affected by significant volumes of rent. The study has helped to answer the following four criticisms: the failure to acknowledge the state-society relationship prior to the advent of the rent income; the lack of dynamism within the theory; the argument that rentierism causes authoritarianism; and the argument that the theory ignores tensions within the élite.

The first criticism is the failure of proponents of rentier theory to take into account the state-society relationship prior to the advent of rent income.[984] Whilst the researcher acknowledges that this criticism has been valid in a number of cases, Jordan provides a perhaps unique study in that the state was established and then constructed through the use of aid. This coincidence helped Emir Abdullah to purchase his initial political legitimacy (or in the words of Weber to use patrimonial power). Thus in Jordan the state-society relationship has effectively unfolded in conjunction with the changing patterns of rent.

Herb criticises what he terms 'simplistic' rentier theory as positing that rentierism causes authoritarianism.[985] However, the claim of rentier theory is that it impedes democracy[986] rather than causes authoritarianism.[987] For example, Huntington in his analysis of the third wave of democratisation following the end of the Cold War argues that the Middle East has been able to resist this move because of its rent

income.[988]   A closely related criticism is that rentier theory cannot account for
political change, although in reality revolutions have occurred in the rentier
economies of Iraq, Libya and Iran.   In addition, the shock of an endogenous or
exogenous crisis in a rentier economy, whether economic (e.g. Saudi Arabia in the
1990s) or political (e.g. Kuwait following the invasion by Iraq), can result in
increased pressures for political change.   The study has illustrated that in Jordan, the
political liberalisation at the end of the 1980s and beginning of the 1990s coincided
with the economic crisis.   However, as the economy has recovered and the rent-
seeking activities have continued so the political liberalisation has been curtailed
with, for example, the promulgation of a less open electoral law (1993), the
cancellation of the November 2001 elections and the introduction of a series of
repressive Press and Publication laws.   Furthermore, the study has provided an
answer to this criticism by highlighting the changing patterns of rent and how the
various actors have adopted new policies in an attempt to maintain control of and
access to the flows of rent—these policies are not claimed to guarantee the
continued success of one group of actors in maintaining control of the rent flows,
nor it is claimed that underlying political structure will remain static.

Finally, Dougherty and Wils argue that the relations of important social actors
are not taken into account.   They contend that the theory not only fails to take into
account tensions within the élite but also wrongly posits a dichotomous relationship
between the economic élites of the public and private sector.[989]   However, the study
has shown how the changing patterns of rent along with the influence of the donor
community have helped to create and/or exacerbate tensions within this élite.
Furthermore, this thesis has used an analysis based on a relatively homogenous
rentier élite (especially in the era of high-level induced rentier state economy),
comprising both the private and public sector economic élites, thus overcoming the
second objection of Dougherty and Wils.

PRACTICAL IMPLICATIONS

Finally, what practical considerations have been highlighted by the analysis? The
first implication concerns the relationship between the state and the rentier élite,
which has previously been relatively consensual as the interests of both actors have
been virtually synonymous. In order to recreate themselves, all states have to walk
the tightrope of extracting sufficient resources from the domestic economy without
upsetting the basis of their political power. Admittedly, in the short term they can
rely on external forms of assistance (grants and/or loans) but this option is not
feasible in the longer run as the case of Jordan has demonstrated. From its
inception in 1921 until at least 1989, the state in Jordan relied to a considerable
extent on the provision of aid, rather than on recourse to local means of extraction.
As has been proved, this option is no longer viable. However, the twin assaults of
the reduction in aid and the conditions set by the donor community have forced the
state not only to increase its tax-raising powers and also to cut-back on its policy of
purchasing political legitimacy. This reduction resulted in the start of the process of
democratisation, although this process has been reversed to a degree in the last few
years as the economic crisis has receded. The state now faces a problem that its
external sources of aid are atrophying, while rent accrues to the private sector in the

form of remittances. This changing pattern of rent means that more resources have to be extracted from the domestic economy—an outcome not appreciated by the rentier élite on whom a considerable portion of the tax burden ought to rest. The scene is set therefore for a divergence of interests between the state as an actor and the rentier élite.

The final point concerns the relationship between the donor community and the state. The SAPs associated with the IMF and the World Bank have been the focus for considerable criticism since their implementation. One strand of the critique has been concerned with the social effects of the policies,[990] as the major losers in the initial stages (at the very least) of the programmes were the disadvantaged members of society due to the cutbacks in government expenditure. A second strand of criticism has been from the economic angle, in which the argument is that the SAPs have tended to be 'one size fits all', i.e. no account is taken of the differing causes of the economic crisis, nor the differing economic structures of the countries involved. The reaction to the Asian crisis of 1997 to 1998 is but one example of this stereotypical approach, with the IMF recommending its 'holy trinity' of government austerity, interest rate rises and liberalisation.[991] This thesis has highlighted the need for a further aspect to be considered by the IMF and the donor community: the lack of a private/public sector dichotomy in an induced rentier state economy. The preponderance of aid helps create a rentier élite which significantly blurs the boundaries between the two sectors. If the aim of the donor community, in particular the heavyweights of the BWIs and the USA, is to reduce rent-seeking activities and implement a 'normal' market economy, then the problems caused by the existence of the rentier élite must be addressed. The present policies have allowed this élite to continue to rent-seek, and have also opened up the possibility of increasing its economic power, albeit at the expense of a slight loss of political power (the democratisation process since 1989).

In conclusion, the medium-term to long-term prognosis for Jordan, as a whole, remains bleak unless the positive aspects of the policy of structural adjustment are delivered to the vast majority of the population and not just restricted to the rentier élite.

Notes

Chapter 2: Theoretical Considerations

1 The gold entering Spain from the Americas in the sixteenth century is an oft-quoted example of an early example of a rentier economy.

2 Beblawi, H., (1987), "The Rentier State in the Arab World", *Arab Studies Quarterly*, vol. 9, no. 4, p.384.

3 Among the different terms used are rentier economy, rentier state, semi-rentier state, allocation state, production state, exoteric state and esoteric state.

4 Beblawi, H. and G. Luciani, (1987), "Introduction", in Beblawi, H. and G. Luciani, (eds.), *The Rentier State*, (London: Croom Helm), p.11.

5 Beblawi, H., (1987), op. cit., p.383.

6 *Ibid.*, p.383.

7 Ibrahim, S., (1982), *The New Arab Social Order: A Study of the Social Impact of Oil Wealth*, (Westview Press: Boulder), p.2.

8 Stauffer, T., (1987), "Income Measures in Arab States", in Beblawi, H. and G. Luciani, (eds.), *The Rentier State*, (London: Croom Helm), p.25.

9 The rent gained from oil extraction in the Gulf States accrues because of the cheap cost of extraction and the high price of the crude oil on the market, i.e. no relationship exists between the cost of production and the sale price, as would be normal according to mainstream economic theories.

10 The term 'donor community' is used in the thesis to refer to the group of official donors (non-official donors, such as NGOs dispense aid but as this type of assistance is not official, it is excluded from the study), whether bilateral or multilateral, which dispense aid.

11 In 1982 Mexico became the first country to default on its debts, leading to a rescheduling of debts throughout the Third World. The debt crisis increased the relative importance of AID to the recipients as the flows of private capital plummeted.

12 The failure of the 1981 Cancun Summit marked the end of meaningful dialogue between the rich and the poor countries. Watkins, K., (1994), "Aid under Threat", *Review of African Political Economy*, no. 66, p.517.

13 Structural adjustment can be defined as "the transition from an unviable economy into a self-sustaining one through altering the structures in the economy." Riddell, R.C., (1987), op. cit., p.96. SAPs were based on the assumption that states interfere with economic efficiency and therefore harm development. Therefore the order of the day was for a slim, efficient, accountable bureaucracy, the aim of which was to create the necessary conditions for a free market economy. To achieve the objective, SAPs use four inter-related components: the

restructuring of incentives; the revision of public investment priorities; an improvement in budget and debt management; and the strengthening of institutions. The policies have been called 'the 3ds' by Cassen (Cassen, R. and Associates, op. cit., p.60) and 'the 4ds' by Lipton and Toye (Lipton, M., and Toye, J.F.J., (1990), *Does Aid Work in India? A Country Study of the Impact of Official Development Assistance*, (London: Routledge), p.101) who add denationalisation to devaluation, deflation and decontrol.

14 OECD, (1995), *Development Co-operation – Development Assistance Committee 1994 Report*, (Paris: OECD), p.12.

15 Stokke, O., (1995), "Aid and Political Conditionality: Core Issues and State of the Art", in Stokke, O., (ed.), *Aid and Political Conditionality*, (London: Frank Cass), p.7.

16 Examples can include tying of goods/services, the size of contribution of the recipient government, and specifying the administrative procedures to be used.

17 Abdel-Khalek, G. and Korayem, K., (1995), "Conditionality, Structural Adjustment: The Case of Egypt", in Stokke, O., (ed.), *Aid and Political Conditionality*, (London: Frank Cass), p.277.

18 Raffer and Singer have identified four phases of IMF conditionality: until 1973 there were none; from 1973 to 1979 there was a 'lenient' phase; until 1982 the conditions became stricter; thereafter the IMF was able to dictate. Raffer, K. and Singer, H.W., (1996), op. cit., p.172.

19 Krueger, A.O., (1981), "Loans to Assist the Transition to Outward-Looking Policies", *World Economy*, vol. 4, no. 3, Sept., p.280.

20 Stokke, O., (1995), op. cit., p.12.

21 *Ibid.*, p.12

22 Although all definitions use the phrase 'country of origin', the case of Jordan is somewhat different in that most of the Jordanian expatriate workers are actually of Palestinian origin, but now have Jordanian citizenship.

23 In 1993 in Bangladesh remittances were equivalent to about 44% of total merchandise exports; in Pakistan about 24% in 1993; and in the Philippines about 22%. Puri, S. and T. Ritzema, "Migrant Worker Remittances, Micro-finance and the Informal Economy: Prospects and Issues", *ILO Working Paper no. 21*, ILO website, www.ilo.org/public/english/employment/ent/papers/wpap21.htm.

24 The definition has three categories, namely: 1) "Workers' remittances, from workers who have lived abroad for more than one year; 2) Compensation of employees or labor income, including wages and other compensation received by migrants who have lived abroad for less than one year; and 3) Migrant's transfers, the net worth of migrants who move from one country to another." Taylor, J.E. and P.L. Fletcher, "Remittances and Development in Mexico", The Center on Rural Economies of the Americas and Pacific Rim website, www.reap.ucdavis.edu/vol_two.html. According to the Migrant News, the third category is not usually included in discussions of remittances. Migrant News, (2001), "Remittances, Trade and Aid", vol. 8, no. 4, April, Migration Dialogue website, migration.ucdavis.edu/mn/Archive_MN/apr_2001-20mn.htm.

25 Taylor, J.E. and P.L. Fletcher, op. cit., p.3.

26 Quoted in Puri, S. and T. Ritzema, op. cit., p.3.

27 Taylor, J.E. and P.L. Fletcher, op. cit., p.3.

28 Beblawi, H., (1987), op. cit., p.384.

29 Mahdavy, H., (1970), "The Pattern and Problems of Economic Development in Rentier States: The Case of Iran", in Cook, M., (ed.), *Studies in the Economic History of the Middle East*, (London: Oxford University Press), p.428.

30 For a comprehensive discussion on the overall problem see Stauffer, T., (1987), op. cit.

31 Although the donor community has tried to remove the state as the direct recipient of AID since the early 1980s, the recipient states have been remarkably resilient in opposing this trend. In Jordan, for example, legislation requires that all external funding must be funnelled

through the Ministry of Planning. Small sums have been directed to the private sector but these have been virtually insignificant.

32 While the phenomenon is acknowledged in most rentier writing as second degree or induced rentierism very little theoretical and practical studies have been undertaken. A notable exception is Chaudhry, K.A., (1989), "The Price of Wealth: Business and State in Labor Remittance and Oil Economies", *International Organization*, vol. 43, no. 1, Winter, pp.101–146.

33 'Production state' is used by Luciani, among others, whereas Chaudhry uses the concept 'redistributive state', indicating one of the ideal aims of taxation is to redistribute wealth from the rich to the poor. 'Extraction state' is a further term based on the state's ability to extract taxes from the population.

34 Luciani, G., (1987), "Allocation vs. Production States: A Theoretical Framework", in Beblawi, H. and G. Luciani, (eds.), *The Rentier State*, (London: Croom Helm), p.73.

35 Vanderwalle, D., (1987), "Political Aspects of State Building in Rentier Economies: Algeria and Libya Compared", in Beblawi, H. and G. Luciani, (eds.), *The Rentier State*, (London: Croom Helm), p.159.

36 Radical economists often challenge these assumptions, but this debate remains outside the scope of the study.

37 Brand, L.A., (1992), "Economic and Political Liberalization in a Rentier Economy: The Case of the Hashemite Kingdom of Jordan", in Harik, I., and D. Sullivan, (eds.), *Privatisation and Liberalisation in the Middle East*, (Indiana University Press: Bloomington), p.168. Abdel-Fadil, in common with others, defines a rentier economy "as one which is substantially supported by the expenditure of a rentier state." As is apparent, this definition ought to refer to a rentier state. Abdel-Fadil, M., (1987), "The Macro-Behaviour of Oil-Rentier States in the Arab Region", in Beblawi, H. and G. Luciani, (eds.), *The Rentier State*, (London: Croom Helm), p.12.

38 Beblawi, H., (1987a), "The Rentier State in the Arab World", in Beblawi, H. and G. Luciani, (eds.), *The Rentier State*, (London: Croom Helm), p.52.

39 Beblawi, H. and G. Luciani, (1987), op. cit., p.13.

40 Chateleus, M., (1987), "Policies for Development: Attitudes toward Industry and Services", in Beblawi, H. and G. Luciani, (eds.), *The Rentier State*, (London: Croom Helm), p.110.

41 Beblawi, H., (1987), op. cit., p.386.

42 Admittedly market forces have a significant impact on the price of oil, but these forces tend not to be controlled by a third party.

43 *Ibid.*, p.385. Emphasis in the original.

44 Beblawi, Chaudhry and Mahdavy use the term 'rentier state', while Luciani and Chateleus use the term 'allocative state'. Indeed, Luciani introduces the concept of the exoteric state as "being states predominantly based on revenue accruing from abroad" as opposed to an esoteric state, which relies on domestic revenue. Beblawi, H. and G. Luciani, (1987), op. cit., p.13.

45 Luciani, G., (1987), op. cit., p.70.

46 *Ibid.*, p.36.

47 Najmabadi, A., (1987), "Depoliticisation of a Rentier State: The Case of Pahlavi Iran", in Beblawi, H. and G. Luciani, (eds.), *The Rentier State*, (London: Croom Helm), p.218.

48 Chaudhry, K.A., (1989), op. cit., p.103.

49 Piro, T.J., (1998), *The Political Economy of Market Reform in Jordan*, (Lanham: Rowman & Littlefield Publishers Inc.), pp.81-83.

50 This style of relationship, particularly in a less than democratic state, makes academic analysis extremely difficult due to the lack of formal records.

51 Chaudhry, K.A., (1989), op. cit., p.116.

52 *Ibid.*, pp.101-146.

53 Brand, L.A., (1994), *Jordan's Inter-Arab Relations: The Political Economy of Alliance Making*, (New York: Columbia University Press), op. cit.

54 A major criticism of donor policy in Zaire was the lack of control of funding, which allowed President Mobutu to transfer funds to accounts in his name in private offshore banks.

55 On occasions, other factors will over-ride this concern, such as in the Second Gulf War when domestic issues that threatened regime stability were of greater concern than maintaining friendly relations with the Gulf States.

56 *Ibid.*, pp.100-101.

57 *Ibid.*, pp.101-146.

58 *Ibid.*, pp.101-146.

59 *Ibid.*, p.103.

60 Interestingly, a similar divide is found in Jordan with the Transjordanians being associated with the state and the Palestinian community being associated with the private sector. However, this divide does not occur at the level of the élite. On the other hand, if Jordan, during its period of state building, had been a private sector rentier state then the subsumption of the private and public sector élites would not have occurred.

61 *Ibid.*, p.104.

62 Gilpin, R., (1987), *The Political Economy of International Relations*, (Princeton: Princeton University Press), p.8.

63 *Ibid.*, p.10.

64 For example, Schwartz, H.M., (2000), *States versus Markets: The Emergence of a Global Economy*, 2nd edition, (Basingstoke: Macmillan Press), p.2.

65 The debate was kicked off by Thomas Hobbes (1588-1679). Held, D., (1983), "Introduction", in Held, D. et al, *States and Societies*, (Oxford: Basil Blackwell in association with The Open University), p.2.

66 Robertson, D., (1985), *The Penguin Dictionary of Politics*, (London: Penguin), p.307.

67 Held, D., (1983), op. cit., p.1.

68 Owen, R., (1992), *State, Power and Politics in the Making of the Modern Middle East*, (London: Routledge), p.3.

69 Owen, R., (2001), "The Middle Eastern State: Repositioning not Retreat", in Hakimian H. and Z. Moshaver, *The State and Global Change: The Political Economy of Transition in the Middle East and North Africa*, (Richmond: Curzon), pp.232-247.

70 Johnson, P.M., "A Glossary of Political Economy Terms", Auburn University website, www.uburn.edu/~johnspm/gloss/index.html.

Chapter 3: Changing patterns of the Rentier Economy

71 *Ibid.*, p.60.

72 *Ibid.*, p.60.

73 Only 3% of the electorate voted in the first election. *Ibid.*, p.48. The low turnout could be seen as indicative of a lack of faith in a foreign imposed, foreign (although Arab) dominated centralised authority.

74 This policy is what Weber calls patrimonial power. Weber, M., (1947), *The Theory of Social and Economic Organisations*, trans., (London: William Hodge).

75 Wilson, M.C., (1987), op. cit., p.2.

76 *Ibid.*, p.2.

77 Khairy, M.O., (1984), *Jordan and the World System: Development in the Middle East*, (Frankfurt: Peter Lang), p.55.

78 Dann, U., (1984), op. cit., p.10.

79 Piro, T.J., (1998), op. cit., p.19.

80 Mazur, M.P., (1979), *Economic Growth and Development in Jordan*, (London: Croom Helm), p.6.

81 mushaa tenure meant that "village lands were periodically reallocated among members of the village, an obvious deterrent to land improvement by a single individual." *Ibid.*, p.6.

82 Dann, U., (1984), op. cit., p.7.

83 Tal, L., (1997), "Jordan", in Sayigh, Y. and A. Shlaim, (eds.), *The Cold War and The Middle East*, (Oxford: Clarendon Press), p.104.

84 For details see Konikoff, A., (1946), *Transjordan: An Economic Survey*, (Jerusalem: Economic Research Institute of the Jewish Agency for Palestine), pp.94-96.

85 Dann, U., (1984), op. cit., p.14.

86 *Ibid.*, p.14.

87 For details see Kingston, P.W.T., (1996), *Britain and the Politics of Modernization in the Middle East, 1945-1958*, (Cambridge: Cambridge University Press), pp. 125-135.

88 *Ibid.*, p.38.

89 Mazur, M.P., (1979), op. cit., p.9.

90 *Ibid.*, p.9.

91 Brand, L.A., (1988), *Palestinians in the Arab World: Institution Building and the Search for State*, (New York: Columbia University Press), p.149.

92 *Ibid.*, p.163.

93 Kingston, P.W.T., (1996), op. cit., p.39.

94 *Ibid.*, p.128.

95 Oren, M.B., (1990), "A Winter of Discontent: Britain's Crisis in Jordan, December 1955 – March 1956", *International Journal of Middle East Studies*, vol. 22, p.171.

96 Tal, L., (1997), op. cit., p.104.

97 Figures as to the annual level of subsidy for the Arab Legion vary with estimates for 1956 ranging from £6m (Satloff, R.B., (1999), "The Jekyll-&-Hyde Origins of the US-Jordanian Strategic Partnership", in Lesch, D.W., (ed.), *The Middle East and the United States: A Historical and Political Reassessment*, (Boulder: Westview Press), p.147) to £10m. (Khairy, M.O., (1984), op. cit., p.58 and Parker, R.B., (1999), "The United States and King Hussein", in Lesch, D.W., (ed.), *The Middle East and the United States: A Historical and Political Reassessment*, (Boulder: Westview Press), p.106.)

98 Vatikiotis, P.J., (1967), op. cit., p.10.

99 *Ibid.*, p.11.

100 The Baghdad Pact was an attempt to create a coalition of countries that could contain the perceived threat of expansion by the USSR. The pact was eventually signed in February 1955 by Iraq, Turkey, the UK, Pakistan, and Iran.

101 As an inducement, Britain promised Jordan £5.5m in arms, substantial economic assistance for developing industry and atomic energy and a favourable revision of the Anglo-Jordanian treaty. Oren, M.B., (1990), op. cit., p.106. Khairy quotes different figures of £3.5m in grants and interest-free loans, excluding the Arab Legion subsidy. Khairy, M.O., (1984), op. cit., p.64.

102 Article 4, The Arab Solidarity Agreement, Foreign Office, (1966), *British and Foreign State Papers, 1957-58*, vol. 163, (London: HMSO), p.401.

103 Foreign Office, (1966), op. cit., pp. 398-401. The share was to be Saudi Arabia £E5.0m, Egypt £E5.0m, and Syria £E2.5m, to be paid in two annual instalments.

104 Kingston, P.W.T., (1994), "Breaking the Patterns of Mandate: Economic Nationalism and State Formation in Jordan, 1951-57", in Rogan, E.L. and T. Tell, (eds.), *Village, Steppe and State: The Social Origins of Modern Jordan*, (London: British Academic Press), p.205.

105 *Ibid.*, table 9.5. Figures exclude military assistance.

106 Kingston, P.W.T., (1996), op. cit., p.138.

107 For details on the inter-donor conflict in this period see *Ibid.*

108 Parker, R.B., (1999), op. cit., p.108.

109 Satloff, R.B., (1999), op. cit., p.118.

110 Parker, R.B., (1999), op. cit., p.108.

111 The first figure from Tal, L., (1997), op. cit., p.104 and Khairy, M.O., (1984), op. cit., p.84. The second from Brand, L.A., (1988), op. cit., p.160.

112 Tal, L., (1997), op. cit., p.104.

113 Brand, L.A., (1988), op. cit., p.160.

114 The resolutions of the conference included the agreement by Saudi Arabia, Kuwait and Libya to pay annual sums of £50m, £55m and £30m respectively in quarterly instalments from mid-October "until the effects of the aggression are eliminated." No mention was made of the amounts to be paid to the beneficiary states. Foreign Office, (1976), British and Foreign State Papers, 1967-68, vol. 169, (London: HMSO), p.323.

115 Gubser, P., (1983), *Jordan: Crossroads of Middle Eastern Events*, (Boulder: Westview Press), p.13.

116 CBJ, (various), *Annual Report*, (Amman: CBJ).

117 For a history of Arab assistance, both bilateral and multilateral, from 1973 to 1989 see van den Boogaerde, P.V., (1991), op. cit.

118 Shihata, I.F.I., (1982), op. cit., p. 204.

119 Brand, L.A., (1994), op. cit., p.96.

120 *Ibid.*, p.98.

121 *Ibid.*, p.97.

122 The Saunders Mission of September 1978, along with the visits of Secretary of State Vance and the National Security Advisor Brzezinski in March 1979 were more overt examples of the courtship.

123 Rivier, F., (1987), "Jordan: A Dependence on a Deteriorating Regional Situation", in Khader, B. and A. Badran, (eds.), *The Economic Development of Jordan*, (London: Croom Helm), p.203.

124 Beblawi, H., (1984), *The Arab Gulf Economy in a Turbulent Age*, (London: Croom Helm), p.30.

125 van den Boogaerde, P.V., (1991), op. cit., p.2.

126 *Ibid.*, p.41.

127 Brand, L.A., (1994), op. cit., p.139.

128 Satloff, R.B., (1992), "Jordan's Great Gamble: Economic Crisis and Political Reform", in Barkey, H.J., (ed.), *The Politics of Economic Reform in the Middle East*, (New York: St. Martin's Press), pp.130-131.

Chapter 4: State-Private Sector Relations: 1921-1989

129 Sha'sha, Z.J., (1991), "The Role of the Private Sector in Jordan's Economy", in Wilson, R., (ed.), *Politics and the Economy in Jordan*, (London: Routledge), p.80.

130 GFCF is the total spending on fixed investment in the economy over a one-year period. The figure excludes capital consumption (fixed capital lost due to wear and tear). Pass, C. and B. Lowes, (1993), *Collins Dictionary of Economics*, 2nd edition, (Glasgow: Harper Collins Publishers), p.228.

131 Livesey, F., (1993), *Dictionary of Economics*, (London: Pitman Publishing), p.91.

132 The classification is based on that used by the 1986-1990 plan. National Planning Council, (undated: d), *The Hashemite Kingdom of Jordan Five Year Plan for Economic and Social Development, 1986-1990*, (Amman: Royal Scientific Society Press), p.95.

133 For example Kingston, P.W.T., (1996), op. cit., p.123.

134 Tal, L., (1997), op. cit., p.103.

135 *Ibid.*, p.103.

136 Wilson, M.C., (1987), op. cit., pp.55-61.

137 Brand, L.A., (1994), op. cit., p.42.

138 Khairy, M.O., (1984), op. cit., p.55.

139 Quoted in Wilson, M.C., (1987), op. cit., p.71.

140 Bannerman, M.G., (1995), op. cit., p.222.

141 Konikoff, A., (1946), op. cit., p.66.

142 Mazur, M.P., (1979), op. cit., p.8.

143 Konikoff argues that expenditure figures for this period understate actual government outlays as a number of costs related to roads, medical services, railways, the High Commissioner, and the Transjordanian Frontier Force were absorbed by the Palestinian government. *Ibid.*, p.96.

144 For years 1924-25 to 1933-34 Naval Intelligence Division, (1943), op. cit., p.500. For years 1934-35 to 1943-44, Konikoff, A. (1946), op. cit., p.95.

145 Konikoff, A., (1946), op. cit., p.97.

146 *Ibid.*, p.77.

147 Abu Nowar, M., (1989),op. cit., p.229.

148 Konikoff, A., (1946), op. cit., p.33.

149 For details of the changes in the taxation system see *Ibid.*, pp.86-92 and Abu Nowar, M., (1989), op. cit., p.229.

150 Interview with Anani, Dr. Jawad, ex-Deputy Prime Minister, Amman, 09/06/99.

151 Brand, L.A., (1988), op. cit., p.149.

152 Kirkbride estimates Jordan was spending around £P40,000 per month on the refugees at the height of the crisis. Quoted in Wilson, M.C., (1987), op. cit., p.191.

153 The UK provided a £1m loan in 1949 and UNRWA (the UN agency created to help solve the refugee problem) did not start work until the 1st May 1950.

154 The problem of re-orienting exports physically and in terms of new markets was paralleled in the events of 1968-71 and 1990-91.

155 Bannerman, M.G., (1995), op. cit., p.233.

156 Piro, T.J., (1998), op. cit., pp.27-28.

157 *Ibid.*, p.29.

158 Anani, J., (1989), "Adjustment and Development: The Case of Jordan", in el-Nagger, S., (ed.), *Adjustment Policies and Development Strategies in the Arab World*, Papers presented at a seminar held in Abu Dhabi, UAE, February 16-18, 1987, (no place: IMF), p.127.

159 Bannerman, M.G., (1995), op. cit., p.226.

160 Brand, L.A., (1988), op. cit., p.159.

161 Brand quotes a figure of 250,000 to 300,000 whereas Mazur puts the estimate higher at 250,000 to 400,000. Brand, L.A., (1988), op. cit., p.157 and Mazur, M.P., (1979), op. cit., p.87.

162 Refugees continued to move into Jordan, with an estimated 65,000 from 1967 to 1989. Winckler, O., (1997), op. cit., p.93.

163 Military spending as a percentage of GDP, which had been falling, increased from 12.3% in 1966 to 19.8% by 1969. Kanovsky, E., (1976), op. cit., p.20.

164 An oil-pipeline from Saudi Arabia.

165 Unrelated to the Civil War, but badly affecting trade, was the decision by India to cut back trade due to Jordan's support for Pakistan at the Islamic Organisation Conference in 1969. Exports to India, a major importer of phosphates, fell from JD1,889,000 in 1968 to JD253,000 in 1970.

166 Piro, T.J., (1998), op. cit., p.61.

167 Jordan Development Board, (1961), *The Hashemite Kingdom of Jordan Five Year Program for Economic Development 1962-1967*, (Amman: Jordan Development Board), p.353.

168 For details of the 'advice war' between the UK, the UN and the USA see Kingston, P.W.T., (1996), op. cit., p.135.

169 Mazur, M.P., (1979), op. cit., p 243.

170 Jordan Development Board, (1961), op. cit., p.19.

171 *Ibid.*, p.25.

172 Jordan Development Board, (undated), *The Seven Year Program for Economic Development of Jordan: 1964-70*, (Amman: Jordan Development Board), p.1.

173 Mazur, M.P., (1979), op. cit., p.243 and p.246.

174 Jordan Development Board, (undated), op. cit., p.8.

175 National Planning Council, (undated: a), *The Hashemite Kingdom of Jordan Three Year Development Plan, 1973-1975*, (Amman: National Planning Council), p.13.

176 *Ibid.*, p.16.

177 *Ibid.*, p.34.

178 The Agricultural Credit Corporation was the result of a merger between the successful Village Loans Scheme (administered by the Jordan Development Board) and the Agriculture Bank.

179 Anani, J., (1989), op. cit., p.127.

180 Dajani, A.T., (1973), *The Industry of Jordan*, 1973, 4th edition, (Amman: ACC), p.23.

181 The JCCC became the Jordan Export Development and Commercial Centres Corporation in 1992, when several new functions were added.

182 *Ibid.*, p.67.

183 National Planning Council, (1971), *Planning Law: Law no. 68 for the Year 1971*, (Amman: National Planning Council), article 9a, p.11.

184 Brand, L.A., (1994), op. cit., p.67.

185 Kanovsky, E., (1976), op. cit., p.8.

186 *Ibid.*, pp.222-223

187 Abu Shair, O.J.A.R., (1997), *Privatization and Development*, (Basingstoke: Macmillan Press), p.136.

188 Mazur, M.P., (1979), op. cit., p.222.

189 From Piro, T.J., (1998), op. cit. The other member is Jordan Fertiliser Industries Company.

190 *Ibid.*, p.45.

191 National Planning Council, (undated: b), *The Hashemite Kingdom of Jordan Five Year Plan for Economic and Social Development, 1976-1980*, (Amman: National Planning Council), p.5.

192 *Ibid.*, p.9.

193 CBJ, (1976), *Monthly Statistical Bulletin*, December, (Amman: CBJ).

194 Abu Shair, O.J.A.R., (1997), op. cit., p.139.

195 Sha'sha, Z.J., (1991), op. cit., p.81.

196 Brand, L.A., (1992), op. cit., p.170.

197 The price of phosphates, Jordan's main natural resource, quintupled resulting in earnings increasing by almost 400% in the period 1973-74. Mazur, M.P., (1979), op. cit., p.85.

198 Abu Shair, O.J.A.R., (1997), op. cit., p.139.

199 *Ibid.*, p.140.

200 Adapted by author from CBJ, (various), *Monthly Statistical Bulletin*, (Amman: CBJ).

201 Interview with Anani, Dr. Jawad, op. cit.

202 Piro, T.J., (1998), op. cit., p.71.

203 Department of Statistics, (1994), *National Accounts 1952-1992*, (no place: Department of Statistics), p.121 and p.125.

204 National Planning Council, (undated: c), *The Hashemite Kingdom of Jordan Five Year Plan for Economic and Social Development, 1981-1985*, (Amman: National Planning Council), p.6.

205 *Ibid.*, p.5.

206 Anani, J., (1989), op. cit., p.129.

207 National Planning Council, (undated: a), op. cit., p.29.

208 *Ibid.*, p.29.

209 *Ibid.*, p.34.

210 Sullivan, M.B., (1987), "Industrial Development in Jordan", in Khader, B. and A. Badran, (eds.), *The Economic Development of Jordan*, (London: Croom Helm), p.137.

211 Brand, L.A., (1994), op. cit., p.75.

212 Khader, B., (1987), "Targets and Achievements of Jordan's Last Five-Year Plans, 1976-1980 and 1981-1985: A Summary", in Khader, B. and A. Badran, (eds.), *The Economic Development of Jordan*, (London: Croom Helm), p.179.

213 National Planning Council, (undated: b), op. cit., pp.37-38.

214 *Ibid.*, p.29.

215 *Ibid.*, p.37.

216 *Ibid.*, p.70.

217 *Ibid.*, p.43.

218 *Ibid.*, p.69.

219 *Ibid.*, pp.39-45.

220 National Planning Council, (undated: c), op. cit., p.7.

221 Committee for Middle East Trade, (1982), *Jordan: The Five Year Plan for Economic and Social Development 1981-85*, (London: COMET), p.5.

222 National Planning Council, (undated: d), op. cit., p.26.

223 National Planning Council, (undated: c), op. cit., p.39.

224 *Ibid.*, p.39.

225 *Ibid.*, p.40.

226 *Ibid.*, p.41.

227 Khader, B., (1987), op. cit., p.186.

228 National Planning Council, (undated: d), op. cit., pp.35 and 49 and authors calculations.

229 Unfortunately, a similar breakdown of the 1976-80 plan is not possible due to the method of presenting the figures in the plan.

230 CBJ, (1983), Annual Report, 1983, (Amman: CBJ), pp.57-58.

231 Free Zones Corporation, (1984), *Free Zones Corporation Law* no. 32 of 1984, (Amman: Free Zones Corporation), Article 3, p.11.

232 *Ibid.*, Article 6, p.12.

233 *Ibid.*, Article 10, p.13.

234 *Ibid.*, Article 13, p.14.

235 *Ibid.*, Article 13, p.14.

236 Free Zones Corporation, "About Us", *Free Zones Corporation website*, www.free-zones.gov.jo/about.htm.

237 *Free Zones Corporation website*, op. cit.

238 Atlas Investment Group, (April 2001), *Jordan: Country Report*, (Amman: Atlas Investment Group), p.28.

239 National Planning Council, (undated: b), op. cit., p.47.

240 Anani, J., (1989), op. cit., p.130.

241 *Ibid.*, p.130.

242 *Ibid.*, p.134.

243 Andoni, L. and J. Schwedler, (1996), "Bread Riots in Jordan", *Middle East Report*, Oct-Dec, p.40.

244 Anani, J., (1989), op. cit., p.131.

245 Of which nineteen were industrial, two transport, four tourism, and one agricultural marketing.

246 National Planning Council, (undated: a), op. cit., p.114.

247 al-Quaryoty, M.O., (1989), "Prospects for Privatization in Jordan", *Journal of Arab Affairs*, vol. 8, no. 2, p.175.

248 Owen, R., (1983), "Government and Economy in Jordan: Progress, Problems and Prospects", in Seale, P., (ed.), *The Shaping of an Arab Statesman*, (London: Quartet Books), p.89.

249 *Ibid.*, p.90.

250 Piro, T.J., (1998), op. cit. p.61.

251 Jreisat, for examples, highlights the "ostentatious display of wealth by many government ministers ... that could never be sustained through legitimate government pay." The author, then argues that, although investigations and parliamentary debates occur, rarely is an official imprisoned or penalised for corruption. Jreisat, J.E., (1997), *Politics without Process: Administering Development in the Arab World*, (Lynne Rienner Publishers: Boulder), p.114.

252 Fathi, S.H., (1994), *Jordan: An Invented Nation? Tribe-State Dynamics and the Formation of National Identity*, (Hamburg: Deutsches Orient-Institut), p.171.

253 Brand, L.A., (1992), op. cit. p.185.

254 Further IMF loans of US$70m in 1986, US$81m in 1987, and US$48 in 1988, as well as US$107m from the IBRD in the period 1985-88 were also agreed. These loans were in addition to other bilateral, multilateral and commercial loans.

255 The civilian uprising of Palestinians against the continued Israeli occupation of the West Bank and Gaza Strip.

256 Satloff, R., (1992), op. cit., p.134.

257 Baram, A., (1994), "No New Fertile Crescent: Iraqi-Jordanian Relations, 1968-92", in Nevo, J. and I. Pappé, (eds.), *Jordan in the Middle East: The Making of a Pivotal State: 1948-88*, (Ilford: Frank Cass & Co. Ltd.), p.128.

258 *Ibid.*, p.171.

259 Brand, L.A., (1994), op. cit., p.76.

260 *Ibid.*, p.175.

261 *Ibid.*, p.175.

262 National Planning Council, (undated: d), op. cit., p.80.

263 *Ibid.*, p.102.

264 *Ibid.*, p.94.

265 Jordanians, including expatriates, contribute 5% of their monthly salaries to the scheme. Brand, L.A., (1992), op. cit., p.176.

266 Moore, P.W., (2001), "What Makes Successful Business Lobbies? Business Associations and the Rentier State in Jordan and Kuwait", *Comparative Politics*, vol. 33, no. 2, Jan., p.140.

267 Brand, L.A., (1994), op. cit., p.58.

268 *Ibid.*, p.58.

269 Brand, L.A., (1992), op. cit., p.174.

270 *Ibid.*, p.178.

271 *Ibid.*, p.173.

272 *Ibid.*, p.173.

273 *Ibid.*, p.173.

274 Anani, J. and R. Khalaf, (1989), "Privatisation in Jordan", in El-Nagger, S., (ed.), *Adjustment Policies and Development Strategies in the Arab World*, Papers presented at a seminar held in Abu Dhabi, UAE, February 16-18, 1987, (no place: IMF), p.219.

275 Economist Intelligence Unit (EIU), (1985c), *Quarterly Economic Review of Jordan*, no. 3, (London: EIU), p.16.

276 EIU, (1985d), *Quarterly Economic Review of Jordan*, no. 4, (London: EIU), p.11.

277 *Ibid.*, p.11.

278 EIU, (1986a), *Quarterly Economic Review of Jordan*, no. 1, (London: EIU), p.16.

279 *Ibid.*, p.14.

280 al-Fanek, F., (1995), "Structural Adjustment in Jordan", in Euchner, W., (ed.), *The Politics of Structural Adjustment: Economic Liberalisation in Arab Countries*, (no place: Konrad-Adenauer-Stiftung), p.212.

281 EIU, (1987c), Jordan Country Report, no. 3, (London: EIU), pp.10-11.

282 Feiler, G., (1994), "Jordan's Economy, 1970-90: The Primacy of Exogenous Factors", in Nevo, J. and I. Pappé, (eds.), *Jordan in the Middle East: The Making of a Pivotal State: 1948-88*, (Ilford: Frank Cass & Co. Ltd.), p.53.

283 Sullivan, M.B., (1987), op. cit., pp.134-135.

284 Anani, J., (1989), op. cit., p.140.

285 Anani, J and R. Khalaf, (1989), op. cit., p.215.

286 *Ibid.*, p.216.

287 IMF, (1988), *Government Financial Statistics Yearbook*, 1988, vol. XII, (Washington: IMF), p.567 and IMF, (1989), *Government Financial Statistics Yearbook*, 1989, vol. XIII, (Washington: IMF), p.374.

288 Brand, L.A., (1992), op. cit., p.167.

289 *Ibid.*, pp.173-174.

290 Piro, T.J., (1998), op. cit., p.59.

291 Abu Shair, O.J.A.R., (1997), op. cit., p.127.

292 Brand, L.A., (1994), op. cit., p.53.

293 Piro, T.J., (1998), op. cit., p.86.

294 Brand, L.A., (1994), op. cit., p.64.

295 Wilson, R., (1991), "Introduction", in Wilson, R., (ed.), *Politics and Economy in Jordan*, (London: Routledge), p.6.

296 EIU, (1987a), *Jordan: Country Report*, no. 1, (London: EIU), p.16.

297 For the role of Arab Nationalist influence in economic development in Jordan during the 1950s see Kingston, P.W.T., (1996), op. cit., and also Kingston, P.W.T., (1994), op. cit., pp.187-216.

298 By 1984, ten of the twenty-two ministries had a degree of influence over economic decision-making. Piro, T.J., (1998), op. cit., p.83.

299 Adapted from Michel Chateleus who termed APC, JPMC, JCFC, JPRC, and JFIC as the big five. However, in 1986 JFIC was subsumed into JPMC. Chateleus, M., (1987a), "Rentier or Producer Economy in the Middle East? The Jordanian Response", in Khader, B. and A. Badran, (eds.), *Economic Development in Jordan*, (London: Croom Helm), p.216.

300 In 1995 the JIC owned shares valued at around US$600m, which comprised nearly 12% of the capital invested in the Amman Financial Market, the Jordanian stock exchange, through some seventy companies.

301 Piro, T.J., (1998), op. cit., p.64.

302 At 1989, nine monopolies existed for two different purposes: sugar, wheat, rice, flour and dried milk to assist the poor; and cigarettes, frozen chicken, lentils and olive oil to protect domestic industries.

303 The 15 years are probably 1974-1989, although Brand does not make this clear.

304 Brand, L.A., (1994), op. cit., p.57.

305 *Ibid.*, pp.57-58.

306 *Ibid.*

307 *Ibid.*

308 Dajani, A.T., (1973), op. cit., p.28.

309 JBA, "The Jordanian Businessmen Association", *JBA website*, www.jba.com.jo.

310 Article 3 of the JBA by-law states: "a) Any private sector Jordanian businessman not less than thirty years of age, enjoying a good reputation and willing to serve the objectives of the Association, may apply for membership provided he shall meet the following conditions:- 1- To be an elected natural member in the board of directors of a public share holding company; 2- To be the chairman or a member of the board of directors of a company with limited liability and with a capital of not less than one hundred thousand Jordanian Dinar; 3- To be the owner of an establishment with a capital of not less that fifty thousand Jordanian Dinar, and has been registered with the companies controller for five years; 4- To be a partner in a company of any kind not mentioned before and his share must be not less than fifty thousand Jordanian Dinar, and the company has been incorporated for five years; 5- To be the director general of a public share holding company; 6- To be a Jordanian expert in the economic affairs and has [sic] participated in the preparation of distinguished economic studies." JBA, "The Jordanian Businessmen Association By-Law", *JBA website*, www.jba.com.jo.

311 JBA, "The Jordanian Businessmen Association", op. cit.

312 *Ibid.*

313 Moore, P.W., (2001), op. cit., pp.135-136.

314 al-Urdan al-Jadid Research Centre, (1999), "Civil Society and Governance: A Case Study of Jordan", (draft mimeograph), p.38.

Chapter 5: The Changing Face of Rentierism: 1989-2002

315 Satloff, R.B., (1992), op. cit., p. 132.

316 CBJ, (various), *Monthly Statistical Bulletin*, (Amman: CBJ).

317 *Summary of World Broadcasts*, (hereafter referred to as SWB), Third Series, ME/0440, 21/04/89, p.A/1-2.

318 al-Fanek, F., (1995), op. cit., p.217.

319 Khader, B., (1987), op. cit., p.187.

320 Baram, A., (1994), op. cit., p.127.

321 The limit of the agreement was only JD185m. Brand, L.A., (1994), op. cit., pp.223-224.

322 By autumn 1989 the debt was over $835m. *Ibid.* p.127.

323 The port at Aqaba had seen the throughput of foot passengers jump from just over 7000 in 1979 to over 823,000 by 1988, most of whom were Egyptian workers in Iraq. Transit exports through Aqaba accounted for less than one-third of 1% of total transit exports in 1978 but by 1988 stood at 27%, again mostly for Iraq. A similar situation was apparent with transit imports, which rose from 5.6% in 1978 to 75.7% in 1988. *Ibid.*, pp.124-7.

324 Political pressures were the over-riding influence on the King's decision.

325 Satloff, R., (1992), op. cit., p.134.

326 Baram, A., (1994), op. cit., p.128.

327 Brand, L.A., (1992), op. cit., p.80.

328 The anticipated cost of food subsidies for 1989, which had been planned to cost JD33m in November 1988, were by March 1989 expected to cost JD60m. *Middle East Economic Digest* (hereafter referred to as MEED), 17/03/89, p.17.

329 IMF, (October 1995), *Jordan – Background Information on Selected Aspects of Adjustment and Growth Strategy*, IMF Staff Country Report No 95/97, (Washington: IMF), p.5.

330 al-Fanek, F., (1995), op. cit., p.217.

331 *Ibid.*, p.217.

332 Satloff, R.B., (1992), op. cit., p. 134.

333 *Ibid.*, p.136.

334 *MEES*, vol. 32, no. 19, 13/02/89, p.B1-2.

335 EIU, (1989a), *Jordan: Country Report*, no. 1, (London: EIU). p.10.

336 *SWB*, Third Series, ME/0399, 03/03/89, p.A/9

337 The Islamic Liberation Party were the only political grouping excluded from the process. Susser, A., (1991), "Jordan", in Ayalon, A., (ed.), *Middle East Contemporary Survey*, vol. XV, (Boulder: Westview Press), p.499.

338 *Ibid.*, p.499.

339 Satloff, R.B., (1992), op. cit., p.147.

340 Susser, A., (1991), op. cit., p.487.

341 *MEED*, 20/09/91, p.15.

342 *The Middle East and North Africa*, 1992, 38th edition, (London: Europa Publications Ltd), p.562.

343 *MEED*, 24/08/90, p.16.

344 Tal, L., (1997), op. cit., p.119.

345 OPEC Bulletin, vol. XXI, no. 10, November/December 1990, p.49.

346 Susser, A., (1991), op. cit., p.486.

347 *Ibid.*, p.486.

348 *MEED*, 28/09/90, p.24.

349 *The Middle East and North Africa*, 1996, 42nd edition, (London: Europa Publications Ltd), p.607.

350 "Expectations Ride High on Peace Hopes", *MEED*, 30/07/93, p.17.

351 The Washington Declaration was a statement by King Hussein and Prime Minister Rabin of Israel announcing the termination of the state of belligerency between the two countries.

352 Under the agreement with Israel Jordanian banks were allowed to open branches in the Occupied Territories of the West Bank, to the anger of Chairman Arafat.

353 *The Middle East and North Africa*, 1995, 41st edition, (London: Europa Publications Ltd), p.582.

354 The breakdown of the peace process meant that the conferences were boycotted by increasing numbers of Arab states. Only five attended the final conference in Qatar.

355 World Bank, (undated), *The World Bank Annual Report*, 1995, (Washington: World Bank), p.97.

356 Authors calculations from CBJ, (various), *Monthly Statistical Bulletin*.

357 Quoted in *Middle East International*, no. 598, 23/04/99, p.16.

358 Prime Minister Rawabdeh was even more optimistic expressing hopes on a live phone-in that Jordan would be forgiven US$2bn of the US$3bn at the forthcoming G7 meeting. Quoted in *SWB Weekly Economic Report*, Third Series, ME/W0591, 01/06/99, p.WME/8-9.

359 Immediate pledges of assistance were received from the USA (US$300m), Japan (US$25.5m), UAE (US$150m), Saudi Arabia (unspecified), and Israel (US$200m). *MEES*, vol. 42, no. 8, 22/02/92, p.B2 and Mideast Mirror, "The Scramble for Jordan", vol. 13, no. 42, 03/03/99, p.16-20.

360 Akeel, O., (1999), "Rawabdeh Lays down to Parliament Jordan's True Economic Position", *The Arab Daily*, 14/06/99.

Chapter 6: Donor Community Involvement: 1989-2002

361 The World Bank is able to issue the occasional small grant.

362 The original value was SDR127.8m (US$181m) but this was augmented by new funds of SDR25m (US$37m) on 14 September 1994 and by SDR36.5m (US$54m) on 13 February 1995. IMF, "IMF approves Augmentation of EFF Credit to Jordan", Press Release no. 95/11, 13/02/95, *IMF Website*, www.imf.org/external/np/sec/pr/1995/ R9511.HTM.

363 The original value was SDR200.8m (US$295m) but this was augmented by further funds of SDR37.24m (US$51.8m) on 11 February 1997. IMF, "IMF approves Augmentation of EFF Credit to Jordan", Press Release no. 97/8, 11/02/97, *IMF Website*, www.imf.org/external/np/sec/pr/1997 PR9708.HTM.

364 IMF, (October 1995), op. cit., p.5.

365 *Ibid.*, pp.5-6.

366 IMF official quoted in *SWB Weekly Economic Report*, Third Series, 25/04/89, ME/W0074 A1/2-3

367 EIU, (1989c), *Jordan: Country Report*, no. 3, (London: EIU), p.11.

368 *SWB Weekly Economic Report*, Third Series, ME/W0074, 25/04/89, pp.A1/2-3.

369 *MEED*, 28/04/89, pp.21-22.

370 *MEED*, 02/06/89, p.16.

371 However the prices of the cheapest powdered milk and cooking fat were increased on 25 April. *MEED*, 28/04/89, pp21-22.

372 *SWB*, Third Series, ME/0439, 20/04/89, p.i.

373 The head of IMF's Middle East Department, Dr. Shakur Sha'lan, quoted in *MEES*, vol. 32, no. 33, 22/05/89, p.B2.

374 The published budgets never included expenditure by the SOEs or military expenditure.

375 *MEED*, 16/03/90, p.25.

376 *Ibid.*, p.25.

377 The Paris Club comprised the majority of official creditors. The members are Austria, Belgium, Denmark, Finland, France, Italy, Japan, Kuwait, Spain, Sweden, Switzerland, the UK, the USA and West Germany, with Canada, the Netherlands and Norway present as

observers. Once the Paris Club agreement is signed, members bilaterally negotiate with Jordan concerning their share of the agreement. The interest rates tended to be agreed on a bilateral basis.

378 The London Club is the umbrella organisation for the 90+ commercial creditors. The six-member committee was established on 06/07/89. The members were Gulf International Bank, the Standard Chartered Bank, the Commercial Bank of Kuwait, the Manufacturers Hanover Trust Corporation, the Union des Banques Arabes et Français, and the Banque Nationale de Paris, with the Arab Bank acting in an advisory capacity.

379 IMF, (October 1995), op. cit., p.6.

380 *Ibid.*, p.6.

381 *Ibid.*, p.2.

382 *MEED*, 07/12/90, p.31.

383 *MEES*, vol. 34, no. 10, 10/12/90, pp.B2-3.

384 The EIU reported a statement appearing in the Jordan Economic Monitor, a publication with invariably accurate inside information. EIU, (1990d), *Jordan: Country Report*, no. 4, (London: EIU), p.15.

385 EIU, (1991c), *Jordan: Country Report*, no. 3, (London: EIU), p.15.

386 On this occasion the rise in fuel prices was met with resignation rather than riots. *MEES*, vol. 36, no. 37, 14/06/93, p.A15.

387 IMF, (October 1995), op. cit., p.8.

388 *Ibid.*, p.8.

389 The figures for foreign and domestic borrowing are obviously incorrect.

390 EIU, (1992a), *Jordan: Country Report*, no. 1, (London: EIU), p.4.

391 *MEED*, 13/03/92, p.16.

392 EIU, (1992d), *Jordan: Country Report*, no. 4, (London: EIU), p.14.

393 *MEED*, 10/06/94, pp.24-25.

394 IMF, "IMF approves Augmentation of EFF Credit to Jordan", Press Release no. 95/11, op. cit.

395 EIU, (1994d), *Jordan: Country Report*, no. 4, (London: EIU), p.12.

396 *MEED*, 23/06/94, pp.12-13.

397 IMF, (October 1995), op. cit., p.11.

398 *Ibid.*, p.11.

399 *Ibid.*, p.20.

400 *Ibid.*, p.39.

401 *Ibid.*, p.40.

402 A food coupon scheme was introduced in September 1990 for sugar, rice and powdered milk but not bread. By 1994 budgetary subsidies had been cut to 1% of GDP from 4% in 1990. IMF, (1995), *Social Dimensions of the IMF Policy Dialogue*, Pamphlet Series no. 47, (IMF: Washington), pp.22-23.

403 IMF, "IMF Approves Three-Year Credit for Jordan", Press Release no. 96/4, 09/02/96, *IMF website*, www.imf.org/external/np/sec/pr/1996/PR9604.HTM.

404 *Ibid.*

405 *Ibid.*

406 *MEED*, 02/02/96, p.21.

407 Camdessus, M., (1996), "The Challenges for the Arab World in the Global Economy: Stability and Structural Adjustment", Speech to the Annual Meeting of the Union of Arab Banks, New York, 20/05/96.

408 World Bank, (1996a), "Consultative Group for the Hashemite Kingdom of Jordan, Paris, July 10, 1996, Chairman's Report of Proceedings", 01/08/96, reference CG 96-39, (mimeograph), annex III.

409 *Ibid.*, p.2.

410 IMF, "IMF Statement on Jordan", News Brief no. 96/5, 21/08/96, *IMF website*, www.imf.org/ external/np/sec/nb/1996/NB9605.HTM.
411 *MEED*, 21/02/97, p.32.
412 IMF, "IMF Statement on Jordan", News Brief no. 96/5, op. cit.
413 IMF, (1997), *Annual Report, 1997*, (Washington: IMF), pp.83-84.
414 *SWB Weekly Economic Report*, Third Series, ME/W0530, 24/03/98, pp.WME/15-16.
415 *SWB Weekly Economic Report*, Third Series, ME/W0553, 01/09/98, pp.WME/9-10.
416 *MEED*, 30/10/98, pp.14-15.
417 IMF, "IMF Approves EFF and CCFF Credits for Jordan", Press Release no. 99/13, 16/04/99, *IMF website*, www.imf.org/external/np/sec/pr/1999/pr9913.htm.
418 *Ibid.*
419 *Ibid.*
420 *Ibid.*
421 *Ibid.*
422 IMF, (1999), *Annual Report*, op. cit., p.77.
423 IMF, "IMF Approves 10.66 Million SDR Outlay to Jordan", News Brief no. 99/68, 05/10/99, *IMF website*, www.imf.org/external/np/sec/nb/1999/nb9968.htm.
424 IMF, *IMF Approves EFF and CCFF Credits for Jordan*, Press Release no. 99/13, 16/04/99, op. cit.
425 *Ibid.*
426 *Ibid.*
427 *Ibid.*
428 *Ibid.*
429 *SWB Weekly Economic Report*, Third Series, MEW/0653, 12/08/00, p.WME8.
430 IMF, "IMF Approves US$39 Million Disbursement to Jordan", News Brief no. 01/83, 29/08/01, *IMF website*, www.imf.org/external/np/sec/nb/2001/nb0183.htm
431 IMF, "IMF Approves US$77 Million Disbursement to Jordan", News Brief no. 02/40, 30/04/02, *IMF website*, www.imf.org/external/np/sec/nb/2002/nb0240.htm
432 IMF, "IMF Approves US$113 Million Stand-by credit for Jordan", Press Release no. 02/31, 03/07/02, *IMF website*, www.imf.org/external/np/sec/pr/2002/pr0231.htm
433 The Committee on the Country Study for Japan's Development Assistance to the Hashemite Kingdom of Jordan, (1996), *Country Study for Japan's Development Assistance to the Hashemite Kingdom of Jordan*, (Tokyo: JICA), p.102.
434 World Bank, (1996b), "Structural Adjustment in Jordan", OED Précis, no.116, *World Bank website*, www.worldbank.org/html/oed/pr116.htm, p.1.
435 *Ibid.*, p.1.
436 *MEED*, 16/05/97, p.13.
437 CBJ, (1994), *Annual Report*, op. cit., p.31.
438 This report will be discussed more fully in chapter 6.
439 World Bank, (1995), op. cit., preface.
440 *Ibid.*, p.4.
441 *Ibid.*, p.ii.
442 *Ibid.*, p.iii.
443 *Ibid.*, p.iii.
444 *MEED*, 09/08/96, p.30.
445 For example interviews with Avédikian, Richard, Director, KfW, Amman, 18/07/99; Hardy, Lawrence, Program Management, USAID, Amman, 21/06/99 and Hasse, Dr. Volkmar, Team Leader, Deutsche Gesellschaft für Technische Zusammenarbeit, Amman, 12/07/99.
446 Interview with Avédikian, Richard, op. cit., and Garces dos Los Fayos, Fernando, First Secretary, Delegation of the European Commission to Jordan, Amman, 09/07/99.
447 *MEED*, 14/06/91, p.24.

448 World Bank, (1992), *Annual Report*, op. cit., p.153.

449 EIU, (1993a), *Jordan: Country Report*, no. 1, (London: EIU), p.17.

450 EIU, (1994c), *Jordan: Country Report*, no. 3, (London: EIU), p.18.

451 *Ibid.*, p.18.

452 Representatives of Belgium, Canada, France, Germany, Italy, Japan, the Republic of Korea, the Netherlands, Norway, Switzerland, Turkey, the United Kingdom and the United States of America attended the meeting. In addition, multilateral institutions of Arab Fund for Economic and Social Development, AMF, EU, EIB, IFC, International Fund for Agricultural Development, IMF, Islamic Development Bank, Saudi Fund, and UNDP were present, along with the OECD as an observer. Those invited but not present included Australia, Austria, China, Denmark, Finland, Kuwait, Oman, Qatar, Saudi Arabia, Spain, Sweden, UAE, Abu Dhabi Fund, Kuwait Fund and the OPEC Fund. World Bank, (1996a), op. cit.

453 *MEED*, 19/07/96, p.20.

454 *MEED*, 21/05/93, p.26.

455 *MEED*, 09/12/94, pp.19-20.

456 World Bank, (1996), *Annual Report*, op. cit., p.124.

457 World Bank, (1989a), "Jordan: Industry and Trade Policy Adjustment Loan Agreement", paragraph 106, (mimeograph).

458 The US$10m loan in 1991 occurred only because of the refugee crisis following Iraq's invasion of Kuwait.

459 As early as 1988, the World Bank argued that adjustment programmes could be designed to "moderate the possible negative effects on the poor." Roe, A., Roy, J. and J. Sengupta, (eds.), (1989), *Economic Adjustment in Algeria, Egypt, Jordan, Morocco, Pakistan, Tunisia and Turkey: Report of a Seminar Held in Izmir, Turkey, March 28-30, 1988*, An EDI Policy Seminar Report, no. 15, (Washington: The World Bank), p.6.

460 *MEED*, 04/04/97, pp.18-19.

461 World Bank, "World Bank US$30 Million Loan to Improve Community Infrastructure in Jordan", News Release no. 98/1443MENA, 21/08/97, *World Bank website*, www.worldbank. org/html/extdr/ extme/1443.htm.

462 *MEED*, 20/06/97, p.27.

463 World Bank, (1998), *Annual Report*, op. cit., p.60.

464 World Bank, (1989a), op. cit., summary of measures.

465 *Ibid.*, paragraph 85.

466 *Ibid.*, paragraph 94.

467 Interview with Anani, Dr. Jawad, op. cit.

468 *MEED*, 13/10/95, p.16.

469 World Bank, (1997), *Annual Report*, op. cit., p.86.

470 *MEED*, 03/01/97, pp.28-29.

471 World Bank, "Jordan Boosts Business and Investment with US$120 million Economic Reform Loan", News Release no. 97/1202MENA, 12/12/96, *World Bank website*, www.worldbank.org/html/extdr/ extme/1202.htm.

472 World Bank, (1997), "Jordan – Third Economic Reform and Development Loan", Report no. PID7066, 20/11/97, p.2.

473 *Ibid.*, p.3.

474 *Ibid.*, p.3.

475 *Ibid.*, p.4.

476 World Bank, (undated), *The World Bank Annual Report, 2001*, (Washington: The World Bank), p.119.

477 *MEED*, 05/11/93, pp.26-27.

478 KfW, (1998), "German-Jordanian Financial Co-operation as of: September 1998", p.5.

479 CBJ, (1994), op. cit., (Amman: CBJ), p.28.

480 *Ibid.*, p.28.

481 *MEED*, 01/07/94, p.20.

482 World Bank, (1994), "Hashemite Kingdom of Jordan, Agriculture Sector Technical Support Project, Technical Annex", Report no. T-6370-Jordan, 18/11/94, pp.1-2.

483 *MEED*, 05/02/93, p.19.

484 *Ibid.*, pp.1-2.

485 World Bank, (undated), *The World Bank Annual Report, 1995*, (Washington: The World Bank), p.100.

486 The government agreed to on-lend about US$19.6m from the proceeds "to support the Government's strategy to improve the efficiency of the housing and housing finance sectors, promote private sector development in land and housing production, and reduce the Government's role in both sectors." World Bank, (1996), *Staff Appraisal Report, The Hashemite Kingdom of Jordan, Housing Finance and Urban Sector Reform Project*, Report no. 15331-Jordan, 02/07/96, preamble.

487 The proceeds were to be on-lent to private banks at market rates of interest. World Bank, (undated), *Staff Appraisal Report, The Hashemite Kingdom of Jordan, Export Development Project*, Report no. 14935-Jordan, p.1.

488 *MEED*, 12/07/96, p.17.

489 World Bank, "Export Development Loan to Jordan to Benefit Private Firms", Press Release, no. 96/11/MEN, 29/03/96, *World Bank Website*, www.worldbank.org/html/extdr/extme/9611men.htm.

490 World Bank, (undated), op. cit., p.1.

491 *Ibid.*, p.1.

492 *Ibid.*, p.1.

493 World Bank, (1996b), op. cit., p.2.

494 *Ibid.*, p.2.

495 World Bank, "World Bank US$32 million Loan Helps Jordan with further Development of Tourism", News Release no. 98/1430MENA, 01/08/97, *World Bank website*, www.worldbank.org/html/extdr/extme/1430.htm.

496 World Bank, "World Bank Committed US$67 Million to Jordan in Fiscal Year 1998", News release no. 99/1892/MENA, *World Bank website*, www.worldbank.org/html/extdr/extme/1892.htm.

497 World Bank, (1999), "World Bank Helps Strengthen Jordan's Health Sector", News Release no. 99/2126/MN, 25/03/99, *World Bank website*, www.worldbank.org/extdr/extme/2126.htm.

498 *Ibid.*

499 World Bank, "World Bank Approves Project to Improve Water and Waste Water Services in Jordan", News Release no. 99/2117/MN, *World Bank website*, www.worldbank.org/extdr/extme/2117.htm.

500 World Bank, "World Bank Board Discusses Jordan Country Assistance Strategy", *World Bank website*, wbln0018.worldbank.org/mna/mena.nsf/All/D4D46C2B71E7CA6C8525694 D0056435D?opendocument.

501 The Bank's CAS, based on its assessment of the country's priorities, past portfolio performance and creditworthiness, sets out the level and composition of financial and technical assistance that the Bank seeks to provide to a member country. Indeed, while the country must 'own' its vision and programme, the Bank must 'own' and be accountable to shareholders for its diagnosis and the programs it supports. The CAS normally takes a three-year focus on Bank activities and is developed in co-operation with the government and, often, with civil society. However, it is not a negotiated document. World Bank, "Strategies", *World Bank website*, www.worldbank.org/whatwedo/strategies.htm#cas. For the World Bank's view on what makes a good CAS see World Bank, "Country Assistance Strategies (CASs)", *World Bank website*, www.worldbank.org/html/pic/cas/tenfeat.htm.

502 World Bank, "World Bank Board Discusses Jordan Country Assistance Strategy", op. cit. Emphasis in the original.

503 *Ibid.*

504 World Bank, "World Bank Approves Loan to Jordan for Higher Education Development", News Release no. 2000/233/MNA, 29/02/00, *World Bank website*, wbln0018.worldbank.org/news/pressrelease.Nsf/5601ca2709466a068525678c00586074/05e5 2417048aa094852568940071d7f1?OpenDocument.

505 *MEED*, 07/08/92, p.14.

506 World Bank, (1993), *Annual Report*, op. cit., p.141.

507 World Bank, (1994), *Annual Report*, op. cit., pp.114-115.

508 World Bank, (1995), *Annual Report*, op. cit., p.98.

509 *Ibid.*, p.98.

510 *Ibid.*, p.99.

511 *MEED*, 03/11/95, p.16.

512 World Bank, (1996a), op. cit.,, p.4.

513 *Ibid.*, Annex III.

514 *Ibid.*, pp.8-9.

515 World Bank, (1997), *Annual Report*, op. cit., pp.86-88.

516 World Bank, (1998), *Annual Report*, op. cit., p.56.

517 *MEED*, 10/07/98, pp.16-17.

518 Quoted in *MEED*, 24/07/98, p.25.

519 *SWB Weekly Economic Report*, Third Series, 08/09/98, ME/W0554 pp.WME/10-11.

520 World Bank, "Statement by World Bank President James D Wolfensohn on the Passing of King Hussein of Jordan", *World Bank website*, www.worldbank.org/html/extdr/extme/ps020799.htm.

521 World Bank, "Annual Report, 2000: Box 4.12 Privatization Initiatives in the MENA Region", *World Bank website*, www.worldbank.org/html/extpb/annrep/bob4_12.htm.

522 World Bank, "Jordan: World Bank Loan Supports Ambitious Public Sector Reform", *World Bank website*, www.worldbank.org/WBSITE/EXTERNAL/NEWS/0,,contentMDK:20052533~menuPK:34455~pagePK:64003015~piPK:64003012~thesite:4607,00.html.

523 Buy-backs were formalised under a system known as Brady Bonds, which restructured debt into tradeable bonds. These bonds are traded at a discount, which allows the government to purchase their own debt at a discount. In 2000, the Jordanian government purchased Brady Bonds with a face value of US$151m, at a discount rate of more than 50%. "Jordan Needs Clear Policy Objectives for Internal and External Debt: A Report by the Export and Finance Bank", Jordan Times internet edition, 11/06/01, *Jordan Times website*, www.jordantimes.com. The outstanding Brady Bonds were liquidated in late 2003.

524 The World estimated that debt-servicing on external debt outstanding at the beginning of 1990 would cost US$976.9m in 1990; US$615.1m (1991); US$1919.7m (1992); US$1214.1m (1993); US$1193.6m (1994); US$1388m (1995); US$1277.5m (1996); US$1132.7m (1997); US$925.7m (1998); US$797.2m (1999); and US$599.2 (2000). Quoted in Merza, A.K., (1992), *A Consistent Macro Framework for Future Alternative Growth Paths in Jordan*, (Amman: Ministry of Planning and UNDP), p.20.

525 *Ibid.*, p.53.

526 *MEES*, vol. 32, no. 37, 19/06/89, p.B2.

527 Principal US$843m, interest US$370m.

528 Principal US$882m, interest US$396m.

529 *MEES*, vol. 32, no. 43, 31/07/89, p.B3.

530 *SWB Weekly Economic Report*, Third Series ME/W0088, 01/08/89, pp.A1/3-4.

531 *Ibid.*, pp.A1/3-4.

532 *MEES*, 18/09/89, vol. 32, no. 50, p.B2.

533 *MEES*, vol. 33, no. 8, 27-11-89, p.B1.

534 *MEES*, vol. 33, no. 9, 04/12/89, p.B2.

535 IMF, (October 1995), op. cit., p.53.

536 *MEED*, 10/08/90, p.13.

537 *MEES*, vol. 33, no. 19, 12/02/90, p.B3.

538 IMF, (October 1995), op. cit., p.58.

539 *Ibid.*, p.54.

540 *Ibid.*, p.54.

541 For official development loans, 20 equal semi-annual payments starting 31/3/03. Other loans, 14 equal semi-annual payments after a nine-year grace period. *Ibid.*, p.54.

542 *Ibid.*, p.54.

543 *Ibid.*, p.56.

544 *Ibid.*, p.58.

545 *MEED*, 08/08/94, pp.26-27.

546 IMF, (October 1995), op. cit., p.55.

547 *MEED*, 11/10/96, pp.32-33.

548 *SWB Weekly Economic Report*, Third Series ME/W0488, 27/05/97, pp.8-9.

549 *MEED*, 06/06/97, p.21.

550 Atlas Investment Group, (2001), op. cit., p.11.

551 *Ibid.*, p.11.

552 *MEES*, vol. 42, no. 22, 31/05/99, p.B5.

553 Ministry of Planning, (1999), "Jordan Reschedules Debt", *Partners in Development*, June, no. 25, p.1

554 *SWB Weekly Economic Report*, Third Series ME/W0653, 12/08/00, p.WME/8.

555 *SWB*, Third Series ME/2044, 11/07/94, pp.MED/12-16.

556 *MEES*, vol. 37, no. 42, 18/07/94, p.C2.

557 *MEED*, 05/08/94, p.23.

558 *MEED*, 12/08/94, p.23.

559 *SWB Weekly Economic Report*, Third Series ME/W0353, 04/10/94, p.WME11.

560 *MEED*, 19/08/94, p.15.

561 *MEED*, 12/08/94, p.23.

562 *SWB*, Third Series ME/2247, 09/03/95, pp.MED/13-1 and *SWB Weekly Economic Report*, Third Series ME/W0385, 23/05/95, pp.A1/4-5.

563 *MEES*, vol. 38, no. 45, 07/08/95, p.B2.

564 *SWB Weekly Economic Report*, Third Series ME/W0306, 02/11/93, pp.A1/4-5.

565 *SWB Weekly Economic Report*, Third Series ME/W0350, 13/09/94, p.WME/9.

566 *MEED*, 03/05/96, p.22.

567 *MEED*, 19/07/96, p.20.

568 In 1999, two debt-swap agreements were signed with France: the first cancelled debt worth FF100m, which had to be invested in projects in water, environment, tourism and training. The second was a an equity swap agreement for FF400m, which was taken up by France Telecom (FF325m) in JTC, Astra Group (FF50m), and Accor (FF25m) in the Ma'in Spa complex. Germany has signed five debt swap agreements totalling DM265.748m, which has been swapped on water sector and social development. Spain has signed two agreements totalling US$22m, while the UK has signed one equity swap for £90m. "Jordan Needs Clear Policy Objectives for Internal and External Debt: A Report by the Export and Finance Bank", Jordan Times internet edition, 11/06/01, *Jordan Times website*, www.jordantimes. Com.

569 These efforts included a letter sent by President Clinton on 05/08/94 to "the leaders of Germany, France, Britain and ten other industrialised nations urging them to grant debt relief to Jordan." Jreisat, J.E., (1997), op. cit., p.123.

570 The following paragraph is based extensively on Prados, A.B., (1997), "Jordan: U.S. Relations and Bilateral Issues", CRS Brief no. 93085, 02/01/97.

571 For a brief history of USAID in Jordan, the fluctuating relationship between the government and USAID, and the relationship between USAID and other donors see Amawi, A.M., (1996), "USAID in Jordan", *Middle East Policy*, vol. iv, no. 4, October, pp.77-89.

572 Significantly, each of these NGOs has a royal patron.

573 *MEED*, 22/02/91, p.13.

574 *MEED*, 05/04/91, pp.24-25.

575 The fiscal year for USAID runs from the 1st October to the 30th September, i.e. FY2000 ends on 30/09/00.

576 Prados, A.B., (1997), op. cit. Date of emergency legislation as given.

577 USA Embassy, Amman, "USA/Jordan, Reflections on Development in Jordan: Panel Discussion", Remarks by USAID/Jordan Mission Director Lewis Lucke, 13/05/99, *USA Embassy Amman website*, www.usembassy-amman.org.jo/USAID/econ.htm.

578 These four points were highlighted in an interview with Thibeault, Steve, USIA, USA Embassy, Amman, Amman, 27/05/99.

579 USA Embassy, Amman, "United States Grants US$50 Million to Support Balance of Payments", *USA Embassy Amman website*, www.usembassy-amman.org.jo/USAID/econ.htm.

580 USA Embassy, Amman, "USAID/Jordan Mission Director Lewis Lucke Opening Remarks at the Rotary Club, Amman, Jordan August 31, 1999", *USA Embassy Amman website*, www.usembassy-amman.org.jo/USAID/rotary2.htm.

581 *Ibid.*

582 The Congressional Presentation is the document in which USAID requests funding for the forthcoming year from Congress. The final budget determined by Congress is not necessarily the same as in the presentation.

583 Congressional Presentation, FY1988, mimeograph.

584 *Ibid.*

585 Zimmerman, R.F. and Hook, S.W., (1996), "The Assault on US Foreign Aid", in Hook, S.W., (ed.), *Foreign Aid Towards the Millennium*, (Boulder: Lynne Rienner Publishers), p.59.

586 For a list of projects associated with economic opportunities see the USA Embassy, Amman, *USA Embassy Amman website*, www.usembassy-amman.org.Jordan/USAID/past.htm.

587 USAID, "Summary of USAID/Jordan Strategy, 1997-2001", (Amman: USAID).

588 USA Embassy, Amman, "USA/Jordan, Strategic Objective Five: Increased Economic Opportunities for Jordanians", *USA Embassy Amman website*, www.usembassyamman.org.jo/USAID/econ.htm.

589 The rest of the paragraph is drawn from *Ibid.*

590 The following paragraph is drawn from *Ibid.*

591 WTO's predecessor, GATT, had established a committee as far back as early 1994 to assess Jordan's application.

592 Congressional Presentation, FY1999.

593 USA Embassy, Amman, "USA/Jordan, Strategic Objective Five: Increased Economic Opportunities for Jordanians", op. cit.

594 Best practices according to USAID include 1) separate operational units dedicated solely to micro-finance; 2) fresh-thinking, well-trained staff dedicated solely to micro-finance; 3) short-maturity loans; 4) rapid response to delinquencies; 5) timely, well-designed loan management systems; and 6) proactive customer service, aggressive outreach, and rapid decision-making. USA Embassy, Amman, "USAID Sponsors Bankers' Workshop on Micro-finance", *USA Embassy Amman website*, www.usembassy-amman.org.jo/USAID/microfin.htm.

595 AMIR, "Business Association Initiative", *AMIR website*, www.amir-jordan.org/bai/bai_mainpage.htm.

596 Funding for the project comes from Canada, the UK, UNICEF, USAID, and Save the Children Fund.

597 Interview with Dababaneh, Rula, Project Management Specialist – Micro-Enterprise, USAID, Amman, 28/06/99.

598 Interview with Nabulsi, A., Founder/Director, Al-Jidara Investment Services, Amman, 07/06/99. Al-Jidara is regularly employed as consultants by the World Bank.

599 The YEA was established in October 1998, and registered the following month. The YEA was created because of the feeling that young people were not represented in business associations, despite being the majority of the population. Members must be under 50, and the majority of them are in their mid-30s. Interview with Alul, Ghalia, Executive Co-ordinator, YEA, Amman, 20/07/99.

600 For example, a discussion was held on "The Jordanian Privatisation Program" at Philadelphia University in December 1998. Executive Privatization Unit, (1999), "Meetings and Activities on Privatization", *Privatization News*, no. 7, May, p.10.

601 For example, the chairman of the Executive Privatisation Unit, Adel al-Kodah, gave four lectures to various audiences throughout Jordan between November 1998 and April 1999. For details *Ibid.*, p.10.

602 For example, the Engineers Association held a seminar in March 1999. *Ibid.*, p.10.

603 For example, a series of three workshops were held at the Centre for Strategic Studies, University of Jordan in April 1999. *Ibid.*, p.10.

604 For example, N. Barqawi of the Executive Privatisation Unit attended a conference on 'Strategic Opportunities in the Developing Electricity Markets' held at the Adam Smith Institute in London, in May 1998. Executive Privatization Unit, (1998), "Meetings and Activities on Privatization", *Privatization News*, vol. 1, no. 5, July, p.12.

605 For example, K. Mirza of the Executive Privatisation Unit attended a training course on 'Building Knowledge and Expertise in Infrastructure Finance' in December 1998 in Beirut. Executive Privatization Unit, (1999), "Meetings and Activities on Privatization", *Privatization News*, no. 7, May, p.11.

606 For example, the chairman of the Executive Privatisation Unit, Adel al-Kodah, appeared on two special programmes on Jordanian TV to explain the benefits of the privatisation of JTC in April 1998. Executive Privatization Unit, (1998), "Meetings and Activities on Privatization", *Privatization News*, vol. 1, no. 5, July, p.11.

607 Six in total up to October 1999, with a further twenty having benefited in other ways. The six business associations were the ACC, the ACI, the Jordan Trade Association, the Business and Professional Women's Club, the Amman World Trade Centre and the YEA. These Business Associations account for the majority of the private sector in Jordan. USA Embassy, Amman, "USAID Sponsors Bankers' Workshop on Microfinance", op. cit.

608 USA Embassy, Amman, "USAID/Jordan Mission Director Lewis Lucke Opening Remarks at the Business Associations Grant Signing Ceremony, Amman, Jordan, October 12, 1999", *USA Embassy Amman website*, www.usembassy-amman.org.jo/USAID/bagrant.htm.

609 USA Embassy, Amman, "$15 Million USAID Grant for Jordan United States Business Partnership will Boost Competitiveness, Productivity, Exports", *USA Embassy Amman website*, www. usembassy-amman.org.jo/USAID/microfin.htm.

610 Jordan-US Business Partnership, (1999), "Summary Statement regarding the Jordan-United States Business Partnership", 15/02/99.

611 One interviewee, who wished to remain anonymous, was highly critical of the media campaign, part of which was being run in the English-speaking press, an area of the media the target audience were unlikely to access.

612 The Institute of Management Consultants (which the JUSBP hoped would take over the programme at the end of the four-year period), the Hotel Association, the YEA, and the association concerned with intellectual property rights.

613 Interview with Shawareb, Maha N., Manager, Business Support Organisations, JUSBP, Amman, 28/07/99.

614 Interview with Katib, Bassam M., Vice-President, Client Services, JUSBP, Amman, 28/07/99.

615 JV2020 is discussed in greater depth in the chapter on the private sector.

616 USA Embassy, Amman, "USAID/Jordan Mission Director Lewis Lucke Opening Remarks at the Rotary Club, Amman, Jordan August 31, 1999", op. cit.

617 Kohama, H., (1999), "Structural Reform and Japan's Co-operation with Jordan", Jordan Times Internet Edition, 22/11/99, *Jordan Times website*, www.jordantimes.com.

618 An undated paper titled "Jordan" given to the researcher by the JICA representative in Jordan.

619 The Committee on the Country Study for Japan's Official Development Assistance to the Hashemite Kingdom of Jordan, (1996), op. cit., foreword.

620 *Ibid.*, p.iv.

621 *Ibid.*, pp.iv-vi.

622 *Ibid.*, p.115.

623 *Ibid.*, p.113.

624 *Ibid.*, p.113.

625 *Ibid.*, p.114.

626 *Ibid.*, p.114.

627 Kohama, H., (1999), op. cit.

628 Interview with Kurkata, Hiroshi, Deputy Resident Representative, JICA, Amman, 19/07/99.

629 Interview with Mustafa, Isam, The Higher Council for Science and Technology, Amman, 23/07/99.

630 The following paragraph is drawn extensively from KfW, (1998), op. cit.

631 *Ibid.*, p.1.

632 Interview with Avédikian, Richard, op. cit.

633 Interview with Hasse, Dr. Volkmar, op. cit.

634 *Ibid.*

635 Interview with Avédikian, Richard, op. cit.

636 Interview with Hasse, Dr. Volkmar, op. cit.

637 The Committee on the Country Study for Japan's Development Assistance to the Hashemite Kingdom of Jordan, (1996), op. cit., p.101.

638 British Embassy, Amman, British Embassy, Development: UK Aid to NGOs (DFID), 1990-1998, *British Embassy Amman website*, www.britain.org.Jordan/development_c.htm.

639 British Embassy, Amman, British Embassy, Development: DFID: Department for International Development, *British Embassy Amman website*, www.britain.org.Jordan/development_a.htm.

640 World Bank, (1996a), op. cit., pp.3-4.

641 *Ibid.*, p.6.

642 *Ibid.*, p.4.

643 *Ibid.*, pp.4, 6 and 8.

644 *Ibid.*, p.5.

645 *Ibid.*, p.11.

646 The EIB is the long-term lending institution of the EU.

647 *Ibid.*, p.9.

648 *Ibid.*, p.9.

649 UNDP Jordan, "UNDP Lends a Hand to Small Enterprises by Fueling 'Engine for Job Creation'", News Release, 24/10/96, *UNDP Jordan website*, www.undp-jordan.org/features 1.html. The remainder of the paragraph is based on this document

650 UNDP assistance for small enterprise development in rural areas was first proposed in the Fourth Country Programme for Jordan, January 1988 to December 1991. UNDP, (1987), "Fourth Country Programme for Jordan, January 1988 to December 1991", reference DP/CP/JOR/4, 12/10/87, paragraph 52, p.12. The planned funding of this project was estimated at US$0.2m, out of the total resources of US$10.1m. *Ibid.*, Annex 3, part I.

651 *Ibid.*

652 UNDP Jordan, "UNDP to Assist Government in WTO Negotiations", News Release, 08/07/98, *UNDP Jordan website*, www.undp-jordan.org/press16.html.

653 UNDP, (1992), "Fifth Programme for the Hashemite Kingdom of Jordan, 1992-1996", reference DP/CP/JOR/5, 11/03/92, paragraph 23, p.6.

654 *Ibid.*, paragraph 32, p.8.

655 Although UNDP documents refer to the process as dialogue, this term is misleading as the agenda for the negotiations is set by the UNDP. For example, prior to the first framework agreement, the UNDP sent an advisory note, which was intended "to convey to the Government UNDP's considered views on the country's current development situation and technical needs, and the choice of priorities for UNDP's future interventions in support of national development aspirations." Indeed, much of the wording in the advisory letter is repeated verbatim in the framework agreement. UNDP Jordan, 'Advisory Note for Jordan', *UNDP Jordan website*, www.undp-jordan.org/programmes.html.

656 UNDP, (1992), op. cit., paragraph 29, p.8.

657 *Ibid.*, paragraph 55, p.13.

658 UNDP, (1997), "First Country Cooperation Framework for Jordan, 1998-2002", reference DP/CCF/JOR/1, 30/06/97, paragraph 12, p.4.

659 *Ibid.*, paragraph 9, pp.3-4.

660 *Ibid.*, paragraph 9, pp.3-4.

661 *Ibid.*, paragraph 20, p.6.

662 *Ibid.*, paragraph 23, p.6.

663 UNDP Jordan, "1999 Annual Report of the UN Resident Coordinator in Jordan: Part One: UN Development Assistance in 1999 – An Overview", *UNDP Jordan website*, www.undp-Jordan.org/ unrc99_1_4.html.

664 UNDP, (1997), op. cit., paragraph 24, p.7.

665 The first protocol (1979-1981) was for ECU40m (US$53m), the second (1981-1986) was valued at ECU63m (US$84m), the third (1987-1991) was ECU100m (US$133m), the fourth (1992-1996) totalled ECU124m (US$165.1m). Almost one-third of the fourth protocol was in the form of grants. In 1991 a one-off Gulf crisis grant of ECU150m (US$200m) was made. *MEED*, 17/07/92, pp.21-22. These protocols were part of wider-ranging Co-operation Agreements.

666 MEDA I covered the period 1996-1999, MEDA II covers the period 2000-2002. Ministry of Planning, (2000), "National Indicative Program for Jordan in the Context of MEDA II", *Partners in Development*, June, no. 37, p.9.

667 Interview with Garces dos Los Fayos, Fernando, op. cit.

668 Interview with Smadi, Dr. Mohammed, Director-General, ACI, Amman, 16/06/99.

669 Interview with Alul, Ghalia, op. cit.

670 Off the record comment to the researcher by a European official concerned with aid.

671 These are countries that America considers do not take sufficient action against counterfeit goods.

672 Only three other countries, Canada, Mexico and Israel, have a FTA with the USA. The FTA will phase out virtually all tariffs on industrial goods and farm products over a period of ten years. Among other aspects the service sector in Jordan will be opened to US companies and Jordan has undertaken to ratify and implement the world Intellectual Property Organisation's Copyright treaty and Performances and Phonograms Treaty within two years. Ministry of Planning, (2000), "The Free Trade Agreement with Jordan", *Partners in Development*, October, no. 41, p.1.

673 Interview with Nabulsi, Dr. M.S., ex-Governor, CBJ, Chairman and CEO, Jordan Investment Trust PLC, Amman, 16/06/99. Dr Nabulsi was with the CBJ during the debt negotiations.

674 A number of the interviewees, such as Riccardo Bocco and Pamela Dougherty were at pains to point out this contradiction. Interviews with Bocco, Riccardo, CERMOC, Amman, 18/05/99 and Dougherty, Pamela, MEED, Amman, 22/07/99.
675 USAID, "Congressional Presentation FY2000: Jordan", *USAID website*, www.usaid.gov/pubs/cp2000/ane/jordan,html.
676 Interview with Gharaibeh, Firas F., Senior Programme Assistant, UNDP, Amman, 03/06/99.
677 Interviews with Avédikian, Richard, op. cit. and Garces dos Los Fayos, Fernando, op. cit.
678 Interview with Avédikian, Richard, op. cit.
679 Interview with Gharaibeh, Firas F., op. cit.

Chapter 7: State, Rentier Elite and Conditionality: 1989-2002
680 Brand, L.A., (1992), op. cit., p.173.
681 Commercialisation or corporatisation includes separating social from commercial objectives, eliminating monopoly protection, capitalising the company, taxing and charging public companies as any other private sector company, and separating policy formulation from regulation. World Bank, (1995), "Private Sector Assessment", Report no. 14405-JO, p.21.
682 Brand, L.A., (1992), op. cit., p.173.
683 Abu Shair, O.J.A.R., (1997), op. cit., p.150.
684 Dougherty, P. and O. Wils, (1999), "Between Public and Private: Economic Élites", (draft mimeograph), p.20.
685 Speech by Finance Minister Basil Jardaneh to bankers in London, 05/07/89. Reported in *MEED*, 21/07/89, p.5.
686 Anani, J. and R. Khalaf, (1989), op. cit., p.220.
687 *MEED*, 13/01/95, pp.24-25.
688 *MEED*, 07/06/96, p.25.
689 Dr Hammour pointed out that a major impediment to the privatisation was the reaction of both the 'street' and parliament. Consequently, the state felt the need to educate these sectors as to the necessity and the benefits of privatisation. Interview with Abu Hammour, Dr. Mohammed, advisor to the Minister of Finance, Amman, 18 July 1999.
690 The report estimated unemployment caused by privatisation to be 50,000 or about 6% of the total labour force. World Bank, (1995), op. cit., p.27.
691 *Ibid.*, p.iii.
692 The suggested number of staff was 10 to 15. *Ibid.*, p.19.
693 *Ibid.*, p.iii.
694 *Ibid.*, p.21.
695 *Ibid.*, p.25.
696 *SWB*, Third Series, ME/2214, 30/01/95, pp.MED/12-22.
697 *SWB Weekly Economic Report*, Third Series, ME/W0357, 01/11/94, pp.WME/7-10.
698 Al-Kodah, A., lecture at the 1997 MENA Economic Conference, Doha, Qatar, 16-18 November 1997, reprinted in Executive Privatization Unit, (1998), "Jordan's Privatization Experience", *Privatization News*, vol. 1, no. 4, Mar., p.8.
699 Figure as quoted.
700 *MEED*, 03/03/95, p.19.
701 EIU, (1995c), *Jordan: Country Report*, no. 3, (London: EIU).
702 *MEED*, 09/08/96, p.12.
703 *MEED*, 21/06/96, p.12.
704 *MEED*, 16/08/96, pp.24-25.
705 Investment Promotion Corporation, (undated), "Jordan as a Venue for Investment", (Amman: Investment Promotion Corporation).
706 *MEED*, 27/06/97, p.15.

707 *MEED*, 22/10/97, p.21.

708 CBJ, (1997), *Annual Report*, op. cit., p.28.

709 *SWB*, Third Series, ME/1104, 21/06/91, p.A1-5.

710 Between 1986 and 1995 at least four studies, costing around US$0.64m, were undertaken merely to establish the assets and liabilities of the company. Abu Shair, (1997), op. cit., p.168.

711 *MEED*, 14/08/92, pp.19-20.

712 *MEED*, 20/01/95, pp.22-23.

713 In 1994, main telephone lines in operation numbered 305,470, with a waiting list of 120,000. The waiting time for a line was close to nine years. Mustapha, M.A., (undated), "Telecommunications in Jordan: Performance, Policy Environment and Reforms Ahead", *World Bank website*, www. worldbank.org/wbi/mdf/mdfl/perform.htm.

714 *MEED*, 27/09/96, pp.13-14.

715 *SWB Weekly Economic Report*, Third Series, ME/W0510, 28/10/97, p.WME/6.

716 *MEED*, 05/05/95, p.23 and *MEED*, 23/06/95, pp.12-13.

717 *MEED*, 19/09/97, p.16.

718 The three companies were awarded four packages. Altawfiq Transport Company gained one package at an annual franchise fee of JD140,000, Asia Transport Company won two packages at JD134,000 and JD196,000 and the fourth package went to Jordan Investment and General Consultancy Company at JD85,000. Executive Privatization Unit, (1998), "Privatization Update and Latest Resolutions on Privatization", *Privatization News*, vol. 1, no. 6, Nov, p.10.

719 In 1992, twenty-five of the thirty-one engines were operational, while only two hundred and eighty-five of five hundred wagons were serviceable. Ministry of Planning, (undated: a), *Plan for Economic and Social Development: 1993-1997*, (Amman: Ministry of Planning), p.80.

720 Executive Privatization Unit, (1997), "Jordan Privatization Program", *Privatization News*, vol. 1, no. 1, May, p.6.

721 *MEED*, 27/09/96, pp.13-14. The project was offered as one of a series of twenty-four projects at the First MENA Economic Summit in Cairo. Ministry of Planning, (1996), "An Overview of Projects: Gateway to Business Opportunities in the Middle East", brochure issued for MENA economic summit, Cairo, p.23.

722 *MEED*, 24/07/98, p.25.

723 *MEES*, vol. 39, no. 39, 22/07/96, p.A14.

724 *MEED*, 12/07/97, pp.17-18.

725 World Bank, (1995), op. cit., p.12.

726 Prime Minister Majali in budget speech to parliament on 20 January 1998. Executive Privatization Unit, (1998), "The Prime Minister's Words on Privatisation in the Jordanian Parliament", *Privatization News*, vol. 1, no. 4, Mar., p.6.

727 *Ibid.*, p.6.

728 Two particular aspects worried the committee at this stage the lack of government control of companies in which the state still had a significant share (e.g. JTC) and also the question of monopolies (e.g. JCFC). *MEED*, 03/04/98, p.14.

729 Kanaan, T.H., (1999), "The Business Environment in Jordan", in Fawzy, S. and A. Galal, (eds.), *Partners for Development: New Roles for Governments and the Private Sector in the Middle East and North Africa*, (Washington: World Bank), pp.57-82.

730 CBJ, (1998), op. cit., p.28.

731 IMF, "Letter of Intent", *IMF website*, www.imf.org/external/np/loi/1999/082899.htm.

732 *MEES*, vol. 42, no. 44, 01/11/99, pp.B4-5.

733 Ministry of Planning, (1999), "The Economic and Social Development Plan (1999-2003)", *Partners in Development*, July, no. 26, p.1.

734 JIC still held 16% of the shares in JCFC.

735 The management of JCFC had started overtly lobbying the government for a reduction in state interference in the industry in 1995. Among the methods of direct government

influence were the fixing of local cement prices at below market rates and insistence on local rather than international sales. The 33% stake was initially targeted for sale in 1997. Ghattas, J., (1997), "Recent Developments and Prospects for Jordan", *ABC Group Economic and Financial Quarterly*, no. 4, September, pp.1-6.

736 The Executive Privatization Commission, "Completed Transactions", *The Executive Privatization Commission Website*, www.epc.gov.jo/completed_transactions.html

737 *MEED*, 17/04/98, p.14.

738 *SWB*, Third Series, ME/3476, 06/03/99, pp.MED/1-5.

739 HM King Hussein of Jordan, "Letter of Appointment", to Prime Minister Abdul Karim Kabariti, 04/02/96, (mimeo), files of Jordan Times.

740 The restructuring included reducing the number of employees from 5592 in 1995 to 4937 at the end of 1998, with a further 100 redundancies in the first four months of 1999. Bin Hussein, M., (1999), "RJ Completes Financial Restructuring Package", *Jordan Times*, 11/05/99.

741 *MEES*, vol. 43, no. 30, 24/07/00, p.B6.

742 The process was not without controversy as the government requested the two leading bids be revised upwards. Aldeasa proved willing to increase their offer from US$52.1m to US$60.1m.

743 The Executive Privatization Commission, "Completed Transactions", *The Executive Privatization Commission Website*, www.epc.gov.jo/completed_transactions.html.

744 *Ibid.*

745 ASE, "ASE – Foreign Investment Regulations; Privatisation", *ASE website*, www.ase.com.jo/pages/privatisation_eng.htm.

746 Naser, A. and S Serhan, (1999), "Cabinet Approves JTC's US$1.25b Sale Scheme", *The Arab Daily*, 1/8/99.

747 Mansur, A.H. and J. Mongardini, (2003), "Stabilization and Structural Transformation of the Jordanian economy", paper presented at conference, *The Jordanian Economy in a Changing Environment*, Center for Strategic Studies, University of Jordan, 22-23 July, p.17.

748 *MEED*, 07/04/95, p.14.

749 *MEES*, vol. 39, no. 58, 04/11/96, pp.A3-4.

750 *Ibid.*, pp.A3-4.

751 *Ibid.*, pp.A3-4.

752 *SWB Weekly Economic Report*, Third Series, ME/W0616, 23/11/99, pp.WME/10-18.

753 Executive Privatization Unit, (1999), "Privatization Update and Latest Resolutions on Privatization", *Privatization News*, no. 7, May, p.7.

754 Prior to privatisation the company employed 1300 workers; only 500 were retained.

755 *MEED*, 20/08/99, p.17.

756 *MEED*, 11/12/98, p.12.

757 Executive Privatization Unit, (1998), "The Privatisation Transaction of the National Electric Power Company", *Privatization News*, vol. 1, no. 6, Nov, p.7.

758 Executive Privatization Unit, (1999), "Meetings and activities on Privatization", *Privatization News*, no. 7, May, p.7.

759 Executive Privatization Unit, (1999), "Privatization Update and Latest Resolutions on Privatization", *Privatization News*, no. 7, May, p.7.

760 These 1,663,523 shares, along with 1,181,750 shares in Jordan Electric Power Company were originally owned by the NEPCO. They were transferred to JIC on 21 July 1997 to be sold to private investors at a later date. Executive Privatization Unit, (1997), "Latest Developments in Privatisation", *Privatization News*, vol. 1, no. 2, Sept., p.2.

761 *MEED*, 15/09/00, p.16.

762 The Executive Privatization Commission, "Ongoing Transactions", *The Executive Privatization Commission Website*, www.epc.gov.jo/ongoing.html

763 *MEED*, 11/04/97, p.24.

764 Off the record statement to the researcher by senior government official. Amman, 1999.

765 *MEES*, vol. 42, no. 17, 22/04/99, p.B9.

766 *MEED*, 03/03/00, p.26.

767 *MEED*, 06/10/00, p.20.

768 These were transferred into a shareholding company in September 2000. Executive Privatization Commission, (2001), "Jordan's Privatisation Program", *Privatization News*, no. 9, Jan., p.3.

769 Executive Privatization Unit, (1999), "Privatization Update and Latest Resolutions on Privatization", *Privatization News*, no. 7, May, p.8.

770 The Executive Privatization Commission, "Ongoing Transactions", *The Executive Privatization Commission Website*, www.epc.gov.jo/ongoing.html

771 *Ibid.*

772 On 16 October 2003, 26% of the shares in APC were sold to Canadian company PCS for approximately US$173m. The Executive Privatization Commission, "Completed Transactions", *The Executive Privatization Commission Website*, www.epc.gov.jo/completed_transactions.html.

773 Executive Privatization Commission, (2001), "Jordan's Privatisation Program", *Privatization News*, no. 9, Jan., p.4.

774 The Executive Privatization Commission, "Completed Transactions", *The Executive Privatization Commission Website*, www.epc.gov.jo/completed_transactions.html.

775 Hamzeh, A.S., "SSC Snaps Up Largest Share of Jordan Press Foundation Shares as Sale Begins", Jordan Times Internet Edition, 31/10/00, *Jordan Times website*, www.jordantimes.com.

776 This part of the programme had first been introduced in late 1996

777 Executive Privatization Unit, (1999), "Privatization Update and Latest Resolutions on Privatization", *Privatization News*, no. 7, May, p.8.

778 *MEED*, 30/04/99, p.18.

779 IMF, "Memorandum on Economic and Financial Policies, 2000", 04/07/00, *IMF website*, www. imf.org/external/np/loi/2000/jor/01/INDEX.HTM, p.23.

780 The fund received JD468m from JTC, JD79.8m from JCFC, JD66m from RJ and JD1.6m from other sales. CBJ, (2003), *Monthly Statistical Bulletin January 2003*, (CBJ: Amman), p.52

781 Adapted from CBJ, (2003), *Monthly Statistical Bulletin January 2003*, (CBJ: Amman), p.47-49

782 *Jordan Economic Monitor*, issue 0201, Feb. 2001, p.5.

783 For example, during a debate on privatisation in the Lower House in March 1998, Deputy Khalil Atiyah expressed fears of Israeli dominance of the economy if privatisation was not strictly controlled. "Lower House Committee Urges Government to Reconsider Privatisation Plans", *Jordan Times*, 26/03/98.

784 Reid, M.F., (1994), "Institutional Preconditions of Privatization in Market-Based Political Economies: Implications for Jordan", *Public Administration*, vol. 14, no. 1, February, pp.65-77.

785 EIU, (1990b), *Jordan: Country Report*, no. 2, (London: EIU), p.13.

786 EIU, (1992d), op. cit., p.14.

787 Quoted in *MEED*, 07/05/93, p.17.

788 Ali Abul Raghib became the second prime minister of King Abdullah's reign in 2000.

789 Quoted in *SWB Weekly Economic Report*, Third Series, ME/W0326, 29/03/94, p.WME/5.

790 EIU, (1994d), op. cit., p.13.

791 *MEED*, 17/03/89, p.21.

792 *Ibid.*, p.21.

793 *SWB Weekly Economic Report*, Third Series, ME/W0067, 07/03/89, p.i.

794 Prime Minister's statement to parliament on economic strategy, reported in *SWB Weekly Economic Report*, Third Series, ME/W0110, 09/01/90, pp.A1/4-6.

795 Prime Minister's statement to parliament on the budget, quoted in *SWB Weekly Economic Report*, Third Series, ME/W0115, 13/02/90, pp.A1/3-5.

796 Ministry of Planning, (2000), "Poverty in Jordan", *Partners in Development*, October, no. 41, p.5.

797 *MEED*, 16/03/90, p.25.

798 *MEES*, vol. 33, no. 28, 16/04/90, p.B5.

799 *SWB*, Third Series, ME/1227, 12/11/91, p.A/17.

800 EIU, (1990d), op. cit., p.12.

801 *MEED*, 26/07/96, pp.12-13.

802 Quoted in *SWB Weekly Economic Report*, Third Series, ME/W0443, 09/07/96, pp.WME/12-13.

803 *SWB*, Third Series, ME/2680, 02/08/96, pp.MED/16-17.

804 *Mideast Mirror*, "Who's Responsible for the Unrest in Jordan", vol. 10, no. 161, 19/08/96, pp.13-20.

805 *SWB*, Third Series, ME/2694, 19/08/96, p.MED/1-2.

806 *Ibid.*, p.MED/1-2.

807 CBJ, (1997), *Annual Report*, op. cit., p.

808 Awwa, R., "2001 budget deficit to reach JD380m—Marto", Jordan Times internet edition, 06/12/00, *Jordan Times website*, www.jordantimes.com.

809 "Jordan-Letter of Intent, Memorandum on Economic and Financial Policies, April 15, 2002", *IMF Website*, www.imf.org/external/np/loi/2002/jor/01/index.htm

Chapter 8: The State-Market Interface: Which Political Economy?

810 For example the letter of designation to the new Prime Minister, Mudar Badran, in December 1989, reported in *SWB*, Third Series, ME/0632, 06/12/89, pp.A/1-3, and in a speech at the opening of the second ordinary session of the 11th Parliament on 17/11/90, reported in *SWB*, Third Series, ME/0925, 19/11/90, pp.A/8-12.

811 *SWB Weekly Economic Report*, Third Series, ME/W0115, 13/02/90, pp.A1/3-5.

812 *SWB*, Third Series, ME/1124, 15/07/91, pp.A/13-18.

813 *SWB Weekly Economic Report*, Third Series ME/W0295, 17/08/93, pp.A1/1-3.

814 *Ibid.*, pp.A1/1-3.

815 Policy address by Prime Minister Shakir to parliament 25/01/95, reported in *SWB*, Third Series, ME/2214, 30/01/95, MED/12-22.

816 *SWB Weekly Economic Report*, Third Series ME/W0463, 26/11/96, pp.WME/7-8.

817 *SWB*, Third Series, ME/3476, 06/03/99, pp.MED/1-5.

818 *SWB Weekly Economic Report*, Third Series ME/W0589, 18/05/99, pp.WME/9-10.

819 See BBC Monitoring Online, 19/06/00, *BBC Monitoring website*, www.bbcmonitoring.co.uk/home/cgi/home.pl.

820 CBJ, (1993), *Annual Report*, op. cit., p.106.

821 *Ibid.*, p.113.

822 World Bank, (1995), op. cit., p.5.

823 King's speech on the opening of the second ordinary session of the 11th parliament on 17/11/90. *SWB*, Third Series, ME/0925, 19/11/90, p.A8-12.

824 Ministry of Planning, (undated: a), op. cit., pp.1-2.

825 *Ibid.*, p.98.

826 *Ibid.*, p.99.

827 *Ibid.*, p.2.

828 *Ibid.*, p.2.

829 *Ibid.*, p.100.

830 *Ibid.*, p.100.

831 *Ibid.*, p.3.

832 *Ibid.*, pp.47-48.

833 *Ibid.*, pp.68-69.

834 *Ibid.*, pp.103-107.

835 *Ibid.*, p.115.

836 *Ibid.*, p.141.

---

837 *Ibid.*, pp.151-152.

838 *Ibid.*, p.170.

839 *Ibid.*, pp.170-174.

840 *Ibid.*, p.188.

841 *Ibid.*, p.188.

842 Wazani, N., (1999), "Five-Year Plan to be the Foundation of the Country's Economy", *The Arab Daily*, 20/07/99.

843 For political reasons, Arab is always distinguished from other foreign investment.

844 Ministry of Planning, (undated: c), *Plan for Economic and Social Development: 1999-2003*, (Amman: Ministry of Planning), (in Arabic), p.6.

845 *Ibid.*, p.6.

846 *Ibid.*, pp.9-10.

847 *Ibid.*, p.21.

848 *Ibid.*, p.41.

849 *Ibid.*, p.23. In the 'Summary of the Plan for Economic and Social Development: 1999-2003', different figures are given: 7.0% for private consumption and 3.6% for public consumption. Ministry of Planning, (undated: d), *Summary of the Plan for Economic and Social Development: 1999-2003*, (Amman: Ministry of Planning), (in Arabic), p.5.

850 Ministry of Planning, (undated: c), op. cit., p.23.

851 *Ibid.*, p.23.

852 The figure given in the table is 1780.9 but this figure does add up. It would seem that a transposition of the 7 and the 8 corrects the discrepancy.

853 *Ibid.*, p.7.

854 *Ibid.*, p.55.

855 *Ibid.*, p.55-56.

856 *Ibid.*, pp.58-59.

857 The list for the Casablanca summit was extremely optimistic with one hundred and fifty-five projects totalling US$19,368m. For the Amman summit the figures were twenty-seven and US$3,511m, respectively. "Projects: Getting Real with revised Priorities", *MEED*, 27/10/95, p.12.

858 The list was almost the same as that presented in Amman the previous year.

859 "New Realism is Hallmark of Wish List", *MEED*, 15/11/96, p.17.

860 Occasionally referred to as the Unified Economic Council.

861 *MEED*, 20/10/89, p.33.

862 King Hussein in his address at the opening of parliament in November 1993. Reported in *SWB*, Third Series, ME/1855, 25/11/93, pp.MED/5-12.

863 EIU, (1989b), op. cit., pp.12-13.

864 *Ibid.*, pp.12-13.

865 Ministry of Planning, (1999), "Economic Consultative Council", *Partners in Development*, December, no. 31.

866 Executive Privatization Unit, (2000), "Privatization: Four Years of Achievements", *Privatization News*, no.8, Jan. p.1.

867 Dougherty, P., (2000), "The Goal is Growth", *MEED*, 18/08/00, p.5.

868 *SWB*, Third Series, ME/2073, 13/08/94, pp.MED/12-13.

869 *SWB*, Third Series, ME/2075, 16/08/94, p.MED/6.

870 Prime Minister al-Kabarati's statement to parliament on 28/02/96, reported in *SWB Weekly Economic Report*, Third Series, ME/W0425, 05/03/96, pp.WME/11-17.

871 Investment Promotion Corporation, (1997), "Investment Promotion Law and Regulations", (Amman: IPC), article 11, p.5.

872 *Ibid.*, article 12, p.6.

873 The three developments, the creation of the IPC, the Higher Council for the Investment Promotion and the investment window, were all part of the 1995 Investment Promotion Law.

These changes had been recommended in the 1995 World Bank Private Sector Assessment Report.

874 Although this move saved businesses from having to contact a number of different government departments, the number of permits, licences and authorisations remained as high.

875 Dr. R. Khalaf, Deputy Prime Minister and Minister of Planning, in an interview printed in "The Hashemite Kingdom of Jordan, Special Report", *First Magazine*, (1999).

876 Investment Promotion Corporation, (1997), op. cit., article 14c, p.7.

877 CBJ, (1994), *Annual Report*, op. cit., p.24.

878 *MEED*, 01/10/93, pp.15-16.

879 Committee on the Country Study for Japan's Development Assistance to the Hashemite Kingdom of Jordan, (1996), op. cit., p. 48.

880 A QIZ is any area that has been specified as a such by the US Government, and which has been designated by local authorities as an enclave where merchandise may enter US markets without payment of duty or excise taxes, and without the requirement of any reciprocal benefits, i.e. goods produced in a QIZ have duty-free quota-free access to the USA. The goods must have a minimum Jordanian and Israeli component. For further details see JIEC, "Qualifying Industrial Zone", *JIEC website*, www.jiec.com/jiec/main_q.html.

881 QIZs have their international recognition as an annex to the US-Israel FTA Act of 1985. Atlas Investment Group, (April 1985), op. cit., p.28.

882 JIEC, "Qualifying Industrial Zone", op. cit.

883 *MEED*, 16/12/99, p.23.

884 Manneh, J., (2003), *Sector Report: Qualifying Industrial Zones*, (Amman: Export and Finance Bank), p.3 & 7.

885 *Ibid.*, p.8.

886 "The Quest for Growth", *MEED*, 23/06/00, p.44.

887 *SWB Weekly Economic Report*, Third Series ME/W0651, 29/07/00, p.WME/10.

888 The start date was actually postponed to the early spring of 2001 because of difficulties completing the necessary formalities in time.

889 Atlas Investment Group, (April 2001), op. cit., p.29.

890 Dougherty, P., (2000), "The Goal is Growth", *MEED*, 18/08/00, p.5.

891 *The Middle East and North Africa, 1997*, 43rd edition, (London: Europa Publications Ltd), p.637.

892 CBJ, (1996), *Annual Report*, op. cit., p.25.

893 ASE, "ASE – Foreign Investment Regulations; Privatisation", op. cit.

894 World Bank, (1995), op. cit., p.48.

895 CBJ, (1999), *Annual Report*, op. cit., p.62.

896 *MEED*, 05/02/93, p.19.

897 CBJ, (1994), *Annual Report*, op. cit., p.28.

898 *MEED*, 19/05/95, pp.14-15.

899 CBJ, (1996), *Annual Report*, op. cit., p.25.

900 *SWB Weekly Economic Report*, Third Series, ME/W0583, 06/04/99, p.WME/9.

901 CBJ, (1999), *Annual Report*, op. cit., p.14.

902 *Ibid.*, p.19.

903 *MEED*, 14/01/94, p.16.

904 CBJ, (1997), *Annual Report*, op. cit., p.7.

905 al-Kouri, R., (2000), "Trade Policies in Jordan, Lebanon and Saudi Arabia", in Hoekman, B. and H. Kheir-el-Din, (eds.), *Trade Policy Developments in the Middle East and North Africa*, (Washington: World Bank), p.144. Note the regulations remain in place and could still be easily re-applied.

906 Customs duties have been a major source of government revenue since the 1970s. The policy of economic liberalisation had resulted in a dual policy being adopted. A gradual

reduction and exemption from the duty on intermediate goods has simultaneously seen the raising of taxes on luxury goods.

907 *SWB Weekly Economic Report*, Third Series, ME/W0668, 25/11/00, p.WME/10.

908 *MEED*, 16/08/91, p.16.

909 Quoted in *Ibid.*, p.16.

910 *MEED*, 05/06/92, p.16.

911 Ghorfa, "Investment Promotion Law and Regulations in Jordan", *Ghorfa website*, www.ghorfa.com/g87.htm, Regulation no. 1 of 1996, article 5.

912 *Ibid.*, article 6.

913 *Ibid.*, article 7.

914 *MEES*, vol. 38, no. 51, 18/09/95, pp.B1-2.

915 *Ibid.*, pp.B1-2.

916 Investment Promotion Corporation, (1997), op. cit., article 3f, p.2.

917 *Ibid.*, p.2.

918 *MEED*, 11/07/97, p.16.

919 Investment Promotion Corporation, (1997), op. cit., Non-Jordanian Investment Promotion Regulation, no 39 of 1997, article 3, p.16.

920 *Ibid.*, article 4, p.16.

921 *The Middle East and North Africa, 1999*, 45th edition, (London: Europa Publications Ltd), p.688.

922 Atlas Investment Group, (April 2001), op. cit., p.36.

923 *MEED*, 23/05/97, p.24.

924 *MEED*, 07/03/97, p.31.

925 CBJ, (1997), *Annual Report*, op. cit., p.7 and p.34.

926 *MEED*, 03/09/99, p.20.

927 The only previous agreements of this nature by the USA were with Canada and Mexico as part of NAFTA and with Israel as part of their special relationship.

928 *MEES*, vol. 43, no. 44, 30/10/00, p.B7.

929 Jordan lacks a proper mechanism to measure FDI. The Atlas Investment Group argues that the official figures are liable to be understated. Atlas Investment Group, (April 2001), op. cit., p.39.

930 Figures adapted from UNCTAD, "Foreign Direct Investment Database", *UNCTAD website*, www.unctad.org/fdi/eng.

931 Executive Privatization Commission, "Completed Transactions", *Executive Privatization Commission website*, www.epc.gov.jo/completed_transactions.html

932 *Jordan Economic Monitor*, issue 0701, July 2001, p.7.

933 SSC, "SSC Law no. 19 of 2001", *SSC website* (in Arabic), www.ssc.gov.jo, articles 9 and 10.

934 al-Fanek, F., (2000), "Consultants to prod the Government", Jordan Times website, *Jordan Times Internet Edition*, 07/02/00, www.jordantimes.com.

935 This paragraph is drawn in the main from "New Partners are Speeding the Expansion", *MEED*, 30/04/99, p.11.

936 The IFC for instance argue that "the factors affecting private sector development include providing the legal and regulatory frameworks necessary for markets to function, the judicial, systems and oversight institutions for their administration, and a level playing field for participants; the financial systems and infrastructure services needed to enable enterprises to grow and be competitive; and a basic commitment to the private sector manifested through protection of property rights and commitment to privatization." These aspects need to be provided by the state. IFC, (2000), *International Finance Corporation: Strategic Directions*, (Washington: IFC), p.2.

937 World Bank, (1995), op. cit., p.11.

938 The totals will not agree with previous table as the agricultural figures have been excluded. The figures account for less than 1% of both totals.

939 See previous footnote.

940 World Bank, (1995), op. cit., p.iv.

941 USA Embassy, Amman, "Strategic Objective (SO) Five: Increased Economic Opportunities for Jordanians", op. cit.

942 USA Embassy, Amman, "Current Projects", *USA Embassy Amman website*, www.usembassy-amman.org.jo/USAID/current.htm.

943 World Bank, (1995), op. cit., p.28.

944 Dougherty, P. and O. Wils, (1999), op. cit., p.28.

945 At this stage the ACI was no longer a nationwide organisation but had been joined by the Zarqa Chamber of Industry and the Irbid Chamber of Industry. However, the ACI remained the most powerful of the three chambers.

946 Atlas Investment Group, (April 2001), op. cit., p.33.

947 The remainder of this paragraph is drawn largely from BBC Monitoring Online, 17/02/00, *BBC Monitoring website*, www.bbcmonitoring.co.uk/home/cgi/home.pl.

948 In 2000, the pharmaceutical industry had become the third largest earner (JD110.8m), overtaking phosphates (JD90.8m), but still behind agricultural (JD116.4m) and potash (JD138m). CBJ, "CBJ Monthly Statistical Bulletin: External Sector", *CBJ website*, www.cbj.gov.jo/docs/bul_4_e. html.

949 *Ibid.*

950 Further updates REACH 3.0 and Reach 4.0 have since been launched. See *The REACH Initiative website*, www.reach.jo.

951 In 1998, 1250 professionals were employed in the sector, with a total estimated domestic and foreign market of US$60m. The REACH Initiative, "Reach 2.0: Final report", *The REACH Initiative website*, www.reach.jo/document.shtml, p.4.

952 Atlas Investment Group, (April 2001), op. cit., p.24.

953 YEA, "News: February 2000", *YEA website*, www.yea.com.jo/ news/2001/february.htm.

954 The REACH Initiative, "Reach 2.0: Final report", op. cit., p.4.

955 *Ibid.*, p.20.

956 Dougherty, P. and O. Wils, (1999), op. cit., p.21.

957 Interviews with Abujaber, Nimer F., Board Member, YEA, and Alul, Ghalia, op. cit., Amman, 20/07/99.

958 Dougherty and Wils, for instance, argue within "the economic élites in particular there is no evidence for particular privileges being associated entirely with regional background." *Ibid.*, p.25.

959 Reported in the *Jordan Times*, "Amman Chamber of Industry Pushes for Transformation to National Body", 19/02/98.

960 By 2001, the ACI had over 10,000 members, the Zarqa Chamber of Industry more than 2500 and the Irbid Chamber around 1000. Awwad, R., (2001), "Industrialists Outside Capital Fear Marginalisation by Proposed National Chamber", Jordan Times Internet Edition, 15/07/01, *Jordan Times website*, www.jordantimes.com.

961 *Ibid.*

962 A German state-funded NGO.

963 YEA, "About YEA", *YEA website*, www.yea.com.jo/objectives.htm.

964 Members must be under fifty years of at the time of application for membership. They must also have acquired entrepreneurial managerial experience, or have been a manager of a private business for at least two years. YEA website, "Join YEA", *YEA website*, www.yea.com.jo/to_join.htm.

965 *Middle East International*, no. 447, 02/04/93, pp.16-17.

966 Despite a number of official censuses, official details are not available on the exact percentage of the population which is Palestinian in origin. Reliable estimates put the figure at over 50%.

967 Brand, L.A., (1996), op. cit.

968 The oil company claimed that US$40m for the second half of 1985 and US$6m for June 1990 remained unpaid. Jordan claimed that the sum had been officially written off. *MEED*, 05/10/90, p.16.
969 *MEED*, 05/10/90, p.16.
970 Andoni, L., "Rock Bottom", *Middle East International*, no. 385, 12/10/90, pp.11-12.
971 *Ibid.*, pp.11-12.
972 *SWB Third Series*, ME/1472, 29/08/92, p.i.
973 *'umrah* is the lesser pilgrimage to Mecca, which can be performed at any time and takes less than an hour. Glassé, C., (1999), *The Concise Encyclopaedia of Islam*, (London: Stacey International), p.410.
974 *SWB Third Series*, ME/1943, 11/03/94, MED/3-4.
975 *SWB Third Series*, ME/1711, 10/06/93, p.i.
976 *MEED*, 14/03/97, p.27.
977 *MEED*, 10/07/98, pp.16-17.
978 *Mideast Mirror*, vol. 13, no. 42, 03/03/99, pp.16-20.
979 "Making the Most of the Potential for Progress", *MEED*, 29/05/98, p.8.
980 *Ibid.*, p.8.
981 Dougherty, P. and O. Wils, (1999), op. cit., pp.28-29.
982 *Ibid.*, p.29.

Chapter 9: Concluding Comments
983 Chaudhry, K.A., (1989), op. cit., pp.101-146.
984 Herb, M., (1999), *All in the Family: Absolutism, Revolution and Democracy in the Middle Eastern Monarchies*, (Albany: State University of New York Press), p.10 and Dougherty, P. and O. Wils, (1999), op. cit., p.3.
985 Herb, M., (2001), "Michael Herb: Assistant Professor, Department of Political Science, Georgia State University", *Georgia State University website*, www.gsu.edu/~polmfh.
986 I argue that democracy historically and at present remains the exception, while authoritarianism tends to be the normal political structure.
987 Ross, M.L., (2000), "Does Resource Wealth Lead to Authoritarian Rule? Explaining the Midas Touch", paper presented to the World Bank Research Group on "The Economics of Political Violence", Princeton University, March 18-19.
988 Huntington, S., (1991), "Democracy's Third Wave", *Journal of Democracy*, no. 2, Spring, pp.31-32.
989 Dougherty, P. and O. Wils, (1999), op. cit., p.3.
990 See Cornia, G.A., Jolly, R. and F. Stewart, (1987), op. cit.
991 For examples of this criticism see Michie, J. and J. Grieve Smith, (eds.), (1999), *Global Instability: The Political Economy of World Economic Governance*, (London: Routledge).

Bibliography

PRIMARY SOURCES

PUBLISHED MATERIAL
Arab Monetary Fund, (1998), *Foreign Trade of Arab Countries, 1987-1997*, vol. 16, (Abu Dhabi: AMF).

_____, (various), *Annual Report*, (Abu Dhabi: AMF).

Amman Financial Market, (various), *Annual* and *Monthly Reports*, (Amman: AFM).

Arab Fund for Economic and Social Development, (various), *Annual Report*, (Kuwait City: AFESD).

Association for Promotion of International Co-operation, (1996), *A Guide to Japan's Aid*, (Tokyo: Association for Promotion of International Co-operation).

Brandt Commission, The, (1980), *North-South: A Programme for Survival—The Report of the Independent Commission on International Development Issues under the Chairmanship of Willy Brandt*, (London: Pan Books).

_____, (1983), *North-South: Co-operation for World Recovery*, (London: Pan Books).

Bruntland, G.H., (1987), *Our Common Future: Report of the World Commission on Environment and Development*, (Oxford University Press: Oxford).

Budget Department, (various), *Budget Law for Fiscal Year*, (Amman: Budget Department).

Cahiers du CERMAC, Les, (1998), *Guides des Centres de Recherche et Documentation en Sciences Sociales en Jordanie*, (Amman: CERMOC), (in French).

Central Bank of Jordan, (1996), *Yearly Statistical Series (1964-1995)*, (Amman: CBJ).

_____, (various), *Annual Report*, *Quarterly Statistical Bulletin*, and *Monthly Statistical Bulletin*, (Amman: CBJ).

Committee of European Economic Co-operation, (1947), *General Report*, vol. 1, (London: HMSO).

Committee on the Country Study for Japan's Development Assistance to the Hashemite Kingdom of Jordan, (1996), *Country Study for Japan's Development Assistance to the Hashemite Kingdom of Jordan*, (Tokyo: JICA).

Congressional Presentation, (various), mimeographs.

Department of Statistics, (1994), *National Accounts: 1952-1992*, (no place: Department of Statistics).

_____, (various), *Statistical Yearbook*, (Amman: Department of Statistics).

Deutsche Gesellschaft für Technische Zusammenarbeit, (various), *Annual Report*, (Eschborn: GTZ).

Dun and Bradstreet, (2001), *Country Report: Jordan, June*, (High Wycombe: D&B).

Economic Intelligence Unit, (various), *Quarterly Economic Review of Jordan*, (London: EIU).

_____, (various), *Jordan Country Report*, and *Jordan Country Profile*, (London: EIU).

Executive Privatization Unit (later editions Executive Privatization Commission), (various), *Privatization News*, (Amman: EPU).

Foreign Office, (various), *British and Foreign State Papers*, (London: HMSO).

Free Zones Corporation, (1984), *Free Zones Corporation Law no. 32 1984*, (Amman: FZC).

General Federation of Jordanian Women, (1999), "Voice of Jordanian Women's Achievement: Final Report of the General Federation of Jordanian Women", 12th Executive Committee, 30/04/93-30/04/99, (in Arabic).

General Union of Voluntary Societies, (1973), *Basic Ordinances*, (Jordan: GUVS).

_____, (1995), *Profiles, Programs, Projects: General Union of Voluntary Societies, 1995*, (Amman: GUVS).

_____, (1995), *Social Development Report on Jordan*, (Amman: GUVS).

Glassé, C., (1999), *The Concise Encyclopaedia of Islam*, (London: Stacey International).

GMA Capital Markets Limited, (1997), *Euro-Mediterranean Partnership: Guide for Investors in Jordan*, (London: GMA Capital Markets Limited in association with Overseas Development Administration).

Government of Jordan, (1999), "Letter of Intent" to the IMF, 28/08/99.

_____, (2000), "Letter of Intent and Memorandum on Economic and Financial Policies" to the IMF, 04/07/00.

Hashemite Kingdom of Jordan National Assembly, (undated), *The Constitution of the Hashemite Kingdom of Jordan*, (Amman: National Assembly).

Higher Council for Science and Technology, (1996), *Japan Week in Jordan: Industrial Policy Seminar*, (Amman: Higher Council for Science and Technology).

_____, (1997), *Industrial Policy Seminar and Round-Table, 30-31/8/1997*, (Amman: Higher Council for Science and Technology).

Hourani, H., Dabbas, H. and M. Power-Stevens, (undated), *Who is Who in Jordanian Parliament, 1993-1997*, (Amman; al-Urdan al-Jadid Research Center).

Hourani, H. and A. Yassin, (undated), *Who is Who in Jordanian Parliament, 1997-2001*, (Amman; al-Urdan al-Jadid Research Center).

Hussein I of Jordan, H.M. King, (1994), *Selected Speeches by His Majesty King Hussein I, The Hashemite Kingdom of Jordan: 1988-1994*, (Amman: Royal Hashemite Court).

International Finance Corporation, (2000), *International Finance Corporation: Strategic Directions*, (Washington: IFC).

International Monetary Fund, (October 1995), *Jordan—Background Information on Selected Aspects of Adjustment and Growth Strategy*, IMF Staff Country Report no. 95/97, (Washington: IMF).

_____, (1995), *Social Dimensions of the IMF Policy Dialogue*, Pamphlet series no. 47, (IMF: Washington).

_____, (1997), *Jordan—Statistical Appendix*, IMF Staff Country Report no. 97/16, (Washington: IMF).

_____, (various), *Annual Report*, (Washington: IMF).

_____, (various), *Government Financial Statistics Yearbook*, (Washington: IMF).

_____, (various), *International Financial Statistics Yearbook*, (Washington: IMF).

_____, (various), *World Economic Outlook*, (Washington: IMF).

Investment Promotion Corporation, (1997), "Investment Promotion Law and Regulations", (Amman: IPC).

_____, (undated), "Jordan as a Venue for Investment", (Amman: IPC).

Islamic Development Bank, (various), *Annual Report*, (Jeddah: IsDB).

Japan International Cooperation Agency, (various), *Annual Report*, (Tokyo: JICA).

Jordan Export Development and Commercial Centers Corporation, (undated), *Jordan: Your Gateway to Business in the Middle East*, (Amman: JPF).

Jordan-US Business Partnership, (1999), "Summary Statement regarding the Jordan-United States Business Partnership", 15/02/99.

Jordanian Development Board, (1961), *The Hashemite Kingdom of Jordan Five Year Program for Economic Development 1962-1967*, (Amman: Jordan Development Board).

_____, (undated), *The Seven Year Program for Economic Development of Jordan: 1964-70*, (Amman: Jordan Development Board).

Konikoff, A., (1946), *Transjordan: An Economic Survey*, (Jerusalem: Economic Research Institute of the Jewish Agency for Palestine).

Kreditanstalt für Wiederaufbau, (1997), "Cooperation with Developing Countries: The Procedures followed in the Financial Cooperation of the Federal Republic of Germany", (Frankfurt am Main: KfW).

_____, (1998), "German-Jordanian Financial Co-operation as of: September 1998", (mimeograph).

_____, (various), *Annual Report*, (Frankfurt am Main: KfW).

Livesey, F., (1993), *Dictionary of Economics*, (London: Pitman Publishing).

Maciejewski, E. and A. Mansur, (1996), *Jordan: Strategy for Adjustment and Growth*, IMF occasional paper no. 136, (Washington: IMF).

Ministry of Finance, (various), *Government Finance Bulletin*, (Amman: Ministry of Finance).

Ministry of Planning, (1994), "Jordan: Tomorrow has arrived ... Investing in People", leaflet issued for MENA Economic Summit, Casablanca.

_____, (1995), brochures issued for MENA Economic Summit, Amman.

_____, (1996), "An Overview of Projects: Gateway to Business Opportunities in the Middle East", brochure issued for MENA Economic Summit, Cairo.

_____, (undated: a), *Plan for Economic and Social Development: 1993-1997*, (Amman: Ministry of Planning).

_____, (undated: b), *Summary of the Plan for Economic and Social Development: 1993-1997*, (Amman: Ministry of Planning).

_____, (undated: c), *Plan for Economic and Social Development: 1999-2003*, (Amman: Ministry of Planning), (in Arabic).

_____, (undated: d), *Summary of the Plan for Economic and Social Development: 1999-2003*, (Amman: Ministry of Planning), (in Arabic).

_____, (various), *Partners in Development*, monthly newsletter of the Aid Co-ordination Unit.

National Planning Council, (1971), *Planning Law: Law no. 68 for the Year 1971*, (Amman: National Planning Council).

_____, (undated: a), *The Hashemite Kingdom of Jordan Three Year Development Plan, 1973-1975*, (Amman: National Planning Council).

_____, (undated: b), *The Hashemite Kingdom of Jordan Five Year Plan for Economic and Social Development, 1976-1980*, (Amman: National Planning Council).

_____, (undated: c), *The Hashemite Kingdom of Jordan Five Year Plan for Economic and Social Development, 1981-1985*, (Amman: National Planning Council).

_____, (undated: d), *The Hashemite Kingdom of Jordan Five Year Plan for Economic and Social Development, 1986-1990*, (Amman: Royal Scientific Society Press).

Naval Intelligence Division, (1943), *Palestine and Transjordan*, (no place: Naval Intelligence Division).

Organization of Petroleum Exporting Countries Fund for International Development, (1998), *OPEC Aid Institutions: A Profile*, (Jeddah: OPEC Fund).

_____, (various), *Annual Report*, (Vienna: OPEC Fund).

Organization for Economic Cooperation and Development, (1996), *Shaping the Twenty First Century: The Contribution of Development Co-operation*, (Paris: OECD).

_____, (various), *Development Assistance: Efforts and Policies of the Members of the Development Assistance Committee, Annual Review*, (Paris: OECD).

Pass, C. and B. Lowes, (1993), *Collins Dictionary of Economics*, 2nd edition, (Glasgow: Harper Collins Publishers).

Private Sector Executive Committee, (1995), *Jordan Private Sector Opportunities*, (Amman: Private Sector Executive Committee).

Queen Alia Jordan Social Welfare Fund, (1985), *Law of the Queen Alia Fund for Social Development: Law no. 37 for the year 1985*, (Amman: no publishers).

_____, (undated), *The Queen Alia Jordan Social Welfare Fund*, (Amman).

Riedel, T., (1993), *Who is Who in Jordanian Parliament, 1989-1993*, (Amman: Friedrich Ebert Stiftung).

Robertson, D., (1985), *The Penguin Dictionary of Politics*, (London: Penguin).

Saudi Fund for Development, The, (various), *Annual Report*, (Riyadh: Saudi Fund).

South Commission, The, (1990), *The Challenge to the South: The Report of the South Commission*, (Oxford: Oxford University Press).

Staff of the Committee and the State Department, (1950), *A Decade of American Foreign Policy, Basic Documents, 1941-49*, (Washington: US Government Printing Office).

United Nations Development Programme, (1987), "Fourth Country Programme for Jordan, January 1988 to December 1991", reference DP/CP/JOR/4, 12/10/87.

_____, (1987), "Small Enterprise Development in Rural Areas, (Phase I)", ILO Preparatory Assistance Mission, May 1987, project JOR/86/004, (Geneva: ILO).

_____, (1992), "Fifth Programme for the Hashemite Kingdom of Jordan, 1992-1996", reference DP/CP/JOR/5, 11/03/92.

_____, (1997), "First Country Cooperation Framework for Jordan, 1998-2002", reference DP/CCF/JOR/1, 30/06/97.

_____, (various), *Development Cooperation Report, Jordan*, (Amman: UNDP).

_____, (various), *Human Development Report*, (New York: UNDP).

UN Economic and Social Commission for Western Asia, (1995), *Survey of Economic and Social Developments in the ESCWA Region, 1995*, (Amman: ESCWA).

UN Economic and Social Commission for Western Asia and Department of Statistics, (1978), *National Accounts in Jordan 1952-1976*, (Amman: Department of Statistics Press).

US Agency for International Development, "Summary of USAID/Jordan Strategy, 1997-2001", (Amman: USAID).

van den Boogaerde, P.V., (1991), *Financial Assistance from Arab Countries and Arab Regional Institutions*, (Washington: IMF).

World Bank, (1957), *The Economic Development of Jordan: A Report of a Mission Organised by the International Bank for Reconstruction and Development at the Request of the Government of Jordan*, (Baltimore: John Hopkins Press).

_____, (1981), *Accelerated Development in Sub-Saharan Africa: An Agenda for Action*, (Washington: World Bank).

_____, (1989), *Sub-Saharan Africa: From Crisis to Sustainable Growth: A Long-Term Perspective Study*, (Washington: World Bank).

_____, (1989a), "Jordan: Industry and Trade Policy Adjustment Loan Agreement", paragraph 106, (mimeograph).

_____, (1991), *Assistance Strategies to Reduce Poverty*, (Washington: World Bank).

_____, (1993), *Implementing the World Bank's Strategy to Reduce Poverty: Progress and Challenges*, (Washington: IBRD).

_____, (1994), "Hashemite Kingdom of Jordan, Agriculture Sector Technical Support Project, Technical Annex", Report no. T-6370-Jordan, 18/11/94.

_____, (1995), "Private Sector Assessment", Report no. 14405-JO.

_____, (1995a), *Claiming the Future: Choosing Prosperity in the Middle East and North Africa*, (Washington: IBRD).

_____, (1996a), "Consultative Group for the Hashemite Kingdom of Jordan, Paris, July 10, 1996, Chairman's Report of Proceedings", 01/08/96, reference CG 96-39, (mimeograph).

_____, (1996b), *Staff Appraisal Report, The Hashemite Kingdom of Jordan, Housing Finance and Urban Sector Reform Project*, Report no. 15331-Jordan, 02/07/96.

_____, (1997), "Jordan—Third Economic Reform and Development Loan", Report no. PID7066, 20/11/97.

_____, (2000), *Privatization: The Jordanian Success Story*, (Washington: World Bank).

_____, (undated), *Staff Appraisal Report, The Hashemite Kingdom of Jordan, Export Development Project*, Report no. 14935-Jordan.

_____, (undated), "Jordan and the World Bank: Working together for Growth and Prosperity".

_____, (various), *World Development Report*, (Washington: World Bank).

_____, (various), *World Bank Annual Report*, (Washington: World Bank).

_____, (various), *Global Development Finance*, (Washington: World Bank).

ELECTRONIC SOURCES

Access to Microfinance and Improved Implementation of Policy Reform Program, *AMIR website*, www.amir-jordan.org/bai/bai_mainpage.htm.

Amman Chamber of Industry, *ACI website*, www.aci.org.jo.

Amman Stock Exchange, *ASE website*, www.ase.com.jo.

British Embassy, Amman, *British Embassy Amman website*, www.britain.org. Jordan.

Central Bank of Jordan, *CBJ website*, www.cbj.gov.jo.

Department of Statistics, *Department of Statistics website*, www.dos.gov.jo.

Federation of Jordanian Chambers of Commerce, *FJCC website*, :www.fjcc.com.

Free Zones Corporation, *FZC website*, www.free-zones.gov.jo.

Ghorfa, *Ghorfa website*, www.ghorfa.com.

International Finance Corporation, *IFC website*, www.ifc.org.

International Fund for Agricultural Development, *IFAD website*, www.ifad.org/governance/ifad/vote.htm.

International Monetary Fund, *IMF website*, www.imf.org.

Johnson, P.M., "A Glossary of Political Economy Terms", *Auburn University website*, www. auburn.edu/~johnspm/gloss/index.html.

Jordan Export Development and Commercial Centers Corporation, *JEDCO website*, /www.jedco.gov.jo.

Jordan Industrial Estates Company, *JIEC website*, www.jiec.com/jiec/main_q.html.

Jordanian Businessmen Association, *JBA website*, www.jba.com.jo.

Ministry of Industry and Trade, *Ministry of Industry and Trade website*, www.mit.gov.jo.

National Information System, *NIS website*, nic.gov.jo.

Noor Hussein Foundation, *Noor Hussein Foundation website*, www.nhf.org.

Organization for Economic Cooperation and Development, *OECD website*, www.oecd.org.

_____, (2000), *International Development Statistics*, CD ROM 2000 edition, (Paris: OECD).

Social Security Corporation, *SSC website*, www.ssc.gov.jo. (in Arabic).

The REACH Initiative, *The REACH Initiative website*, www.reach.jo.

United Nations Development Programme, Jordan, *UNDP Jordan website*, www.undp-jordan.org.

USA Embassy, Amman, *USA Embassy Amman website*, www.usembassy-amman.org.jo/USAID/econ.htm.

US Agency for International Development, *USAID website*, www.usaid.gov/pubs/cp2000/ane/jordan,html.

World Bank, *World Bank website*, www.worldbank.org.

Young Entrepreneurs Association, *YEA website*, www.yea.com.jo.

INTERVIEWS

Abu-Hammour, Dr Mohammed, Advisor to the Minister of Finance, Amman, 30/06/99.

Abujaber, Nimer F., Board Member, YEA, Amman, 20/07/99.

Alul, Ghalia, Executive Co-ordinator, YEA, Amman, 20/07/99.

Anani, Dr Jawad, ex-Deputy Prime Minister and ex-Minister, Amman, 09/06/99.

Avédikian, Richard, Director, KfW, Amman, 18/07/99.

Awadallah, Dr Bassem I., Director of the Economic Department, The Royal Hashemite Court, Amman, 31/07/99.

Ayoubi, Dr Zaki, Business Association Component Leader, AMIR, Amman, 15/06/99.

Barghouti, Rasha J., Director, Business and Professional Women Club, Amman, 22/07/99.

Bdour, Maisoon, Director, Organisations and International Relations, Ministry of Social Development, Amman, 27/07/99.

Bocco, Riccardo, CERMOC, Amman, 18/05/99.

Dababaneh, Rula, Project Management Specialist—Micro-Enterprise, USAID, Amman, 28/06/99.

dos Los Fayos, Fernando Garces, First Secretary, Delegation of the European Commission, Amman, 09/07/99.

Dougherty, Pamela, MEED, Amman, 22/07/99.

el-Hamad, Jawad, Director, Middle East Studies Centre, Amman, 20/07/99.

Gharaibeh, Firas, Senior Programme Assistant, UNDP, Amman, 13/06/99.

Ghawi, Salem, Assistant Secretary-General, Ministry of Planning, Amman, 10/07/99.

Hammad, Waleed, National Centre for Human Resources Development, Amman, 30/06/99.

Hardy, Lawrence, Program Management, USAID, Amman, 21/06/99.

Harmarneh, Dr Mustafa, Director, Centre for Strategic Studies, Amman, 02/06/99.

Hasanat, Abdullah, Executive Director, Jordan Times, Amman, 29/05/99.

Hasse, Dr. Volkmar, Team Leader, GTZ, Amman, 12/07/99.

Hourani, Hani, Director, al-Urdun al-Jadid Research Centre, Amman, 17/05/99.

Husseini, Amin Y., Secretary General, FJCC, Amman, 29/07/99.

Ifram, Dr Ghassan, Head of Research Department, CBJ, Amman, 04/07/99.

Katib, Bassam M., Vice President, Client Services, JUSBP, Amman, 28/07/99.

al-Kodah, Adel Ahmed, Chairman, Executive Privatisation Unit, Prime Ministry, Amman, 24/07/99.

Kurakata, Hiroshi, Deputy Resident Representative, JICA, Amman, 19/07/99.

Mango, Dr Ahmed, Economic Advisor to Prince Hassan, Amman, 16/07/99, by telephone.

Mango, Hind-Lara, Freelance Reporter, Amman, 16/07/99.

Mansur, Dr Yusuf, ex-Minister and Director General, Telecommunications Regulatory Commission, Amman, 13/06/99.

Mustafa, Eng. Isam, The Higher Council for Science and Technology, Amman, 23/07/99.

Nabulsi, Awni, Founder/Director, Al Jidara Investment Services, Amman, 07/06/99.

Nabulsi, Dr. M. Said, ex-Governor Central Bank of Jordan, Chairman/CEO, Jordan Investment Trust PLC, Amman, 16/06/99.

Nsour, Dr Maen, Director, Aid Co-ordination Unit, Ministry of Planning, Amman, 03/06/99.

Qattoum, Ribhi, Director of Research Centre, GUVS, Amman, 07/06/99.

Sabbagh, Amal A., Secretary General, Jordan National Commission for Women, Amman, 08/07/99.

Saifi, Rana, Development Officer, British Embassy, Amman, 23/05/99 and 05/07/99.

Salti, Dr Amer O., Deputy General Manager, Arab Banking Corporation, Amman, 20/06/99.

Salti, Rebecca, Director of Royal Society for the Conservation of Nature, Amman, 03/06/99.

Samman, Moayad, Assistant Director General, JEDCO, Amman, 02/08/99.

Sara, Martha, Director's Assistant, Konrad Adenauer Foundation, Amman, 05/07/99.

Shawareb, Ms Maha N., Manager, Business Support Organisations, JUSBP, Amman, 28/07/99.

Smadi, Dr Mohammed, Director-General, ACI, Amman, 16/06/99.

Sweis, Dr Rateb, Institute of Diplomacy, Amman, 06/07/99.

Thibeault, Steve, United States Information Agency, US Embassy Amman, Amman, 27/05/99.

Vogts, Dr. Ulrich, Representative of Friedrich-Naumann-Stiftung, Amman, 01/06/99.

Zakhary, Evelyn R., Director, The Jordanian Hashemite Fund for Human Development, Amman, 11/07/99.

PANEL DISCUSSION

"Reflections on Development in Jordan", US Embassy, Amman, 13/05/99.

SECONDARY SOURCES

BOOKS

Abu Jaber, K., (ed.), (1983), *Major Issues in Jordanian Development*, (Amman: The Queen Alia Jordan Social Welfare Fund).

Abu Nowar, M., (1989), *The History of the Hashemite Kingdom of Jordan Volume 1: The Creation and Development of Transjordan: 1920-1929*, (Oxford: Ithaca Press).

Abu Shair, O.J.A.R., (1997), *Privatization and Development*, (Basingstoke: Macmillan Press).

Adams, N.A., (1993), *Worlds Apart: The North-South Divide and the International System*, (London: Zed Books).

Aldcroft, D.H. and R.E. Catterals, (1996), *Rich Nations—Poor Nations: The Long Run Perspective*, (Cheltenham: Edward Elgar).

Ayalon, A., (ed.), (1991), *Middle East Contemporary Survey*, vol. XV, (Boulder: Westview Press).

Ayubi, N.N., (1995), *Over-stating the Arab State: Politics and Society in the Middle East*, (London: I.B. Tauris).

Baldwin, D., (1985), *Economic Statecraft*, (Princeton: Princeton University Press).

Bandow, D., (ed.), (1985), *US Aid to the Developing World: A Free Market Agenda*, (Washington: The Heritage Foundation).

Barkey, H.J., (ed.), (1992), *The Politics of Economic Reform in the Middle East*, (New York: St. Martin's Press).

Barakat, H., (1993), *The Arab World: Society, Culture and the State*, (Berkeley: University of California Press).

Barratt Brown, M., (1970), *After Imperialism*, (London: William Heinemann Ltd).

_____, (1993), *Fair Trade: Reform and Realities in the International Trading System*, (London: Zed Books).

Bauer, P., (1991), *The Development Frontier: Essays in Applied Economics*, (London: Harvester Wheatsheaf).

Beblawi, H., (1984), *The Arab Gulf Economy in a Turbulent Age*, (London: Croom Helm).

Beblawi, H. and G. Luciani, (eds.), (1987), *The Rentier State*, (London: Croom Helm).

Bobiash, D., (1992), *South-South Aid: How Developing Countries Help Each Other*, (New York: St. Martin's Press).

Brand, L.A., (1988), *Palestinians in the Arab World: Institution Building and the Search for State*, (New York: Columbia University Press).

————, (1994), *Jordan's Inter-Arab Relations: The Political Economy of Alliance Making*, (New York: Columbia University Press).

————, (1998), *Women, the State and Political Liberalization: Middle Eastern and North African Experiences*, (New York: Columbia University Press).

Breizat, M., (1995), *Jordan's Diplomacy: Balancing National Survival with National Revival*, (Amman: Center For Strategic Studies).

Brown, L.C., (ed.), (2001), *Diplomacy in the Middle East: The International Relations of Regional and Outside Powers*, (London: I.B. Tauris).

Burnell, P., (1997), *Foreign Aid in a Changing World*, (Buckingham: Open University Press).

Caporaso, J.A. and D.P. Levine, (1992), *Theories of Political Economy*, (Cambridge: Cambridge University Press).

Carnoy, M., (1984), *The State and Political Theory*, (Princeton: Princeton University Press).

Carty, R. and V. Smith, (1981), *Perpetuating Poverty: The Political Economy of Canadian Foreign Aid*, (Toronto: Between the Lines).

Cassen, R. and Associates, (1994), *Does Aid Work? Report to an Intergovernmental Task Force*, 2nd edition, (Oxford: Clarendon Press).

Chelkowski, P.J. and R.J. Pranger, (eds.), (1988), *Ideology and Power in the Middle East: Essays in Honor of George Lenczowski*, (Durham: Duke University Press).

Cho, G., (1995), *Trade, Aid and Global Interdependence*, (London: Routledge).

Clayton, A., (ed.), (1994), *Governance, Democracy and Conditionality: What Role for NGOs?*, (Oxford: Intrac).

Colman, D. and F. Nixson, (1986), *Economics of Change in Less Developed Countries*, 2nd edition, (Oxford: Philip Allan).

Committee for Middle East Trade, (1982), *Jordan: The Five Year Plan for Economic and Social Development 1981-85*, (London: COMET).

Cook, M., (ed.), (1970), *Studies in the Economic History of the Middle East*, (London: Oxford University Press)

Coote, B., (1992), *The Trade Trap: Poverty and the Global Commodity Markets*, (Oxford: Oxfam).

Corbridge, S., (1986), *Capitalist World Development: A Critique of Radical Development Geography*, (Totowa: Rowan & Littlefield).

————, (ed.), (1995), *Development Studies: A Reader*, (London: Edward Arnold).

Cornia, G.A., Jolly, R. and F. Stewart, (1987), *Adjustment with a Human Face: Volume 1 Protecting the Vulnerable and Promoting Growth*, (Oxford: Clarendon Press).

Crabb, Jr., C.V., (1982), *The Doctrines of American Foreign Policy: Their Meaning, Role and Future*, (Baton Rouge: Louisiana State University Press).

Crush, J., (1995), *Power of Development*, (London: Routledge).

Cunningham, R.B. and Y.K. Sarayreh, (1993), *Wasta: The Hidden Force in Middle Eastern Society*, (Westport: Praegar).

Dajani, A.T., (1973), *The Industry of Jordan, 1973*, 4th edition, (Amman: Amman Chamber of Commerce).

Dann, U., (1984), *Studies in the History of Transjordan, 1920-1949: The Making of a State*, (Boulder: Westview Press).

Eatwell, J., Milgate, M. and Newman, P., (eds.), (1987), *Economic Development— The New Palgrave*, (London: Macmillan).

Euchner, W., (ed.), (1995), *The Politics of Structural Adjustment: Economic Liberalisation in Arab Countries*, (no place: Konrad-Adenaüer-Stiftung).

Evans, P.B, Rueschemeyer, D. and T. Skocpol, (1985), *Bringing the State Back In*, (Cambridge: Cambridge University Press).

Fathi, S.H., (1994), *Jordan: An Invented Nation? Tribe-State Dynamics and the Formation of National Identity*, (Hamburg: Deutsches Orient-Institut).

Fawzy, S. and A. Galal, (eds.), (1999), *Partners for Development: New Roles for Governments and the Private Sector in the Middle East and North Africa*, (Washington: World Bank).

Ferrel, R.H., (1966), *The American Secretaries of State and their Diplomacy, vol. XV, George C. Marshall*, (New York: Cooper Square Publishers Inc.).

Fischer, S., Rodrik, D. and E. Tuma, (eds.), (1993), *The Economics of Middle East Peace*, (Cambridge: The MIT Press).

Frank, A.G., (1981), *Crisis: In the Third World*, (London: Heinemann).

Frieden J.A. and D.A. Lake, (1995), *International Political Economy: Reflections on Global Power and Wealth*, 3rd edition, (London: Routledge).

Führer, H., (1996), *The Story of Official Development Assistance: A History of the Development Assistance Committee and the Development Co-operation Directorate in Dates, Name and Figures*, (Paris: OECD).

Garfinkle, A., (1992), *Israel and Jordan in the Shadow of War: Functional Ties and Futile Diplomacy in a Small Place*, (New York: St. Martin's Press).

Ghatak, S., (1995), *Introduction to Development Economics*, 3rd edition, (London: Routledge).

Gills, B., Rocamora, J. and R. Wilson, (1993), *Low Intensity Democracy: Political Power in the New World Order*, (London: Pluto Press).

Gilpin, R., (1987), *The Political Economy of International Relations*, (Princeton: Princeton University Press).

Gubser, P., (1983), *Jordan: Crossroads of Middle Eastern Events*, (Boulder: Westview Press).

Griffin, K., (1999), *Alternative Strategies for Economic Development*, 2nd edition, (Basingstoke: Macmillan Press Ltd).

Haggard, S., (ed.), (1995), *The International Political Economy and the Developing Countries*, vol. 1, (Aldershot: Edward Elgar).

Haggard, S. and R.R. Kaufman, (1992), *The Politics of Economic Adjustment: International Constraints, Distributive Conflicts and the State*, (Princeton: Princeton University Press).

Hakimian H. and Z. Moshaver, (eds.), (2001), *The State and Global Change: The Political Economy of Transition in the Middle East and North Africa*, (Richmond: Curzon).

Hammed, W., (1999), *Jordanian Women's Organisations and Sustainable Development*, (Amman: al-Urdan al-Jadid Research Centre).

Harik, I. and D.J. Sullivan, (eds.), (1992), *Privatization and Liberalization in the Middle East*, (Bloomington: Indiana University Press).

Havrylyshyn, O. and D. McGettigan, (1999), *Privatization in Transition Countries: Lessons of the First Decade*, Economic Issues, no. 18, (Washington: IMF).

Hayter, T., (1971), *Aid as Imperialism*, (Harmondsworth: Penguin Books Ltd).

Held, D. et al, (1983), *States and Societies*, (Oxford: Basil Blackwell in association with The Open University).

Herb, M., (1999), *All in the Family: Absolutism, Revolution and Democracy in the Middle Eastern Monarchies*, (Albany: State University of New York Press).

Hettne, B., (1995), *Development Theory and the Three Worlds: Towards an International Political Economy of Development*, 2nd edition, (Harlow: Longman).

Hewitt, A., (ed.), (1994), *Crisis or Transition in Foreign Aid*, (London: Overseas Development Institute).

Hoekman, B. and H. Kheir-el-Din, (eds.), (2000), *Trade Policy Developments in the Middle East and North Africa*, (Washington: World Bank).

Hook, S.W., (1995), *National Interest and Foreign Aid*, (Boulder: Lynne Rienner Publishers).

_____, (ed.), (1996), *Foreign Aid Towards the Millennium*, (Boulder: Lynne Rienner Publishers).

Hourani, H. and B.K. Neal, (eds.), (1998), *The Jordanian Economy in its Regional and International Framework*, (Amman: al-Urdan al-Jadid Research Center).

Ibrahim, S., (1982), *The New Arab Social Order: A Study of the Social Impact of Oil Wealth*, (Westview Press: Boulder).

Jabbra, J.G., (ed.), (1989), *Bureaucracy and Development in the Arab World*, (Leiden: EJ Brill).

Jalée, P., (1968), *The Pillage of the Third World*, translated from the French by M. Klopper, (New York: Monthly Review Press).

Joffé, G., (ed.), (1999), *Perspectives on Development: The Euro-Mediterranean Partnership*, (London: Frank Cass).

Jreisat, J.E., (1997), *Politics without Process: Administering Development in the Arab World*, (Lynne Rienner Publishers: Boulder).

Kanovsky, E., (1976), *Economic Development of Jordan: The Implications of Peace in the Middle East*, (Tel Aviv: University Publishing Projects).

Kazziha, W., Hill, E. and K. Sakai, (1997), *Civil Society and the Middle East*, M.E.S. series no. 43, (Tokyo: Institute of Developing Economies).

Khader, B., (1989), *Jordan's Economy, 1952-1989: Past Achievements and Future Challenges*, (no place: Centre d'Etude et de Recherché sur le Monde Arabe Contemporain).

Khader, B. and A. Badran, (eds.), (1987), *The Economic Development of Jordan*, (London: Croom Helm).

Khairy, M.O., (1984), *Jordan and the World System: Development in the Middle East*, (Frankfurt: Peter Lang).

Khan, M.H. and J.K. Sundaram, (2000), *Rents, Rent-Seeking and Economic Development: Theory and Evidence in Asia*, (Cambridge: Cambridge University Press).

al-Khazendar, S., (1997), *Jordan and the Palestine Question: The Role of the Islamic and Left Forces in Foreign Policy-Making*, (Reading: Ithaca Press).

Killick, T. with Gunatilaka, R. and A. Marr, (1998), *Aid and the Political Economy of Policy Change*, (London: Routledge).

Kingston, P.W.T., (1996), *Britain and the Politics of Modernization in the Middle East, 1945-1958*, (Cambridge: Cambridge University Press).

Korany, B., Brynen, R. and P. Noble, (eds.), (1998), *Political Liberalization and Democratization in the Arab World: vol. 2: Comparative Experiences*, (Boulder: Lynne Rienner Publishers).

Krueger, A.O., Michalopoloulos, C. and V.W. Ruttan, (1989), *Aid and Development*, (Baltimore: The John Hopkins University Press).

Lappé, F.M., Collins, J. and D. Kinsey, (1980), *Aid as Obstacle: Twenty Questions about our Foreign Aid and the Hungry*, (San Francisco: Institute for Food and Development Policy).

Lavy, V. and Sheffer, E., (1991), *Foreign Aid and Economic Development in the Middle East: Egypt, Syria and Jordan*, (New York: Praegar).

Lele, U. and Nabi, I., (eds.), (1991), *Transitions in Development: The Role of Aid and Commercial Flows*, (San Francisco: ICS Press).

Leopold, R.W., (1962), *The Growth of American Foreign Policy: A History*, (New York: Alfred A. Knopf).

Lesch, D.W., (ed.), (1999), *The Middle East and the United States: A Historical and Political Reassessment*, (Boulder: Westview Press).

Leys, C., (1996), *The Rise and Fall of Development Theory*, (Oxford: James Currey).

Lipton, M., and Toye, J.F.J., (1990), *Does Aid Work in India? A Country Study of the Impact of Official Development Assistance*, (London: Routledge).

Liska, G., (1960), *The New Statecraft: Foreign Aid in American Foreign Policy*, (Chicago: The University of Chicago Press).

Long, D. and B. Reich, (eds.), (1995), *The Government and Politics of the Middle East and North Africa*, (Boulder: Westview Press).

al-Madfai, M.R., (1993), *Jordan, the United States and the Middle East Peace Process, 1974-1991*, (Cambridge: Cambridge University Press).

Magdoff, M., (1969), *The Age of Imperialism: The Economics of US Foreign Policy*, (New York: Monthly Review).

Mazur, M.P., (1979), *Economic Growth and Development in Jordan*, (London: Croom Helm).

Merza, A.K., (1992), *A Consistent Macro Framework for Future Alternative Growth Paths in Jordan*, (Amman: Ministry of Planning and UNDP).

Michie, J. and J. Grieve Smith, (eds.), (1999), *Global Instability: The Political Economy of World Economic Governance*, (London: Routledge).

Milson, M., (ed.), (1973), *Society and Political Structure in the Arab World*, (New York: Humanities Press).

Moseley, P., Harrigan, J. and J. Toye, (1995), *Aid and Power: The World Bank and Policy-Based Lending*, vol. 1, 2nd edition, (London: Routledge).

Myrdal, G., (1970), *The Challenge of Poverty*, (London: The Penguin Press).

el-Nagger, S., (ed.), (1989), *Adjustment Policies and Development Strategies in the Arab World*, Papers presented at a seminar held in Abu Dhabi, United Arab Emirates, February 16-18, 1987, (no place: IMF).

Nelson, J.M. et al, (1989), *Fragile Coalitions: The Politics of Economic Adjustment*, (New Brunswick: Transaction Books).

Nevo, J. and I. Pappé, (eds.), (1994), *Jordan in the Middle East: The Making of a Pivotal State: 1948-88*, (Ilford: Frank Cass & Co. Ltd.).

Norton, A.R., (ed.), (1995), *Civil Society in the Middle East*, vol. 1, (Leiden: E.J. Brill).

Ohlin, G., (1966), *Foreign Aid Policies Reconsidered*, (Development Centre of the OECD, Paris: OECD).

Owen, R., (1992), *State, Power and Politics in the Making of the Modern Middle East*, (London: Routledge).

Piro, T.J., (1998), *The Political Economy of Market Reform in Jordan*, (Lanham: Rowman & Littlefield Publishers Inc.).

Preston, P.W., (1996), *Development Theory: An Introduction*, (Oxford: Blackwells Publishers).

Raffer, K. and Singer, H.W., (1996), *Economic Assistance and Development Co-operation*, (Cheltenham: Edward Elgar).

Ramanadham, V.V., (ed.), (1989), *Privatisation in Developing Countries*, (London: Routledge).

Randel J. and T. German, (eds.), (1996), *The Reality of Aid: An Independent Review of International Aid*, (London: Earthscan).

_____, (eds.), (1997), *The Reality of Aid: An Independent Review of International Aid, 1997-1998*, (London: Earthscan).

Richards, A. and J. Waterbury, (1990), *A Political Economy of the Middle East: State, Class and Economic Development*, (Boulder: Westview Press).

Riddell, R.C., (1987), *Foreign Aid Reconsidered*, (London: James Currey and Overseas Development Institution).

Robins, P., (2004(, *A History of Jordan*, (Cambridge: Cambridge University Press).

Rogan, E.L. and T. Tell, (eds.), (1994), *Village, Steppe and State: The Social Origins of Modern Jordan*, (London: British Academic Press).

Rostow, W.W., (1960), *The Stages of Economic Growth: A Non-Communist Manifesto*, (London: Cambridge University Press).

Roxborough, I., (1979), *Theories of Underdevelopment*, (London: The Macmillan Press Ltd).

Salibi, K., (1993), *The Modern History of Jordan*, (London: I.B. Tauris).

Salamé, G., (ed.), (1994), *Democracy without Democrats? The Renewal of Politics in the Muslim World*, (London: I.B. Tauris).

Satloff, R.B., (ed.), (1993), *The Politics of Change in the Middle East*, (Boulder: Westview).

Sayigh, Y. and A. Shlaim, (eds.), (1997), *The Cold War and The Middle East*, (Oxford: Clarendon Press).

Schuurman, F.J., (ed.), (1993), *Beyond the Impasse: New Directions in Development Theory*, (London: Zed Books).

Schwartz, H.M., (2000), *States versus Markets: The Emergence of a Global Economy*, 2nd edition, (Basingstoke: Macmillan Press).

Schwedler, J., (ed.), (1995), *Toward Civil Society in the Middle East: A Primer*, (Boulder: Lynne Rienner Publishers).

Seale, P., (ed.), (1983), *The Shaping of an Arab Statesman*, (London: Quartet Books).

Shafik, N., (ed.), (1998), *Prospects for Middle Eastern and North African Economies: From Boom to Bust and Back?*, (Basingstoke: Macmillan Press).

Shihata, I.F.I., (1982), *The Other Face of OPEC: Financial Assistance to the Third World, Energy Resources and Policies of the Middle East and North Africa*, (London: Longman).

Shwardan, B., (1959), *Jordan: A State of Tension*, (New York: Council for Middle Eastern Affairs Press).

Sluglett, P. and M. Farouk-Sluglett, (1993), *The Times Guide to the Middle East: The Arab World and its Neighbours*, 2nd edition, (London: Times Books).

Sørensen, G., (ed.), (1983), *Political Conditionality*, (London: Frank Cass in association with EADI).

Stewart, F., (1995), *Adjustment and Poverty: Options and Choices*, (London: Routledge).

Stokke, O., (ed.), (1989), *Western Middle Powers and Global Poverty: The Determinants of the Aid Policies of Canada, Denmark, The Netherlands, Norway and Sweden*, Norwegian Foreign Policy Studies no. 64, (Uppsala: The Scandinavian Institute of African Studies in co-operation with the Norwegian Institute of International Affairs).

_____, (ed.), (1995), *Aid and Political Conditionality*, (London: Frank Cass).

_____, (ed.), (1996), *Foreign Aid Towards the Year 2000: Experiences and Challenges*, (London: Frank Cass & Co. Ltd.).

Strange, S., (1996), *The Retreat of the State: The Diffusion of Power in the World Economy*, (Cambridge: Cambridge University Press).

Streeten, P., (1994), *Strategies for Human Development*, (Copenhagen: Handeslshoskolens Forlag).

Sundrum, R.M., (1983), *Development Economics: A Framework for Analysis and Policy*, (Chichester: John Wiley and Sons).

Thirlwall, A.P., (1994), *Growth and Development, with Special Reference to Developing Economies*, 5th edition, (Basingstoke: Macmillan Press Ltd.).

Todaro, M.P., (1994), *Economic Development*, 5th edition, (New York: Longman).

Toye, J., (1993), *Dilemmas of Development: Reflections on the Counter Revolution in Development Economics*, (Oxford: Blackwell).

al-Urdan al-Jadid Research Centre, (2000), *Professional Associations and the Challenges of Democratic Transformation in Jordan*, (Amman: al-Urdan al-Jadid Research Centre).

van der Beugel, E.H., (1966), *From Marshall Aid to Atlantic Partnership: European Integration as a Concern of American Foreign Policy*, (Amsterdam: Elsevier Publishing Co.).

Vandewalle, D., (1998), *Libya Since Independence: Oil and State-Building*, (London: I.B. Tauris).

Vatikiotis, P.J., (1967), *Politics and the Military in Jordan: A Study of the Arab Legion 1921-1957*, (London: Frank Cass).

al-Wazani, K.W., (1994), *Stabilization and Structural Adjustment Policies: Jordan's Experience*, (Amman: al-Urdan al-Jadid Research Center), (in Arabic).

Weber, M., (1947), *The Theory of Social and Economic Organisations*, trans, (London: William Hodge).

Weissman, S. et al, (1975), *The Trojan Horse: A Radical Look at Foreign Aid*, (Palo Alto: Ramparts Press).

Wilson, M.C., (1987), *King Abdullah, Britain and the Making of Jordan*, (Cambridge: Cambridge University Press).

Wilson, R., (ed.), (1991), *Politics and the Economy in Jordan*, (London: Routledge).

_____, (1995), *Economic Development in the Middle East*, (London: Routledge).

Winckler, O., (1997), *Population Growth and Migration in Jordan, 1950-1994*, (Brighton: Sussex Academic Press).

Wuyts, M., Mackintosh, M. and T. Hewitt, (eds.), (1992), *Development Policy and Public Action*, (Oxford: Oxford University Press).

Yapp, M.E., (1996), *The Near East Since the First World War: A History to 1995*, (London: Longman).

Yorke, V., (1988), *Domestic Politics and Regional Security: Jordan, Syria and Israel: The End of an Era*, (Aldershot: Gower).

Zeylstra, W.G., (1975), *Aid or Development: The Relevance of Development Aid to Problems of Developing Countries*, (Leyden: A.W. Sijthoff).

THESES AND DISSERTATIONS

al-Ahmad, A.K., (1992), "Economic Effects of Foreign Aid: Case of Jordan", (PhD Thesis, University of Missouri).

Knowles, W.M., (1996), "Safawi: A Study in Oleaginous International Relations", (MA Dissertation, University of Durham).

Mubaideen, M.A., (1995), "The Influence of Foreign Aid on Jordan's Foreign Policy, 1921-1970", (PhD Thesis, Newcastle University).

Saifi, R., (1996), "Non-Governmental Organisations and the State: Economic, Political and Institutional Contexts as Determinants of their Modes of Interaction", (MSc Dissertation, SOAS, Centre for Development Studies).

Salah, M.J., (1991), "Foreign Aid Efficiency in Jordan during the Three Cycles of the Five Year Development Plan, 1976-1990", (PhD Thesis, University of Strathclyde).

ARTICLES

Abu Rish, M., (undated), "Report on the Economy", paper prepared for British Embassy, Amman.

Abu Sheika, A. and G. Assaf, (1983), "Poverty and its Implications for Development", in Abu Jaber, K., (ed.), *Major Issues in Jordanian Development*, (Amman: The Queen Alia Jordan Social Welfare Fund), pp.47-69.

Adams, L.S., (1996), "Political Liberalization in Jordan: An Analysis of the State's Relationship with the Muslim Brotherhood", *Journal of Church and State*, vol. 38, no. 3, pp.507-528.

Akel, M.M.A., (1999), "Expectations for the Jordanian Economy under the Rule of His Majesty King Abdullah II", *The Arab Bank Review*, vol. 1, no. 1, October, pp.9-17.

Amawi, A.M., (1996), "USAID in Jordan", *Middle East Policy*, vol. iv, no. 4, October, pp.77-89.

American Chamber of Commerce in Egypt, (1996), "A Comparative Study of Egypt, Jordan, Syria, Lebanon, Palestine and Syria".

Amerah, M., (undated), "Trade Liberalization and Foreign Investment in Jordan", *Economic Research Forum for the Arab Countries, Iran and Turkey*, working paper 9611.

Anani, J. and R. Khalaf, (1989), "Privatisation in Jordan", in El-Nagger, S., (ed.), *Adjustment Policies and Development Strategies in the Arab World*, Papers presented at a seminar held in Abu Dhabi, United Arab Emirates, February 16-18, 1987, (no place: IMF), pp.210-233.

Anderson, L., (1987), "The State in the Middle East and North Africa", *Comparative Politics*, October, pp.1-18.

Andoni, L. and J. Schwedler, (1996), "Bread Riots in Jordan", *Middle East Report*, October-December, pp.40-42.

Atlas Investment Group, (April 2001), *Jordan: Country Report*, (Amman: Atlas Investment Group).

Barguthi, A., (1997), "The Economic Summit for the Middle East and North Africa", *Middle East Studies Centre*, report no. 23. (in Arabic).

Bauer, P. and B. Yamey, (1981), "The Political Economy of Foreign Aid", *Lloyds Bank Review*, October, pp.1-14.

Baylies, C., (1995), "'Political Conditionality' and Democratisation", *Review of African Political Economy*, no. 65, pp.321-337.

Beblawi, H., (1987), "The Rentier State in the Arab World", *Arab Studies Quarterly*, vol. 9, no. 4, pp.383-397.

Beck, M., (1997), "Can Financial Aid Promote Regional Peace Agreements? The Case of the Arab-Israeli Conflict", *Mediterranean Politics*, vol. 2, no. 2, Autumn, pp.49-70.

Bienen, H. and J. Waterbury, (1989), "The Political Economy of Privatisation in Developing Countries", *World Development*, vol. 17, no. 5, pp.617-632.

Brand, L.A., (1995), "Palestinians and Jordanians: A Crisis of Identity", *Journal of Palestine Studies*, vol. XXIV, no. 4, Summer, pp.46-61.

Brett, E.A., (1993), "Voluntary Agencies as Development Organisations: Theorizing the Problem of Efficiency and Accountability", *Development and Change*, vol. 24, pp.269-303.

Bruce, J., (1995), "Waiting for the Helping Hands", *Janes Defence Weekly*, 1st July, pp.19-21.

Brynen, R., (1992), "Economic Crisis and Post-Rentier Democratization in the Arab World: The Case of Jordan", *Canadian Journal of Political Science*, vol. XXV, no. 1, March, pp.69-97.

Burki, S.J. and R.L. Ayres, (1986), "A Fresh Look at Development Aid", *Finance and Development*, March, pp.6-10.

Burnside, C. and D. Dollar, (1997), "Aid Spurs Growth in a Sound Environment", *Finance and Development*, December, pp.4-7.

Camdessus, M., (1996), "The Challenges for the Arab World in the Global Economy: Stability and Structural Adjustment", Speech to the Annual Meeting of the Union of Arab Banks, New York, 20/05/96.

Centre d'Etudes et de Recherches sur le Monde Arabe Contemporain, (1985), "Study Day on the Economic Development of Jordan", *Cahier*, no. 34.

Chaudhry, K.A., (1989), "The Price of Wealth: Business and State in Labor Remittance and Oil Economies", *International Organization*, vol. 43, no. 1, Winter, pp.101-146.

Chenery, H.B. and A.M. Strout, (1966), "Foreign Assistance and Economic Development", *The American Economic Review*, vol. 56, no. 4, part 1, September, pp.679-733.

Collier, P. and J.W. Gunning, (1999), "The IMF's Role in Structural Adjustment", *The Economic Journal*, no. 109, November, pp.F634-F651.

de Janvry, A., E. Sadoulet and E. Thorbecke, (1993), "Introduction", *World Development*, vol. 21, no. 4, pp.565-575.

Doherty, C.J., (1994), "Foreign Aid Bill Wrapped up after Fight over Earmarks", *Congressional Quarterly*, 30th July, pp.2155-2157.

Dollar, D. and J. Svensson, (1998), "What Explains the Success or Failure of Structural Adjustment Programs?", draft.

Dougherty, P. and O. Wils, (1999), "Between Public and Private: Economic Élites", (draft mimeograph).

al-Fanek, F., (1999), "The Predicament of Economic Growth in Jordan", paper presented at the *Jordanian Forum for Economic Development*, al-Urdan al-Jadid Research Center. (in Arabic).

Garfinkle, A., (1981), "Negotiating by Proxy: Jordanian Foreign Policy and US Options in the Middle East", *Orbis*, vol. 24, Winter, pp.847-880.

Ghattas, J., (1997), "Recent Developments and Prospects for Jordan", *ABC Group Economic and Financial Quarterly*, no. 41, September, pp.1-6.

Grant, R., (1995), "Japanese Foreign Aid to the Middle East and North Africa", *JIME Review*, no. 31, Winter, pp.5-21.

Griffin, K., (1991), "Foreign Aid after the Cold War", *Development and Change*, vol. 22, pp.645-685.

Griffin, K. and J. Gurley, (1985), "Radical Analyses of Imperialism, The Third World, and the Transition to Socialism: A Survey Article", *Journal of Economic Literature*, vol. 23, September, pp.1089-1142.

Hilal, T., (1997), "Overview of Jordanian NGOs", paper prepared for DfID, Amman.

Hinnebusch, R., (1993), "State and Civil Society in Syria", *Middle East Journal*, vol. 47, no. 2, pp.243-257.

al-Humaidhi, B., (1989), "Twenty-Eight Years of Development Cooperation: The Kuwait Fund for Arab Economic Development", *American-Arab Affairs*, no. 31, Winter, pp.11-14.

Huntington, S., (1991), "Democracy's Third Wave", *Journal of Democracy*, no. 2, Spring, pp.12-34.

Hussein of Jordan, H.M. King, (1993), "Securing Peace in the Middle East?", *RUSI Journal*, no. 138, October, pp.1-3.

Jaber, T.A., (undated), "Key Long-Term Development Issues in Jordan", *Economic Research Forum for Arab Countries, Iran and Turkey*, working paper 9522.

Kaplan, S.S., (1975), "United States Aid and Regime Maintenance in Jordan", *Public Policy*, vol. 23, no. 2, Spring, pp.189-217.

Karsh, E., (1997), "Cold War, Post Cold War: Does it make a Difference for the Middle East?", *Review of International Studies*, vol. 23, pp.271-291.

Katanani, A.K., (1985), "Development Problems and Prospects of non-Oil Arab Countries: The Case of Jordan", *Dirasat*, vol. 12, no. 5, May, pp.49-63.

el-Khatib, A., (1994), "The Experience of NGOs in Jordan: A Brief Description", paper presented at the NGO's experts meeting on *Strategies for Strengthening NGO Networking and Research in the Middle East*, Arab Thought Forum, Amman, Jordan, 26/03/94, (Amman: GUVS).

―――――, (1995), "The Status of NGOs in Jordan", paper presented at the *Conference on Canada and the Middle East: Developing a NGO Vision*, Carleton University, Ottawa, Canada, 05-06/10/95, (Amman: GUVS).

―――――, (1996), "The Impact of the Third Sector on the Economic Development of Jordan", paper presented to the *ISTR Second International Conference*, 18-21 July, El Colegio de Mexico, Mexico City.

Kingston, P.W.T., (undated), "Failing to Tip the Balance: Foreign Aid and Economic Reform in Jordan, 1958-1967", (mimeograph).

Knowles, W.M., (2000), "Retooling Jordan's Economy", *Middle East Insight*, vol. XV, no. 6, November-December, pp.89-92.

Krueger, A.O., (1981), "Loans to Assist the Transition to Outward-Looking Policies", *World Economy*, vol. 4, no. 3, September, pp.271-286.

Leftwich, A., (1994), "Governance, the State and the Politics of Development", *Development and Change*, vol. 25, pp.363-386.

Lipton, M. and S. Maxwell, (1992), "The New Poverty Agenda: An Overview", *Institute of Development Studies*, DP306, October.

McKinlay, R.D. and Little, R., (1977), "A Foreign Policy Model of US Bilateral Aid Allocations", *World Politics*, vol. 30, no. 1, October, pp.58-86.

_____, (1978), "The French Aid Relationship: A Foreign Policy Model of the Distribution of French Bilateral Aid, 1964-1970", *Development and Change*, vol. 91, no. 3, July, pp.459-478.

_____, (1978), "A Foreign Policy Model of the Distribution of British Bilateral Aid, 1960-1970", *British Journal of Political Science*, vol. 8, pp.313-332.

_____, (1979), "The US Aid Relationship: A Test of the Recipient Need and Donor Interest Models", *Political Studies*, vol., 27, no. 2, June, pp.236-250.

Maizels, A. and Nissanke, M.K., (1984), "Motivations for Aid to Developing Countries", *World Development*, vol. 12, no. 9, pp.879-900.

Majdalani, R., (1996), "The Changing Role of NGOs in Jordan: An Emerging Actor in Development", *Jordanies*, no.2, December, pp.119-134.

Meijer, R., (1997), "Jordan: The Precarious State", *JIME Review*, Summer, pp.69-86.

Mikhail, W.M., (1991), "Growth and Inflation in Jordan's Adjustment Program", *The Middle East Business and Economic Review*, vol. 3, no. 2, pp.1-13.

Moore, P.W., (2001), "What Makes Successful Business Lobbies? Business Associations and the Rentier State in Jordan and Kuwait", *Comparative Politics*, vol. 33, no. 2, January, pp.127-147.

Morrisey, O., (1991), "An Evaluation of the Economic Effects of the Aid and Trade Provision", *The Journal of Development Studies*, vol. 28, no. 1, October, pp.104-129.

Moseley, P., (1987), "Conditionality as Bargaining Process: Structural Adjustment Lending, 1980-86", *Princeton Essays in International Finance*, no. 168, October, pp.1-36.

Moseley, P., Hudson, J. and S. Horrell, (1987), "Aid, the Public Sector and the Market in Less Developed Countries", *The Economic Journal*, vol. 97, September, pp.616-641.

Najjar, O.A., (1988), "The Ebb and Flow of the Liberalisation of the Jordanian Press: 1985-1997", *Journalism and Mass Communication Quarterly*, vol. 75, no. 1, Spring, pp.127-143.

Openskin, B.R., (1996), "The Moral Foundations of Foreign Aid", *World Development*, vol. 24, no. 1, pp.21-44.

Oren, M.B., (1990), "A Winter of Discontent: Britain's Crisis in Jordan, December 1955 – March 1956", *International Journal of Middle East Studies*, vol. 22, pp.171-184.

Pillai, V., (1982), "External Economic Dependence and Fiscal Policy Imbalances in Developing Countries: A Case Study of Jordan", *The Journal of Development Studies*, vol. 19, no. 1, October, pp.5-18.

Poe, S.C. and J. Meernik, (1995), "US Military Aid in the 1980s: A Global Analysis", *Journal of Peace Research*, vol. 32, no. 4, pp.399-411.

Porter, R.S., (1986), "Arab Economic Aid", *Development Policy Review*, vol. 4, pp.44-68.

Prados, A.B., (1997), "Jordan:U.S. Relations and Bilateral Issues", CRS Brief no. 93085, 02/01/97.

al-Quaryoty, M.O., (1989), "Prospects for Privatization in Jordan", *Journal of Arab Affairs*, vol. 8, no. 2, pp.159-190.

_____, (1989a), "Reconciling Development Planning with Privatization: The Case of Jordan", *Public Enterprise*, vol. 9, no. 1, pp.53-64.

Regan, P.M., (1995), "US Economic Aid and Political Repression: An Empirical Evaluation of US Foreign Policy", *Political Research Quarterly*, vol. 48, no. 3, September, pp.613-628.

Reid, M.F., (1994), "Institutional Preconditions of Privatization in Market-Based Political Economies: Implications for Jordan", *Public Administration*, vol. 14, no. 1, February, pp.65-77.

Roberts, J.M., (1991), "Prospects for Democracy in Jordan", *Arab Studies Quarterly*, vol. 13, nos. 3 and 4, Summer/Fall, pp.119-138.

Roe, A., Roy, J. and J. Sengupta, (eds.), (1989), *Economic Adjustment in Algeria, Egypt, Jordan, Morocco, Pakistan, Tunisia and Turkey: Report of a Seminar Held in Izmir, Turkey, March 28-30, 1988*, An EDI Policy Seminar Report, no. 15, (Washington: The World Bank).

Ross, M.L., (2000), "Does Resource Wealth Lead to Authoritarian Rule? Explaining the Midas Touch", paper presented to the World Bank Research Group on "The Economics of Political Violence", Princeton University, March 18-19.

Sengupta, A., (1993), "Aid and Development Policy in the 1990s", *Economic and Political Weekly*, 13th March, pp.453-464.

al-Shababi, S., (1987), "OPEC Aid: Issues and Performances", *OPEC Review*, Spring, pp.45-70.

Shihata, I.F.I. and R. Mabro, (1979), "The OPEC Aid Record", *World Development*, vol. 7, no. 2, pp.161-173.

Singer, H., (1994), "Aid Conditionality", *Institute of Development Studies*, DP346, December.

Stiglitz, J., (1997), "The State and Development: Some New Thinking", edited transcript of paper presented at International Roundtable on the Capable State, Berlin, Germany, 08/10/97.

Stiles, K.W., (1990), "Conditionality: Coercion or Compromise?", *World Development*, vol. 18, no. 7, pp.959-974.

Sullivan, P, (1999), "Globalisation: Trade and Investment in Egypt, Jordan and Syria since 1980", *Arab Studies Quarterly*, vol. 21, no. 3, pp.35-72.

Susser, A., (1991), "Jordan", in Ayalon, A., (ed.), *Middle East Contemporary Survey*, vol. XV, (Boulder: Westview Press), pp.482-519.

Uphoff, N., (1993), "Grassroots Organizations and NGOs in Rural Development: Opportunities with Diminishing States and Expanding Markets", *World Development*, vol. 21, no. 4, pp.607-622.

al-Urdan al-Jadid Research Centre, (1999), "Civil Society and Governance: A Case Study of Jordan", (draft mimeograph).

_____, (1999a), "Jordanian Civil Society in the Nineties", *Civil Society*, March, pp.16-19.

Watkins, K., (1994), "Aid under Threat", *Review of African Political Economy*, no. 66, pp.517-523.

White, H., (1992), "The Macroeconomic Impact of Development Aid: A Critical Survey", *The Journal of Development Studies*, vol. 28, no. 2, January, pp.163-240.

Williams, M.J., (1976), "The Aid Programs of the OPEC Countries", *Foreign Affairs*, vol. 54, no. 1, pp.308-324.

Wills, O., (1998), "Foreign Aid since 1989 and its Impact on Jordan's Political Economy: Some Research Questions", *Jordanies*, no. 5-6, June-December 1998, pp.100-120.

Wilson, M.C., (1994), "Jordan: Bread, Freedom or Both?", *Current History*, vol. 93, no. 580, February, pp.87-90.

Wiktorowicz, Q., (2000), "Civil Society as Social Control: State Power in Jordan", *Comparative Politics*, vol. 33, no. 1, October, pp.43-61.

Wood, R.E., (1980), "Foreign Aid and the Capitalist State in Underdeveloped Countries", *Politics and Society*, vol. 10, part 1, pp.1-34.

Yorke, V., (1990), "A New Era for Jordan?", *The World Today*, vol. 46, no. 2, February, pp.27-31.

Zahariadis, N., Travis, R. and P.F. Diehl, (1990), "Military Substitution Effects from Foreign Economic Aid: Buying Guns with Foreign Butter", *Social Science Quarterly*, vol. 671, no. 4, December, pp.774-785.

Zak, M., (1996), "Israel and Jordan: Strategically Bound", *Israel Affairs*, vol. 3, no. 1, Autumn, pp.39-60.

ELECTRONIC SOURCES

BBC Monitoring Online, *BBC Monitoring website*, www.bbcmonitoring.co.uk.

Herb, M., *Georgia State University*, www.gsu.edu.

Jordan Times Internet Edition, *Jordan Times website*, www.jordantimes.com.

Migrant News, (2001), "Remittances, Trade and Aid", vol. 8, no. 4, April, *Migration Dialogue website*, migration.ucdavis.edu/mn/Archive_MN/apr_2001-20mn.htm.

Mustapha, M.A., (undated), "Telecommunications in Jordan: Performance, Policy Environment and Reforms Ahead", *World Bank website*, www.worldbank.org/wbi/mdf/mdfl/perform.htm.

Puri, S. and T. Ritzema, "Migrant Worker Remittances, Micro-finance and the Informal Economy: Prospects and Issues", ILO Working Paper no. 21, *ILO website*, www.ilo.org/public/english/employment/ent/papers/wpap21.htm.

Taylor, J.E. and P.L. Fletcher, "Remittances and Development in Mexico", *The Center on Rural Economies of the Americas and Pacific Rim website*, www.reap.ucdavis.edu/vol_two.html.

PERIODICALS AND NEWSPAPERS

The Arab Daily.

First Magazine.

Jordan Economic Monitor.

Jordan Focus.

Jordan Times.

The Middle East and North Africa.

Middle East Economic Digest.

Middle East Economic Survey.

Middle East International.

Mideast Mirror.

OPEC Bulletin.

Summary of World Broadcasts.

Summary of World Broadcasts
    Weekly Economic Report.

Index